HOLY GRADUEL

A TRUE LIFE STORY

By: Christine J. Haven

© 2007 Christine J. Haven
All Rights Reserved.
No part of this publication may be reproduced, stored in a retrieval system, or transmitted, in any form or by any means, electronic, mechanical, photocopying, recording, or otherwise, without the written permission of the author.

First published by Owl Creek Press

ISBN: 978-0-6151-4403-0

Printed in the United States of America

Holy Graduel

By: Christine J. Haven

    The word Graduel is a French word meaning gradual. To seek the Holy Graduel is to seek for self-discovery, a symbol for self-improvement for enlightenment and spiritual power. Graduel is a step-by-step process and not something to be attained. It is the perfection and development on ones human spirit and is a great challenge for anyone to find. The true path of the Graduel is marked by questions which forces you into deeper contemplation. Questions are more important than the answers when seeking Eternal truth and God. It is impervious to rational thought. Hence, peace of mind is worth the truth.
    The Holy Graduel is the true life story of David A. Haven and his quest to find God. This book is written in two sections. The first section, *Together Forever Before the Light* tells of Dave's life in the sixties and his deep love affair with Joan Lee Harris.
    During the mid nineties, he was able to accept her death and it was Jo, her Entity, who was the only person that he would trust and she convinced him of God. She was able to turn their love into Divine Love as she slowly introduced him to Gabrael, Michael and Jesus and together they brought him to God.
    The second section of this book, *God's Forgotten Guiding Love*, continues with Dave's learning of God's Concepts of Life. He brings to you in his own words the teachings he has received from Jo and the other Angels. This section answers many of the questions we have about life, love, why are we here, who is God, and what is God. Most importantly you will learn "Peace of mind is worth the truth". Live Free, Live Free, Touch Free, Love Free, Be Free!

IN LOVING MEMORY OF JOAN LEE HARRIS

She gave her love and now shares her knowledge with the world.
God is the Light, and she is now part of the Light.

CHAPTERS

TOGETHER FOREVER BEFORE THE LIGHT

1. PREAMBLE 1

SUMMER OF '65

1. MEETING JO 6
2. THEIR FIRST DATE 12
3. THE HIDE-A-WAY 17
4. DAVE'S CAREER 21
5. TOGETHER 23
6. JOAN 27
7. THE MOVIE 30
8. THE NIGHT PICNIC 38
9. "I WANT YOUR BABY" 41
10. JO'S NEW APARTMENT 45
11. DIVORCE PAPERS SERVED 48
12. THE WARNING 51
13. GOING TO DAVE'S MOM'S 55
14. A SAD JO 58
15. A HAPPY JO 62
16. AN ANGRY AND MYSTERIOUS JO 67
17. THEIR FINAL DATE 73
18. DEEPLY DEPRESSED 79
19. THE DEATH OF QUEEN VICKIE 84
20. HARD TIMES 87
21. SHE'S GONE 90

THE SEARCH

1. RETURN TO MARION 93
2. THE PHONE CALL 101
3. DAVE KNEW 103
4. CHRISTINE LEARNS ABOUT JO 105
5. DAVE TELLS MORE 110
6. CHRISTINE RECALLS JOAN'S CALL 114

THE HAUNTINGS

1. GRANADA HILLS, CALIFORNIA 117
2. PALMDALE, CALIFORNIA 122
3. LANCASTER, CALIFORNIA 126

LEARNING

1. BETTY WAY 129
2. "SHE WON'T ANSWER, SHE'S DEAD" 132
3. BITS AND PIECES START COMING 136
4. DAVE'S ACCEPTANCE 140

CIVIL WAR DAYS

1. INNOCENT LOVE 145
2. PLANS FOR THE FUTURE 148
3. DAVE JOINS SHERMAN 150
4. GUILT 152
5. HIS PROMISE IS KEPT 154

UNDERSTANDING

1. JO'S LIFE 156
2. NO MORE HAUNTINGS 160
3. CHRISTINE SHARES THEIR LOVE 162
4. GOOD-BYE BETTY WAY 164
5. THE FINAL WAIT 166

IN DAVE'S OWN WORDS

1. JO 168

OTHER LIVES

1. TRIALS OF OTHER LIVES 171
2. THE LO 172
3. OTHER LIVES 178
4. FAREWELL 183

IN CHRISTINE'S OWN WORDS

1. FEELINGS FOR JO 185
2. DAVE 188
3. I SHARED THEIR LOVE 190
4. JO REMAINS WITH US 192
5. THEY WON'T BE BACK 194

GOD'S FORGOTTEN GUIDING LOVE

1. GOD'S FORGOTTEN GUIDING LOVE 196

WHO WE ARE

1. THE DOG 208
2. THE ANGEL WITHIN 216
3. THE SOUL 222
4. GUARDIAN ANGELS 226
5. EQUAL 234
6. NON-CONFORMED ONES 240
7. UNGUIDED ONES 244
8. FAMILIAR SPIRITS 250
9. THEORY OF LIFE 254

THE CONCEPT OF LIFE

1. TO LEARN AND EXPERIENCE 258

2. COMPASSION 260
3. UNDERSTANDING 269
4. FORGIVENESS 277
5. LOVE 282
6. WISDOM 303
7. CHERISHMENT 309
8. JUDGMENT 312
9. COVENANT 323

"AND THE ANGEL JO SAID UNTO ME..."

1. IT CAME TO PASS 326
2. CYCLES 329
3. GENESIS 331
4. CREATION 339
5. THE OTHER SIDE 346
6. THE LIGHT 350
7. KNOWLEDGE 356
8. TO SAY GOODBYE 362
9. FOLLOW YOUR HEART 368
10. HEAVEN AND HELL 375
11. LIVE FOREVER 382
12. NEVERTHELESS 388
13. RULES 392
14. BLASPHEMY 399
15. RELIGIONS 401
16. CHURCH 405
17. PRAYERS 408
18. HUMAN PRIDE 411
19. DOMINATION 415
20. SIN 421
21. DO NOT BE AFRAID OF DEATH 428
22. SYMBOLISM 433
23. FAITH AND BELIEF 435
24. THE FINAL DAY 437

AND THE ANGEL JO ASKED

1. KILLING OF OUR CHILDREN 442
2. SADNESS 446

CONCLUSION

1. PSYCHIC POWERS 451
2. THE FUTURE 456
3. EPILOGUE 460
4. THE FINAL TEACHINGS 464

TOGETHER FOREVER BEFORE THE LIGHT

PREAMBLE

It was May, 1996, and once again lunchtime rolled around at the large candle factory in the San Fernando Valley where Dave worked with Bob, Fred and Jose.

Dave had been with the company for almost six years as their truck and electric forklift mechanic.

Every day at noon, Fred, who was the company's machinist, would walk by the large covered "patio" where Dave did his repairs to the factory's vehicles to alert him of the time.

Fred was a tall Texan in his mid-fifties. He loved trains and always wore bib-overalls as he thought the train engineers wore.

Dave would grab his lunch and they would head toward the smoke shack, which was really their lunch room in the rear of the factory's yard complex. It was the smaller room of the original two-room factory, which now was reserved for the smokers where they ate lunch, played penny ante poker and told their stories within its nicotine stained walls.

Dave and the guys would gather around the old wooden table and reminisce about old flames while they ate their lunches. Of course each one of them had to have a better story about how good or bad an old girlfriend was in bed. It was almost a ritual that they would share stories.

After the usual comparison of who had what for lunch, Bob began the conversation of past self-indulgences, "Speaking of lunch," he grinned.

He was the younger of these old friends. And Dave thought Bob came from northern California, but was not sure.

Bob stood about 5 foot 8 inches tall, dark skinned and around 45 years old.

"I had these neighbors a long time ago. Damn, I can't remember what their names were. Anyway, this lady would call me up on the phone and start talking sexy to me," Bob said.

"How the hell do you talk sexy, Bob?" asked Jose, "I thought women looked sexy."

Jose was from south of the border, somewhere in Central America, and around 50 years old. His dark skin and hair showed he was from Latin America, but his English was superb.

"Shut- up dickless," replied Bob as the others laughed.

Looking around the room to make sure all were listening, Bob continued, "Anyway, I didn't know if she was really trying to be sexy and coming on to me or what, so I asked a buddy of mine what he thought. He told me I should take her out for lunch or dinner, just the two of us. You know, without her husband or my wife. Well a couple of days later while my wife was gone, here comes this lady to my door. She wasn't a bad looking gal either. She was about five-five with dark hair and brown eyes. She wasn't fat but she wasn't skinny either and best of all, she had a great set of boobs on her. Anyway, she comes in and sits down on the couch. I took one look at her, jumped on her and gave her the kiss of her life. She fought and struggled free from me, and then she hit me right in my mouth."

Dave, Fred and Jose roared.

"Yea, she did," laughed Bob as he continued. "You know, about a month later my wife invited these folks over to the house for dinner. Just when we sat down to eat I got a phone call so I took the call in the bedroom. Now our bedroom was down the hall from the kitchen just past the bathroom. I had just hung up the phone and looked around and there she was. She said not to worry because she had locked the bathroom door. Our bathroom had a connecting door to the bedroom. Anyway, she let her sun dress fall to the floor, and she didn't have anything on under it, exposing this body that you would not believe with the nicest looking set of tits you have ever seen. She gives me this very seductive look and tells me how much she wants me.

I said, "Man, are you nuts? No way! My wife and your husband are just in the other room.

"I just could not believe this was happening to me. Anyway, about a month or so later they moved away and I never saw her again."

"Ooo! The one that got away," laughed Fred, Jose and Dave.

"Did you know," asked Fred, "that the reason I had to marry my first wife was because she was the only woman I ever met that could keep up with me drinking."

"Oh, he's going to tell us some shit now, boys!" Bob chuckled.

"No! I'm serious," said Fred. "One week-end we drank nine cases of beer and screwed all week-end... I mean we did it everyway you could think of. After that, I knew that this was the girl for me. Within the week we were married. After about a year, we were divorced. She started slowing down. She didn't want to screw so much either. That's when I knew it was time to move on and find someone else who could keep up. Of course, you've got to remember that that was in my younger days."

"Oh, what a stud," laughed Dave.

Jose added, "I used to date this girl that didn't have much, but utilized every ounce she had."

As they all burst into laughter and urged Jose to elaborate, Dave's mind began to wonder. Usually, Dave had the best of the stories. He had always been a tough one to out-do. He laughed with the others, but presently his mind was elsewhere. He was thinking of someone that he had never told anyone about and would never tell anyone about. And also he thought that if the truth were known, most men do talk to other men about their past flings and love affairs. He figured it was sort of like "locker room talk" that helps keep old men's egos up after years of being married and finding old age creeping up on them. Women, on the other hand, would merely wonder if her ex-lover ever found true love and if he was happy. It was amazing to Dave how two completely different lines of thought could be conceived on the same subject by opposite genders... Just then, out of the blue, there she was again. Her memory plagued Dave's mind once again.

"Oh God," Dave thought to himself, "I am so sorry."

Engulfed in his own thoughts of her Dave was startled as the 12:30 whistle blew that summoned them back to work.

"Well, I guess it's time to do it again," said Bob as he stood up from the table.

"It's reach and get'er time again," Dave added, and crushed out the cigarette that he unconsciously lit, grabbed his coffee jug and headed back to his little shop.

As he walked an eerie feeling filled his body as a cold chill ran down his back. Once again she filled his mind and his head with pain as though his soul were set on fire. With the thoughts of her still in his mind, Dave started again with the needed repairs to a company forklift.

"How's that forklift coming?" asked Matt.

Matt was Dave's boss, but Dave rarely ever saw Matt.

"She'll be ready by the end of the day," replied Dave.

"There wasn't a doubt in my mind that it wouldn't be," smiled Matt as he waved to Dave and headed back to his office.

As Dave watched Matt heading back to his office and with her thoughts still fresh in his thoughts, he saw Fred approaching walking toward his shop.

Holy Graduel

"What the hell you doing?" yelled Dave at Fred as he entered Dave's shop.

Dave always greeted fellow employees with this line.

"I just came to check out your Playboy calendar again," said Fred.

Dave wiped his hands on a shop rag and watched as Fred flipped through Dave's Playmate calendar and made his usual frivolous comments about each Playmate. Suddenly, Dave shuttered as Fred flipped to August.

That eerie feeling filled him again. It was her. Not really Jo, but her grin and almost identical facial features stirred up those thirty-year-old memories again.

The rest of the afternoon passed swiftly for Dave as he finished up his repairs on the forklift. Before he knew it, the three o'clock whistle was sounding. He was definitely ready to call it a day. Clocking out, walking across the parking lot, Dave opened the door to his old '79 Mercedes and set his coffee jug on the passenger car seat and started his sixty mile journey home to Lancaster, California.

As Dave drove, he thought about how he loved living in the high desert and about his life. Here he was, fifty-two years old, in a comfortable marriage for twenty-one years and raising two wonderful sons. What a lucky man he was!

In December of 1992, Dave had had a massive heart attack. It was touch and go for the first forty-eight hours. His condition was very critical with one artery blocked 100% and two others 60% blocked. The 100% blockage caused the bottom right part of his heart to die. This part of his heart became scar tissue. He was a very sick man. For the next three years, he tried to keep working his regular forty to fifty hours a week as a tractor/trailer and electric forklift mechanic. Finally in September of 1995, Dave had a triple by-pass. Now he could only work thirty to forty hours a week.

As Dave headed north up the 14 Freeway towards Lancaster, he began thinking about how short life was.

Not only was he fifty-two and having heart problems, but he also was about thirty pounds overweight with very high cholesterol, which the doctors were having trouble bringing down even with medication. Dave knew he was living on borrowed time.

Jo had been plaguing his mind all day, and all of a sudden, there she was again.

"That was a long time ago," Dave thought to himself.

This was not the first time Dave had thought about her, but something was really tugging at him this time. He could not quite put his finger on it.

Once again, Dave started thinking back to over thirty years ago when

Christine J. Haven

he first met her.

SUMMER OF '65

MEETING JO

It was March of 1965. Dave had recently been discharged from the Army. Due to in-law problems, he found himself with a son and in a rocky marriage. He had to find work to support his family. The only work the young twenty year old Dave had ever done beside the service, was working in the oil field as a roughneck on drilling rigs.

Dave left his family with his in-laws in Wooster, Ohio. Driving his 1956 Crown Victoria Ford, he headed for Mt. Gilead, Ohio.

Dave was quite proud of his car, it cost him $25.00 and she was a jewel, which had a big V8 engine and a four-barrel carb. She was red and white with shiny chrome bumpers and purred like a kitten. She would do 120 and rarely ever saw anything under 80.

A big oil boom was going on in Mt. Gilead, Ohio at that time. People were so oil crazy that they tore down their garages and drilled oil wells in their yards. Even the elementary school had an oil well drilled on its playground.

The Mt. Gilead boom was wilder and crazier than any Texas or Oklahoma oil boom ever was. And it resembled an old west town with a cattle drive coming through it.

In actuality, it was a sad time for Mt. Gilead. The oil promoters oversold percentages of the wells to investors. The promoters would bring their investors out to watch their wells being drilled. They would wine and dine them, and feed them empty promises about how much money they were going to make, knowing fully in advance which wells that they planned to plug and abandon. Even today, these promoters are going back re-drilling those abandoned wells and producing them, using their own money, without the investors. Thus, the promoters are now making profits from the original investors' investment. Those investors did not and will not ever see any of the profits from those wells.

Unable to find cheap lodging in Mt. Gilead, Dave headed west on Route 95, looking for a place to live.

Passing through several small towns, he drove into the next county to a medium size town called Marion.

It was as though something was guiding him. Dave drove straight through the heart of Marion toward the western edge of town where he pulled into the parking lot of the Pacific Union Hotel. It was an old wooden two story run-down hotel by the railroad tracks.

As he turned off his engine, he knew this would be his home until he could find steady work and get settled in, and then he could bring his family "home."

Dave spent days driving from one drilling rig to another, searching for work. Sometimes he would find work for a day or two by filling in for someone who was sick, injured or just wanted a day off.

The rigs worked eight or twelve hour shifts, seven days a week and fifty-two weeks a year. If a roughneck took a day off without finding someone to replace him, he would be fired.

Dave "chased" drilling rigs every eight hours, checking with each shift in the hope that someone may be looking for another hand.

Most of the rigs he found work on were poor-boy companies and their equipment showed it. Dave was really looking for a good company needing a good steady hand but accepted part-time work on any rig even the poor-boy rigs.

Less than one block up the street from the Pacific Union Hotel there were two bars; Casey's Bar and the H&H Bar and Grill. Both bars were in the same run down older brick building.

For some reason, unbeknown to Dave, he was pulled to the H&H nightly.

As Dave pulled into the dirt parking lot at the side of the bar, he had a feeling that it was natural for him to be going to the H&H, even though whenever he would enter the area that included Mt. Gilead and Marion before, he always was overcome by a sadness or gloom, a sickening feeling, but that did not occur on this trip.

The door to the H&H was to the left of a large plate glass window with cafe curtains. It was a fairly large place with hardwood floors and was finished in dark wood. The bar ran the length of the room on the left. Booths lined the right, a jukebox stood in the right rear corner and about five to ten tables filled the rest of the room. The place was dimly lit by Strohs and Old Dutch Beer signs that hung on its walls.

Shot glasses were neatly lined on the shelf below a shelf that whiskey bottles sit on behind the bar.

Mary, the owner of the bar, was a tall, thin, mid-fifties woman with graying and tightly curled hair. She held her age well and one could tell from looking at her that she was not one to allow any problems in her establishment.

Most of the clientele was from the railroads with a few older guys from the surrounding neighborhood.

Lunch time would draw the men from the neighborhood factories as well. The H&H Bar and Grill was famous for their greasy hamburgers and their open-face sandwiches.

During the first two weeks, it became a ritual with Dave to "chase" the drilling rigs then spend the early part of the evenings at the bar.

Back in those days you could sit and drink all night for a couple bucks. A long neck bottle of beer only cost twenty-five cents.

That Wednesday evening, just as any other evening, Dave walked into the bar about six-thirty.

"Hi, Dave, how's it going?" asked Mary as she brought him his usual bottle of Strohs Beer, "You haven't met my new barmaid yet. This is Jo."

As Dave looked at Jo, his heart began to pound. This was the most beautiful woman he had ever laid eyes on. He was surprised that such a young and innocent looking girl would be working in a bar like this.

Jo was about five feet tall with brown shoulder-length hair which was pulled back from her face with tortoise-shell combs. She could not have weighed much over a hundred pounds.

Jo smiled as Dave looked into her light blue eyes and he said, "Hi, Jo! I'm Dave."

There was something about her eyes. They were so light that they were almost as white as the clouds. But it was more than that… it was as if Dave had looked into her eyes before.

Dave and Jo hit it off right away. For some strange reason Dave thought that they seemed to feel completely comfortable and relaxed together.

"Who is this woman?" Dave wondered. "Why do I feel like I could talk to her about anything?"

Mary went to wait on another customer, as Jo washed some glasses she turned her head and looking over her shoulder at Dave and asked, "So, you come in here often?"

"Not really. Just about every night," laughed Dave.

"I see! A real native, huh!" she replied.

Just about then an older woman, named Sarah, wearing a tattered sun dress came raging through the wooden screen door as she did almost every night about this time.

"This has got to stop. I've had your supper on the table for over an hour now. I'm telling you right now..."

Trying to calm the scene, Gus replied, "Why Sarah, I'm just sitting here having a drink with my good friend, Bobby. Now what's the harm in that?"

Gus did whatever his wife asked of him, and rarely did anything on his own that his wife knew about. Gus was a guy that liked to drink, but barely made enough money to support his wife and family. Gus was a short, fat, older man, who wore pants that were held up by a set of old suspenders and usually had the left side of his shirt hanging out over his trousers.

"You're drunk again, Gus," Sarah yelled at him.

"No, I ain't drunk," slurred Gus as he fell back into his chair while trying to stand up.

"Well, I'm not helping you home tonight. You've got ten minutes to get your butt home or you won't have a home to come home to." Sarah slammed the door as she stormed out.

Mary asked Bobby, "Bobby, why don't you see to it that Gus-Gus gets home, okay?"

"Sure thing, Mary," replied Bobby, as he took the last swig of his beer and stood up.

Bobby was an older man that maybe at one time would have been considered good looking by the women. He was a thinner man that rarely shaved anymore. His clothes were old but well taken care of.

"But I don't want to go home. I'm not done with my beer. Who does she think she is anyway?" said Gus.

Mary walked over to Gus and Bobby's table.

She put her hands down on the edge of the table, "Now, Gus-Gus, you know as well as I do that you don't want to keep Sarah waiting. Go on and let Bobby take you home now. You've been here since three today. You need to rest up for tomorrow."

"Okay, I'm going. See you tomorrow, Mary, and watch out for that sweet little thing you hired," Gus timidity replied.

Bobby helped Gus up and together they headed out the door as everyone yelled good-night to them.

"Holy smoly," said Jo, "I thought we were going to have a real problem there."

Dave laughed. "You mean Gus-Gus and Sarah? Get used to it. It happens just about every night. Gus-Gus gets off work at three and comes straight over here. Then about seven-thirty, Sarah comes looking for him. I guess this has been going on for years."

"You're kidding!" replied an astonished Jo.

Mary set down another tray of glasses for Jo, "At least for the last eight

Holy Graduel

years that I know of. Don't worry Jo, they're pretty harmless."

As Mary walked away, Dave turned back to Jo and said, "No, I'm not."

With a puzzled look on her face, Jo asked, "No, you're not what?"

"Before the shit hit the fan with Sarah and Gus, you asked me if I was a native. No, I'm not," he smiled.

"Oh my gosh, I forgot. I like that, you're good," laughed Jo.

Dave passed the evening by making small talk with Jo and Mary. His day started at five in the morning so by ten Dave was ready to call it a night.

As Dave stood up and headed for the door, Mary asked, "Leaving already?" as she wiped down a table.

"Yep! I better go get some sleep so I can get after it again in the morning," he answered.

"I would say be good and stay out of trouble, but I know you won't be good, so just stay out of trouble. See you tomorrow," chuckled Mary.

Jo was cleaning up the tables nearest the door. "You're not leaving are you?" she asked.

"Yea, gotta get up pretty early in the morning," replied Dave as he stopped by Jo to tell her goodnight.

"Oh!" pouted Jo and she looked down at the table she was wiping.

Dave thought, "What the hell, I ain't looking for work tomorrow."

"Tell you what. How about I take you to lunch tomorrow?" he asked.

Jo smiled and looked deeply into Dave's dark blue eyes and said, "You're on."

"I'll pick you up about noon," Dave said as he glazed back into her eyes.

"See you at noon," she smiled.

"Goodnight," Dave said with a smile and wave as he left.

Within a few seconds the door swung open, and Jo looked up.

"Where do I pick you up at?" Dave asked.

"I'll meet you in the parking lot. I have a place above Casey's, just next door," Jo replied with a big smile.

"See you at noon then," Dave said as he once again said goodnight and walked out the door.

Driving back to the hotel, Dave thought how strange it was. He felt like he had known Jo forever, but right now all he wanted to do was get a hot bath and go to bed. There would be no "chasing" drillings rigs tonight or tomorrow.

The thought of Jo's voice echoed through Dave's mind as he was suddenly jolted back to reality.

"Damn," Dave thought as he neared his exit, "I can't remember driving this far."

It was a little after four when Dave pulled into the garage.

He sat there in his car for a few minutes and thought back to 1965 and said out loud, "I'm sorry, I didn't mean it to happen like it did."

Then slowly he got out of the car and walked into the house as he changed his sad face into a happy face.

"Hello!" he yelled as he walked into the kitchen.

"Hello!" replied Dan as he walked into the kitchen from the dining room to greet his dad. "How was your day?"

"Okay," said Dave, "How was yours?"

"Pretty good and my homework's all done," Dan replied.

Dan was Dave's twelve year old son, who stood almost as tall as his 5ft. 6in. Dad.

Dan was a good kid that helped his Mom and Dad whenever he could, even though he had asthma and was a little over weight.

They sat and chit-chatted for a few minutes before Dan took off to ride his bike. Dan knew he had to be back home by five o'clock when Tony, his older brother - Dave's other son, got home from baseball practice because their Dad would have dinner ready for them.

Christine, their Mother and Dave's wife, did not get home until close to seven.

After dinner, Dave poured his usual cup of coffee, lit a cigarette and went out onto the patio to just sit and relax.

Watching the colorful sun set in the California sky, Dave's thoughts turned once again to Jo as his mind drifted back to Marion, Ohio, and their first date.

THEIR FIRST DATE

Dave pulled into the parking lot of the H&H a few minutes before noon. There was Jo, standing in a full-skirted, knee-length, white dress with a blue floral design. She looked like a little doll standing there all alone. Jo turned and smiled as she saw him pull into the parking lot.

"Need a ride?" Dave smiled as he got out and opened the car door for Jo.

"Why yes, thank you," Jo smiled as she slid past Dave into the car.

Dave drove out of town towards a small cafe he knew of in the center of Mt. Gilead.

As they drove, Dave had asked Jo what brought her to Marion.

"Well," she began, "I was born and raised here. My family has been in this area for generations. I've known Mary most of my life. I was looking for a job and Mary said that she sure could use some help at the bar, so...here I am. Hey! How about some music?" she added as if to change the subject.

"Sure!" Dave turned the radio on.

Jo scooted over a little toward Dave and turned the radio to what she called a good country station.

They contentedly listened to country music for the rest of the drive to Mt. Gilead.

Unlike Dave, he kept his speed under the highway speed limit of sixty miles per hour. He wanted to savor every moment he could with Jo and found himself looking more at her than the road.

After ordering a couple of cheeseburgers, Jo looked deep into Dave's blue eyes and smiled.

Dave's heart pounded as it did when he first laid eyes on her.

"Well," she asked, "if you're not a native of Marion, what brought you here?"

"The oil field," replied Dave, "I'm looking for a good company to latch on to. I usually go 'chasing' rigs at night when it's dark and you can see their lights."

"What exactly do you do on a rig?" she asked.

"Usually throw chain. You see, there's a guy who goes to the top of the rig and he sort of steers the drill pipe over to the pipe sticking out of the well. The driller, the guy who operates the rig, lowers the pipe into the other pipe. I screw the pipe together with a chain. Then the guy running the tongs, who's called the tong hand, finishes tightening the pipe up. Nothing to it," he said.

Dave thought he better not make it too complicated for her to understand.

"I've never seen one of those rigs up close," said Jo.

"Well, if it ain't little Davy. How's it going, man?" asked a completely soiled and unshaven man who reeked of diesel fuel.

"Well, what are you up to Johnny?" asked Dave.

"Just stopped in to get a bite before I head out for my tour," Johnny replied.

A "tour" in oil field slang means shift.

"Looks like you're doing okay for yourself, boy," Johnny said as he smiled at Jo.

"I'll catch ya later, Davy," he said through a toothless grin as he winked at Dave and walked away with two other men who were dressed similar to him.

"You work with those guys?" asked Jo.

"Sometimes, but don't worry. They're harmless." Dave assured her, "They're pretty good old boys."

"You just don't look like you fit in with them," Jo replied.

After they finished their lunch, Dave paid for their lunch and waited for Jo as she slid out of the booth.

"It sure is a beautiful day," Jo said to Dave as he held the cafe door for her.

Stepping outside, Jo waited for Dave to get beside her and then slipped her hand into his.

Her touch was electrifying. Dave thought of how tiny and fragile her hand was. He gave her hand a light squeeze.

"It sure is," Dave replied.

The sun brightly shined down on the street full of stop and go mud covered oil field trucks and cars as they strolled down the street toward his car.

When he opened the car door for her, Dave asked, "So what now?"

"I really don't have anything pressing to do," Jo said as she slid closer to Dave as he started the engine of the car.

Dave smiled at her and drove, at the edge of town he turned left onto a small dirt road that could barely be seen through the trees.

"How beautiful," Jo exclaimed as the view of a lake became visible through the trees.

Dave just smiled at her.

After stopping, getting out and walking around to her side of the car and opening her door, he extended his hand to help her out of the car.

"How did you ever find this place?" She asked.

"Oh, I get around," replied Dave.

Actually, Dave knew that he had just lucked out. He had never been to this lake before in his life. But for some reason he drove right to it.

The air had an aroma of fresh cut grass. The trees were tall and fully embellished with their shapely green foliage. Through the trees, as though at the end of the horizon, was the silvery glitter of the lake.

Yes, Jo was right. This was very beautiful.

Dave and Jo held hands as they strolled down one of the worn paths to the lake.

The sunlight glistened through the treetops as a Fox Squirrel ran out on a limb and jumped to another tree.

Jo laughed as she watched the tiny creature stop and barked at them, and then it ran and hid as they walked under the tree to the graveled shoreline of the lake.

It was so quiet and peaceful there. There was a small boat out on the lake with what appeared to be a couple of guys fishing. At the same time, Dave and Jo smiled at each other then both picked up a rock and skipped them across the lake. Dave thought that it was almost as if Jo could read his mind.

"I love this place," Jo said as she looked deeply into Dave's eyes.

His arms went around her tiny waist as she raised her arms up and around his neck. Time stood still while they seemed to swallow each other with their eyes. Just then, a man and two small boys came walking by. Dave and Jo released their embrace, but still held hands while they bid them good afternoon. Jo watched the small boys until they went out of sight. Then they continued to quietly walk the shoreline.

Dave spotted a huge log lying near a big weeping willow tree.

Dave sat down on the log.

"I don't want to get my dress all dirty," Jo said.

"You don't have to," Dave replied as he patted his lap, "You can sit right here."

Jo laughed like a little girl as he pulled her onto his lap.

Dave stroked the side of Jo's face and once again they were unable to take their eyes from each other.

Dave's heart pounded as he lightly touched her full lips with his.

Neither one said a word. Their actions were so natural they didn't have to talk.

Hearing ducks, they turned and watched ducks swimming by out on the lake.

With Dave's arm around her waist and Jo's arm resting on his shoulder, they were both content.

A gentle breeze began to blow through the trees, the willow's long limbs swayed as his lips touched hers again.

Dave's heart pounded like never before. The feeling was almost too electrifying to comprehend for Dave as Jo seemed to have lost her breath, too.

They spent the next hour sharing their passionate kisses, breaking only to watch the ducks and to just enjoy the afternoon as the long limbs of the giant willow danced to the flow of a gentle breeze.

Finally they headed back up the path to the car.

Jo was the first to break the silence. "You know, I was wondering, why does everyone call Gus, Gus-Gus? That sounds so stupid."

"From what I understand," began Dave, "He got it years ago when he first started working for the railroad. He was short and fat and silly. I guess he reminded everyone of the little fat mouse in the Cinderella movie, so they started calling him Gus-Gus."

Jo roared with laughter, "Oh my God, You're kidding."

The echo of Jo's laughter in Dave's mind was broken by Christine's, "Hi, Honey, I'm home."

Then, Christine walked out onto the patio.

"There you are," she said to Dave as she brushed his lips with her own.

"How was your day?" She asked.

Christine was a petite and beautiful woman, who was thirty-nine, with short brown hair and brown eyes, and knew how to dress.

"Okay, how about yours?" Dave answered.

"Alright, I guess, just the same old stuff. I was just really busy. I'm not going to eat anything tonight, I'm too tired. I'm going to get a cup of coffee. Do you want some more while I'm going in?" she asked.

"Thank you," Dave replied with a smile as he handed Christine his empty cup.

After she disappeared into the house, his thoughts drifted back to 1965 and he thought, "Jo, I'm sorry…I wish it wouldn't have happened."

And then he put out his cigarette and lit another before Christine returned.

"Here you go," said Christine as she handed him his coffee.

"Thanks," he said with a kiss.

"You know, Hon, you can't beat these warm desert nights. Just look at that sky," he said gazing into the sky.

"Yea," answered Christine as her eyes searched the sky while she gently slipped her arm through his arm and around his waist, "Sure wish that I could see a falling star tonight. I always miss them."

"You're always looking some place else. I see one and tell you, but by the time you look, it's gone. You have to keep watching," Dave jokingly replied while they gazed at the stars together.

"Can you believe that in just a few weeks we will be heading for Ohio for our vacation, I can't wait. I need a vacation from work," she exclaimed.

"It won't be long now, Babe," Dave said.

They sat out on the patio and discussed their up-coming trip along with their day's events over their cups of coffee and a few more cigarettes.

"Well Honey, its nine-thirty," Christine began, "I'm going to get things ready for work tomorrow and then I'm going to bed," she told Dave.

She paused as she looked at him and then picked up her empty coffee cup and headed for the door.

"Yea, let's do it," Dave said as he followed behind her.

Dave found himself staring at the darkened ceiling while Christine lay sleeping peacefully beside him.

A feeling of restlessness overcame him that he could not shake or put his finger on.

"This is silly," he thought to himself, "I may as well get up and have another cigarette."

Lighting up a cigarette, Dave closed the front door quietly behind him so as not to wake anyone up as he walked out front of their house.

A shooting star briefly lit up the sky.

How he longed to be there with it. And once again his thoughts turned to Jo and the year of '65.

THE HIDE-A-WAY

Dave had been "chasing" drilling rigs all afternoon, still searching for that one good company he so desperately hoped to find.

He got back to the hotel around six o'clock, took a bath and just hung out in his room. Dave did not want Jo to know that he could not afford to sit and drink all night long.

He arrived at the H&H around nine-thirty.

"How's it going, Dave?" Mary called from behind the bar when she saw him walk through the door, "Any luck today?"

"No, not today," answered Dave, "But there is always tomorrow."

Dave sipped on a couple of beers until the bar closed. He and Jo were to ascend on their second date when she got off work.

"You kids go on. I'll lock up," Mary told Jo while Jo started to go over her checklist to make sure everything was off.

"Are you sure, Mary?" Jo asked with a smile that would have lit up any room.

"I'm positive. Now, go on and get before I change my mind," responded Mary.

Jo grabbed Dave's hand and said, "Let's go while the gettin's good…"

"Thanks Mary," Jo yelled as they went out the door.

Dave opened the car door for Jo and she slid across the seat.

Heading south out of town, Jo latched on to Dave's right arm and laid her head against his shoulder. From this time on, this would be her usual position when he drove.

The full moon cast its luminous glow across the land as they drove down the highway. A late night breeze, filled with the smell of freshly bailed hay swept through the car while the Wilburn Brothers sang, "It's Another World" on the radio.

Dave drove about fifteen to twenty miles before turning off to the right.

Along this lonely dirt road, lined with cornfields, Dave drove another few miles then turned left into one of the cornfields. He went about another quarter of a mile along the edge of the cornstalks before stopping.

After turning off the engine, Dave turned to Jo.

Without saying a word, his lips crushed hers as she pulled him tighter to her. Passion filled their bodies; they seemed to become one. It seemed to be an eternity before they caught their breath.

Dave smiled at Jo, opened his door and stepped outside the car.

As he held out his hand to help Jo out, he said, "It sure is a beautiful night."

Jo smiled and grabbed his hand. Her arms automatically went around his neck. Dave grabbed her around her small waist and pulled her toward him. His eyes burned with desire. His lips pressed against hers while she arched her pelvic against him. Dave squeezed her closer to him. They held on to each other like there was no tomorrow. They searched each others eyes between kisses. No words were needed. Somehow, Dave knew Jo felt the same way.

"Come on," Dave said as he lifted Jo on to the hood of his car.

He jumped up beside her, and they scooted back and rested their backs against the windshield while staring at the clear star filled sky. Dave sat with his arm around Jo and she rested her head on his shoulder.

"You know, here we are on our second date and we really don't even know much about each other," Dave said, "Tell me about Jo," he smiled.

"Well, I'm twenty-seven," Jo began as she looked at Dave, "How old are you?"

Not wanting her to think of him as a kid, he replied, "I'm twenty-one."

Jo continued while turning her head back to the stars, "I'm married, but my husband left and took our nine children with him."

Suddenly she rose up and pointed skyward. "There goes a shooting star!" She exclaimed, "Did you see it?"

"It was beautiful," Dave replied, "But so are you."

He reached up and pulled her back to him again.

She continued searching the sky in silence and Dave realized she did not want to talk about the past anymore. He knew that from that point on, if she wanted to tell him anything, she would. As it were, nothing more was ever said about Jo's or his past.

Dave leaned over and kissed Jo on the cheek. Jo turned her head and gave him a quick kiss on the lips.

Trying to break the silence, he asked, "Did you hear that noise the car was making when we were driving in here tonight? She's missing a little. I think I better give her a service and tune up."

"Her!" exclaimed Jo, "Why do you say 'her'? What kind of car is this?"

"She's a '56 Ford Crown Victoria."

"Okay! From here on she shall be known as Queen Vickie," Jo said in her childlike playful way.

"You're crazy," chuckled Dave as he hugged her closer to him.

After about another twenty minutes or so, they decided to sit in the car where the seats were much more comfortable than the hood.

Dave felt so content just sitting there as he lit up a cigarette. He turned to Jo and asked, "Would you like to drive Queen Vickie?"

"I don't have a license. I never learned how to drive, but thanks anyway," she replied as she gave Dave a little peck on the cheek.

With her hand in his, Jo leaned against his side while propping her feet up on the dash as Dave slowly puffed on his cigarette.

Dave thought, "What a strange perfume she wears. It has the fragrance of wildflowers."

They sat silently watching the stars as the moon slid across the sky.

All of a sudden Dave found himself looking down at a field followed by another field, then a weed covered fence. All of the scenery below was brightly lit by the rising sun.

Looking down to the left, then to the right Dave saw scattered trees and rolling country side as a cornfield approached. Near the rows of cornstalks, sat a car with its doors opened. As Dave flew to the right of the car and circled left over the cornfield while descending towards the car, he realized that it was Queen Vickie.

And then, Dave felt a pressure on his lips. He opened his eyes and it was Jo.

They now lay on the front seat of Queen Vickie with their arms and legs entwined instead of setting up together on the front seat of the car as he last remembered.

Dave held her tight as he pressed hard against her lips.

"I must have fallen asleep," he thought.

"Have you ever seen such a sunrise?" Jo asked as she looked out towards the horizon with a sigh of contentment.

Jo saying, "Have you ever seen such a sunrise?" sung out over and over again in his mind as he stared into the sky from the front porch of his home in Lancaster, California.

In the darkness and stillness of the night, he stood there alone and lit up another cigarette and remembered thinking about that sunrise, it was the most beautiful sunrise he had ever seen. It was not just the sunrise, though. It was having Jo there beside him and them sharing in the experience. He never actually asked her, but somehow he knew that she felt exactly as he felt.

"What about the flying?" Dave thought to himself, "I always thought it was a dream. I recalled that when I was a young child I almost died a couple of times from pneumonia. And during those illnesses I always thought that I flew many times in a dark and starlit place, but I always thought that it was just hallucinations from my fevers…I was always alone and sad in those flights. This was the first time that I can really recall flying without being sick and burning up with a high fever. And this was also the only time that I ever flew in the daylight and was not alone. I felt someone was to my right and back just a little, but I did not see who it was."

With the thoughts of Jo still in his mind, he turned and headed back into the house, and once more looked up into the starlit skies and said, "I'm sorry…I didn't mean that to happen," as he closed the door behind him and went to bed.

DAVE'S CAREER

When Dave was sixteen, his older sister married a man who's family owned a small drilling company. And prior to the Mt. Gilead boom, Dave had worked for his brother-in-law on a drilling rig. But that company was really a poor boy company and their equipment was junk.

Dave had worked for his brother-in-law full time and had made good money, but they worked twelve hours per day and seven days a week. Dave knew his place was in the oil field drilling wells. He also knew there had to be good companies to work for, but he only needed to find one of those companies.

During the spring, summer and early fall of 1965, in the Mt. Gilead oil boom, Dave had been able to get a couple days of work here or there on one of the rigs, filling in for a hand who wanted a day or two off. He usually averaged two or three days of work a week. This brought him more money than most factory workers brought home working a forty hour week.

Dave's dream was to eventually work for a big drilling company in the oil fields in other countries around the world. Years later, Dave would see his dreams come true, working in such places as Libya and Algeria, besides all around the United States.

But those were trying and complex days for Dave in 1965.

Daily he checked with the desk clerk at the hotel to see if he had any messages or phone calls from his wife, but there were never any. He called home every three or four days.

"Home" was where his wife and young son were staying with his in-laws.

"Home," Dave thought, "Rich bitches who always put me down."

No matter what Dave did or how hard he tried, nothing he ever did was quite good enough for them.

He was married to a woman he could have loved, but she always let her family stick their noses into hers and Dave's business.

In 1965, Dave had found a woman that he started falling in love with.

Jo had all the qualities that he ever wanted in a woman. She didn't care about how much money he had or about his past. In fact, she never asked him about his past. Jo didn't talk about the future or what she wanted to buy in the future such as a house or a new car or anything like that. All she wanted was to be with him.

Every week or so Dave would drive to Wooster and give his wife his money. He would spend the day playing and visiting with his boy and then the nights with his wife while listening to his in-laws bitch about his chosen career.

They would tell him how he should forget the oil field, find a nice factory job and settle down in Wooster. They even offered to give Dave the down payment for a house if he would only do like they wanted him to do. Needless to say, these trips to Wooster became less frequent and the smell of divorce was soon in the air.

TOGETHER

After getting into bed Dave silently kissed Christine on her cheek and soon was asleep. And as he slept, soon Jo returned into his dreams and he dreamt about her and their love affair in 1965.

He got off work at three o'clock, and it took him about forty minutes to drive back to the hotel.

Dave went straight to his room, got a bath and cleaned up.

After eating a can of cold chicken noodle soup for supper, he decided to lie down and get a little sleep before going over to the H&H to see Jo.

Dave got up about midnight and drove on over to the bar to wait for Jo to get off work.

"Hi, Hon. How did your day go?" Jo said as she blew him a kiss across the bar.

Returning her kiss, Dave replied, "Alright. How's yours?"

"The usual, Gus-Gus and Sarah going at it again as always," Jo said with a Ha Ha.

"Are you about ready to get out of here?" he asked.

Jo turned and looked at the clock and sighted, "In about two hours. Wish we could go now."

Dave sat there slowly sipping on a beer and watched Jo serving customers while the two hours dragged by.

After locking up, they drove straight to their newly found hide-a-way in the cornfield.

Dave turned off the engine, turned to Jo and said, "Boy, I missed you today."

Jo smiled as she slid her hand across the side of his face to the side of his neck and then rested it at the nape of his neck. Pulling him closer to her, she looked longingly into his eyes.

Just before his lips touched hers, she whispered, "I couldn't get you off my mind all day either."

Dave felt like they were melting into one. Dave's tongue touched against hers as it darted in and out of her luscious mouth. Jo began to quiver as both of them grasped for air.

Releasing her, he gently kissed Jo and said, "Wait here. I'll be right back."

Dave went to the trunk of the car and pulled out a quilted blanket and pillow. He walked back and opened her car door and extended his hand out for her.

Hand-in-hand, they walked together to the old oak tree near the grassy edge of the cornfield.

Jo held the pillow while Dave spread the blanket out under the tree. Kneeing down on the blanket, he turned and looked up at her, and she held out her hand to him.

Dave reached up and caressed her hand pulling her down on her knees, and in the same motion began kissing her neck.

Jo's breathing quickened and she dropped the pillow.

Dave continued lightly kissing up and down her neck. She tossed her head back, grabbed the back of his head and pulled him tighter.

Dave stopped kissing her and pulled away. He sat back on his legs.

Smiling, he unbuttoned his shirt while he looked deep into Jo's light blue eyes. He dropped his shirt on to the blanket, exposing his muscular torso.

Jo smiled as she ran her eyes over his body. Then she stared directly into his eyes, and slowly she removed the combs from her hair, shaking her head and letting her hair fall onto her shoulders.

Her hands moved to her top button as she began to remove her blouse. As it fell, Jo unhooked her bra and allowed it to fall beside her.

Dave's eyes roamed over her body. Seeing that the bottom of her right breast was surgically removed, he asked, "What happened?"

With one word she answered, "Cancer," as she extended her arms out to him.

Nothing more was ever said about her cancer.

Their bodies came together. Dave felt the warmth of Jo's breasts against him as his tongue went deep into her mouth.

Embraced with a kiss, Dave gently laid her down, resting her head on the pillow as she kicked off her shoes. Dave undid her shorts and removed them along with her panties.

As Dave stood up to take off what was left of his clothes, she looked like a Goddess to him in the moonlight.

Dave rejoined her on the blanket.

Jo gave him a loving kiss while wrapping her arms and legs around him.

Her fire burned deep into his soul.

She tightened her grip as they blended into one.

Dave raised himself up as if doing a push-up over her body.

She began thrusting her pelvic harder at him. Her breath quickened and her legs tightened as she purred in ecstasy and her whole body shivered with pleasure. His thrust began to increase as she moved with him, trying to keep pace.

Suddenly he stopped moving, and then her arms went up around his neck, and she pulled him back down to her and quickly kissed his face all over, Dave began moving his hips once again as his mouth covered hers. He felt her tongue finding its way around his.

The time seemed to stand still as their inner souls merged while their feeling of pleasure, fulfillment, desire and passion rose from a woman and a man, making love on a blanket, under a tree, at the edge of a cornfield around three o'clock in the morning, under a star filled sky, on a warm summer night in June of 1965, they exploded together.

After holding each other for a few minutes, Dave kissed Jo and got up to get dressed. She followed his lead.

"Come here," said Dave as he pulled Jo back down on to the blanket with him. She kissed his cheek and then snuggled comfortably in his arms.

"Listen! Do you hear that?" he asked her.

"Crickets," she replied, "I hear frogs, too. There must be a farm pond around here. But what's that other sound? I've never heard that before."

"Sounds like raccoons," Dave responded.

After watching the stars and listening to all of the night sounds for awhile, they gathered up the pillow and blanket and walked back to the car. With both car doors opened, Dave slid the front car seat back and Jo lay down on the seat. Dave crawled onto the seat facing her. He gave her a kiss and then they contently slept in each other's arms.

"Good morning," Jo said with a kiss as Dave opened his eyes.

The sun was making its way over the horizon.

"Good morning. Hungry?" Dave asked.

"Not really, but I sure would like a cup of coffee," Jo smiled.

They stopped at a small coffee shop on the way back into town, then Dave drove Jo home.

"You don't need to pull into the parking lot," Jo said to Dave, "It's closer if you just park on the street between Casey's and H&H."

Dave pulled up to the curb just past Casey's. He had never noticed the doorway between them before.

Jo led the way, holding on to Dave's hand as they made their way up the old, unpainted, wooden steps. Jo's room was a few steps to the left at the top of the stairs.

Without saying a word, Jo unlocked the door and Dave followed her inside.

It was a very small room with just a bed, dresser and a small round table with two wooden chairs. As Jo looked up into Dave's eyes, he stooped down to kiss her. Even though he was only five foot-six, he was very tall compared to her, she was only four foot-nine.

"This is hard on my back, bending down like this to kiss you," Dave said to Jo as he gently took her hand and led her to one of the chairs by the table.

"Here, sit on my lap," he said as he scooped her onto his lap.

"You're just so tall," laughed Jo.

As their eyes met, Jo pulled Dave's head toward hers. His lips met hers with a burning passion. Jo's mouth opened up as to summon Dave to enter.

He could not explain the feeling he had when he was with Jo. It was as though whenever they touched, they became one.

Jo's eyes slowly closed and then her grip loosened.

Dave thought about how beautiful she was.

"Jo," he said quietly.

"Jo," he said again as he kissed her cheek.

"I better go now," he told her as she opened her eyes.

"Okay! I'll walk you down to the street."

After they descended down the stairs, Jo stopped on the bottom step as Dave stepped on to the sidewalk. He turned to her and put his arms around her waist. Jo put her arms around his neck and kissed him.

Dave looked into those extraordinary light blue eyes and said, "Hey, this is perfect. I don't have to bend or stoop to kiss you. I can look you right in the eyes like this," looking directly into her eyes.

"I can't help it that you're so tall," laughed Jo.

This became their standing joke that they always laughed about.

Dave pulled Jo closer to him and kissed her passionately.

"I'll see you tonight," Dave said. He quickly kissed her one more time before he left.

The vision of Jo's eyes burned into Dave's mind as he heard the grandfather clock in the living room striking midnight. Rolling over in bed and thought, "She was so special."

"Where are you tonight, Jo? You know, I'm really sorry… Goodnight, Jo," he said to himself as he drifted off to sleep.

JOAN

Dave felt like he had just fallen asleep when he heard the alarm.

The day seemed to drag. He could not get Jo off of his mind. Even at lunch with all the guys, Dave was quiet.

Everyone kept asking him if he felt all right.

It was unlike Dave not to be pulling little pranks and joking, and he thought three o'clock would never get there.

Traffic was heavier than usual today. Dave found it hard to keep his mind on his driving because his thoughts kept returning to Jo.

He repeatedly found himself looking to his right, feeling as though he would find her sitting there.

"This is crazy," Dave thought to himself, "Why does her memory keep haunting me so? Am I still in love with her after all those years?"

Dave was totally bewildered.

Dave got home about ten minutes later than usual. Tony and Dan were both watching television. The three of them decided to order pizza for dinner.

After dinner, Dave fell into his usual routine, talking with the boys while waiting for Christine to get home.

Dave still could not shake this strange feeling that he had and nor could he keep Jo from his thoughts, but before he knew it, Christine was home.

As she ate, she told him about her day and they talked about their upcoming vacation they were planning for early July.

After lying down in bed, Dave was on the verge of what he thought would be a good night's sleep when he felt something touch his arm. He opened his eyes and brushed his arm.

He thought it must have been a fly. He tossed and turned, but sleep would not come because he could not stop thinking of Jo.

When he closed his eyes, he saw her face. When he opened his eyes, he saw her face.

Not wanting to wake Christine, he decided to go have a cigarette and sit out on the patio for awhile.

Dave looked upward at the stars and his mind drifted back once again to thirty years ago.

He thought about how he and Jo spent their nights.

Every night they were together. They would go to either their special hide-a-way and make love, and watch the stars until day light or they would go to her place and she would sit on his lap and then make love. But it seemed like they only made love once a night.

"Why didn't we do it two or three times in one night? We acted like old married people. Why didn't we have oral or exotic sex? I had it with other women before Jo and I had it with other women after her. What was so different about Jo? Maybe she wasn't the type to like oral sex, but why didn't I try to go down and give her oral sex?"

He remembered that Jo did not work on Sundays, so Dave tried not to either.

Their Sundays were spent riding around in Queen Vickie with all her four windows down and Jo sitting next to him, holding his arm against her body and with her legs curled up under her.

They would usually stop and eat lunch or dinner, but they always went to one of the various parks in the area.

They enjoyed their Sunday afternoon strolls through the parks, walking hand-in-hand, occasionally sitting on a park bench while stopping for a kiss or two.

Jo never wanted to talk about the past or the future. It was like today was the past while it was also the future, as though that moment and them were all that existed.

Dave remembered one Sunday in particular. He and Jo were holding hands and walking in a park. Dave sat down at a picnic table with his back against the table. Jo sat on his lap facing to the right where kids were playing on a playground area. Jo watched the kids running and playing.

Moms and dads were playing with their kids also, and they were all laughing and yelling.

Dave tried, to no avail, to get Jo's attention. He would kiss her on the cheek. She would turn her head, returning his kiss to his lips, and then quickly turn her attention back to the kids.

Finally, Dave gave up trying to get her mind off the kids and just sat there staring at the side of her face.

Dave thought about how much he loved her and he knew that she must be a wonderful mother and that she really missed her kids. He also knew that he could not ask her about her kids. All he could do was try to comfort her because his playful gestures could not change her line of thought.

After about an hour everyone left.

The park became silent and lonely. Dave and Jo sat there for a few more minutes, in silence, before they also left.

Then Dave's memory drifted to her name and recalled how Jo's name seemed to fit her. At times she acted like a fourteen year old tom-boy. But there were other times when she was as feminine and delicate as a princess.

Dave remembered one slow night when the H&H had only a few customers. Jo asked him to play G-4 on the jukebox.

As Eddy Arnold started singing, "Make the World Go Away," Jo came out from behind the bar holding out her arms to Dave and said, "Let's dance."

Dave put his arms around her while Jo's arms encircled his neck.

They swayed to the music as Jo rested her head on his chest and her hair gently touched his face. Her smell of wildflowers made his heart pound.

Breaking the silence, he asked, "What does Jo stand for?"

"Joan," she replied with her cute little smile.

"How do you do, Joan? Glad to meet you," he smiled.

Jo laughed. "Well, I'm happy to meet you too, David."

This was the only time Dave ever called her Joan. To him, she would always be his Jo.

THE MOVIE

As Dave stared at the sky, he thought, "Jo never told me her last name. How odd to spend an entire summer with a woman, to be completely in love with each other, and I didn't even know her last name... I don't think she knew mine either... how odd!"

As Dave took a big drag from his cigarette, he thought to himself, "She must have loved me. Just like the note..."

It was a Saturday night, about nine-thirty, and the H&H was busier than usual.

Dave was not quite sure why they were so busy that night, but he thought maybe it was the 4th of July.

As he walked into the bar, he saw that the stools that lined the front of the bar were all full. Even his usual place had already been taken.

Dave spotted an empty stool at the short end of the bar, so he claimed it.

Jo and Mary were working so fast that they were almost running. He ordered a Strohs and watched Jo as she brought him his beer and hurriedly served other customers.

After about ten minutes a stranger walked into the bar, scouting for a bar stool. With none to be found, he stood between Dave and the guy sitting next to him.

The stranger ordered a beer and downed it pretty fast. As Jo approached the end of the bar the man ordered another beer. When he paid Jo for the beer, he also handed her a note.

Without even looking at it, she handed it to Dave.

"What's this?" Dave asked.

"I don't know. He just handed it to me," she said as she tipped her head towards the stranger standing next to Dave.

Dave unfolded the note and read it.

It was a note asking Jo out.

Dave turned to the stranger and said, "Sorry, We're going together."

Gripping his beer with both hands, the stranger dropped his head and stared at his beer.

As Jo started to walk away, she looked over her shoulder and gave Dave a loving grin as the stranger sat his almost empty beer bottle down and left.

Feeling a little threatened by the idea of someone trying to move in on his girl, Dave stayed at the bar until they closed, even though he had to get up and go to work early the next day. It was one of those Sundays that he could not help but work.

Dave cleared the glasses as Jo wiped the tables down. It was still almost three o'clock by the time they finished cleaning up.

Dave went with Jo up to her room. Once inside, almost as if in one motion, Jo locked the door and threw her arms around his neck and practically knocked him down with her passion.

"Wow," Dave said as he regained his balance.

He led her over to a chair by the table and then lifted her onto his lap.

"Now, where were we?" he said as he pressed his lips against hers.

Dave slowly moved his mouth from her lips and down her neck while gently maneuvering his hand under her blouse and bringing it to rest on her breast.

"Oh Baby," Jo breathed as she rolled her head on his shoulder. "It's that time of the month for me, but if you don't mind, I don't either."

"I don't mind," Dave whispered between kisses.

"Come on... Let's get comfortable," Jo said as she got up from his lap and lead Dave to her bed. She pulled back the blankets.

Dave peeled off his clothes and then he watched as Jo stripped down to her panties.

She jumped onto the bed and crawled across to the middle of the bed. Dave watched as her tight, light blue panties outlined her voluptuous cheeks as they wiggled at him. Jo turned to face him.

She rested her head on her left hand and patted the bed while she seductively looked at him with a devilish grin.

Dave shook his head as if to say "No".

Jo's grin turned into a pout as she lowered her head and then looked up at Dave with the saddest little puppy dog eyes.

Dave laughed and jumped onto the bed, almost landing on Jo.

He pressed her burning lips with his mouth and she vigorously wrapped her arms and legs around him. Jo moaned her approval as Dave's tongue quickly found hers. Their heads moved in unison. Dave felt Jo's tongue searching around his own.

"Oh God," Dave moaned as he returned her gesture.

Dave began kissing Jo's neck passionately, working his way down to her breast.

"Oh, Baby," Jo cried as he began to move his tongue on her nipples.

Jo started kissing Dave all over his face and neck. They began to roll around on the bed. Somehow, Jo ended up on top.

Suddenly Jo jumped up.

"Stay right there. Don't move," she whispered as she climbed off the bed.

She grabbed a towel from the towel rack and spread it on the bed.

Dave rested on his side and watched as Jo slid her panties off.

She stretched out on the towel. She reached her arms for Dave and said, "I can't take it anymore. I have to have you now."

Jo screamed as Dave mounted her.

As he grew within her, Dave felt a tingle spread up the small of his back. The tingle turned into an electrifying shock that grew with intensity as it raced up his back, raising the hair on the back of his neck then shooting out the top of his head and exploding somewhere in outer space.

Jo's grip remained tight as she kissed his lips.

They lied in this position for another five or ten minutes, kissing and hugging each other with Dave still inside her. Finally Dave dismounted Jo.

She got up and wiped herself off with the towel. Handing the towel to Dave she said, "Here! You better wipe off, I'm flowing pretty good."

Putting her panties back on, Jo returned to Dave's waiting arms where they laid and talked until the sky grew lighter outside.

"I best go, Babe," Dave said.

Dressed, they walked with his arm around her, down the steps to the street. Stopping on the last step she threw her arms around his neck and lowered her head.

"I don't want you to go," she sighed.

Dave gently raised her head up with his right hand and kissed her lips, "I must go to work. I'll see you this afternoon. Now go back to bed and get some sleep."

"Okay! See you later," Jo said.

With another kiss, Dave released her, "I'll walk you up to your door."

Hand in hand and with her head leaning against his arm, they slowly climbed the stairs once again.

Unlocking her door, Jo smiled with her girlish look on her face and said, "You want to come in for a few minutes?"

"I better go," Dave gave her a light kiss and left.

Stopping at the top of the stairs, Dave paused for a moment then looked back and waved, she returned his wave and then he was gone.

Dave got off work at three o'clock. He stopped by the hotel, got cleaned up and then went over to Jo's place.

Before he could even knock, Jo opened the door and flung her arms around him.

"Hi, there!" she greeted him with a kiss and a smile.

"Hello," Dave said as he hugged her.

"So, where do you want to go today?" she asked with enthusiasm.

Jo seemed to love their Sunday afternoon drives. Dave loved their Sunday outings too, but today he was hoping to do something different.

Dave had not had much sleep. He had worked all day yesterday, slept for a couple of hours, got up and went to see Jo, stayed awake with her all night making love and then went straight to work. Now, here he was and what he really wanted to do was to lay on Jo's bed and take a little nap.

"Let's do something different," Dave said, almost hoping Jo would want to just stay home.

Jo stretched her arms out around his neck and in her childlike way she asked, "Do you want to go to the movies? Alfie is playing. I really would like to see it."

Dave looked into those pleading light blue eyes. How could he possibly tell her he was too tired, but then, Dave was sure she knew what he would say.

He never refused her anything she asked for, just as she never refused him anything that he asked of her.

Dave winked at her and Jo gave him a big kiss, kicked her shoes off and dashed to her closet.

Slowly he drugged his tired body to his chair at the table.

Jo pulled out five or six dresses. Holding the first one up to her, she asked, "Do you like this?" as she held the dress to her shoulders and pulled it tight against her waist so Dave could get the real picture.

"Looks great, Babe," he answered as Jo threw the dress on her bed and held up the second dress in the same manner before Dave could even finish his answer.

Jo went through this with all the dresses that she had pulled out as Dave continued to tell her how good each looked. Finally Jo dug through the pile of dresses she had thrown on the bed and held up the second or third dress again.

"I think I'll wear this," she smiled sexually at Dave.

Dave watched through half shut eyes as Jo peeled off her blouse and slid her shorts over her shapely hips, wiggling her little behind as her shorts fell to the floor.

Jo dug into her dresser drawer and pulled out a girdle, then slipped it on.

She then proceeded to dig deeper in the drawer until she found a pair of nylons.

She smiled, sitting on the edge of the bed and quickly put on and pulled up the nylons, then hooked them into place.

"Are the seams straight?" she asked Dave as she stood turning with her back to him.

"Perfect," he replied in amazement.

Jo grabbed the royal blue, sequenced dress. She eased it over her head, wiggling into it as she pulled it down.

"Zip me up, please," she said as she walked over and turned her back to Dave.

"What a fit," he whistled.

Jo smiled as she grabbed the other chair and set it in front of the dresser.

Dave's eyes opened a little wider as they roamed over every curve of his lady.

She pulled the combs from her hair and shook her head, then quickly brushed her hair out.

Dave was flabbergasted as he watched how fast and perfectly Jo applied her make-up.

As she picked up her lipstick she noticed Dave watching her.

She set the lipstick back down, hurriedly walked over, gave him a big kiss on his lips, then returned to the mirror and applied her lipstick.

Jo pulled a small jewelry box towards her and picked out a delicate gold chain with a pair of dangle earrings. In one swift motion, she latched the necklace in front, and then slid the latch to the rear of her neck as she flipped her hair over the necklace.

Moving her head from side to side, she screwed on her earrings.

Standing up, she went back to her closet, dug through a pile of shoes and pulled out a pair of blue high-heeled shoes to match her dress.

Spraying on her perfume and letting out a deep sigh, she said, "I'm ready," as she twirled a couple of times, stopping so Dave got a good look.

Dave took in the view and thought how beautiful she was.

Jo was short, but she had long legs compared to the rest of her body... Everything was proportioned perfectly. She looked like a doll, like a fragile china doll. He thought how much he was in love with her.

"You look great, Babe!" Dave whistled.

"Let's go," smiled Jo.

She locked the door behind them and handed Dave her key because she did not want to carry her purse.

He traded sides with her when they got to the bottom of the stairs so he was walking on the outside, nearest the street.

"Let's walk to the show," she suggested, "It's such a nice afternoon and it's only about three blocks or so."

They walked hand-in-hand to The Palace, which was the name of the movie house.

Once there, they found that they had an hour to kill before the movie started again.

"There's a nice little restaurant just up the street," Jo said to Dave. "Why don't we go have some supper, then we'll come back for the movie."

"Sounds great," he replied.

He just picked at his supper, making sure he ate light. He knew if he ate too much, he was going to fall asleep.

After supper, they walked back to The Palace and settled in mid-row about halfway down the isle in the theatre.

Dave put his arm around Jo, and she held his hand that draped over her shoulder.

She nestled up against him as he rested his head against hers.

Hard as he tried, Dave could not help but to doze off and on throughout the movie. The lack of sleep was starting to catch up to him, but there was no way he could deny his lovely lady this afternoon out.

When they came out of The Palace, the sun had just set and the street lamps started to light as they slowly walked back to Jo's place.

A car with five young guys passed blowing their horn and whistling at Jo.

As the car sped out of sight, Jo released Dave's hand then quickly walked ahead exaggerating her every movement with her steps.

Dave could not help getting aroused as he watched her hips sway from side to side. About fifteen or twenty feet ahead of Dave, she stopped and twisted her body in a way to look back at Dave over her right shoulder and gave him one of her familiar sexy grins while letting Dave catch up to her.

Dave drank in the site of this beautiful woman, dressed in her skin tight, royal blue, low cut in the back as well as in the front, mid-length dress with matching high-heeled shoes.

Dave burned the vision of this moment into his mind forever because no matter what the future held for them, he knew that he had this picture of her that he would carry forever in his mind.

He caught up to her, kissing her intensely as he wrapped his arm around her shoulder and she placed her arm around his waist.

As they continued their stroll, she still exaggerated her hip sway.

She covered her mouth with her other hand and giggled because her swaying made it difficult for Dave to walk close to her.

She smiled up at him and gave him a kiss.

Hand-in-hand, they continued their walk back to her place.

Dave pulled out her keys from his pocket and unlocked the door of Jo's place.

They stepped inside and all of a sudden sleep was the last thing on his mind.

He pulled her to him and kissed her so hard that she grasped for air.

It was not long before they were both out of their clothes and in Jo's bed.

In one swift move, she rolled herself over, grabbed a towel and spread it on the bed.

Jo shivered as Dave gently tantalized her erect nipples with his fingers while he kissed her neck.

Her wanting eyes looked deep into Dave's as he mounted her.

Without any guidance by either, his manhood found its own way into her.

Once again, they seemed to melt into one, and with their eyes locked, they needed no words.

Together they cried out in blissful harmony as they both climbed to the end of the universe and climaxed out of control while their pounding hearts steady matched rhythm.

They laid in each others arms for what seemed to be only a few minutes. Dave glanced at the clock sitting on her dresser.

"God," Dave thought, "We have been back from the movie for well over three hours now. I better go."

"I best go, Baby," he said as he softly kissed her, "I have to work tomorrow."

"Do you have to?" she asked in that little girl's voice.

"I'm filling in for a guy for the next few days on a rig outside of Mt. Gilead. I'll come and see you at the bar tomorrow night." He tried to sooth her sad-eyed pout.

"Promise," she asked.

"Promise," he smiled.

Quickly they cleaned themselves up.

"You know, there's a bigger apartment that will be available after Tuesday," she began as they dressed, "I told my landlord that I wanted it. It has a couple more windows and a kitchenette."

"Well, why don't you wait until Thursday and I'll help you move. Don't do it yourself, okay?"

"Okay," she answered.

Dave kissed her goodnight at her door.

As always, she walked Dave down to the street.

They kissed for a while, and then Dave walked Jo back up to her door, gave her another goodnight kiss and left.

Dave thought how lucky he was as he walked to his car.

Once he walked into his room at the hotel, he laid done in bed and quickly fell asleep reminiscing of this evening with Jo.

THE NIGHT PICNIC

Before he knew it, his alarm was going off at five o'clock.

Dave hurriedly got dressed, stopped by the coffee shop for a quick bite for breakfast then rushed off to work.

Even though he did not have to be at work until seven, the crews always try to relieve the crew on tour fifteen minutes early.

Dave made it a point to be at work a few minutes earlier than necessary. He was always one for promptness.

The crew and Dave changed their clothes and went to work.

Even though it was a beautiful day, it drug on.

Dave was disappointed when he thought for sure it must be about noon but then found that it was only nine-thirty.

Everywhere he looked, he saw Jo's face and he could not wait to hold her again.

Dave listened to the guys tell tall oil field stories and lie about the wild times they had. Dave never told them about Jo.

She was sacred and not to be shared in this manner.

Finally, it was two forty-five and the next crew was coming on to the rig.

Dave wasted no time washing up, changing his clothes and heading to the Union Hotel.

Instead of going directly to the hotel, he pulled into the parking lot behind Jo's place where the tenants parked.

He ran up the stairs and knocked on Jo's door.

When she opened it, he grabbed her and kissed her.

"I just couldn't wait 'til tonight to see you," he said to her.

"You poor thing... You look so tired," Jo said as she led him inside, "You haven't had much sleep, have you?"

With his arms around her waist, Dave looked down into Jo's eyes through his blood shot eyes and mumbled, "Enough," then he kissed her wanting lips again.

"I just had to stop and see you before getting some sleep. I'll be out in the parking lot, sleeping in Queen Vickie, when you get off. Wake me up, okay?" He followed with another kiss to her lips.

"Okay, Hon," Jo shook her head and walked with Dave to her door.

With a good-bye kiss, he headed off to the hotel and much needed sleep.

Dave got up around midnight. After getting a bath and shaving, he thought he would go down to the coffee shop to get something to eat.

Once he got there, he decided that instead of eating there, he would buy a couple cold ham and cheese sandwiches to take with him, one for Jo and one for him.

After pulling into the parking lot, Dave turned off the engine and lay down across the front seat.

It seemed like he just closed his eyes when he felt someone shaking him.

"Hey, good-looking," he heard as he opened his eyes.

"Well," Dave said as he sat up and got out of the car to let Jo in, "What took you so long?" He laughed as he kissed her.

They stopped by a gas station on the way out of town to get a couple of cokes to go with their sandwiches.

"It's such a clear night," Jo began as Dave turned into the driveway that led back to their hide-a-way, "Just look at those stars."

"Sure is nice," he said as he parked the car, and then he grabbed the blanket and pillow while Jo carried the cokes and sandwich.

Spreading the blanket under the oak tree, they sat facing one another while smiling at each other and ate silently.

"This is good but I'm stuffed," Jo laid down her half-eaten sandwich.

Dave reached for Jo, "Come here."

He pulled her to him while lying back onto the pillow.

"The stars are just unbelievable tonight," Jo remarked as she nestled down and rested her head on his chest.

Dave kissed the top of her head.

They laid there, content to just watch the stars and steal a kiss now and then.

Before they knew it, the dawn began to break and a new day commenced.

They looked towards the east and saw a beautiful sun rise.

"Is that a sight or what?" Dave said as he pulled Jo up to him and kissed her cheek, "But I guess we better head back so I can get to work."

"Work," Jo exclaimed, "When do you ever sleep?"

Holy Graduel

"Oh, I manage," He smiled at her.

They folded the blanket then headed back to town.

"I'll walk you up," Dave said as he helped Jo out of the car.

When they reached her door, he slipped his arm around Jo's waist and gently kissed her goodnight.

The sound of sirens in the distance jolted Dave back to reality. As he put out his cigarette, he shook his head and wondered why things ended the way they did.

He wished he could just hold her one more time.

Dave started to go back into the house to go to bed but then he stopped and glanced up into the night sky one last time. He longed to tell Jo what he should have told her so long ago.

Through teary eyes he said, "I'm really sorry, Baby… Goodnight Jo."

"I WANT YOUR BABY"

The next morning, after getting up, Dave headed to work as he drove down the 14 Freeway, his thoughts of Jo once again filled his mind and throughout the day.

Something was happening to him. There was a feeling inside of him that he just could not quite grasp.

The day slowly passed as Dave went through his daily routine. He had his smoke breaks with Bob and Fred and joined all of the guys for lunch. He wanted nothing more then to get through the day and go home.

When three o'clock finally came, he said his good-byes and headed up the 14 Freeway. Jo rode along in his mind.

Nearing Lancaster, Dave got off the Freeway and pulled into the Palmdale Car Wash just as he did every Wednesday.

"The works, please," he told the attendant.

After paying the cashier, Dave sat outside and waited for his car to be finished.

He sipped a Coke that he just bought, and he noticed a sign that read, "Senior's Special Wednesday."

Special Wednesday stuck in his mind. Dave remembered the night that it happened as clear as if it were yesterday and he always thought of it as Their Special Wednesday.

That...Their Special Wednesday, Dave had to work the daylight tour.

After cleaning up, he ate a can of cold chicken noodle soup and lay down for a while before going to see Jo.

He walked into the H&H around ten o'clock.

"Hi, Babe," Jo said as Dave took his usual spot at the bar.

Dave sipped on a couple of beers, and he talked with Jo until the bar closed.

After locking up, she turned to Dave and kissed him.

"I missed you today," she said.

"I missed you, too," he pulled her to him, gently kissing her as he massaged the small of her back.

Grabbing his hand, Jo led Dave up the rickety stairs to her place.

Once inside, she turned and looked deeply into his eyes. She stood in front of him as close as she could.

Dave smiled as she removed the combs from her hair, and then slowly she brushed the hair from her face, without moving her eyes from his.

He softly tilted her chin upward, lifting her lips to meet his.

He gently picked her up and kissed her enticing lips as he laid her onto the bed.

Their eyes were still locked. He smiled as he slowly removed her clothes, then his own.

The street light cast its glow across Jo's beautiful face, lacing golden highlights in her dark hair.

Her soft red lips invited his as he knelt between her shapely thighs, feeling the smoothness of them as his body joined with hers.

Jo's warm moisture engulfed him as he steadily entered her sacred depths.

Their passion for each other mounted higher and higher.

She clinched her fist as she started pounding him on his back.

"Give me a baby! I want your baby! Give me your baby! Give me a baby!" she commanded.

"Okay, Honey... I love you," Dave whispered into her ear.

"I love you, too," Jo breathed.

They climbed to a new height of pleasure as Dave swelled within her.

She tightened her grip around him while their fluids exploded together inside her, causing their bodies to shake as one.

Quickly she covered his face with kisses.

Dave tried fruitlessly to return her kisses.

Between kisses, she kept repeating, "I love you."

In response, Dave kept repeating, "I love you, too".

Finally, with one big kiss to his lips, Jo held Dave tight and placed the side of her head against the side of his head. She squeezed him tightly with her arms and legs still wrapped around him.

Time stood still as they lay in this position. After awhile, she released her grip and Dave rolled off of her. Jo lay with her head on his chest and silently played with the hair on his chest and stomach.

Dave ran his hand up and down her back and thought of how much he loved her. This is the woman he wanted to be with forever.

As the room lightened with the coming of dawn, the birds began to sing.

"Let's go to breakfast," he said.

"Sure, Hon," Jo purred as she finger-wrote the letters, 'J' and 'O' on his chest.

Over a table at their usual coffee shop, they held hands while eating breakfast with their other hand.

Once again, words were not needed as they looked deeply into each other's eyes and smiled at one another between bites.

After finishing breakfast, Dave drove Jo back to her place.

He noticed how tired Jo looked as they slowly climbed the stairs and she unlocked the door.

"Aren't you coming in?" Jo asked Dave who stopped at the doorway.

"No. I want you to go inside and get some sleep. Honey, you can hardly hold your eyes open. I'll be back at one o'clock to wake you up and help you move, okay?"

"I'm not..."

Dave silenced her with a deep long kiss.

"I love you," he said with a final squeeze.

"I love you, too. Promise you'll be back at one?" Jo asked with a pleading look in her eyes.

"I promise," Dave smiled.

"All right, here," Jo said as she dangled her apartment keys in front of Dave, "Wake me up when you get here," She winked.

Dave grabbed the keys and ...

Startled by the sound of a car horn, Dave came out of his daze and saw that the attendant was flagging that his car was ready.

As he pulled out of the car wash, heading home, he wondered about that Wednesday night again.

"Why did Jo ask me to give her a baby? I never used any protection. Didn't she know that? Did she use some protection? I am not sure. What I am sure of is she was in complete control of that particular situation, and she could have easily gotten pregnant anytime without my permission. Why did she command me to give her a child? And yet it is almost as if she seemed to need my approval...

And he thought that from that point on, it became a ritual that we made love daily. Jo no longer climaxed two or three times before we united. Now, we always came together. Our passion burned deep as our souls seemed to combine into one every time we made love... We were trying to conceive a life. And that was the first time that I ever told Jo that I loved her and that was also the first time that she told me, and from that point on, we always told each other "I love you." It was like I didn't want her just for sex, I

Holy Graduel

wanted for us to truly love one another.

JO'S NEW APARTMENT

Dave and the boys had just finished their dinner when Christine got home.

"Hi, guys!" she said as she threw her briefcase and purse on the sofa.

"Hi!" they all replied.

"You ready for some dinner?" Dave asked her as she walked into the kitchen.

"No, I just want some coffee right now," Christine said as she poured herself a cup of coffee.

The evening past swiftly, and around nine o'clock they all headed to bed.

Dave was unable to sleep again.

Around eleven-thirty, he looked over at Christine sleeping so peacefully.

He loved Christine, but he could not get Jo out of his mind, and her memory would not let him rest.

"If I could only turn back the time, Jo," he thought, "If I could only hold you in my arms once again."

Her memory burned stronger and stronger in his mind.

Everywhere he looked, he saw her face, and soon he was with her once again in his mind as he fell asleep.

After unlocking Jo's room, he walked over to her bed, and he stared down at Jo restfully sleeping in her bed.

She was so innocent looking. He loved her and knew he wanted to protect his little baby forever.

"Good morning," he said softly as he leaned down and kissed her forehead.

"Hi!" she whispered as she stretched, smiled and she opened her eyes.

She wrapped her arms around his neck and said, "What a great way to wake up."

Dave's lips went immediately down on her lips ever so gently.

"Are you going to sleep all day?" he laughed, "Come on sleepy head, we've got some packing to do."

Jo got up, combed her hair and freshened up a little.

"I can't wait to get moved in to my new place," she grinned.

They began packing up her things. It really did not take long because there was not a whole lot to pack.

With their arms loaded with boxes, they walked down the hall to the other end of the same building.

Jo set down her box and unlocked the door.

As the door swung open, she quickly picked up her box and entered.

Dave could not help but notice how Jo beamed as she set her box down on the little wooden table in her kitchenette.

She spread her arms out, showing Dave her new place.

"So, what do you think?" she said.

He set his boxes down and took in the view. He looked straight ahead and he saw that there was a step down to the kitchenette and to the left of that was a small bathroom, and directly to the left of him was the bed and dresser.

"Not bad, it's something how much more light you get with just a couple of more windows," he nodded his head in approval as he told Jo who stood gleaming with pleasure at her new place.

She was like a little kid with a new toy.

Jo turned toward Dave and threw her arms around him. She hugged his neck. "You know, I feel that I love this place almost as much as I love you," she teased as she kissed him quickly on the lips.

Dave smiled and returned the kiss, "We better get the rest of your stuff moved before I forget what we are doing and get side-tracked. The bed looks inviting."

They had everything moved into Jo's new apartment within the hour.

Dave set down the last box and stretched his tired back.

"Well, that's the last of it," he said.

Jo had pretty well put things in their place while he moved them in.

"Thanks for helping me," Jo said, standing on her tip toes and gave Dave a kiss.

"No problem," he said as he pulled her closer to him and looked deeply into her eyes.

Her lips met his with a burning desire as they stood by the bed and Dave held her tighter, feeling her body pressing against his.

"Maybe we had better try out your new bed," he suggested.

"Maybe we should," Jo smiled and then released her grip around Dave's neck.

Then stepping back from Dave, she began to undress.

It did not take long for Dave to follow.

In a passionate rush, they clung to each other like glue.

Dave pulled Jo up on to the pillow as they fell to the bed together.

"I love you," Dave whispered in a pant as he mounted Jo.

Suddenly, they both stopped their actions simultaneously. Jo's new bed squeaked enormously.

"Wait! I have an idea," Jo said as he got off of her.

He seemed to read her mind.

They both grabbed the blankets and pillows from the bed and laid them out on the floor.

Jo laid down and put her head on the pillow. She reached out her arms to him and asked with that familiar little grin, "Now, where were we?"

Dave kissed her deeply.

Jo pulled him closer, grinding her hips against his in a circular motion as he whispered, "I love you."

Dave's mouth covered hers as their tongues met.

"I love you too," Jo responded as he lifted himself up on his arms, and he smiled down at Jo and gently entered her.

Dave could not take his eyes from Jo's beautiful face as she whimpered with pleasure.

Dave felt himself growing inside of her, and together, they exploded to a new height of their climax.

Awaken by Christine turning over in her sleep brought Dave out of his memories of Jo.

Dave glanced at the clock. In four hours, he would have to get up for work.

"Why do you keep haunting me?" he wondered of Jo as he got up to take some NyQuil. He thought the NyQuil would help him find sleep as it had so many other sleepless nights.

"I loved you so much, Jo. I would have done anything for you... I'm sorry for what happened," he whispered to himself.

Carefully, Dave turned over in bed, hoping that he would not wake Christine.

"Damn it!" He brushed his shoulder, "These flies. Tomorrow I'm going to buy some fly spray. Every night one lands on me when I'm trying to go to sleep. Hell, I might as well have a cigarette."

DIVORCE PAPERS SERVED

Dave sat halfway up on the bed, lit a cigarette and recalled the rest of the week after he helped Jo moved.

After they made love that Thursday afternoon, she had to go to work.

Dave told her that he had to stop by the rig to pick up his paycheck, then run to Wooster to take care of some business and would be back Sunday morning.

Dave stopped by the rig and picked up his check, and then drove straight to his in-laws.

He missed his son and was looking forward to seeing him.

"Nobody's home," Dave's father-in-law yelled from the porch as Dave walked up the sidewalk.

"Where are they?" Dave asked.

"They all went shopping or something. Then they're gonna have supper and go to the movies. I don't expect them 'til late."

"Well Hell, I'm going to go down and visit with my mom and dad. I'll come back later," Dave said as he told the old man good-bye.

As he drove down to his folk's place, Dave thought his father-in-law acted like he didn't want Dave to come in. Then again, there was never any love lost between him and his in-laws.

Dave's mom and dad were happy to see him.

He called his in-law's place a couple of times but no one answered.

As usual, Dave and his parents spent the evening laughing and talking over cups of coffee and they topped it off with a large pizza, before finally going to bed fairly late.

"Well, morning," Dave said to his mom as he walked into the kitchen.

"Good morning, how about some coffee?" she started to get up from the kitchen table.

His mom was short and a heavier older woman who never dressed very well; she never wore anything else besides dresses that always were tattered, and she rarely wore shoes inside.

Dave held up his hand and said, "Sit down, I'll get it, I know where everything is, what about you, do you want some more?"

"I'll take just a dab more, thanks. How about if I fix you up some eggs and bacon," she said.

"No, I really don't want anything," Dave smiled sipping on his hot cup of coffee.

Just then, they heard someone walking across the long wooden porch in a hurriedly long stride. The footsteps stopped at the kitchen door and then came a knock on the door.

Dave got up to answer it as his mom looked toward the door.

"Good morning, sir," a Sheriff started as Dave opened the door.

Dave closed the door behind him as he went out onto the porch.

After a few minutes, Dave returned inside again.

"What is it?" Dave's mom asked as she saw a discerned Dave close the door behind him.

He glanced at the legal looking paper he had just signed for.

"I've been served divorce papers," Dave said solemnly as he went into the living room to call his wife.

The phone rang and rang.

"Where are you," Dave wondered to himself while pictures of his son flashed through his mind. And then he hung the phone up after about fifteen rings.

Dave waited for about an hour before he decided to drive over to his in-laws. The house looked deserted and cold. No one answered the door bell and no cars were in the drive.

Dave's dad arrived home from work shortly after twelve o'clock.

He was a dark thin man, who stood 5foot 7. He always wore some kind of baseball cap and his company's uniforms.

Dave spent the afternoon with his mom and dad, periodically trying to call his wife on the phone.

Finally, late Saturday afternoon he was able to talk with his wife.

"What's going on?" Dave asked her.

"I just can't take it anymore," she said, "You're always gone. You're never home. I want more out of life..."

"I want to see my boy!" Dave told her.

"Forget it. If you can't be here all the time, then don't bother," he heard her say as the phone went dead.

Dave's heart sank because he loved his boy more than anything in the world.

Not wanting his mom and dad to know how angry he was with his wife and how hurt he was about not to be able to see his boy, Dave had another cup of coffee with them before he left, promising to see them soon.

Dave headed straight for the Pines, a bar just about two miles outside of Wooster on the east side.

The Pines was a rough bar known to have a lot of fights. They had a cheap but loud country band, where the women were wild and the place was always packed.

Dave did not go there very often because it was not his kind of place. But tonight, he was pissed.

He could not believe what his bitch of a wife was trying to pull now.

She was threatening him with his own kid.

The more he drank, the angrier he became.

Dave drank all night long, and then he started thinking about his life.

"What the Hell am I doing?" he wondered. "Jo is the most wonderful thing that ever happened to me and I love her more than life itself. But what kind of future do we have? I'm twenty-one and with a kid, she's twenty-seven years old with nine kids. Will I ever be able to support ten kids and a wife? Will I ever see my boy again?"

(This occurred in August and Dave had turned twenty-one on June 12th.)

Dave was so confused. He drank until he was so drunk nothing mattered.

Dave was not sure how he got there, but when he awoke, he was at a roadside rest on I-71, heading for Marion. He looked at his watch and saw that it was near eleven o'clock in the morning... Sunday morning.

He would not have much time to clean up once he arrived at the hotel in Marion, before he was suppose to meet Jo.

Dave decided to clean up there at the roadside rest instead of driving back to the hotel first. This way, he could drive straight to Jo's place.

THE WARNING

It was fifteen before noon as Dave pulled in front of the H&H.

His heart fluttered as he raced up the stairs.

Life with Jo was always so simple. He could not wait to hold her in his arms again. And when Jo opened the door, she practically fell into his embrace.

Without a word, she kissed him long and hard.

"I love you, and it felt like you were gone a lifetime," Jo said as they went inside.

"I love you and missed you, too," he told her with another kiss.

Reaching up with her left hand, she placed it on the back of Dave's neck and pulled him down to her. She placed his forehead against hers.

Their eyes were just inches apart. She looked deeply into his eyes and while running her index finger around the outside of his left ear, she asked, "Hon, I would like for us to go to my sister's place today, okay?"

She smiled her little girl smile.

"Okay," Dave answered.

Jo jumped up and down a couple times as she clasped her hands together.

"Let's go!" She exclaimed excitedly, and she grabbed her purse as they headed out the door.

She held Dave's hand as she practically ran to Queen Vickie.

This time she did not wait for Dave to open her door. She just opened the car door herself and slid in.

She sat on her legs and she held Dave's arm tight to her with both of her arms after he started the car.

Jo smiled, shrugged her shoulders up as she pulled Dave's arm tighter to her side.

Unlike herself, she talked all the way to her sister's. Besides giving

Dave directions of turns and bridges coming up on the road, she talked about houses she liked or disliked as well. She was almost like a little kid going to see Santa at the Mall.

But very much to her character, she never said a word about the past or the future.

Dave thought how different Jo was than his wife.

"Slow down, we'll miss their drive. Their driveway is just up a little on the left," Jo said excitedly.

They pulled down a long gravel driveway.

Dave barely had stopped the car and turned off the engine before she slid across the seat, opened the door and ran around to Dave just as he closed his door behind him.

Holding hands, they hurriedly walked up the long sidewalk together.

They entered the house through the kitchen.

Dave stopped in the dining room that held a big long table.

Jo ran into the next room laughing and yelling.

There were kids everywhere, who also laughed and yelled.

She bent down and kissed and hugged each one of them.

They practically knocked her down while they all tried to hug her at the same time.

This scene reminded Dave of an old home Christmas.

With her arms still around the kids, who were yelling as they clung to her, Jo shouted introductions of Dave to her mother, her sister Linda, her brother-in-law John and John's brother Jerry.

These guys looked like they could hunt bears with a stick.

The women all started talking together.

"What do you guys say we go outside where it's not quite so noisy," laughed John to Dave and Jerry.

Both men chuckled and agreed as they followed John outside.

"Sure is a nice day today," Jerry said as they walked along the sidewalk toward the gravel drive.

"It sure is," replied Dave.

"So Dave, what do you do for a living?" asked John as he picked up a piece of wood lying near the picnic table under the broad maple tree near the edge of the drive.

"I work in the oil fields," Dave answered in wonder.

John pulled out a pocket knife as he sat on the top of the picnic table and began to whittle on the piece of wood he had found.

Dave stood in front of John, watching him whittle as Jerry stood to the left of him facing Dave.

"You know Dave we all *really* love Jo," John began without looking up from his handy work, "Her husband was an ass. He treated her real bad. Now, we don't care who she sees or who she goes with, just as long as who ever it is, as long as she's happy."

Dave didn't say a word as John slowly looked up at him.

John and Jerry both grinned at him as Dave stamped out the cigarette he just finished.

Then Dave heard that familiar voice behind him, "Hey, are you ready to go?" Jo was calling to Dave as she came out of the house.

"Yea, we probably ought to. It was nice meeting you guys," Dave said without a handshake from John and Jerry.

John and Jerry just nodded their heads and didn't say a word.

Dave opened the car door for Jo.

She pulled the back of her front seat forward.

The three kids piled into the back seat. Then Jo slid in on her side of the front seat, sitting a modest six to twelve inches from Dave with her hands folded on her lap.

This was the one and only time that Jo did not hang on to Dave as he drove.

As they headed back to her place, Dave stopped at a tee in the road. And suddenly, one of the two little girls in the back seat sprang forward and pointed, with her arm extended between Dave and Jo, at the graveyard across the street. "Look!" she exclaimed, "There's President Harding's tomb."

"Oh, that's Harding's tomb, huh," Dave remarked as Jo smiled at the little girl and then at Dave.

He turned right, onto a cross street and drove straight to Jo's place.

It seemed like no time at all and then they were back at Jo's.

Dave stopped the car in the parking lot behind the H&H, Jo got out and flipped her seat forward and helped the kids get out.

"You guys wait for me," she said as they got out of the car.

Dave never got out of the car.

After the last little one was out, Jo put the seat back up and looked into Dave's eyes with a smile.

Neither one had to say anything.

"I'll see you tomorrow," Dave smiled back.

"Okay," she said as she closed the car door and shrugged her shoulders.

Dave was sort of glad that he did not go in with them. Unbeknown to Jo, he had one bad hangover and really wanted to just get some sleep.

"What a picture," Dave thought as he gazed in amazement at his princess in her short sleeved checked shirt, which was tied up in the front, revealing a slice of her back above her white shorts. He noticed that she was not much taller than the kids surrounding her as they walked across the dirt parking lot. Dave watched as they all disappeared up the wooden stairs, then he drove away.

All of a sudden, Christine quietly slumbered out of bed to turn off the alarm.

Christine had purposely placed their alarm clock across the room on the dresser because she had gotten into a bad habit of hitting the snooze button.

It was then that Dave realized that he had sat in bed all night only thinking of Jo.

"Shit," he said, "I'm so tired. I don't think I'm going to go in to work today."

Looking in on Dave before she left, Christine asked, "Did you get a hold of Matt?"

"I left a message on his voice mail."

"Alright, I'm going to go now. See you tonight."

"See you tonight. Be careful. Love you," Dave said to Christine.

"I love you, too," Christine replied as she closed the bedroom door behind her.

GOING TO DAVE'S MOM'S

Dave finally fell asleep again.
It was a little afternoon when he woke up to a quiet and empty house.
He poured a cup of coffee, sat down at the dining room table and lit up a cigarette, and his thoughts once again drifted back to the summer of '65.
After he had dropped Jo and the kids off at her place, he drove back to the hotel and thought of his Jo.
He only wished that he was holding Jo in his arms instead of needing to sleep off the night before because she had become the most important person in his life, and contently think of Jo soon he drifted off to sleep.
The next three weeks passed quickly. He would always go back to the hotel after work, get a bath, sleep for a few hours, and then go to the H&H to see Jo.
When she would get off from work, they would either go to their special hide-a-way or they would go to Jo's place. And their Sundays remained reserved for their Sunday afternoons in the parks.
Dave had just walked in to the hotel.
"Good afternoon, Sir," the desk clerk said to Dave as he stopped by the desk to pick up his messages. Dave had received a message from his mom that his paycheck was mistakenly sent home instead of being held at the rig.
"Thank you," he said to the desk clerk and headed to his room.
It had been a very long day for Dave. He was beat. He took his bath, and then crashed onto the bed until his alarm went off at nine-thirty.
Dave walked into the H&H about ten o'clock that night.
"Hey, Babe!" Jo said from behind the bar as she got Dave a beer.
"Hello, Beautiful," he smiled and took a sip of his cold beer and added, "How are you doing tonight?"
"Better now that you're here," she reached across the bar toward Dave for a kiss.

"Are you having a bad day?" he asked her.

"Not really. I just missed you."

Dave smiled at her with a wink and said, "Hey! My mom called today. My paycheck was sent to her house by mistake, so I have to go pick it up. You want to go with me?"

"Me... when are you going?" she asked.

"I thought we could go when you get off work."

"You don't mind waiting for me?"

Dave was sure that Jo knew the answer to that. He would wait until the end of the world for her if he had to.

It was near three o'clock in the morning by the time Jo had everything cleaned and locked up at the bar.

They had about a sixty to seventy mile drive ahead of them.

Jo seemed to be pretty excited about the trip to Dave's Mom's.

She stayed awake for the first few miles, and then decided to curl up on the seat and take a little nap before they got there.

Dave noticed how small and delicate Jo was as he watched her sleeping so peacefully.

"You're so beautiful," he quietly whispered, laying his free hand on her shoulder.

She was so tiny... she looked like a little girl lying there on the seat.

With Jo sleeping, he ran Queen Vickie at more of his normal speed, which was around a hundred.

Dave pulled into his mom's before four o'clock.

He pulled into the alley and parked under the apple tree in the back yard where he always parked. Jo never woke up.

She was sleeping so soundly that Dave could not find it in his heart to wake her up. She was so tired that he decided to just run in by himself.

He picked up his paycheck and talked with his mom for a few minutes. He told her that he had to go to work, but he would be back again soon.

He went back out to the car. Jo was still sleeping.

She must have been even more tired than he had imagined because she slept all the way back to Marion.

Dave parked in the back parking lot of the H&H, and Jo never budged.

He went around to her side of the car and opened the door. He took her apartment key from her purse and sliding her purse over his shoulder, and then he gently picked her up.

"Are we there yet?" a sleepy Jo asked through half opened eyes.

"We've already been there, and now we're back home," Dave told her quietly as he pushed the car door shut.

"You should have woke me up," Jo said as her eyes slowly shut once again.

Dave carefully carried her up the stairs while she slept like a baby. He unlocked the door, walked in and laid his precious cargo down on her bed.

He slipped her shoes off and pulled the blankets snugly up around her.

He kissed her gently on her forehead and then he whispered, "Goodnight, Baby."

He laid Jo's keys beside her purse on the dresser so she would see them, and then quietly closed the door behind himself as he left.

Dave stopped at the top of the stairs and lit up a cigarette.

The sun was just starting to lighten the sky.

He walked slowly down the stairs to Queen Vickie and decided that he would go to the coffee shop and have a couple cups of coffee.

He knew that if he lay down at all, he would never get up in time for work.

A SAD JO

Dave was working pretty steady by then. He was getting known and was being offered more daylight shifts to work. And so, it became that during the evenings he slept a few hours, and then went to see Jo every night. And their love seemed to grow stronger and stronger every day.

No matter how tired they were, they seemed to always come to life when Jo got off work and they would once again come together as one.

The love they shared was not sexual only. Their love was a bond between a man and a woman; two Souls united as one.

Dave recalled that one Sunday in particular.

Jo just did not seem to be herself at all that day at the park.

"What's the matter?" Dave had asked her several times.

"Nothing," Jo would always answer with a quick kiss to his lips.

Dave could definitely sense sadness in her, though. Not just in her voice, but in her whole being.

Jo sat close and held Dave's arm in her usual way, but stared straight ahead during their drive back to her place.

Dave wondered what was wrong as they walked hand-in-hand up to her apartment.

"Come here, Baby," he said as he sat at his usual spot at Jo's table and pulled her onto his lap.

He looked tenderly into her eyes.

She smiled and gave him a quick kiss.

She hugged him so hard as if she were afraid to let go.

"I love you," Dave said tenderly.

"I love you, too," she whispered as she leaned her head against his.

Dave began kissing her neck, working his way up toward her pretty face, and he thought how good she smelled.

Jo placed her hand on the back of his head as he slowly found his way to her lips. He pressed against hers ever so gently as his hand softly rubbed her inner thigh.

Taking a deep breath from his kiss, Jo whispered, "I started flowing today, but that's okay, if I'm not..."

"We don't need to do anything, as long as I am with you," Dave interrupted and followed with a kiss.

He held her in his arms, then carried her over to the bed and laid her gently down.

After turning on the radio, Dave laid down beside her.

There he held Jo in his arms as he lightly stroked her arm.

Dave was completely content to just lay there holding Jo, listening to the country music as the room darkened while the evening became night.

Dave glanced at his watch and saw that it was almost ten o'clock.

"Well, Babe," he said, "I better go."

"Do you have to?" Jo asked.

"I have to get up early in the morning, and you need to get some sleep, too. Neither one of us have had much sleep this week," he said as he kissed her forehead before getting up from the bed.

Jo followed Dave to the door.

"I love you," she said as she put her arms around his neck.

"I love you and I'll see you tomorrow," he kissed her one more time.

"Goodnight," Jo said as she closed and locked the door.

Dave went back to the hotel and went straight to bed for a much needed night of rest. Sundays were usually the only night that he and Jo got a good night's sleep.

Dave felt refreshed when he woke up Monday morning.

He thought of Jo all day.

He hated leaving her last night. She was so fragile. It hurt him badly inside to see her so sad. He knew that when she was ready, she would tell him whatever it was that made her feel so down.

"My God, why did I cut her off in mid-sentence when she started to tell me?" Dave asked himself, "She was ready to tell me."

The week passed swiftly.

Dave saw Jo every night, she seemed a little down, but never said what had made her feel bad. They spent the nights just laying together, holding each other like there was no tomorrow, as they listened to the radio until it was time for Dave to go to work.

Friday night, around nine-thirty, Dave walked into the H&H.

Jo had just served drinks to a couple at the back booth near the stool where Dave always sat.

"Hi, Babe!" Jo said with a kiss to Dave as she passed by him.

Dave thought about how nice it was to see her happy once again.

Jo grabbed a beer from the cooler from behind the bar and popping the cap, she sat it down in front of Dave.

"Let's go to our special hide-a-way tonight," she said with smiling eyes.

"Okay!" winked Dave.

Jo was ready to leave at two-thirty.

"Don't you have to lock up?" Dave asked her.

"No. Mary's locking up for me tonight. Let's go," she quickly responded.

Jo sat close to Dave, holding his arm tightly while occasionally rubbing her head against him. And they gazed at the lit road ahead as Queen Vickie streaked through the darkness.

Dave pulled Queen Vickie near the huge oak tree which they always would lay under.

He barely turned off the engine when Jo said, "Give me the keys," as she reached down and pulled the keys from the ignition.

In one swift motion, she slid across the seat and jumped out of the car.

By the time Dave got out, she was already getting the blanket and pillow from the trunk.

Dave helped her spread the blanket under the tree.

As their eyes met, Jo reached her arms out to Dave.

He fell to his knees as he took her hands in his. He pulled her gently down to him. Their lips met in wild passion.

Dave slowly moved his hands up and down the small of her back, resting them on her buttocks.

"I love you," Dave told Jo, laying her down onto the blanket.

"I love you so much," she said as she looked into his eyes as if she were searching for his inner soul.

He crushed her luscious parted lips while her hips began to grind against his moving pelvic.

Dave's desires hungered for Jo.

Five days he had patiently waited for her to tell him what was bothering her, which she never did. However, now life had returned to his princess.

Jo hurriedly helped Dave remove his clothes, and then they both removed hers as they fell back down onto the blanket together.

Jo showered Dave with kisses all over his face until she finally found his lips. Their lust burned deep as they both gasped for air. They both cried out in intense delight and the love flowed from within them as they blended into one.

They both just laid there for what seemed to be an eternity while they caught their breath. Dave could feel Jo's heart pounding against him.

"I love you," she said as she rubbed her foot up and down the calf of his leg.

"I love you," he softly repeated to her before kissing her again.

After getting dressed, Dave held Jo in his arms as they lay on the blanket and stared up at the stars.

Jo smiled with contentment as she let out a big sigh.

"What?" Dave asked her with curiosity.

"Oh nothing," Jo turned and looked up into his eyes, "I just love being with you. I love everything about you."

Dave shook his head and smiled as he tenderly kissed her.

A HAPPY JO

Just before daylight, Jo held out her hand, "Did you feel that?"
"What?" he asked.
"I felt rain drops," she said as she wiped her hand and extended it back out again.

Raindrops began to fall lightly. They jumped up and quickly grabbed their pillow and blanket, laughing and running they dashed to the car.

"This is crazy! There's no clouds in the sky and the stars are out, but it's raining," Dave exclaimed while Jo was still laughing.

"We had better get out of here before we get stuck," he said as he hurriedly started the car, drove out of the field and headed back toward Marion.

"I'm hungry. Let's go get some pie and coffee," Jo chuckled as she held her hand over her mouth and tried not to let Dave see her still laughing.

"Well, Hell! We may as well. It's almost time for me to get and go to work anyhow."

"Get and go to work? Or do you mean, Get up and go to work," Jo burst into roaring laughter.

Embarrassed, Dave lit up a cigarette and remarked, "You know what I meant."

They pulled into the parking lot of the little coffee shop that they frequently stopped at.

"Hi there, Dave," Betty, the morning waitress, yelled, "You brought Jo with you this time, huh? I guess we have to be good today. Oh, Hi Jo. How are you doing?" Betty laughed.

Dave was lost for words.

Jo threw her arms around Dave's waist and pulled him to her side, "Don't you be trying to steal my guy," Jo smiled at Betty and then at Dave.

Dave and Jo walked over to their favorite booth, the last one in the corner, and sat down.

Betty set their water on the table and then pulled her pad out from her apron pocket.

"You kids want some coffee?"

"Yea, and how about a couple pieces of your homemade apple pie to go with it," Jo beamed.

They finished their pie and coffee, and then they headed back to Jo's.

As usual, Jo stopped on the first step of the stairs so she could look directly into Dave's eyes.

His hands rested on each side of her hips as Jo wrapped her arms around him.

As they looked into each other's eyes, their lips came together for the longest time, then briefly breaking apart followed by another long kiss as their tongues lightly touched.

Dave grabbed her hand and said, "Come on. I'll walk you to your door."

With a smile on her face, Jo stared at Dave all the way up to her door.

They stopped at her door as she unlocked and opened it.

"I have to go to work," Dave softly said.

She threw her arms around his neck and pulled him down to her.

Their lips met in a tender kiss. She broke her lips away from his and pulled his head down along side of hers by squeezing his neck.

"I had a wonderful time tonight," she whispered.

She did not release him from her grip.

"I had a great time too," Dave whispered.

He gave her another kiss and then pulled her arms loose.

"I best get going now. You go on inside and get some sleep and I'll see you tonight."

Dave got to work right just in time.

He was happy that it was Saturday and his last day on this rig. He was not going to ask anyone else if they wanted him to fill in for them because this rig was junk, a real man killer. Dave only hoped that his paycheck from this rig would not bounce.

Dave was glad to see the other tour coming up the steps onto the drilling rig at two forty-five.

"Well guys, see you later," he told the driller. He just wanted to get the hell away from this junk.

Dave headed back to the hotel but decided to drop in on Jo to see her before she went to work.

He parked Queen Vickie in the back parking lot and ran up the steps to Jo's door and knocked on it.

Jo opened the door in surprise.

"My gosh! What happened to you?" She asked wide-eyed as she gave him a quick up and down look.

"What? Oh shit!" Dave looked down at his clothes, "I forgot to change after work."

Jo laughed until tears came into her eyes.

"You know, you kind of look like those guys we met in the cafe on our first date. But that's okay. I love you anyway."

"I just wanted to come by and see how you were feeling before you went to work. Don't touch me. I don't want you to get all dirty."

As he stepped back, he blew her a kiss, "I'll see you later."

"I missed you, too. Love you," she said as she blew him a kiss back.

Dave went down to his car and changed his clothes in the parking lot.

He could not believe that he was in such a hurry to get away from that junk that he forgot to change and he certainly did not want to go into the hotel looking like that.

As soon as he entered the hotel lobby, he walked directly to the pay phone, and dialed zero.

After a couple rings, "Operator, may I help you?"

"Hello, operator, this is a collect call," Dave replied.

"Area code and number you wish to call, please."

"The area code is 216, the number is 555-1312," Dave answered back just as coldly as the operator talked.

"Your name, please," the monotone voice asked.

"Dave *please*," oh shit, thought Dave.

Dave could hear the telephone at the other end ringing.

"Hello," Dave heard his Mother say.

"Will you accept a collect call from Dave Please?" the operator asked in her dead calm voice.

His mother asked, "From who?"

"Will you accept a collect call from Dave Please?" repeated the operator. This time she put a little life into her voice.

Dave broke into their conversation, "Mom, this is Dave calling. Operator, she will accept the call, okay?"

"Of course I'll accept a call from Dave. He's my son. Operator, why didn't you say Dave was calling? I don't know any Dave Please. And if I did, why would he be calling collect?"

"Hello, Mom," Dave answered.

"Is there something wrong, Dave?"

"No, I just called to see how you and Dad are." Dave was trying not to worry his Mom.

"We are okay Dave. How about you? You aren't sick are you?" She asked worriedly.

"No Ma. I'm okay. I just needed you to get me an old friend's number. Remember Bob Wert? I want to call him. It's in the phone book under Attorneys."

"Wait a minute... here it is, it's 555-5234. Are you in trouble Dave? Is there anything we can..."

Dave interrupted her, "Everything is fine. I just need to talk with him, that's all. Well, Mom, I better go. Don't want to run your phone bill up. Tell Dad I said Hi."

"Okay, Dave. You be careful, good-bye."

The phone went dead. Dave brought the phone away from his face and just stared at it.

"He won't be in his office today, it's Saturday. I'll call him Monday. Maybe he can help me get my boys back," Dave thought.

Dave dashed upstairs to his room to get cleaned up, eat another can of cold chicken noodle soup and to get some sleep.

In no time at all, Dave drifted into a deep sleep.

He dreamt of Jo; the sky was blue and the sun burned hot on the pavement as Queen Vickie's wheels sang on the soft blacktop. The speedometer's needle pointed past one hundred and twenty. With all of the windows down, Jo sat close to him with her legs curled under her, holding his right arm tightly against the side of her breast, and country music blared while they raced down the road.

Dave slowed Queen Vickie down, pulled over to the side of the road under a big shady tree. Putting the drive selector into park, he turned to Jo, put his arms around her and brought his slightly parted lips down to hers. His tongue lightly touched the tip of hers....

Dave jumped at the sound of the alarm on his clock.

He looked around and realized that he was in his hotel room and that it was dark outside and he had been sleeping.

He got up and stretched and yawned.

He walked over to the dresser, pulled a cigarette out of the cigarette pack and lit it.

He took a couple of deep puffs from his cigarette and thought, "I think more about Jo than I do of my son. I love him and I won't let anyone take my boy from me, no way! But I sure love Jo a lot."

Dave got dressed and drove over to the H&H.

He went inside to find the same happy Jo that he saw earlier that day.

He took his usual seat at the bar and drank his regular limit of two beers.

After the bar closed, Dave and Jo went to her place and made love.

He returned to his hotel room about five o'clock in the morning.

They had made plans to meet at Jo's around one in the afternoon for their Sunday drive.

After spending the afternoon in the park, they went for a long drive out around the country side and just enjoyed the evening and being together.

Dave dropped Jo off at her place about eleven o'clock that night, which was a little later than they normally stayed out on Sunday.

As she stood on the bottom step with her arms around Dave, Jo's eyes gleamed with pleasure. "You know, I love you!"

"Yea and I love you, too!" he responded and tenderly kissed her.

Dave walked her up to her door and kissed her good night and said, "I'll see you tomorrow."

"Okay, Babe. Are you sure you don't want to come in?"

"No, I'm going to get some sleep tonight. I want you to get a good night sleep, too, before you get sick. I love you."

Dave gave her another quick kiss and headed down the stairs.

AN ANGRY AND MYSTERIOUS JO

Dave slept in until about nine o'clock on Monday morning. He could not believe that he slept that long, but it sure felt good.

He got dressed and went to the hotel lobby to use the pay phone to call his friend Bob.

"Dave," exclaimed Bob. "How the hell are you? Haven't heard from you in quite a while," he added.

"Not bad! I need your help though."

"What's going on?"

"Well, Rose served papers on me. She won't let me see my boy. I want to see my kid. Can you make her let me see him?" and then Dave briefly told his old friend about the problems he was having with Rose and her family.

"Gee, Dave, I'm real sorry to hear that. Let me look at my calendar. Hmmmmm! The earliest that I can see you is going to be the first Wednesday in September."

"Damn! That's over two weeks from now."

"I know, but I'm booked. I've got a lot of court dates scheduled."

"Okay... I'll see you then, Bob," agreed Dave.

"Be here around ten-thirty, see you then," replied Bob as they both hung up.

Dave turned around, stood there and stuck his hands his pockets.

"Damn," he thought, "Lawyers are just as heartless and cold as those damn telephone operators. Well Hell, it's such a nice morning. Think I'll walk over and see what Jo is doing."

He walked out of the hotel lobby and greeted the desk clerk on his way.

The sun was shining and the trucks and cars rumbled along Center Street as Dave walked the block to the stairway beside the H&H, that led up to Jo's place.

The lighting on the steps and halls made them look different. He had never seen them at this time of the morning before.

Dave stopped at Jo's door and knocked.

Within a few seconds the door opened.

"I knew it was you," Jo smiled and gave him a kiss.

He returned her kiss as they entered her apartment and walked into her kitchenette.

"I just got up. How long have you been up?" Dave asked.

"I've been up for hours now," Jo answered as Dave sat down and she sat down on his lap, giving him another kiss but this time a much longer kiss.

They spent the rest of the day until Jo had to go to work, just talking and laughing and enjoying each other's company.

Finally, Jo had to go to work.

Dave walked with her down to the back door of the H&H.

"I'm going rig chasing for a little bit. I'll be back soon," Dave promised.

"Okay, Hon. I'll be here," she said with a good-bye kiss.

She opened the door, walked inside and waved as she went through the kitchen and into the bar.

Dave took his time walking back down the street.

He stopped to light a cigarette and then he continued his leisure walk back to the hotel.

Dave walked over to his car in the parking lot of the hotel, unlocked the door and got in. He rolled down the window and started Queen Vickie up. And once again, he headed toward Mt. Gilead, to chase drilling rigs.

He stopped by four rigs before finding five days work, working evening tour this time. He would be getting off at eleven instead of three in the afternoon.

"Alright, I can spend more time with Jo," he thought. "I don't need to get a lot of sleep tonight. I can visit with Jo, get to the hotel by five in the morning, sleep until one and be at work by two forty-five and back with Jo by eleven."

By now it was around seven o'clock in the evening.

Dave decided to head straight for the bar to see his little Jo.

Dave pulled into the bar parking lot near eight o'clock.

"Not a lot of cars for this time of evening," he thought.

It had been awhile since Dave had visited the H&H this early in the evening.

Stopping his car near the end of the lot, he turned off the engine.

He lit a cigarette while he walked along the building to the sidewalk.

As Dave passed the bar's window, he could see Jo serving Gus-Gus and

Bobby at their usual table close to the men's restroom.

Dave opened the screen door and walked into the bar.

Jo looked around to see who came in.

"Hi, Dave," she beamed. "You're here early tonight."

"I couldn't help myself. This is where it's at," Dave smiled.

"Well, lookie who's here." Gus-Gus waved at Dave, "My good friend Davy, give him a drink on me."

"No! You ain't buying drinks for nobody. It's time to get your ass home, you good for nothin'," Sarah yelled. She had walked in right behind Dave.

"Now woman, I'll buy drinks for whoever I want to!" Gus said. He reached into his pocket for his billfold.

The place went silent as all eyes were on Sarah and Gus.

"Okay, buy him a drink and then you get on home," Sarah turned and walked out the door.

Dave was seated on his regular stool by this time.

Jo handed Dave a beer.

Dave turned on his stool towards Gus and said all he could think to say, "Thanks."

"Think nothing of it kid," Gus answered.

He stood and placed money for the beer on the table and staggered for the door.

"Bobby!" Jo pointed to Gus with her head.

"Okay, I'm right behind him. I'll make sure he gets home."

Bobby finished his beer and set the empty bottle down on the bar as he went out the door behind Gus.

"Boy, I thought we had trouble there," Jo told Dave.

"Yes, I've never seen him talk to her like that," he added.

The rest of the night went pretty smooth. Jo and Dave were able to talk between her serving customers.

Dave was happy that he could sit and visit with his Jo without worrying about getting up early in the morning.

Mary showed up around mid-night and helped Jo until two-thirty. Then she told Jo she would close up.

Jo locked the front door, and then she and Dave went out through the kitchen door.

Hand-in-hand, they shared a kiss or two as they walked over to the apartment's stairs.

Sitting about half way up the stairs was a woman who was crying her heart out.

Jo dropped Dave's hand and ran up the stairs to the crying woman.

"What's wrong?" Jo asked.

"You know big Fat Sam, our landlord, he said he wants to go out with me and if I don't go, then I gotta move," the crying woman said between sobs, and then she dropped her face back into her hands.

"Where's he at?" Jo demanded.

"He's somewhere in the building now," the crying woman said.

"I'll take care of him. You don't worry," Jo exclaimed.

She grabbed Dave's hand and headed off to find the landlord.

She walked so fast that Dave had a hard time keeping up with her. Up the stairs they went, along the hall, down the other set of stairs.

"I know he's here. His car was in the back parking lot when we came out of the bar," Jo said to Dave as they hurriedly walked around to the front of the building.

They ran up the front stairs, across the hall and then down the back stairs again.

Jo stopped and said, "He left. His car's gone."

Dave jumped, pulled from his thoughts of Jo by the phone ringing. He didn't know how long it had rung before he realized it was ringing. He half ran over to the phone and picked it up.

"Hello," he answered.

"Hi, Hon, how are you feeling?" Christine asked.

She had become very concerned about Dave's health ever since his heart attack.

"I'm okay," Dave replied.

"I just wanted to make sure you were alright."

"Love you, see you tonight," Dave said.

"Love you," Christine said before she hung up the phone.

Dave hung the phone up, went into the kitchen and poured himself a cup of coffee, walked over and sat down at the dining room table.

Dave thought, "Christine is some woman worrying about me like she does…Jo was some woman, too. When Jo said, 'I'll take care of him', she didn't say anything about kicking his ass or beating him up. All she said was, 'I'll take care of him.' What did she mean?"

Dave recalled seeing that crying woman later. She didn't have to move. He didn't think she ever went out with Fat Sam either.

Dave also remembered one evening just after he and Jo started going together. He was sitting in the H&H drinking as usual. A couple factory workers began talking to him. They talked about the factories they were working at, and then one of them asked Dave where he worked.

Dave told them he worked in the oil fields on drilling rigs.

They started shooting shit about how bad roughnecks were.

They said all roughnecks were white trash, and told Dave stories they had heard about how oil field trash would come into towns, throwing their weight around, spending money, and stealing married women, drinking and fighting, tear the towns up then leave the women behind.

Of course, Dave had to make comments about factory workers. His favorite line was, little bittie factory workers.

There was no love lost between roughnecks and factory workers back in those days.

Dave got up from this conversation and went to the restroom.

As he walked out of the restroom about four factory workers gathered around him. They started moving in closer to him and calling him white trash.

Dave looked around.

They had surrounded him.

He reached into his pocket for his hawk billed knife. If he was going down, he would take a few with him, he thought.

Just then, Jo came out from behind the bar and walked through the crowd of factory workers that surrounded Dave.

"That's enough!" she said, "Go sit down or get out."

Those guys shut up real fast and went and sat back down just like Jo told them to do.

Dave left after telling Jo that he would see her later.

Dave never had anymore problems with the factory workers again. She or he never talked about this incident just like they never talked about what she did or had done to Fat Sam.

How could this little girl, Jo, have power over people like she did?

Did her husband have money or power in town?

Dave recalled that day when Jo got ready to go to the movies. She had a lot of expensive clothes.

Who paid for them?

How could a married young woman and man afford nine children and buy all those clothes she had?

Her husband must have been a rich man, maybe he was an older man. Who knows?

And why didn't she drive?

Did she have servants that did her bidding for her?

But her hands were a little rough and red from working at the bar. Things just did not fit.

Dave never saw Jo heading for the Laundromat with dirty clothes. But he had seen hand washed under clothing hanging in her bathroom.

And she never had dirty dishes in her kitchenette, and in fact, she never cooked for him.

He never found anyone at her place, not even her sister or her mother.

Dave knew he must find Jo not only to tell her how sorry he was, but to get answers for all these questions he should have asked years before.

THEIR FINAL DATE

Then Dave then heard the unlocking of the front door.

Dan opened the door and entered their house.

"Hi, Dad, I didn't know you stayed home today," Dan said as he closed the door and re-locked it.

"Yea, I didn't sleep too good last night," Dave replied, "I was just too tired to go in this morning. How was your day?"

"Fine, no problems," Dan smiled and went into the kitchen for a snack.

"That's good," commented Dave.

"As soon as I finish eating, I'm going over to John's, okay? I'll stay close," Dan stated as he grabbed some cookies and a glass of milk.

"Okay, just stay close." Dave smiled back at him.

With another cup of coffee and a newly lit cigarette, Dave headed for the patio.

Dave sat down in a patio chair, crossed his legs and looked into the cloudless sky.

"I sure miss her... You were a fool, Dave," he thought as his thoughts returned back to 1965.

Things were going along great for Jo and Dave.

She kept him from thinking about his boy, stupid Rose and those rich bitchie in-laws of his. If Jo hadn't been there for him, he probably would have gone crazy with worry or worse.

Dave was saving all the money he could for lawyer fees.

He neglected servicing Queen Vickie like he should have.

She had obtained a little miss, her tires were wearing out and she needed a good cleaning. But Dave only spent money on lunches and dinners for Jo and himself. And whenever he ate alone, he stuck to his regular cold soup meals.

The nights started to get a little cooler. The corn at their hide-a-way was tall and soon would be ready for harvest.

Dave remembered... After Jo and Mary closed up the H&H, hand-in-hand, Jo's head leaning against Dave's arm, they walked over to Queen Vickie. Dave opened the driver's door. She got in and slid across the seat. Dave got in beside her.

"I love you," Jo said as she brought her lips to his.

"You know, I love you, too," Dave replied, "I love you so much Jo. I could not stand to be without your kisses and I couldn't stand life without you."

She placed her hands on either side of Dave's face. Jo smiled at him and brought him to her and kissed him passionately. Their tongues slightly touched through opened lips while their arms wrapped around each other.

Dave thought, "After my divorce, we'll leave this town and get our own place together and you will never have to work in a bar again, I promise."

After a few minutes, they broke their kiss. Dave released her and started the car.

Queen Vickie shook and missed.

"She's ready for another tune-up," Dave stated as he let her warm up before he put her into drive.

"I wondered what was going on with Queen Vickie," Jo replied, "Maybe we shouldn't go very far tonight. I would hate to break down somewhere."

"No, she's okay... she's just cold," Dave reassured her, "The old Queen wouldn't let us down, not on her life."

Queen Vickie's worn out wipers streaked the early morning dew across her windshield as they drove out of town towards their hide-a-way.

A full golden early fall moon shown ghostly in the western sky.

They turned onto that drive which took them to their hide-a-way.

The tall brownish corn stalks looked cold and dead to Dave.

"Looks like summer is just about over," Dave remarked to Jo.

"I'm cold. Please turn on the heater," she asked.

Dave reached over and turned on the heater for her, "Sure Hon."

Dave slowly drove down the dirt drive, carefully dodging the mud puddles. He did not want to get stuck out here in the middle of nowhere.

"The heat feels good," Jo said as Dave stopped Queen Vickie at their usual parking spot.

"It sure does," he responded and turned off the headlights but let the engine run to keep them warm.

Coming together, they kissed. And then he ran his lips down her neck, then under the edge of her collar.

Their passion grew higher and higher as he returned to her lips, and their tongues raced faster and faster around and over the other'.

Dave felt Jo tighten her grip with her arms and legs.

Together they climbed and erupted simultaneously.

Still hugging, they showered kisses over the other's face, "I love you," they both kept repeating.

Finally, still lying on top of Jo, Dave thought, "How natural and comfortable it is to be laying on top of Jo with her arms and legs wrapped around me."

They put their clothes back on and then Dave turned off the engine. He got the blanket out of the trunk, and then they lay covered on the seat of the car. Dave looked up and out through the windshield, watching the stars as Jo laid her head on his chest. Soon, they were asleep.

Once again, the rising sun woke them up.

After their good morning kiss, they headed back to town. Of course, Jo rode as always, sitting next to Dave as she held his arm tightly to her body. They stopped for coffee before they proceeded back to Jo's place.

At the bottom of the stairs, Jo again stood on the first step while Dave stood on the sidewalk. They kissed their good-byes, and then walked hand-in-hand up to her door for their last kiss.

"I'll see you tonight," Dave smiled.

"Okay, Hon. I love you," she responded.

"I love you, too."

Dave walked to the stairs, turned and waved to her. Jo returned the wave and he was gone.

Dave drove back to the hotel and checked for messages, none of course.

In two days he was meeting with Bob Wert in Wooster.

"Then watch all Hell break loose with Rose when I get my boy back!" he thought.

He slept until one and then arose from the bed. He cleaned up, headed for a coffee shop then work.

The day's work on the drilling rig was the usual for drilling a lime stone formation. Slow drilling with plenty of time for cleaning and painting of the equipment. The day dragged by.

But eventually it was time for them to change their clothes and start watching for the morning tour to show up.

Ten forty-five, morning tour was not there yet.

Eleven o'clock, still no morning tour.

"Damn it, boys, we might as well change back into our greasers, they ain't coming to work tonight," the driller told his crew.

They changed back into their work clothes, kept working, but still watched for the headlights of the morning tour.

Morning tours were noted for quitting and not telling anyone. Also they were known for just getting drunk and not showing up for work.

"Dave, I appreciate you staying with us," the old driller told Dave.

"I can't leave you guys short handed, beside, I might want to work for you again someday," Dave laughed.

Dave was really trying to make all the money he could to pay his attorney in his divorce case. So this extra overtime shift would not hurt him at all.

Dave thought of how this was the first night in about three weeks that he hadn't been with Jo. He sure did miss her.

Before long, the sun was rising and here came the daylight crew.

Before they could get out of their car, Dave had changed back into his civvies and gave the daylight crew a "Hi," as he passed them and headed for Queen Vickie.

It didn't take long for Dave, driving his normal speed, to get back to Marion.

He parked his car in front of the H&H, ran up the stairs and knocked on Jo's door.

Jo opened the door and quickly threw her arms around his neck.

"What happened? I thought something happened to you! I thought I would never see you again!" Jo exclaimed as she pulled him tightly to her.

"Damn morning tour didn't show up so I had to stay," Dave answered.

He patted Jo on her back while he held her as tightly as she held him.

"Don't do that to me!"

"I will always be with you, I love you," Dave tried to assure her while he kissed her on her lips.

Dave released his grip around her and then grabbed Jo's hand and they walked over into the kitchenette.

Dave rambled on about crews not showing up for work all the time and about how many times he had to pull double shifts. He sat down on a chair and pulled Jo down onto his lap.

"I'm sorry about being late, but you know I love you..."

"I love you, too," she replied with a kiss.

She became cheerful after she got over his lateness, and she playfully tried to tickle his side.

"Don't!" He squirmed in his chair, almost dropping Jo as she laughingly poked Dave in one side and then the other.

He grabbed her by her arms.

She looked into his eyes as his lips came down upon hers.

Soon their passion for each other began to rise.

He released her arms and her arms went around him. His hands dropped to her butt. He rubbed them through her shorts.

"Let's go," she whispered in his ear, "I started again today, but this time I am only spotting."

Jo pulled her head back a few inches from his and beamed.

"She's pregnant," Dave thought, "My baby's pregnant. She is carrying my child inside her!"

He felt wonderful.

Gently Dave stood up and her head rested on his shoulder as he carried her over to the bed.

Very easily Dave laid her down, and he then removed her clothes and then his own.

Carefully as not to hurt his precious lover, Dave covered her with his body.

She held his face in her hands, "I love you," she said as she deeply kissed Dave on his lips.

"I love you too, Hon," he replied.

He found his way into her and wrapped his arms around Jo. He softly pushed his pelvis against hers. Their emotions grew together as the old bed springs squeaked.

Soon, neither Jo nor Dave could last anymore as their height of total climax was accomplished and their fluids mixed.

Their body motion stopped.

Dave continued a deep and loving kiss to her lips, the woman he loved. They held the embrace while they kissed over and over again.

When Dave's racing heart slowed down, he carefully got off Jo and out of bed.

Dave got dressed and sat there watching her run around in the nude while Jo looked through her closet for something to wear for work. She was the most beautiful woman he had ever seen.

"Hon, I have to go to Wooster tonight," Dave started, "I have some very important business to take care of."

Jo looked around at him as if something was wrong. "Going... when will you be back?"

"I'll be back Thursday afternoon," Dave promised, "I'll only be gone tomorrow and Wednesday."

Jo found the clothes she wanted to wear and got dressed while they talked.

She had to be at work in about one half hour, so Dave decided he better leave now and head for Wooster.

Jo came over to Dave, hugged him while they kissed their good-byes and said, "Remember that I love you."

Dave shut and locked the door as he left.

Dave walked towards the stairs; paused and lit a cigarette, and then his old indescribable saddened feeling started filling his stomach.

The farther down the stairs he went, the worse and deeper the feeling became.

"Its over, I'll never see Jo again," he thought. He turned, ran up the stairs and stopped almost at the top, "That's silly, why wouldn't I see her again? I'm only going to Wooster for a few days. Nobody can keep me from Jo. I love her too much to let anyone stop me."

Confident again, Dave turned and headed for his car.

As he headed out of Marion, that old familiar sickened feeling once again returned and stayed with Dave as he drove towards Wooster.

Then it came into his mind, "My job is over, I was only to give Jo my baby."

Tears filled Dave's eyes, "I won't let this happen! I will be back. I promised her, I will be back!"

"First I get my boy back, then I'll return to Jo and then we will leave. We'll all move to a better place. I know I can find good steady work in the oil fields somewhere," Dave's mind raced.

DEEPLY DEPRESSED

When he arrived at Wooster, Dave drove passed his in-laws place.
He wanted to see his son, maybe he would be outside playing. No such luck. No one was outside, but Rose's car sat beside her mother's Chevy in the drive.
Dave decided not to make a scene by going up to their door and demanding to see his boy.
"Be cool Dave," he thought, "Don't give them a chance to have you arrested. The bastards would love that."
Dave tried to stay within the town's speed limit. He drove cautiously across town to his parents' house.
He parked behind their house under the old apple tree.
He gathered up his dirty clothes from the trunk of Queen Vickie. He laid them down beside the washer and dryer, inside their enclosed back porch, before he entered the kitchen.
His Mom looked up from the newspaper she was reading.
"Dave, I'm so happy to see you," she smiled, "How about some coffee?" She stood up from her chair at the table and started for the cupboard.
"I'll get it, Mom," he responded, "Sit down, do you want some more?" Dave added while he filled his cup.
Within a few minutes, Dave's dad walked into the kitchen, leaving his TV playing in the living room.
The old man loved watching sports on television. He didn't care what kind of sports he watched or who was playing as long as it was sports.
The rest of the day flew by as they talked about work and everything else they could think of. Dave did not tell them about Jo or his love for her.
He would never tell them about Jo, even though his mind kept drifting back to her while they talked. Also, nothing else was said about his

separation with Rose, even though they knew what was going on.

When Dave went to bed, he could not help thinking about that bad feeling he got earlier when he was leaving Jo.

"No! It can't be! I won't let it happen! I will be back! Jo and I, along with my boy, will start a new life together," he thought.

He fell to sleep and dreamed of the three of them and their wonderful life that lay ahead.

He cleaned up the next morning and put on fresh clothes.

He was ready to meet with Bob.

Bob greeted Dave as he walked into Bob's office.

"Glad to see you again, Bob," Dave warmly shook Bob's hand.

"Have a seat, Dave," Bob sat down behind the huge desk faced Dave.

As Dave sat down, Bob continued, "I've talked with Rose's attorney. Dave, you have problems here."

"I know that. How can I get my boy back? Divorce she can have, but I want the boy," Dave responded.

"You don't understand," Bob said as he looked down at the papers he held in his hands, "You've got problems here. Abandonment, non-support, beating Rose..."

Dave stood up quickly, "What do you mean abandonment, non-support and beating her. I didn't do those things at all!" Dave protested.

"Just sit down, let's talk about them."

Dave sat down again and shook his head.

"These are the grounds she's divorcing you on. They say you haven't been home in over a month. You never even send her money. She doesn't know where you are living. And she claims that you slapped her around. By this, you are a regular ass, Dave," Bob paused and then laid down his glasses.

Bob continued, "Women always get the children in divorce cases. You'll be lucky if you get visitation rights on Sundays. The judge will throw the book at you, Dave," Bob said as he stared at Dave.

Dave dropped his head and said, "So, you are saying, if I want to keep my boy, I better go back to the bitch!"

"Yes Dave, go back to Rose," Bob re-affirmed.

Dave stood up and said, "Thanks, Bob, send me your bill."

Then he walked out of Bob's office.

Dave walked down the street.

"Shit, everything is falling apart. Keep my boy and lose Jo, or keep Jo and lose my son. There must be a way to keep them, my boy and Jo," he thought.

He knew Bob was right but he could not give up Jo.

Dave needed a drink. He stopped in Silver Dollar Bar to help clear his head. As he headed for a bar stool, an old wino asked Dave to buy him a drink.

"Go to Hell," Dave answered as he sat down on a barstool.

"Bring me a Strohs!" he told the barmaid.

Dave sat there drinking, looking straight ahead and thinking about his problems. Before long the sun was setting and little bittie factory workers started packing the bar.

"I've had enough of this shit," he thought.

Dave stood up and staggered out of the Silver Dollar.

Somehow, a drunken Dave drove to the Pines.

Now he planned to really get drunk as his depression deepened. Dave destroyed Rose's life, his boy's life and now Jo's life.

How could his wife find another husband that would treat his son fair?

How could his boy grow up without his dad?

What would Jo do?

Dave knew he wasn't worth a shit. He shouldn't have been born.

After driving to the Pines, he staggered up to the bar and said, "Give me a fucking Strohs Beer," he demanded to the bartender.

"Give you a what?" The bartender laughed as he placed a Strohs in front of Dave.

Someone in the crowded bar said, "I didn't know Strohs did that."

Everyone laughed.

Dave turned and glared at the people sitting around the room at their tables.

"Go to Hell," he thought.

By closing time, Dave was "high centered" on his bar stool.

In other words, he was very drunk.

Some ugly woman had been trying to pick Dave up and had sat beside him while he bought her drinks. She listened to his woes most of the night.

Dave and this woman staggered out toward his car.

She gave Dave a big wet kiss as he felt her tits and rubbed her crotch. She was hot and wanted him.

"But not now," he thought, "I gotta go see Jo."

He left the ugly woman standing in the parking lot and headed back to Marion.

Dave awoke in the parking lot of the H&H. He could not remember driving here or how long he had slept or even where he had slept. His head hurt with a real bad hang-over. And he somehow managed to get out of Queen Vickie and staggered into the bar.

The place was empty of customers. Mary was sweeping the floor. Dave walked over and sat down at the bar. He looked at the clock; it showed ten twenty-four.

"Now what do you want!" Mary demanded.

"Give me a Strohs, please," Dave requested.

She leaned her broom up against a table, walked over behind the bar, got out a long-neck and sat it down in front of Dave.

She looked around and then started, "You know, Jo needs to go back to her husband and kids. She wants to go back to them. You are keeping her from her kids. Why don't you let her go?"

Dave didn't say a word he just looked down at the label on his beer.

"If you were a real man, you would let her go. There are plenty of other women you can screw. Jo's a nice girl. She deserves better than oil field trash."

Dave stood up and poured the rest of his beer down his throat. He knew Mary was right. He had to leave Jo. He was just no good to anyone.

Dave gently sat his empty bottle down on the bar and walked out without saying a word.

He opened the door of Queen Vickie, stopped and looked up towards Jo's apartment and said, "Good-bye Jo, you know I love you and always will, but I must let you go back to where you belong, with your husband and children."

Dave got in and drove away. He didn't even stop by the hotel to pick up his things, he just drove out of town and Jo's life forever.

Somewhere on the other side of Arkon, Ohio, Dave unconsciously pulled off the highway onto a dirt road that lead to a drilling rig.

He walked up onto the rig floor and someone yelled, "Hi, you looking for a job? I'm Dean Mills."

Dean Wills stood about 5 foot 7, his face gave the appearance of a teenager looking to get into mischief, but in reality he was about thirty years old.

"Yea, I sure am, I'm Davy," Dave replied.

Dean and Dave would become the best of friends, a friendship that would last for years to come.

"Davy this is Harold the driller, and Glen the derrick hand, they are my brothers, we work together," Dean stated as he introduced Dave to his brothers.

Harold was the oldest of the three brothers. He must have been nearly forty for you could see time had weathered his face and he had graying hair.

Glen was the youngest of the three. He was thin and muscular with wavy dark hair and always on the go.

"Welcome aboard, Davy," Harold said as he shook Dave's hand.

"Did you bring some work clothes?" Harold added.

"These are okay," Dave stated as he pointed down at the clothes he wore.

"Okay then, Dean showed Davy around."

Dean grabbed a grease gun and then Dave and Dean headed off to service the rig.

Dave's memory was brought back to the present time by, "There you are," Christine stated as she walked out on to the patio, "What's wrong, Hon? You feel okay?" she added.

"No, I'm fine," Dave replied.

He stood up and gave her their usual little, "Hello" kiss.

"I'm going to change my clothes and get a cup of coffee. I'll be right back," Christine said as she went back into the house.

"Damn, I loved her so much, why did I leave. I'm so sorry Jo. Please forgive me," Dave thought as he fought back the tears that started to fill his eyes.

Then backing away from his memory of Jo, he followed Christine into the bedroom, and through a forced a smile he said to Christine, "So, how was your day?"

THE DEATH OF QUEEN VICKIE

Christine could not cheer Dave up all evening. She did not know what was wrong and kept asking him if he was okay.

Dave talked to Christine, but he could not get his mind off of Jo. He only wanted to sit at their dining room table and smoke cigarettes and drink coffee.

Soon it was bedtime again.

Dave declined on going to bed when Christine went to bed. He said that he just wanted to sit up for awhile longer.

He left just the kitchen light on and sat there in the darken dining room with his memories of Jo. And then he remembered his first day working with the Mills brothers.

At two forty-five, the evening crew came on to relieve them.

Finding out Dave had no where to live, Glen suggested he move into the rental trailer behind his. They all lived in a trailer park near Alliance, Ohio, which was about fifteen miles from the rig.

Dean rode with Dave back to Alliance. On the way, Dean explained all about Nye Drilling Company; they were based in Denver, paid every two weeks, etc., etc.

Davy had no problem with money or with waiting two weeks for his first paycheck. He had saved a lot of money that he had planned to pay his attorney with. So he had no problem renting the little trailer beside Dean's trailer which was located behind Glen's.

Later that evening, Dave knew what he must do to keep his boy. Reluctantly, he drove to a pay phone and called his in-laws. He heard the sound of Rose's voice on the phone as she said, "Hello."

"Don't hang up, it's me. I've got to talk to you," Dave responded.

"Okay, then talk," she told him coldly.

"I've made a big mistake, would you please have supper with me tomorrow night? Maybe we can work this out. Think of our son," Dave pleaded.

After a pause of silence came "Alright, see you about five tomorrow," she replied then she hung up.

As he hung up the phone, Dave felt like an ass. He left the woman he really loved to keep his kid. Dave knew he would win over Rose and talk her in to coming back to him. Jo would have to wait until somehow he and his boy could leave Rose.

During supper with Rose, she decided for her and their son to move to Alliance with Dave and she would drop her divorce procedures against him.

They ran by his in-laws, picked up their boy and their belongings and headed for Alliance.

All four families got to know each other over the next few weeks.

Dave became well acquainted with Dean's wife.

She was a little over weight with dark shoulder length hair, not a bad looker. He found out she would screw anyone and like to be abused during the act, but he never nailed her.

Glen's wife, Vickie, was the best looking of the three Mills' wives.

Vickie was a younger slim woman with a nice butt. Dave often thought about getting into her pants, but never did.

Harold's wife Jean was the older of the women. She and Harold had five kids so Dave thought of her as the mother of the Mills brothers.

Dave's home life was Hell.

Sex with Rose wasn't any better than having sex with a log. He longed to be back with Jo once again.

Almost daily, Dave would talk the Mills boys into stopping at a bar after work as they headed home. Their home lives must have not been any better than his because they never refused his offer to buy a round or two.

Once they started drinking, they would stay at the bar until eleven or so. Rose didn't like having sex with a drunk so Dave tried to stay that way.

Sometime in October, Dave found out that the rig was going to be down and they were going to be off work for a day or two.

Putting his plan to work, Dave talked Rose into going to visit with her family that same day.

After Rose and their son had left, Dave packed his clothes into Queen Vickie and headed to Marion once again.

He hoped old Queen Vickie would make it. He had neglected her.

Her oil was old, her tires were bald and she missed badly, but down the road he roared, happy once again.

He was finally going home to Jo.

"To Hell with Rose," he thought.

He loved his son, but he could not live without Jo. Dave loved Jo more than anything else in the world.

He passed though Wooster and headed toward Marion.

All at once Queen Vickie made a loud banging noise, and then she went silent. Dave coasted the old girl over to the side of the road.

Smoke rolled out from under her.

Dave jumped out, ran around and opened her hood.

After the smoke cleared, he could see a big hole in the side of her engine block. Queen Vickie was done. She had thrown a rod which came out her side.

Dave's heart sank.

He loved her and now she was gone too.

She was the only thing he owned that Jo and he had shared.

Queen Vickie's sides may have been rusty and she had a few dents but to Dave, she was a lovely old girl.

Queen Vickie was the only one who knew Dave's secret of Jo and how lonely he was without her.

He gathered up his clothes and hitch-hiked back to Wooster, leaving a dead Queen Vickie for the junk yard along side US Route 30.

Dave obtained a ride from some old farmer back to Dave brother's used car lot in Wooster.

Dave told his brother about his car blowing up and he bought a '57 Lincoln, and with most of his money used to buy a car, he reluctantly headed back to Alliance.

He hoped Jo would be okay until he had another chance to get back to her.

The old wore out Lincoln just barely made it back to Alliance when it blew its engine. Dave ended up walking the last few miles back to the trailer park.

Within the week, Dave bought a real Junker, a '57 Ford convertible. The engine's valve lifters rattled and its top was all ripped up. Dave made a top out of canvas for it. But the tired old Junker got Dave back and forth to work.

HARD TIMES

The winter of '65 and '66 was harsh and cold.

Roughnecks found their rigs shut down more than working. The economics of the oil industry played a big roll in the slow down of drilling along with the weather element of that winter.

Dave found the little bank roll that he had saved from working the Mt. Gilead oil fields was gone and the money that he was now making didn't last long.

Rose loved to spend money. Giving her his paycheck was like giving a wino a bottle of wine to hold for you. Needless to say, she kept him broke.

Roughly, it took about seven to ten days to drill a 5,000 foot well. Starting the drilling of a new well in the middle of the week and finishing in the middle of the following week, no over time was paid for either week. Then the drilling companies would start to drill another well in the middle of the third week. This way, cutting the cost of labor lowered the cost of drilling wells.

Dave was one of the many unfortunate roughnecks caught up in the economics of that winter plus his spendthrift wife didn't help his financial problems either.

He would adventure out to a silent drilling rig and fill two five gallon buckets with diesel fuel from the rig's tanks. Then carefully, he would carry the full buckets back to his rented trailer, to use as heating fuel.

Whenever he did work, his lunch was only one sandwich consisting of two slices of bread and bologna which was half frozen whenever he had time to eat. And without money to buy heavy winter work clothes and unable to afford to wash his work clothes, soon all Dave's clothes became his work clothes. Before long, Dave looked worse than those guys Jo saw in the cafe on their first date.

Dave made sure Rose and their son did not go without, instead, he went without.

Before winter's end, Dave would end up with all his fingers tips, forehead and the back of his neck being frost-bit.

Is it any wonder with Dave's money problems, driving a junk car, not working full time, bad sex at home with a woman he didn't want to be with and Jo's memory burning in his mind, why he did start drinking and running around with women?

Dave only stayed home just enough to keep Rose off his back.

Dave's son wanted one of those Aluminum Christmas Trees that year. Trying to make his boy happy, he bought one. He even got one of those rotating color lights to go with it.

A few days before Christmas, Rose decided to visit her mother. Rose and their son were spending the night and would not be back until the following evening.

With his family gone, Dave decided to go down to Canton and do a little serious drinking.

While Dave was sitting at a bar minding his own business, who walks up and sits down beside him, but his cousin's future bride.

She was about three months pregnant and as ugly as a mud fence. Dave wasn't trying to put the make on her or anything like that but he was unable to shoo her away so he spent the evening talking with her.

Just about closing time, some guy walked up to Dave and asked, "Are you taking her home? If not, I will."

Dave looked at the guy and said, "Yes, I am taking her home."

By now with Dave being pretty well drunk and reminded by this guy that this ugly, pregnant, soon to be his cousin by marriage home was a woman, he decided to take her home and screwed her in Rose's bed.

The next morning Dave drove her back to the bar, where her car was and left her there.

Rose never found out about Dave screwing this woman, let alone in their own bed.

Dave had hit the bottom of the barrel with the rest of the scrum. Nothing mattered anymore.

But somehow, he had to get back to Marion and Jo. He did not know how or when, but he knew that he would have to figure that out.

He could still see the look on Jo's face when he told her, "I'll be back. I promise."

Dean Mills and Dave became drinking buddies quickly after meeting for the first time in September.

Dean didn't run around much on his wife, but he would have liked to.

Dave hung around Dean only when Dave wanted to drink and was not looking for a new ass to screw.

Dave recalled one night in particular, Dean and Dave drank heavy all evening. By closing time, both men could hardly walk to Dean's 1959 Ford Fairlane.

Dean gassed the Ford and pulled unto the street and fish tailed, almost went into a one-eighty.

He backed off the throttle just enough to keep her under control and then they proceeded down the street. Somehow, Dean was able to stop his car behind another car at a red traffic signal.

After they sat there a few moments, Dean became impatient.

"To Hell with it," Dean exclaimed.

He pushed the car into the intersection so they could turn left.

As the other car crossed the intersection, the fellow driving the car, stuck his arm and head out his window. He waved and grinned at Dean and Dave.

Dean was just as crazy as Dave had become. Those two got into fights with others, but we won't go into that now.

During February, the drilling started to pick back up again.

Glen went to drilling Morning Tour, and Dave went along with him as his derrick hand. So now instead of Dave drinking nights, he could drink in the mornings and all day if he wished to.

SHE'S GONE

The money situation did not become any easier for Dave; He gave his paychecks to Rose, who would give him ten dollars a week to spend. And he still drove his old broken down '57 Ford Convertible and didn't have any good clothes left.

Dave just worked, drank and kept thinking about his Jo.

Rose started talking to Dave about Vickie going on a visit to Illinois. The Mills' were all from there including their wives. So Vickie was going back to see her family. Rose told Dave how nice it would be if she and their boy could go with Vickie. Rose said they would only be gone a little over a week.

"Alright!" Dave thought, "I will have a full paycheck coming. I could get the Hell out of here. Leave Rose and I will go back to Jo. Jo and I could leave Ohio, go somewhere where no one knew us and start over!"

It didn't take long for Dave to agree to let Rose and their son go to Illinois with Vickie. The trip was being planned for March, next month.

Dave hurriedly serviced his old Ford. Nothing he did made her run any better. She still knocked and rattled. Dave even somehow found the money to buy used tires for her.

Now he just had to wait until Rose left.

He was like a kid looking forward to Christmas coming, but he could not and did not tell a soul about his coming "Christmas".

In fact, Dave had kept Jo his secret and never told anyone about her until just before the writing of this book.

Just owning work clothes by now, Dave needed only to buy one change of clothes. Something nice, something Jo would like to see him wear. Maybe a nice pair of blue jeans and a light colored shirt. Even get a hair cut, his hair was getting pretty shaggy. He hadn't had it cut in over five months.

While he waited for Rose to leave, Dave still drank to keep away from Rose, but stopped chasing women for his woman waited for him in Marion,

Ohio.

Finally, the big day came. Rose had packed her things and the boy's things the night before.

Happy and laughing Vickie and Rose watched Glen and Dave load up Vickie's car as Dave's son and their daughter ran around playing.

Soon they backed out of the drive, and everyone waved good-bye and they vanished around the corner.

"Great, she is gone!" thought Dave.

As he and Glen walked toward Glen's mobile home, Dave said, "You know, I've gotta get away for a few days. I need to go see my parents. In two days we get paid. I'll get Don, the Daylight derrick hand to fill in for me for one day, and I'll get Steve, the Evening Tour derrick hand to fill in for me also, if you don't mind?"

Glen smiled and looked at Dave, "She must be pretty special giving her two days. Who is she anyway?"

Dave looked down, moved his foot back and forth in the dirt, "No, it's not a woman, wished it was. I just need to go see my family, that's all."

"Sure, why not," agreed Glen.

Dave's heart jumped with joy, but he tried to act natural and calm with Glen around.

"I'm out of here!" Dave thought to himself.

The next two days dragged by for Dave. He did not have the need to drink. He just worked, slept and thought of Jo.

Pay-day finally arrived. Around nine o'clock in the morning, their boss, the rig's Tool Pusher, brought their checks out to the drilling rig.

After very few words of small talk, Dave was out of there and headed for the bank.

He cashed his check at the drive-up window, and then stopped by a barber shop and got a hair cut. His next stop was the K-Mart down the street.

Dave picked out a pair of jeans, a nice looking short sleeve shirt and then headed back to his trailer, and took a shower and put on his new clothes.

Dave jumped into his car with only his shaving gear. That was all he had besides his work clothes, which he always kept in the trunk of his car.

His old Ford cranked and cranked and then finally fired up. She wasn't much of a car and he just hoped she would make the trip without breaking down. He pulled out of the trailer park around ten-thirty in the morning. It would take him about two hours to drive to Marion.

Around one o'clock in the afternoon, Dave pulled into the parking lot of the H&H.

Holy Graduel

Excited he finally made it back, he almost ran into the bar.

Quickly he looked around the familiar place. Dave did not see Jo.

"Oh, she doesn't start work until later. It's too early for her to be here now," Dave thought.

Trying to act cool, Dave slowly strolled up to the bar and his old favorite stool.

Mary was working behind the bar.

"Hi, Mary, give me a Strohs, please," Dave said.

"Well, Dave, I haven't seen you in a long time. Where have you been?" Mary smiled at him.

Dave didn't answer her question, instead he asked, "Where's Jo?"

"Oh, she's gone," Mary replied and then continued, "She left a long time ago. She got pregnant and went south."

Dave was stunned. He could not say anything. He was lost for words.

Mary walked away to serve other customers.

Dave's mind went wild, "South, but where? Columbus? Dayton? but where?"

He tried to act calm as he finished his beer and left.

"Where do I look for her? I can't even recall her last name. If I could remember where her sister lived I could go ask her, but I can't remember how to get to her sister's house," Dave's heart sank.

He knew this was the end. He would never be able to find his Jo again. She would never be anymore than memories in his mind forever. "OH God, I wish I could find her. I love her so much!"

Dave got into his old car and sat there for a while and looked up at what used to be Jo's apartment window.

"Why didn't I call her? She would have waited for me... I know she would have waited. Why didn't I try to contact her?" Tears filled his eyes and he cried.

After about a half hour, Dave started up his old car and headed back to Alliance.

Like the song said, "The future becomes the past," so it was with Dave.

Within the next few years, Rose did divorce Dave. And she married a fat, older, little bittie factory worker.

Dave went through another marriage which lasted only one year before he met and married Christine.

Dave placed his memories of Jo and their "Summer of '65" deep within a small corner of his mind. Frequently he visited her in "their hide-a-way" part of his mind where he would relived those days that Jo and he were together. But he never revealed Jo or their undying love to anyone for thirty years.

THE SEARCH

RETURN TO MARION

While tears rolled down Dave's face, Christine walked toward him from their bedroom.

"Hey Babe," she said as she reached for the light switch, "It's dark in here. Its nearly midnight, aren't you coming to bed?"

"Don't turn it on. I was just getting ready to come to bed anyway."

He did not want Christine to see that he had been crying.

Christine walked in front of Dave as they walked down the hall toward their bedroom.

"I'll be right there," Dave told her as he closed the door to the bathroom behind him.

"I've got to find her. I gotta find Jo!" He looked into the mirror.

His eyes were slightly swollen and red from crying.

He thought, "Damn it! I can't let Christine see me like this. She'll know something is wrong."

He flushed the toilet for Christine's benefit. Then he rinsed his face and eyes with cold water.

"That's better," he told himself, "Now, I've got to get my mind off of Jo."

He took a big swig of NyQuil, let out a sigh and headed off to bed.

He slid into bed beside Christine and gazed at the ceiling.

"Did you realize that in just a few days we'll be leaving on our vacation?" he asked her as she lay with her head on his arm.

"I know. I can't wait either. We really need to get out of here for awhile."

Dave kept staring at the ceiling as he and Christine talked about their upcoming trip.

Dan was as excited as them that they would soon be heading back east.

But they both felt bad that Tony could not go with them because he had school.

Friday came faster than Dave thought it would.

It had been a very busy week trying to make sure everything that needed to be done at work was completed, and getting the car serviced and making sure that they had everything they needed for the trip.

Anticipation filled Dave as they finally had their van all loaded up and ready to go.

He had to be very careful though that Christine thought the anticipation was from the trip and not what he was going back to do.

The first few days of the trip seemed to drag for Dave as they drove through Wyoming, seeing things that Dan and Christine wanted to see. Finally, they arrived in Ohio at Christine's Mom's.

Dave had planted the seed in Christine's head, that while they were back there, he wanted to look up some of his old oil field buddies one day while Christine visited with her mother.

As it turned out, Christine had some high school friends who wanted to get together with her.

"Perfect!" Dave thought to himself.

Dave told Christine, "Why don't you go ahead and take Dan and spend the day with your old high school friends tomorrow and I will run to Wooster and see if I can't find a few of my old friends?"

It was set. Dave did not have to worry about Christine wanting to go to Wooster with him. He had pulled it off. Now the search began.

Dave left for Wooster early the next morning. Christine was not to meet with her girl friends until noon, so he knew that he had all day to try and find some of these guys.

"Old roughnecks are a close-nit group of guys. Those boys will help each other out whenever needed. Just call on one and all will be there to help you. They can also help you find someone, someone like Jo," Dave thought.

He went around to several of the oil field supply companies. He knew that they were a good source of leads to finding a few of his old friends.

Dave found out that 'Fat-Boy Floyd', who got his nickname from being big and fat, had a heart attack and died. 'Cat Fish Richard', who was all mouth and had no ass, had left Wooster and went back home. No one was sure where home was, but they thought maybe Indiana or Kentucky or some place like that.

However, Dave did get a phone number for 'Puss-Gut Bobby', who got his name from having a big belly without an ounce of fat anywhere on him.

No one answered Dave's phone call to 'Puss-Gut's' house.

Feeling a little bleak, he decided to stop at a restaurant and get a cup of coffee.

As he walked into the restaurant, he noticed that the place resembled an old '50 café with stainless steel on the wall behind its counter and vinyl covered stool and booths that lined the long room.

The waitress was already bringing the coffee pot and a glass of water as Dave slid into one of the booths in the back.

"Good morning," she said as she set down the water, "Coffee?" she asked as she handed him a menu.

"Just coffee," he told her as he waived off the menu.

"Alrighty," she said as she poured. "Just let me know if you change your mind."

"Thank you," he smiled.

Dave lit up a cigarette and noticed a man sitting in the booth in front of him, who was staring at him every now and then. He kind of looked familiar, but Dave could not place him which was not unusual. After all, Dave was born and raised in Wooster. A lot of people looked familiar to him. He may have gone to school with him or met him through a mutual acquaintance sometime through the years.

"I'm gonna find you, Jo. It may take me a little longer than I thought, but I'm gonna find you. Where do I go from here?" he wondered, "Maybe I'll just..."

"Well, I'll be damned. Is that really you, Davy?"

Dave looked puzzled as he saw the man from the booth in front of him walking over to his table.

"Oh, my God..." Dave began with a laugh. Finally he recognized the man who had been staring at him, "If it ain't ol' 'Seal Beams'... Have a seat."

'Seal Beams' was a thin tall man who now had lost some of his hairline. He dressed well and always was the nervous type that never could sit still for very long.

"Can't call me 'Seal Beams' anymore, Davy, I wear contacts now," he laughed as he slid into the booth facing Dave and he added, "So where in the Hell have you been? I ain't seen you in ages."

"I live in California now."

"California? Living in the fast lane, huh! You are just back visiting family?" he asked.

"Not really. My mom and dad both passed away a few years ago. I'm looking for a girl."

Suddenly, out of the blue, Dave remembered that 'Seal Beams' wife was from Marion.

"You still married to Claire?" Dave asked.

"Yep! I decided to keep the ol' girl around after all," he chuckled.

"Maybe you can help me. I'm looking for a woman named Jo. She worked at the H&H over on West Center Street in Marion during the summer of '65," he told 'Seal Beams' as he lit another cigarette.

"More coffee?" the middle-aged waitress asked as she cheerfully refilled both cups before either of the two men could say a word.

"Thank you," they chimed together.

After he poured a little cream in his coffee, 'Seal Beams' looked at Dave with a devious grin on his face he said, "You sly dog. You ain't changed a bit. Still driving the women crazy are you?"

"Nah, it's nothing like that. I just need to talk to her."

"You got a last name for this mystery lady?"

"No! That's all I can tell you. Think you can help me?"

"Well Davy, let me do some checking and see what I can come up with. Maybe some of Claire's family might know of this lady or know someone who may have known her. Why don't you give me your phone number and I'll give you a call and let you know what I find out."

Dave wasted no time in grabbing a paper napkin and wrote down his work phone number on it for 'Seal Beams'.

"Thanks, I owe you one. I'll be back to work on Monday morning, the fifteenth of July. I'm there from seven in the morning until three in the afternoon," Dave handed 'Seal Beams' the napkin.

He took the napkin as he swallowed the last of his coffee.

'Seal Beams' smiled at Dave, "Davy it was great seeing you again."

Then he slid out from the table, stood up and reached his hand out to Dave.

"I'll see what I can find out for you and give you a call," after he shook hands with Dave, 'Seal Beams' left.

Dave began to ponder what his next move should be. He knew that he could not just sit and wait for 'Seal Beams'. After all, he did not really give him a lot to go on.

"Dave, old boy, it's time to take a trip to Marion. You did not come this far just to wait on someone else to call you."

Dave slid out from the booth, paid his bill and headed for Marion.

Around Mansfield, Dave started getting that same old sad feeling back again. It was a sadness coming from deep within him. It made him feel sick. He hated this feeling. He still did not understand what made him feel this way whenever he was in this area.

"Concentrate Dave... You're on a mission. Just go do what you have to do."

Dave's thoughts now turned back to Jo. What would he find when he got to Marion? Would he find Jo? Would the old H&H still be there? It has been thirty years! A lot can happen in thirty years.

It was as if he could feel Jo all around him.

"Am I going crazy?" Dave asked himself, "Why, after thirty years, is this girl forever haunting my mind? She wasn't my first woman and she wasn't the last."

Dave knew he had a lot of women before Jo and plenty more after her. Then there was Christine.

He loved Christine very much and Jo was a long time ago.

"So, why is she driving me crazy now?" he wondered.

Just then it dawned on Dave what he had to do.

He had to find Jo and tell her he was sorry, but how?

And once he found Jo, would he tell Christine?

And what if he found Jo and they hit it off again?

Was he willing to give up all that he has had with Christine and the boys? "NO!"

Could he just walk out of their lives? "NO!"

But what if he found Jo and they were still as much in love today as they were thirty years ago?

Could he just re-appear back into her life and then just walk right back out again? Could they separate a second time, and what about Jo?

Would she be willing to give up everything that she has? "NO!"

She is probably still married. And she had kids, so by now she must have grandchildren and what about her friends and maybe a job?

Would she be willing to give up people and all of those things and move to California? "NO!"

When she was twenty-seven years old, she did not have a driver's license. She did not know how to drive then. Did she ever get a driver's license? "Probably not."

Would she fit in with this hard, fast paced life in Southern California? "No!"

Then Dave wondered, "Besides giving up my family, my job, my insurance and my friends, could I once again live in a small town in Ohio? "NO!"

Could I even get insurance back there? "NO!"

I've had a heart attack, I've had a by-pass, my eyes aren't too good anymore and I'm overweight. Matt understands my health problems. He doesn't push me, could I find another job where my boss would understand it if I can't work forty hours a week, probably not."

Dave knew that he could not tell Christine about Jo. He would have to find her secretly.

And once he found Jo, he would have dinner with her... In a nice restaurant, seated across the table from her, he would reach out and hold her hand and say "Jo, I am so very sorry that things didn't work out for us. I am also very, very sorry for what I did. Please forgive me."

Maybe she would allow me to give her one last kiss. Maybe one last hug and I would say, "I wish things would have been different."

He wondered how life with her for the last thirty years would have been. Her having breast cancer... "Cancer," Dave thought.

"OH my God! That's why her husband took the kids and left. She never ran around on him. She was always true to me. That's why she never cried. She was all cried out. That's why she never talked about the past or the future. She thought she had no future. That's why she watched those kids so intensely that Sunday in the park when I couldn't get her attention. That's why we never lived together. She wanted her freedom, and she didn't want to burden me with all her problems.

"Her husband bossed her around and treated her bad. That's why her brother-in-law and his brother said what they did on that Sunday at her sister's house. They must have really loved her. And they knew that she had cancer.

"Jo was a very loving person and must have been a very loving mother. She never kissed me or held on to me on that Sunday, the one and only time I ever met her kids.

"Breast cancer in the 60's... but she can't be dead! Her life was so sad. I must find her. I have to tell her how sorry I am."

Dave could not deny how content Jo had made him feel. There was such a sense of peace and comfort that she brought over him back then, when he was going through some rough times with his first marriage.

He sensed that he also gave Jo that same feeling of peace and comfort.

The way that she would just lay her head on his shoulder, sitting on his lap and resting in his arms so tranquil, that was a nightly scene that was undeniable. That was real.

Nothing mattered except for the true love that they shared.

The age difference did not matter.

To be together, forever, was all they wanted and needed.

Now, more than ever, Dave was convinced that no matter what the outcome may be, he had to find her. Even if she now hated him so much that she would just slap him, come hell or high water, he would find his princess, Jo.

He only wanted to see her and to tell her how sorry he was that he did not return as he promised her he would.

Realistically, he knew that he never would leave Christine for anyone not even for Jo.

"Please be there, Jo. I only want to talk to you."

Although it had been better than an hour, it seemed like no time at all when he was entering the Marion City limits.

He found himself having a hard time remembering where things were because so many of the old buildings were gone.

Dave found Center Street and drove down it. He parked about two blocks past The Palace Theater. Then he walked down the street towards where the H&H once stood.

He spotted a small tavern and decided to go in for a beer and see what he might be able to find out.

The old bar was empty except of a couple sitting in one of the booths along the wall. The bar itself was badly worn wood, and on its walls hung the signs of today's brands of beer.

Though he never got her name, it did not take him long to strike up a conversation with the barmaid, who was a heavier woman about his age with graying hair pulled back into a pony tail.

They talked about the town and how so much had changed in the last thirty years. She told him that the H&H and the hotel had been torn down years ago.

He finished his beer, Dave bid the old woman a good-day and left.

He walked down past where he thought the H&H used to be, then on down to where the old Union Pacific Hotel once stood. For sure the old hotel was gone. But maybe one of those old buildings once held the H&H. He looked around trying to get his bearing back again because everything looked different, newer buildings stood everywhere.

In order to really figure out what was where, Dave decided to go to the Library to get the true addresses of the H&H and the hotel.

The Librarian helped him to locate the 60's Business Directories.

Dave pulled out the 1965 Business Directory. He put on his glasses sat down at a table and began his research.

He wrote down the addresses of the H&H, Casey's and the Union Pacific Hotel.

Then it flashed through Dave's mind that Jo had told him she was a local girl. That meant that she went to school there, but she never said if she finished high school or not.

She was twenty-seven years old when he knew her in '65. That means that she would have been eighteen years old and have graduated in '56. Therefore, he must check the high school Yearbooks from 1955 through 1957.

He did not find any Joans or anyone who resembled Jo in those year's books. He then began looking in older year books.

Located in an old 1947 Yearbook, he found three Joans; Joan Patterson, Joan Clayton and Joan Harris.

Patterson and Clayton's pictures were full front view. They definitely did not look like Jo. The Harris' picture shot from her back with her head turned as she looked over her left shoulder was Jo! She had short, bleached-blonde, Doris Day style hair-do. The 1948 and 1949 Yearbooks did not show any record of Joan Lee Harris. And the 1950 Yearbook only had pictures of Patterson and Clayton as graduates.

Dave could vaguely remember something about Jo's last name being Harris. It might have been when Jo introduced him to her mother as, "Dave, this is my mother, Mrs. Harris."

Dave began thinking. A sixteen year old, nine kids plus one year of Cancer equals thirty-one years old!

BINGO!

She must have quit high school when she was sixteen.

He has at last found her.

He knew that Joan Harris had to be his Jo.

"She wasn't twenty-seven like she said she was when we first met; she was actually thirty-two because she was born on June 27th 1932. We met about two months before our birthdays. She had lied about her age because I was so much younger than she. But Hell, I also lied about my age as well," Dave thought.

He looked at his watch and saw that it was getting late.

He had to get back to Christine's Mom's before they started to worry about him. He was sure that Christine was back by now.

The rest of their vacation went by rather quickly. Dave's mind kept drifting back to Jo and about what he would say to her when he found her.

THE PHONE CALL

Two weeks had gone by since they had returned from their vacation.

Dave thought that ol' 'Seal Beams' must not have been able to find out anything or he would have called by now.

His mind seemed to be going a mile a minute.

Every spare moment he had, he tried to figure out how he was going to find Jo. What made it even worse was that he had to do it without Christine finding out.

Then about another week later, he received a phone call at work.

"This is Dave," he said as he answered the phone.

"How you doing, Davy? This is Seal Beams."

Dave's heart stopped for a minute but he replied not trying to sound too anxious.

"Just hanging in there, how about you?"

"Same old shit. You know how that goes."

Dave nervously chuckled. "Well, did you do any good?"

"Sort of... I found a woman who knew of this Jo. Davy, I don't want to see this woman get hurt. I gotta know why it's so important that you find Jo."

"I need to know if she had my child."

"Oh shit! Okay. Take down this number..."

'Seal Beams' gave Dave a phone number to call in Marion, Ohio, and told him to call that number in two days at this same time.

Dave just about went crazy with anxiety for the next two days.

At last he was going to find his Jo.

Finally, it was time to make the call. Dave went to a pay phone and dialed the number that 'Seal Beams' gave him to call.

"Hello!" 'Seal Beams' answered the phone.

"Hi, it's Davy."

"Hey, Davy, I've got the woman I told you about here with me, I'm gonna put her on so you can talk directly to her, okay?"

"Thanks."

"Hello?" came from the soft sound of a young woman's voice.

"Hello," followed Dave.

"I understand what you want to know. Yes, I know a woman named Jo, who did work for the H&H during the summer of 65. Yes, she did have a child in '66. No, you are not the father and she doesn't know you."

"She doesn't remember me?" Dave asked.

"No, she does not know you. Maybe it was another Jo that worked at the H&H about the same time."

"Did this Jo that you know have the bottom part of her right breast removed because of Cancer?"

"Breast Cancer!" came back the surprised voice, "I don't know, but I'll ask."

"My Jo was a local girl. There were only three local Joan's in that age group. They were Patterson, Clayton and Harris. Patterson and Clayton both graduated. Harris quit as a sophomore. She was sixteen years old in the tenth grade. Joan Lee Harris is the Jo I'm looking for."

The phone went silent for a few seconds.

Dave asked, "Hello, are you still there?"

"Yes, yes, I'm here," replied the woman's voice.

"If I send a letter to her through Seal Beams, would you pass it on to Jo?"

"Yes, I will."

"Okay, let me talk to Seal Beams again," Dave requested.

Seal Beams gave Dave his address for the letter that Dave was going to send for Jo, promising Dave that he would pass the letter on to the woman.

After hanging up, Dave realized that Seal Beams nor the woman ever said who the woman was that Dave had been talking to.

Dave wasted no time in writing the letter to Jo. It contained little things like going to the movies, their special hide-a-way and the time that they went to her sister's house. He also told her about their last conversation when she told him she was only spotting... pregnant.

Dave stated in the letter that he would be coming back there again in October. He asked her to please contact him because he really needed to talk to her. In closing, he gave her his address and work phone number.

Once again, Dave found himself playing the waiting game. He never heard anymore from 'Seal Beams' or the woman. As if that was not bad enough, he never received a response from the letter he had written to Jo either.

DAVE KNEW

Once again, Dave was on his own.
"I can't give up. I won't give up. I must find you. You must know the truth."
Dave got the phone number for Wells Investigation Agency in Marion. But when he called them, all he got was an answering machine.
"Damn!" he thought, "I need to talk to a person."
As much as Dave hated leaving messages on "those things," he left a message stating he needed to talk to someone about finding a person there in Marion. He asked them to please call him back at their earliest convenience and gave them his work number.
There was no response.
After a few days, Dave called Wells again and left the same message, and once again no response.
By now, Dave was feeling pretty depressed.
"Jo, where are you? Why can't I find you? Why is it every time I think I'm going to finally talk to you, something happens. I get no response from anyone. I loved you so much and I know you felt the same about me. And I know you would not deny me now."
Deep in his heart, Dave knew the answers but refused to listen. He did not want to hear what he knew was the truth.
The answer was... Jo was dead.
However, Dave refused to believe that Jo was dead.
Now he knew that he must return to Marion because no one was going to help him. He was going to have to find Jo by himself.
"Oh God! How in the world am I going to tell Christine that I have to go to Marion to look up an old girlfriend?" He thought.
He knew for sure that Christine would flip her lid, kill him or throw him out.

But there was no other way.

He was going to have to wait for just the right moment to tell her. He would also have to be very careful to tell her in just the right way.

While still hoping to hear from the people he had contacted back east, Dave waited for the right moment to tell Christine.

He thought about what would happen when he finally saw Jo again and how she would look.

Would she be a three hundred pounder and wrinkled with glasses.

He knew she would have gray hair. After all, she would be sixty-three years old now. She had ten kids and certainly would have a handful of grandchildren.

Would she be married?

Nah! She was too headstrong and independent. She would not have re-married.

What would she think of him?

Now he's fifty-two, graying and starting to lose his hair. Dave now had some wrinkles and his belly stuck out a little. He dressed a lot better and drove a Mercedes these days. He had a lot more money now than he did back then, and his personality had completely changed.

Would they still love each other like they did back in 1965 or would they hate one another?

Dave wondered, "How in the world am I going to find her? Could her sister still live in the same place? How could I ever find that house again? The only part of the directions I can remember was when the little girl in the back seat pointed out Harding's Tomb that day coming back from Jo's sister's. I can barely even recall what the house looked like."

He knew that Jo never left Marion, and he knew he would find her still in Marion.

CHRISTINE LEARNS ABOUT JO

Dave realized that he had to get a plan if he was going to find Jo. And he needed something concrete to go on and right now.

He began thinking about hypnosis.

This may be the only way he could remember how to get to Jo's sister's house.

He had read about detectives using hypnosis on witnesses to obtain license plate numbers in hit and run cases. Also, doctors used it to help patients recall things from their childhood to help straighten out their lives. So, perhaps hypnosis may work on him.

Dave checked the Lancaster Phone Book for Hypnotists. He did not find any.

He decided that he would check out the phone books of Los Angeles that he had at work.

The next morning at work, Dave went through the front office of the factory where he worked. He checked his box to see if he had any memos.

"Hello, Dave. How do you feel today?" greeted Norma the receptionist.

Norma was a good person who is a good looker. She was one of those people who looked good and had a personality to go with it. And yet she did not let them go to her head as most women would have done.

"Hi, Norma, I feel great today. How do you feel?"

They always greeted each other with, "How do you feel today?" because of Dave's heart problems and Norma had a brain tumor that was surgically removed a few years ago.

Dave looked to his left and then to his right to see if anyone was around. He then looked Norma straight in the eyes, serious with no smile on his face, and asked, "How would you like to get married today?"

Norma stared back at him with a puzzled look on her face, and answered, "No!"

A big smile covered his face, "Good! I didn't either. Tonight we'll just fool around," Dave laughed.

Norma laughed with Dave.

They were always kidding with each other like that.

Dave picked up a phone book, walked out of the office and into the clock room.

He sat down at the table and opened up the San Fernando Valley Yellow Pages.

There were four or five listings under Hypnotists. They were all clinics except for the last one, Betty Way.

Something just seemed to grab him about her name. He wrote her number down so he could call her later.

He walked back down to the pay phone by his shop, and dialed the number for the hypnotist.

The phone rang then, "Hi! This is Betty Way..."

He shook his head and hung up the phone.

"Another answering machine," he thought.

He did not leave a message. He waited until he arrived at home from work before trying to call her again.

At home, once again he got her answering machine.

Doubts of using a hypnotist to locate Jo began to fill his mind. Dave put off trying to call Betty Way again.

He poured a cup of coffee and walked outside thinking to himself, "Now what am I going to do. How am I going to find you, Jo? I guess I'm really on my own for good this time."

Dave looked at his watch and knew that Christine would soon be home.

"I'm going to go back there in October. What am I going to tell Christine?" He thought.

He knew he had some serious thinking to do now.

Dave went back into the house to get a little more coffee as Dan hung up the phone.

"Hi, Dad, I ordered us up a pizza. It'll be here in about thirty to thirty-five minutes."

"Alright," Dave responded with a smile.

Within a few minutes, Christine came through the door.

After dinner, Tony left for his late college classes while Dan went into the living room to watch television.

Dave watched Christine as she poured them both another cup of coffee.

"Thank you," he smiled as he reached for his coffee.

Christine kissed him on the cheek, "I love you."

Later that evening, after they finished talking about their day's events, he pushed back his chair and picked up his coffee and then looked at Christine, "Let's go outside. I need to talk to you about something."

Dave led the way as they went out to the patio together.

He lit up a cigarette, "I love you," Dave began, he exhaled another puff, "Christine, there's something that I have to do. I'm going to tell you about something that happened a long time ago... way before I met you."

Christine lit up a cigarette as Dave drew another puff and continued.

"Now, just listen to me before you say anything. About thirty years ago I was working down in the Mt. Gilead oil boom... me and this girl fell in love. I was twenty and married to Rose at the time, but we were separated. This girl was thirty-two... She had nine kids. Her husband took the kids and left. We pretty well spent the summer together."

He took another puff of his cigarette in order to give Christine a chance to let his statement sink in, "I believe that she was pregnant when I left. I think I have a twenty-nine year old kid that I have never met. I want to find them." Dave paused and looked at Christine, "And I'd like to see her again before I die."

Calmly, Christine asked him, "What do you want to do?"

"I want to go back there in October. I have to find her, Christine."

"Okay, but you know that I will have a hard time getting off work, or do you want to go by yourself?"

"I think it's best if I go by myself," he put his arm around her. "Let's go to bed. It's getting late. We'll talk more about it later."

The following evening, after dinner, Dave and Christine went out on the patio to talk some more.

Dave gazed off into the evening sky and then he turned to Christine.

"I've been thinking... if I find this child, how am I going to tell our boys? How am I going to introduce him to Tony and Dan, 'Oh, boys, this is your twenty-nine year old half-brother that I forgot to tell you about.' That would go over like a lead balloon, huh?"

"Well first, let's see if there is a child. Then we'll figure out how to tell the boys," she responded.

"You're right. I'm not sure if we had a child, and I'm not really sure what the girl's last name was. She may be dead. She had breast cancer..."

"Breast cancer, oh my God," Christine interrupted.

"Yea, breast cancer, she had the complete lower right breast gone... removed by surgery. You know, Christine, I've always been an ass. This is a girl that I really cared about in my life, besides you. I left this girl pregnant. I didn't want to, but that's the way things turned out. I need to find her and tell her that I'm sorry for what I did."

"You left and never said anything? Never called, never wrote... just walked out on her?" Christine looked at Dave in wonder.

"I tried to get back, but I always failed. I'm not going to tell you anything else right now."

Christine took both of their coffee cups and went silently inside to get them more coffee.

She found Dave gazing at the stars when she came back out.

She had decided that he would tell her all he wanted her to know in his own time.

Now, Christine waited for Dave to talk the same way Dave had always waited for Jo to talk.

Dave and Christine continued their discussion but talked only about their day's events while watching the stars until it was time for bed.

"Well, I guess it's time to do it," Dave told her as they finished off their coffee.

After getting in bed, Christine laid on Dave's arm while he smoked a cigarette.

"You know, I never meant to hurt her. We got along so well... We never fought about anything. I can't even remember us ever being mad at each other."

"How did you meet her?" Inquired Christine as Dave rubbed her upper arm.

"There was this bar I used to go to all the time in Marion. I walked in there one day and there she was. I don't know why, but we just seemed to hit it off."

"I thought you were working in Mt. Gilead."

"I was. I couldn't find a place in Mt. Gilead to live that I could afford, so I drove straight to the Union Pacific Hotel in Marion..."

"Marion," interrupted Christine, "We used to go there to visit with some friends when I was a kid living in Barberton, Ohio."

"Boy, you were only ten years old at that time. If this girl was your mother, she was thirty-two then, you could have ended up being my step-daughter," laughed Dave.

"I gotta turn over and go to sleep," Dave stated as he put out his cigarette.

Christine snuggled up against Dave's back.

"Damn it!" Dave exclaimed.

"What's the matter?" Christine asked.

"Those Damn flies, every night one lands on me as I try to go to sleep. I'm going to spray in here tomorrow," Dave replied as he covered up his legs and arms.

"There are no flies in here. You must be imagining things."

Dave wondered, "Why is it every night something touches me as I am going to sleep, summer, winter, spring or fall?"

Like all nights, Dave could not sleep without dreaming of Jo. As always, he would wake up every hour or so and look around the room to see if anyone was in their bedroom. He never found anyone, but he continued his nightly vigilance.

DAVE TELLS MORE

The next day, after getting home from work, Dave decided to try to call Betty Way one more time.

Once again he got her answering machine. For some reason this time, he left a message for her.

Within an hour, Betty Way had returned his call. Dave was very surprised.

In talking with Betty on the phone, he found out that not only was she a licensed hypnotist and therapist, but she was also a Cherokee Medicine Woman and had dealt a lot with parapsychology in her practice, and she was clairvoyant.

Dave made an appointment to see Betty Way, on the following Monday.

After he had hung up the phone, he thought, "Good! Maybe she'll be able to help with all the other problems my family has been having besides helping me find Jo."

About an hour after they had hung up, Betty called back again.

"Dave," she started, "This is Betty Way again."

"Oh Hi, Betty."

"You know, I was just talking to my daughter on the phone. She reminded me of my busy schedule on Monday and that I probably would need more time with you, so if it is okay with you, I would like to change our appointment to Wednesday."

"Okay, Wednesday… same time?" He added.

"Yes, if that will fit in with your schedule alright?"

"Oh, yea, that will be fine. I'll see you on Wednesday then. Good-bye."

As he hung up the phone, Dave thought of how this would give him a week to think of everything he wanted to talk to her about. He began to feel like maybe help was on the way.

After dinner, Dave and Christine went out on to the patio to have their coffee and enjoy the beautiful summer evening.

"Oh, Dave, just look at those stars, isn't that a beautiful sky?" Christine smiled up at the stars.

"It's something. You can't beat these California skies or weather," he replied.

After he paused for a minute, Dave decided that it was time to tell Christine a little more about what was going on. After all, he had to tell her about his appointment with Betty Way. What if Christine got home before he did, and he also did not want Tony and Dan worrying about him when he did not get home at his usual time.

"Christine," Dave started, a little unsure of how to approach the subject, "You know when we were in Ohio on our vacation, I ran into an old boy I used to work with. We called him 'Seal Beams'," Dave chuckled as Christine stared at him.

"Seal Beams?" She asked.

"Yea, well, we started out calling him 'four-eyes' because he wore glasses, but too many people used 'four-eyes', so we came up with 'Seal Beams'."

"Was he one of your friends that you went to see when I went and spent the day with the girls?" she asked.

"Sort of, I couldn't really find the guys I was looking for, so I stopped by a coffee shop and there he was. I remembered that his wife was from Marion so I asked him for his help in finding this woman."

Dave waited for Christine's response because it was difficult for him to try to read her face.

"You went to Marion when we were back there, didn't you?" Christine asked.

There was really no expression on her face. She wasn't mad and she wasn't happy either, she simply asked a question.

"I had to," Dave answered.

Christine nodded her head as she lit up a cigarette. "So, what happened? Was he able to help you?"

"Well, he called me at work and he said he had found some woman that knew of the woman I was looking for..."

"'Seal Beams' called you at work?" asked Christine.

"Yes," answered Dave as he continued, "I told him I wanted to see her about the child," Dave stopped and lit up a cigarette.

"He instructed me to call this number in two day at the same time, which I did. When I called, 'Seal Beams' answered the phone and then he put this woman on the phone. She said this woman that she knew, who' name was Jo said, 'Yes, she did work at the H&H during the summer of

'65,' and 'Yes, she did have a child in '66,' and, 'No, I am not the father of her son,' and, 'No, she did not remember me.'"

Dave paused as he took a big puff off his cigarette.

"What did you say to her?" asked Christine.

"I asked her if this woman also had breast cancer because the woman I knew had the bottom part of her right breast surgically removed because of cancer. Then the woman said, 'Cancer? I don't know. I'll find out if she did and let you know.'"

"Did you hear anything from her after that?"

"No, but you know that she said that maybe it was another woman with the same name that worked at that bar back in '65. There's no way. I was in that bar all the time. We were always together. I would have known if there was someone else that worked there with the same name. Christine, I have to go back. I have to find out if she is dead or not."

"You weren't able to find anything out when you went there while we were on vacation..."

"No! I went into Marion, but so much had changed... I never knew her last name, so I decided to go to the library to see if maybe I could find something out about her there. The lady in the library gave me some old high school Yearbooks..."

Dave took another drag from his cigarette and then continued, "There were three girls with Joan as their first name. Two of them graduated from high school. The third one had no record after the tenth grade."

Neither Christine nor Dave said anything for a moment.

"How did she afford all those clothes?" he continued.

Christine had a puzzled look as Dave spoke.

"I mean, this girl had the clothes. I remember one time we went to the movies. She wore this tight-fitting, low-cut, knee length, sparkling blue dress with matching high heeled shoes. I remember walking down the street and she started walking ahead of me shaking that butt. Then she just stopped and looked over her shoulder at me with so much love in her eyes, and then she gave me this sexy grin. This girl knew how to dress and she loved me. There is no way she could have forgotten me."

"How about some more coffee," Christine asked as she picked up their cups.

"Yes, then come back out and I'll tell you some more," Dave responded.

Before long, Christine had rejoined him again with cups of fresh hot coffee.

"There is no way, she would not remember me. Hell, we were in love. Getting serious, too," Dave added.

"She even took me to meet her family," he reminisced, "One Sunday afternoon we drove out to her sister's house. She introduced me to her sister, mother, brother-in-law and some other guy, who I believe was her brother-in-law's brother. There were kids everywhere. We even took three of the kids back to her place in my car. She would not have forgotten me."

Christine sat quietly and listened to Dave.

"I even took her to meet my mom," Dave added.

"To meet your mom and you were still married to Rose at the time?" Christine inquired.

"Yes, but she was so tired and slept all the way to Wooster. I let her sleep and only ran in for a minute to visit with Mom. She never woke up. She was so little... she curled up on the front seat beside me. She was so tiny... she did not even touch me or the door. I remember how little she looked laying there beside me. I didn't have the heart to wake her at Mom's. She also slept all the way back to Marion."

Dave paused and lit up another cigarette. He had become a heavy smoker, almost chain smoking for the last few months.

"Yea, we were serious," Dave gazed at the distant stars in the sky.

"I'll say you were serious, taking her to your mother's and meeting her family," Christine added.

That was all Dave would tell Christine tonight. Dave knew that this was the best way to break all of this to Christine. He wanted to give her a little bit at a time so she could digest it before he told her more. She seemed to be handling it well this way.

He changed the subject and they talked about Tony's pitching for the college baseball team.

CHRISTINE RECALLS JOAN'S CALL

The next evening, after Dan had gone to bed, Dave and Christine took their coffee and went out on to the patio.

"Christine," Dave began, "I've been thinking about getting a hold of a hypnotist to see if maybe they could help me remember the directions to the sister's house, so I found one located in Burbank and I made an appointment."

Christine looked over at Dave, "I thought you didn't think that anyone could ever put you under. What made you decide to call a hypnotist?"

"That's how important it is to me to find her. I called this woman named Betty Way. I just opened up the phone book and there were four or five hypnotists listed. For some reason her name caught my eye. I think maybe it was because all of the rest of them sounded like clinics. Hers was just her name and phone number."

Dave took a sip of coffee and lit a cigarette before he answered her questions.

"More than likely she won't be able to put me under, but I have to at least try. There are actually two reasons why I'm going to see her. One, like I said, to see if she can help me remember the directions to the sister's house, and the second, to see if she can help us with all the problems we've had with the ghost that's been around us all these years."

"You think she can help with that?" Christine asked.

"Well, let me tell you, in talking with her on the phone, I found out that she is not only a licensed hypnotist, but she is also a Cherokee Medicine Woman and has dealt in parapsychology... I told her about this girl and the child and why I needed to find her. Then she told me about herself. I then told her a little about some of the strange things that have gone on with us. We originally made the appointment for Monday, but she called me back and said that after talking to her daughter, she thought she should change it to Wednesday so she could spend more time with me."

"That is really weird. She must think she can really help you if she feels she needs to spend that much time with you. You never know, Dave, maybe this lady can help you find the answers that you need."

Christine lit a cigarette and looked at Dave as he watched the stars.

"Damn it, Christine, there was too much there for her not to remember me. I remember one night we were making love and she took her fist and started pounding me on my back, demanding me to give her a child. I was with her through three menstrual cycles. The first two, she was flowing pretty heavy, but we didn't care. That didn't stop us from making love. The third one was really strange."

Dave took another sip of coffee and went on.

"She told me that it was her time, but she was only spotting. I mean she was proud and happy that she was only spotting. I knew then that she was pregnant... I knew the girl was pregnant."

Christine was silent as Dave continued, "There was one night when I was at the bar and she came over to me and said, 'Let's dance.' I wasn't going to tell you her name, but now is the time for you to know her name. Her name was Jo, so when we were dancing, I asked her what Jo was short for. She told me Joan. I don't recall her ever telling me her last name and I don't think I ever told her mine."

"Joan?" Christine's eyes widened.

She knew from what Dave had told her that this girl may have died years ago because she had breast cancer. Research has come a long way in the last fifteen years or so, but back then they both knew that if you had breast cancer, the odds were not very good that you would survive.

Christine picked up their cups and went inside for refills.

As she sat Dave's cup in front of him, she asked, "Dave, don't lie to me. I'm going to ask you something and you have to tell me the truth. Did you know any other Joan?"

Dave thought for a moment, "No! I never knew any other Joan, not even as a friend. Why?"

"You're absolutely sure?"

"Yes! Why?"

"Well, I told myself along time ago that I would never tell you about this. Tony was only about a week old at the time. We were living in that trailer in Wooster, and you were working for the Petroleum Supply Company. Well, one night while you were at work I got a phone call from a woman."

Dave and Christine looked at each other intensely now.

"Dave, she said her name was Joan."

"No, Christine, I didn't know any other Joan. What else did she say?"

"She asked me to set you free. She said that the two of you were in love and that you didn't want to hurt me. She knew that we just had a baby. I can't remember how many kids she said that she had. But I know it was a lot. I thought five or so. She was begging me to set you free."

"I'll be damned! It had to be her. Remember all the other strange phone calls? Remember when Tony's friends called and my dead mother would answer the phone and talk to them, and to you recall that some other girl claimed my mother talked to her, too. She wouldn't tell Tony or us what this old woman said to her, but do you recall that my mother had died long before that. You remember all those other people telling us they talked to someone on the phone at our house when we were gone. It had to be Jo. If Jo was alive, she couldn't have found us… She didn't know my last name. I wonder if my other wives ever received calls from her?" Dave rambled on, "Maybe Betty Way can help us."

Dave looked at his watch. He grabbed his cup and told Christine, "Well, it's getting late. We better go in and get things ready for work tomorrow."

Dave locked the door behind them and changed the subject to what was going on at work as they got things ready for the next day and then they went to bed.

THE HAUNTINGS

GRANADA HILLS, CALIFORNIA

After a hard day at work, Dave drove his Mercedes up the 14 Freeway for home.

"I'm sure glad that it's Friday and next week I'll be seeing Betty Way," he thought to himself.

His mind drifted back to Jo again while he tried to make sense out of the things he had been finding out in the past few days, such as Christine telling him about that strange phone call from Joan.

Before he knew it, he was home.

He and the boys had decided to get Chinese food for dinner instead of cooking. And after he put on some coffee, he went out on to the patio to have a cigarette and wait for the boys to come back with dinner.

He lit up a cigarette and thought to himself, "I've got five days to think of everything I want to tell Betty Way."

Dave thought about the first house they had bought in Granada Hills.

Tony was only five years old at the time. The first night in the house did not go without incident. They woke the following morning to find all the lights in the front of the house on. At first, they thought that maybe Tony had turned them on. But there was no way he could have reached the light above the stove.

Many times they heard the patter of little feet running in the hall during the night. Their house had hardwood floors, no carpet anywhere. They thought it was Tony, but Dave or Christine would get up to find Tony sound asleep in his room and the rest of the house was very cold and silent.

Dave recalled the incident with the big velvet painting.

Christine had it hanging in the living room above the Elgin Pendulum stand that had a house plant on top of it.

When they got home from work that day, they found the painting had been removed from the wall and carefully placed behind the door which led to the back hallway. Immediately thinking their house had been broken into, they checked all the doors and windows. Everything was still locked. Nothing was missing from within the house. No one had broken in.

The picture did not just fall off the wall and then bounce over behind the door because the Elgin Pendulum and the plant that was directly under the stand were not damaged.

Many mornings they woke to find the sliding patio door unlocked, yet the pole that was placed across the bottom of the door for security had not been removed. And many days they would come home from work or from one of Tony's baseball games and they would find the same thing.

When Dan was born, he was a very sick baby.

The doctors could not find what was wrong with their son. He just seemed to be in pain a lot of the time. Dan would want them to pick him up, but it seemed to hurt him when they did.

Dave remembered one night when they didn't know what to do. Dan cried and cried. Christine laid him down on to the couch. Dan got a dazed look on his face. He was no longer crying.

Christine became very upset and wanted to call the doctor.

Dave told her not to. He recalled telling Christine that Dan was okay. He knew Dan was flying. He had left his body. Dave reminded Christine of the times when he was little and very sick and left his body to escape the pain. Within a few minutes, Dan was back and no longer crying. He was his playful self again.

Dave went into the house to get a cup of coffee. He then went back outside, lit up a cigarette and continued thinking of the other occurrences that happened in the house in Granada Hills.

Dan was about two or three. He was sitting on the love seat in the living room watching television. Christine and Dave were sitting just outside the patio door where they were only a few feet from him. Suddenly, Dan began to cry, repeating, "Stop it! Stop it!"

They looked in at Dan and saw his little head bobbing back and forth as if someone were pushing it.

They rushed inside. Dan cried and wanted to be held. Christine picked him up and comforted him.

Dave often wondered about the old Sea Captain that Christine had seen in the backyard while hanging laundry.

This ghostly old gent wore a captain style cap and a dark blue coat. One arm hung by his side while his other hand was in his coat pocket. He just looked at Christine then vanished. She would not go back out there after dark again. She had seen him a couple times.

Then there was the ball.

On three different occasions, Christine had told Dave about a colorful light in the shape of a ball that she had seen in her rearview mirror as she drove. She had told him that the colors were the basic colors. The top edge was sort of a whitish yellow that turned into orange and the bottom part was red.

At first, she thought it was some kind of a reflection from the sun, but even when she would make a turn and head in a different direction, the ball remained in the same spot. It always disappeared when she got home. This happened while they lived in Granada Hills; once in their Toyota Landcruiser and once in their GMC Van. The third incident occurred when Christine was driving home from work to their home in Lancaster in her Chrysler New Yorker.

But that third time was a little different.

Christine stated that the inside of her car became deathly cold and its windows began to frost over, and its electronic instruments quit working. Then a few miles from home, everything went back to normal. Christine said she was never so afraid in her life.

Dave could not remember exactly when the elephant sounds started, but all of them kept hearing it.

One night the yelling continued so much, Dave finally shouted, "Shut up, I need to get to sleep."

He rolled over away from the noisy elephant sound and immediately he felt a warm little hand on his bare shoulder as if trying to pull him back over.

A few times Dave recalled hearing this strange elephant sound going deep into his ear as though it was entering his brain.

Then there was the night that Christine woke up and found Dave screaming in a woman's voice.

He could not remember what Christine had told him he was saying, but he did remember how scared she was.

Before Dave's mom died, she had come to visit them in 1982.

She slept in the guest room. This was not the first time she had come to stay with them, but for some reason, after the first few nights, she had asked them if it would be all right if she left her light on all night. She never told them why or what had happened.

It was strange the way these things always seemed to start acting up in the fall. They had moved into this house a week before Thanksgiving in 1980.

When Tony was about seven years old, he had a pretend friend named Peter, whom he said lived in his closet. Tony was always playing with his friend and talking to him.

Dave was not sure if it was Peter, but he remembered Tony telling him that while he was in his room he saw a boy standing in the hall.

The boy told Tony, "I gotta go now."

Then he turned, walked down the hall and disappeared.

There was also the pot roast that disappeared.

Christine had set out a roast for dinner.

Dave remembered that they got into some kind of argument about the roast. For some reason he did not want it, but he could not remember why.

For some strange reason, the roast just disappeared. They never did find it.

Many times they could hear aircraft communications on radios that were turned off.

After Dave's mom had passed away, Dianna, his daughter who was killed in a car accident years later, had told Dave about talking to her grandmother, Dave's Mom, on the phone.

He also recalled how that house always had cold spots.

Dave thought about the phone call to his brother Phil, who was near death because of lung cancer.

Phil and Dave never got along and had not spoken to each other in a long time.

Yet, after Phil's death, Dave's other brothers thanked him for calling Phil just before his end.

They said that before Dave's call, Phil was in a lot of pain. Phil never told them what he and Dave talked about, but his pains were eased after he hung up the phone.

Dave knew that he never called Phil, "To Hell with the bastard," is what Dave thought, "Rot in Hell!" was how Dave cared about Phil.

There was also a strange whistling that would be heard throughout the house. This whistling would occur night or day. They would run from room to room trying to find its source, which they never did find.

There was another time when Dave had a bad toothache. Nothing would help.

He remembered taking different kinds of pain pills and toothache medicine and finally, he lay down and said, "It's now or never!"

When he awoke the next morning, his toothache was gone.

Christine told him how he had walked the floors all night long, but Dave swore that he slept all night and he recalled feeling very rested, as though he had had a good nights sleep.

When they decided to sell, with the house on the market for sale, Dave recalled two perspective buyers and the realtor telling him that they saw two

Entities walk through the wall. The realtor refused to handle the house and canceled their contract. Dave and Christine were able to find another realtor that sold their house within two weeks.

After the house was finally sold, Dave recalled a conversation with Christine... He, Tony and Dan had taken a load of furniture to storage and Christine was getting the last bit of their things ready for storage. All of a sudden, in a crackling voice, she said she heard a tiny soft voice say, "I... go... too?"

Christine did not know what to do or say. She said that she felt sad inside and very sorry for the thing. Dave and the boys also felt the same way about the Entity.

It was also strange that they never had any problems for the three months that they lived in their motor home in Castaic after they sold their home. They were supposed to be there for only two weeks, but their new home in Palmdale was not completed until the end of March.

PALMDALE, CALIFORNIA

Right from the start, things were not right as with the unexplained high electric bills. Though their house was large and had a pool and spa, their electric bills were high enough for two homes.

Dave had some knowledge of electricity, so he checked out the amperage use of the pump motors plus all other electric appliances in their house. It did not add up to the amount of electric they were using.

Dave even thought that maybe their neighbor's house was wired through their meter. The electric company came out and checked their meter. Everything looked okay. No reason was ever found for the enormous electrical usage.

Jewelry, which Dave had bought for Christine in Spain that had disappeared several years prior reappeared on Christine's dresser.

Still friends told Dave, Christine and Tony that they had called and left messages with some old woman. No old woman lived with them.

One night after going to bed, Dan screamed.

Christine and Dave ran into his bedroom.

Dan was crying, stating that something just hit the wall over his head.

They looked and saw that just inches above him there was a hammer like impression in the wall. It seemed like Dan was bothered more than the rest of the family by these unusual happenings.

One school Holiday while Christine and Dave were at work, Dan was having problems with the ghost again.

Tony was walking into Dan's room, telling Dan that there are no ghost, and something hit Tony on his chin, "like a fist," and knocked him against the wall.

Day or night, you could hear people walking around upstairs in the attic. Sometimes you would hear water being run or a toilet being flushed and you might hear chains rattling up there, too.

Many times they heard doors opening and closing. More than once when they came home they found TVs and/or radios turned on.

One of their last Christmas' spent in their Palmdale home, after days of endless noises and seeing things everyone was so afraid that they all slept in the family room for four nights and they left all the lights on in the house. On a morning of one of those days, they found on the floor of their "bedroom" a jeweled cross that was all bent up. This jeweled cross belonged to Christine, who kept it in her jewelry box upstairs, but the cross was not bent before.

Sometimes as they sat in their back yard enjoying their pool or spa, they would look up and see someone walk past the window of their upstairs master bedroom.

Now Dave could laugh about that night that he got so mad at the happenings in their house that Christine and he actually went into Dan's bedroom and Dave cussed out this ghost. He remembered giving it a good old oil field cussing as they heard it shifting its weight from one foot to the other in Tony's bedroom. The creaking of the floor made it sound very heavy. Dave demanded it to fight him. The thing never did, and Dave was kind of glad that it did not accept his challenge.

One afternoon, the smell of roses filled the house. Christine and Dave raced from room to room trying to find out where the smell was coming from. In the kitchen, in an area of about a three foot circle, the rose smell was the strongest. It was so strong that the smell was sickening. It lasted for about one half hour before the odor disappeared.

They all used to laugh while watching their little pet dog as he would look around the room as if he were watching someone or something fly around. They laughed at him until they once saw him fly across the room and land on the couch.

One night, Dave and Christine lay in bed and they could hear someone walking in the attic above. The next morning, in their walk-in closet they found the lid to the attic was twisted like it had been opened.

On another night, Dave waited for Christine to come to bed. All of the lights were turned off and the street light shown on the wall. Then all of a sudden writing appeared on the wall. Dave was unable to figure out what it said before it disappeared.

Dave was not sure if he saw the eyes the same night he saw the writing on the wall. The incident with the eyes was similar to the writing. While he waited for Christine, Dave saw two large red eyes appear on the ceiling of their bedroom. The eyes appearance lasted for a few minutes then they were gone.

One of Tony's girl friends, Lisa, told a strange story, the same story that Dave's sister had told Dave and Christine years before.

Holy Graduel

Lisa was sleeping in her room, and all at once she woke up.

A round ball was on her wall that was the same colors of the ball that had ridden in the cars with Christine.

Dave was missing. No one knew where he was. Lisa and Christine cried because they were worried about Dave. A little ghost appeared and told them he knew where Dave was and that he would take Christine to him. Christine refused out of fear but Lisa said she would go with him.

Hand-in-hand, the ghost and Lisa entered the ball of light on the wall.

They flew over a house that Lisa did not know. In the side yard, stood a group of people looking at a crack in a step to the back door of this house, near them Dave lay dead. Not one of the people cared about Dave.

Lisa had described Dave's mother's house. Those were his brothers and sisters she had seen. She had described a house and people that she had never seen or met before. Lisa knew and told exactly the same story that Dave's sister had told them years prior, but she never met Dave's sister. Tony couldn't have told Lisa this story because he had never heard this story before. How did she know the story unless it really happened to her?

Dave knew his brothers and sisters did not care for him. Out of eleven kids, Dave kept in touch with two sisters. The rest of his family was like strangers to him.

Dave's family troubles stemmed from his brother Phil. Phil could have been a good brother except in his younger days he listened to what everyone said; His older brothers talked him into quitting school to play music in their band. He never worked at any other kind of job. He never had a girl friend that Dave knew of and he never moved out of their parents' home.

Their mother would carry meals up to Phil's room. He didn't want anyone to see him. His teeth rotted out and he grew thin. He bragged he only needed to use a cigarette lighter once in the morning and then he chained smoked the rest of the day. He kept a loaded shotgun next to his bed. They claimed he would kill and had threatened all of his brothers and sisters.

Dave tried to get Phil professional help, but their mom kept saying there was nothing wrong with Phil. Phil ruled and controlled their mother and father. He destroyed any relationship that Dave could have had with his parents.

The last ten years or so that Phil lived, he demanded money from his mom, and she gave him all he wanted.

Phil died in Buffalo, New York, at a hospital on Halloween from lung cancer at the age of forty-nine.

Phil was one of the reasons Dave left home and joined the Army. Was there any wonder why even today Dave still hated Phil.

Many other strange things happened when they lived in Palmdale too. While working the graveyard shift for a pharmaceutical company one of these Entities went to work with Dave.

The ghost whistled at him in the locked maintenance shop. Dave ran around and looked for whoever whistled, no one could be found.

One of the workers while sizing vitamins looked up to see an old woman standing and staring at him. The building had security with closed circuit TV. No one could have entered the building without being seen. Security searched everywhere for the old woman. They never found her, and the guy quit his job immediately.

While doing apartment maintenance, an Entity once again went to work with Dave. The assistant manager saw the old sea captain outside her window one night. She described the same sea captain that Christine had seen in Granada Hills. The assistant manager lived on the second floor.

The manager of the apartments and Dave were going to check out a vacant apartment. She tried to open the door, the door was pushed shut from the inside. Again she tried to open the door, this time the door opened. They both ran inside and looked for whoever shut the door. No one was there. The windows were closed and they all had screens on them. Again, this apartment was on the second floor.

Late one night, Dave was driving home on the freeway when the car filled with the smell of beer. The odor only lasted a few minutes and then was gone. Dave had quit drinking years before and no beer was ever carried in this car.

LANCASTER, CALIFORNIA

"Things didn't get any better after moving in there," Dave thought to himself while he lit another cigarette.

Dave started to recall things that Tony had told him about, such as pennies flying off of his desk and landing beside him on his bed.

Unlike Dan, Tony would take these things in stride and tried not to let them scare him.

"Either that or he didn't want me to know how afraid he was," Dave chuckled to himself.

Dave remembered Tony telling him about going on a date one night. His girlfriend was complaining that it was cold in the car so Tony turned the heater on. He kept it on high, but the car just would not warm up the way it normally did. He looked into his rearview mirror and saw his grandmother, Dave's mom, who had passed away seven years earlier, sitting in the back seat.

On another occasion, Tony was in his room doing something and he saw his grandmother again. This time, she was sitting in the easy chair in his room, she sat there as she did in the car, looking straight ahead and never said anything.

And then, about a year or so ago, Tony was home alone. Their little dog ran into the dining room barking. The little dog stopped barking and sat down, looking up and started wagging his tail about five feet from a corner of the room. Tony walked over to the dog and bent down to pick him up. As Tony stood up holding the dog, he saw his deceased grandfather, Dave's Dad, standing in front of him.

The smoke like Entity said, "Do not be afraid," and disappeared.

Dave's dad had died fourteen months after his mom had passed away. Tony was very close to both of his grandparents.

And there were a few times that Tony came home to find his room tore up. Things would be thrown and scattered everywhere.

Then there was Dan.

He seemed to be more prone to strange occurrences than Tony.

He always slept with his light on and did not like to be alone for very long. In fact, Dan always liked to be where he could see someone at all times.

He had seen Entities all over the house. He had seen them walking up and down the stairs. He even had gone into the garage and seen one sitting in one of the cars. Dan had told Dave about these sightings several times. He did not like to go into the garage unless someone went with him or he left the door from the house to the garage open.

Dan was very meticulous about where he put things and how he had them arranged. And many times he had gotten up in the mornings to find a lot of things in his room had been rearranged. And he had also seen things move by themselves in his room.

Dave recalled how Dan would come running down stairs because one of his toys turned themselves around or moved across the room. Also there were times when Dan would be in bed and his little toy Gargoyles would shoot their suction cup darts at him.

More than once, Dan saw a woman dressed in white walk across the living room, down the hall and then vanish through the closed door to the master bedroom.

Christine also saw the woman, but that time the woman standing near the living room fireplace. Christine remembered the woman was about five foot tall and was wearing a full skirted knee length white with some kind of blue floral print dress with short puffy sleeves. When Christine described this woman to Dave and Tony, Tony exclaimed, "That's the same woman I saw in our house in Granada Hills when I was six years old."

Not once in all these years did Dave see any ghost or Entities. He heard many strange noises but never saw anything.

Over the years, Dave had always said, he was studying these ghosts and he didn't want them to leave just yet.

He felt that he learned how they moved from room to room in the house, traveling down electric wire like roads. He thought they live in low electric like diodes, computers chips used in communication and other household appliances. Their reflections what we see is actually off the low end of our color spectrum, and they are really low levels of electric energy.

Dave thought over the years Entities had entered his mind to "live" his life. As they relived his daily routine, he thought that he was reliving their lives.

Dave could recall being upstairs in an old wooden house.

Suddenly he hears someone coming up the stairs. Panic stricken he runs over and tries to hide inside of a wall. He can see cobwebs and dust that has settled on the harden plaster that oozed out between the wooden slates. He stood there still, hoping the human will not see him. The guy comes into the room and looks around. Not seeing anyone, he leaves. Dave was relieved he was not seen.

Dave could also recall flying with someone else.

They are playing some sort of tag. He was being chased by this other person. Flying fast and hard, Dave slams into the ground. Down into the earth he goes then turns upward. All of a sudden he stops and looks around. He is inside of a coffin. A dead man's forehead is pressed to the lid. The skin on his neck has pulled his mouth open, and some of the lining of the coffin is hanging down. The casket is cast in a bluish white light. The light is coming from Dave... He is glowing. Dave feels real sad about this old dead man. All of a sudden, the other Entity has caught him. She is also sad about the man. After a moment they continue their game and fly away.

Dave also remembered flying straight up out of a house into the night sky, faster and faster he flew straight up until he could see the complete Earth far below him. How beautiful the world and universe looked from there.

Dave had thought he learned the experiences of these of Entities, but now he realized he was only remembering things that he had done.

But now these Entities started to disrupt his family's daily lives. Maybe, Betty Way could help get rid of these ghosts once and for all.

Dave had a lot of things to talk to Betty Way about but if she only helped him remember how to get to Jo's sister's house, he would be happy.

LEARNING

BETTY WAY

At last Wednesday was here.

All day long, Dave kept thinking of everything he wanted to tell Betty Way. His mind kept wandering. Would she be able to help him? Would she be able to hypnotize him? What kind of person is she? What if she was some kind of weirdo?

"I guess I'll find out at three-thirty," he thought.

All of a sudden, a really scary thought went through his mind, "Boy! What if she puts me under and I do too much talking. She sure would have a lot to gossip about."

Dave thought back over the years about his sex life and how it had been kind of wild. He sure would be embarrassed, but then, so would a lot of women.

Before he knew it, it was two forty-five.

Dave took off a little early so he would have time to stop and get something to eat before his appointment with Betty. Knowing he would be getting home late because of rush hour traffic and all, he pulled into Jack-In-The-Box and ordered a hamburger, fries and a Coke to go. This would be dinner tonight.

Dave parked across the street from her house.

Looking at his watch, he realized that it was only a ten minute drive from his work to Betty Way's house which was located near the Burbank Airport. He still had twenty minutes to wait because it was only ten after three.

Betty's office was in her home. Although most of the area reminded Dave of a commercial or industrial area, he found the streets to be lined with fifties style homes.

There was one car setting in her driveway. Two other cars sat in front of her house on the street. He noticed that one of the cars had a spider web that went from its bumper down to the street.

Betty's house fit in with the rest of the homes in this little neighborhood. It was small and sat about twenty feet back from the sidewalk. The grass was uncut and a little shaggy looking but a couple of neatly looking plants sat by her door. All in all, there was still a warm glow radiated from her home.

He was not sure what was going on in there. He did not know if she had another client with her or not. He decided that he would wait until exactly three-thirty before he knocked on her door.

Precisely at three-thirty a car sped down the street and pulled into Betty's driveway.

There was just one woman in the car.

As she was getting out of the car, a tall thin man came out from inside of the house and started talking to her.

She was about five foot six with straight black hair that came about halfway down her back. She was a tall good looking woman.

Dave could tell she had Indian blood in her from her high cheekbones and her dark eyes. It was hard to tell her age, though. She was probably somewhere between thirty-five and forty. Dave knew that this had to be Betty Way.

He put out his cigarette, got out of his car, locked it and headed across the street.

The man who was talking to the woman had grabbed a couple of bags from the car and went back into the house. The woman grabbed another bag from the back seat and closed the car door.

As Dave neared her, he said, "Hi! You must be Betty Way."

She looked at him, smiled and answered, "Yes, and you must be Dave."

She rambled on about a friend having the flu and she had gone over to help her out, and was very sorry that she was running late.

"That's okay. No problem," Dave assured her as he held the door to her house open for her.

"Thank you. I just hate running late like this, but when friends call... well you know how that goes."

Dave followed Betty through the house as she rambled on.

Betty opened the door to a step-down office. She turned the lights on and then dimmed them down some.

"Why don't you just make yourself comfortable and I'll be right back," she added.

Betty walked out and left Dave standing there.

Her office was sort of a long narrow room.

Dave got a warm feeling about this room with its decor of earth tones. In front of him and to his right was an easy chair. Across the room and to his left, was a large picture window with thick drapes that were closed.

A small desk with a computer and lots of papers spread on top of it sat in front of the picture window. To the left of the desk was a small, freestanding, three shelf stand. Indian relics had been carefully placed on top of the stand.

There was a bookcase in between the desk and the chair on the right.

Instead of books, the bookcase was full of more Indian artifacts. It held items such as a peace pipe, dream catchers and pictures of wolves. These types of items were all over the room.

Dave sat in the easy chair in the dim lit room, and he tried to relax.

He was still wondering if this was going to work or not. He knew that in order for her to be successful, he had to be confident with her. She would have to have complete control of him.

After about fifteen minutes, Betty came back into the office.

"I am so sorry that I am running late, Dave. I'm not usually this rushed. I just cannot apologize enough."

"Those things happen. Don't worry about it," Dave chuckled.

Betty sat down on the chair at her desk.

"Would you like an ice tea or water or something before we begin?" she asked Dave as she set some sort of large drink for herself down on the desk.

"No thanks," Dave said.

"SHE WON'T ANSWER, SHE'S DEAD"

Betty picked her drink up, took a sip and pointing to her degree hanging on the wall, said, "As I told you on the phone, I'm a licensed hypnotist."

She went on to tell Dave about how she became a Medicine Woman. After her father died, she lost faith in the Cherokee ways then later reclaimed her faith.

She then told Dave how her husband had always wanted to be a pilot and she told him to quit his job and do it. She knew that God would take care of them and direct her in helping other people with her abilities to communicate with the Other Side.

Then she asked, "How may I help you?"

"I need your help to remember how to get to a house that I visited thirty years ago."

"Why do you want to go to this house?" Betty inquired.

Dave answered, "I need to find an old girlfriend of mine, I believe she had my child... She was older than I. She had breast cancer and I need to find out if she had my child. I want to tell her that I'm sorry for leaving her and why I left."

"How do you know that she's alive? I see a woman standing to your left... she's about five foot tall with shoulder length brown hair..."

Dave interrupted, "No, she wasn't that tall. That might be my daughter..."

Betty came back with, "No, your daughter went into the Light. She's happy, but it might be someone else. You have an older son that just moved out and I believe you have a younger son who is quite ill. Have you been to see your doctor lately or are you going in soon? You need to get in. You need to go see him."

She turned in her chair and took another sip of her drink.

"Tony, my older son, still lives at home. He's going to college and should be signing a baseball contract next May. My younger son, Dan, had some health problems, but I think he's okay now," Dave went on to explain his heart condition.

Betty stated other things relating to his family which were true, but these things were unknown to Dave; Tony had signed up with the Marines last month, and Dan was still having health problems.

"Dave, what happens if you go back there and find this woman?" Betty asked, "I've helped other people go back to find old sweethearts or friends, who were not the same people they were a long time ago."

"I don't know what I'll do. But I do know that I wish to take her out to a nice dinner and tell her I'm sorry for leaving. I know she couldn't change her life and move out here with me. Also, I know I couldn't change my life and move back there to her. I'm fifty-two years old now and she's sixty-four, things just wouldn't work out. I just would like to see her one more time before I die."

"Okay! What else would you like to remember besides directions to this house?"

"I was only at her sister's house once, so I need to remember directions for that, and I'd like to remember what Jo's last name was. I called her Jo, but her real name was Joan," Dave replied.

Betty brought her chair over to the left side of his and turned down the lights. She instructed Dave to pull the lever on the right side of the easy chair so that it would recline back. She told him to rest his arms on the arms of the chair and lay back, close his eyes and just relax.

"Now, Dave, just relax and think about being a young small boy again. You are running and playing in a park... you're kicking leaves and playing with the leaves falling from the tree."

Betty went on telling Dave that he sees a man with balloons and the man ties a balloon around his left wrist. She talked of the detail about his arm feeling lighter as the man kept tying on more and more balloons.

Dave realized that his arm now was floating in the air.

She placed her hand on his forehead and told Dave that his forehead and his floating hand were magnets and they were coming together. As his hand started coming toward his forehead she removed her hand from his forehead.

Bang, his hand hit his forehead.

He's was under hypnosis.

Betty continued instructing Dave, "In the park, you come upon a garden, as you walk into the center of the garden, you see a bench. Sitting on the bench is your Guardian Angel. Ask him what his name is."

Dave saw someone sitting on this park bench, dressed in white, surrounded by many other people.

"She won't answer," Dave replied.
"Why?" Betty asked.
"They won't let her."
"Who won't let her?"
"All the people standing around her," he answered.

Tears started to form in Dave's eyes because he knew why they would not let her answer.

"Who are all those people standing around her?" Betty asked.
"People that someone in my family killed," he said.
"Who in your family killed these people?"

Now the tears really began to run down his face, "I did."
"Why did you kill them?"
"I didn't want to... They made me... I killed them in the Civil War," he sobbed.

Betty instructed Dave to go back to when he killed the people.

Dave saw a black man and a white man, two women and a small boy standing in front of a large house. The soldiers raped the older women and then drug the younger woman off. The black man ran. Dave and others were ordered to fire. He could see and smell the smoke from his gun as the man, the older woman and the small boy fell down to their death.

Dave's heart began to race. His breathing quickened.

Betty commanded Dave to relax, instructing him that he was only watching this scene on a big screen TV as though he was not there but only watching the event.

She asked, "What happened to Dave?"

Dave could see himself standing in some bar, taking a drink of whiskey and then an ex-Rebel shoots him, which he relayed to Betty.

"Okay Dave, remember going to Jo's sister's house?"
"Yes, I do," Dave now smiled.
"Do you remember the directions?"
"No, I can't. It was so long ago."
"That's okay. Remember Jo sitting beside you when you drove there? Do you remember her giving you directions?"
"I can't remember all of her directions," Dave replied.
"That's okay. Remember her sitting beside you... now you are driving to her sister's house. Listen to the directions she's giving you."

Dave answered, "All I can remember is leaving her place."

In anticipation of what questions Betty was going to ask, Dave nervously started moving his right leg and foot back and forth and waving his left hand in a circular motion. All at once he could see Betty looking at his hand and foot in motion as if he was standing in front of himself and

Betty, and he stopped moving immediately.

Betty commanded, "Jo is sitting beside you. Look at her and ask her directions to her sister's house."

Dave could see Jo sitting on her legs on the car seat beside him.

She was holding his arm tight to her body and smiling up at him. She would not answer his questions. She just kept smiling.

Once again, tears rolled down Dave's face as Betty asked him, "Why won't Jo answer you?"

"She's gone. She's on the Other Side... She's dead. Jo said to remember where her daughter pointed to President Harding's Tomb, just go straight out that road. The house is on the left just before the big right curve on the road."

"Ask her how you can find your child."

Dave replied, "The birth record. Jo put her maiden name down as mother and my first name and her husband's last name down as father. Check out the birth records."

Finishing up, Betty brought Dave out of hypnosis.

"Maybe this information will help you," Betty told Dave.

"I'm going back. I have to go back and see for myself. I was planning on going in October anyway," Dave stood up from the easy chair.

"Let me know what you find out."

She walked Dave to the door,

"After a good session, we always hug," she gave him a hug at the door.

As Dave headed for his car, he glanced at his watch and realized that the session with Betty took three hours. It was now six-thirty.

He got into his car, headed home and thought about everything that he had just learned.

BITS AND PIECES START COMING

As Dave parked his car in the garage and was getting out, he suddenly thought to himself, "Damn it! I didn't talk to Betty about the ghosts. Shit!"

Christine was just pouring herself a cup of coffee when he came through the door.

"How did it go? Is she for real?" she asked after Dave said hello, kissed her on the cheek and asked her to pour him a cup, too.

"Oh yea," Dave exclaimed, "I didn't think it was really possible, but she was able to put me under. Let's go sit down and I'll tell you about it."

They each took their cup of coffee and went into the dining room. As they sat down, Tony walked into the room.

"Hi, Dad, I didn't hear you come in," Tony said to Dave as he sat down at the table with them.

"Tony, did you ever read or study anything in the Civil War about any kind of civilian killings?" Dave asked.

Tony proceeded to tell Dave all about Sherman's March to the Sea. He told of how ruthless Sherman was because he could not fail this time. This was a big battle for him and he had to be successful, no matter what the price. Tony said how Sherman ordered his men to burn everything and to kill anyone who got in their way, be it man, woman or child. Tony went on to say many innocent people were killed.

"Well, let me tell you what happened," Dave began as he told Christine and Tony about the Civil War part of his hypnosis.

Neither one of them could believe it. They all talked about how odd it was that Dave never knew about Sherman's March to the Sea.

After Tony and Dan had gone to bed, Dave and Christine slipped out to the patio with their coffee and cigarettes.

"Christine," Dave began, "This sure did open my eyes to a lot of things, but it also left me with a lot of questions."

"What about the directions? Were you able to remember how to get to the house?" Christine asked him.

Dave told her about Jo telling him to remember her daughter pointing to Harding's Tomb and staying on that road. The house would be on the left where the road had the big curve to the right.

"But it won't do any good to find the house," Dave told her, "Everyone is gone."

Something happened to Dave in that session with Betty Way. It seemed that little by little he was getting the answers to all his questions. He knew that Jo was with him and she was giving him all the answers a little at a time. Although he did not want to admit it at first, he knew that it was because at last he had accepted Jo's death.

There were times when Dave felt like he must be going crazy. At times, he almost wished that were the case, but deep down he knew Jo was dead. His beautiful Jo was dead and she was trying to help him to understand. Over the next three weeks, Dave got bits and pieces of information, and he told Christine about most of them.

One night, Dave revealed to Christine that it was Jo who was sitting on the bench in the garden when he was under hypnosis. She wore a knee length, full skirted, lacy dress. It was sort of low cut with puffy sleeves. She sat there with her hands folded on her lap, ankles crossed and swinging her feet backwards and forwards with a big smile on her face.

"But, you know what I can't understand," Dave told Christine, "is why everyone's faces were blurred. Even when I was under at Betty's, and Jo was sitting beside me in the car, I knew it was Jo, but I couldn't really make out her face... The conversation we had in the car was strange, too. She would answer my question before I ever asked it. It was like she was reading my mind. Then when she answered, she never opened her mouth. I could hear her answer, but she never really spoke."

"That is so bizarre, Dave," Christine started as she looked at Dave, "I'm so sorry for all the pain you're feeling. I don't know why, but I really feel sorry for Jo, too."

A few days later, Dave was thinking about his session again. He realized that all those people that were standing around Jo in the park were not all dressed in Civil War time clothes. He did not kill all of those people. They were from different time periods, including the present... There were people in Rebel uniforms, two in Union uniforms and men, women and children of all ages just milling around her. They all stared at him when he was there, but no one said anything.

The Civil War along with what he had done during and after the Civil War was what made him not get along and hate people in his present life. He knew what people were capable of doing, and he knew what they were about to think before they thought about it. Dave also knew the Soul was not evil, the flesh was evil.

He always knew that "something" was helping him, and now he knew that it was Jo. She had been protecting him since at least 1968 or '69. Dave had gone through four severe car accidents which had completely totaled his cars, but he never got hurt. He always thought that was strange and knew that someone must have been on his side, especially since he was never one to wear seat belts.

She could not stop his death, but she could stop or warn him about being injured. For sure she could ease his pains because back in 1986, his doctor had asked him about how he broke both wrists. Dave recalled back in 1969, being in a car accident where he had hurt his wrists, but did not know that he had broken them.

Many times she had kept him from getting hurt on the drilling rigs; he would be in a situation, and she would warn him about something that was going to happen, and sometimes he could actually feel the pain of getting hurt and could see the injury occurring. The accident would always happen, but he did not get injured or hurt as badly.

Dave eventually found out within these three weeks that it was Jo touching him every night when he went to bed, but before he thought it was a fly.

Jo also revealed to Dave that they were Soul Twins, and every time they came back to experience their dream of living as man and wife and raising a family, something would happen to prevent it. People would always stop them. She explained to Dave that that was the reason he tried to do so many things in this life, for they would never be back again.

Over the years he had become quite good in many different professions. He had traveled the world to places of interest to him, and he knew, partied and dined with music stars, actors and actresses.

He did all of these things and more because subconsciously he knew that he was not coming back again. But through the years he had first refused to believe it though, this is what Jo told him.

Dave started to remember things about, "the Other Side" and "the Light". But at this point, he had not told Christine a lot about these things.

Jo also told him about her coming by and they would go flying on this side and the Other Side together. She also reminded him of their special hide-a-way along the wall on the Other Side and displayed to him her secret treasure of jewelry that she had collected over the years.

Dave had been going back and forth about which car he should take on his trip back to Ohio. He could not decide if he should take the Van or his Mercedes. Jo let him know that she wanted to take the Mercedes.

During these weeks of remembering bits and pieces of the past, Dave serviced his Mercedes and prepared for his trip.

But daily, Dave still looked for a letter from Jo.

He still could not believe she was gone. Nor did he really believe in reincarnation, which he always thought was stupid. He thought once life was over, it was over... There may be something after death, but who cared what happened after you die. Now, he was learning things were different than what he previously thought.

"But, why am I learning these things now? And what will I find in Marion?" Dave thought.

DAVE'S ACCEPTANCE

The Friday to leave finally arrived.
Dave took off work early, stopped by Pep Boys Auto Parts Store and picked up extra Diesel Fuel Additive. He knew it would be needed in Ohio, because the weather was starting to turn cold.
His Mercedes was originally owned by the wax company that Dave worked for before he bought it, and it was driven by the company's sales manager who took care of it. The sales manager had gotten it repainted its original silver gray color and re-chromed just before Dave got it.
Many times, Dave had taken the trip to Ohio. It was nothing for him to drive it. Besides his regular coffee and food stops, he needed only to stop once in Oklahoma for fuel because his Mercedes had two fuel tanks that held over 50 gallons of fuel. And if he could stay awake, he could drive to Ohio, in around thirty-six hours. And he knew Jo would keep his old car running like she had many times before.
Jo's help was needed only once during the trip.
Somewhere in Arizona the Mercedes started knocking and blowing out blue smoke through its exhaust. Dave just knew for sure he had lost its piston. Within the next few miles, the old engine straightened out and ran perfect again, and Dave did not see any more smoke coming out.
Around three o'clock the next morning, Dave had to stop for sleep. He pulled into a rest area and lay back in his seat. He had just closed his eyes when the car shook and he heard Jo say, "Let's go!"
Sitting back up, he pulled out of the rest area and continued the trip.
Whenever Dave stopped, he would get a funny feeling when he would pull back onto the freeway. The feeling was like he had forgotten someone. He would look around the car for a passenger but could not see anyone. He was traveling with his "Ghostly" Jo. Because he could not see her, he felt like he had left her behind.
The weather was good for traveling, and the rest of the trip went

without incident. Dave arrived just outside of Columbus, Ohio somewhere after midnight on Saturday night.

His room at the motel in Marion was reserved for one week beginning on Sunday, so he decided to pull into a roadside rest and get a little sleep. He knew that if he kept driving, it would put him in Marion about two o'clock in the morning on Sunday, and he did not want to arrive that early in the morning.

Dave woke up Sunday as the morning sun began to shine into his car and he knew it was still pretty early.

He needed to kill some time so he went into a restaurant to have some breakfast instead of just eating while driving like he usually does.

Dave got to the motel around ten-thirty in the morning. The desk clerk told him that his room would not be ready for another three hours.

Dave told her that he would come back later to check in.

"Well," Dave thought to himself as he stopped at pay phone, "I guess I can try to call that number that 'Seal Beams' gave me to contact that woman who knew Jo."

Dave dialed the number only to get a recording telling him that the number had been changed to a non-published number. Thinking he might have dialed wrong, Dave hung up and tried the number again. He got the same recording.

"Shit!" he said as he hung up the phone.

Dave had 'Seal Beams' address with him, so he decided that he would call information and get his number. He could not believe it when he got the same sort of recording stating that the number he was requesting was a non-published number.

Dave quickly brushed away any thought of going to Wooster to talk to 'Seal Beams'. After all, they knew that Dave was coming and they also knew where he would be staying.

Feeling a little disappointed, he walked back to his car.

Dave decided that he would go looking for the road to Jo's sister's house.

He found Harding's Tomb, but could not recognize the road. Everything was built up new.

Suddenly, he got the notion to just start driving and let what he always thought was his gut instinct but now knew was Jo, guide him. She had never let him down throughout the years.

He just kept driving and would turn left or turn right where and whenever he thought he should turn. All of a sudden, he turned on to this straight, old country, paved road.

To his left on a curve, way off of the road, he saw the house. He knew it

Holy Graduel

was the house that Jo's sister had once lived in, but it did not look the same. It had been remodeled over the years.

Dave kept on driving for he knew there was no use in stopping because the sister did not live there any more.

Before long, he drove into a small town by the name of Cardington. At a stop sign, Dave saw a road sign that read, "LANCASTER - 26 MILES."

Now he remembered.

Sherman was from Lancaster, Ohio. Dave used to live around here before the Civil War. He also knew that what had happened during his Civil War life was the reason that he always got that uneasy, sadness and sickening feeling whenever he was in this area. It was guilt that made him feel that way.

Dave turned the car around and began to retrace his steps back to the motel in Marion. As he came upon the house where Jo's sister used to live, he stopped and looked at it for a few minutes as memories flooded his head, then sadly he headed back to the motel.

When Dave arrived at the motel, he found that his room was ready. He gave the clerk his credit card and signed the registration form. He was checked in.

Later that afternoon, carrying the addresses of the H&H and the old Hotel with him, Dave drove to Center Street.

It was raining slightly, almost a snow, as he got out of his car.

Dave shivered at the cold as he began to walk. He located the spot where the Pacific Union Hotel used to stand. It was now just an old empty lot.

Walking along Center Street, he found where Casey's and the H&H used to be.

"I'll be damned!" Dave thought to himself.

The building was still standing. He remembered the barmaid he had spoken with back in July had told him that it had been torn down.

There were different stores in the building now, but it was the same old building. Dave noticed that the driveway curb for the parking lot of the H&H was still there.

Slowly he walked down through the parking lot to the back of the building like he had done so many times in the past.

The old stairs that lead to Jo's apartment were still there. A few of the wooden steps had been changed, but it was definitely the same old stairs.

He looked up and could see the window of her apartment.

The inside of the window was covered with something that appeared to be plywood. It looked like no one lived there. And once again, a million memories filled his head.

Dave stood there for five or ten minutes in the misty cold rain as tears rolled down his cheek.

Sundays were their special days. This day... this Sunday was completely different; there was no sunshine, there was no Jo to greet him and no Queen Vickie to whisk them away to the parks or their hide-a-way.

Queen Vickie had laid her head down and died while trying to carry him back to Jo in an October, thirty-one years ago.

Finally, he turned and slowly walked back to his car and drove back to the motel where he spent the night.

Sleep did not come easy to Dave that night for he could not help but think of his loneliness without Jo. But when he did fall asleep, his dreams were of his Jo and their summer of 1965.

Monday morning, Dave woke up around seven o'clock. He wanted to be at the library when they opened. He could not remember when they opened but figured that they probably did not open until nine.

After taking a shower and cleaning up, he decided to go get some breakfast and kill some time until the library opened.

Dave got to the library a little after nine.

"Even this place looks differently than it did just a couple of months ago when I was here," he thought to himself.

There were all kinds of construction going on.

Dave approached the Librarian and asked her if she could help him. He told her that he needed some old high school books and directories from the sixties.

"Oh, I'm terribly sorry but that section of the library is not available to the public at this time. Everything has been packed up and stored until after the completion of the construction."

Dave thought that maybe what he could do was find out what her last name became after she was married.

He asked the Librarian if he could look at old newspapers on microfilm.

She showed Dave where the microfilm was and how to set it up and use the machine.

He started looking in 1948 for wedding and engagement announcements. After about a half-hour had passed, it hit him that this was not needed. He was just wasting his time. He knew what had happened. He put everything up that the Librarian had given to him and went outside.

Previously before this trip, Dave had called the Bureau of Vital Statistics in Columbus, Ohio.

They had told him that in order for them to verify the date of Jo's death, they would need to know her married name.

Dave thought that maybe he could go into the Marion Court House and find records of her children's birth, but then even that was not worth it.

The rest of the day he just walked around town, reminiscing about the 'Summer of '65' and everything that had happened to him this year since May.

Finally, it all became clear to Dave. He had accepted everything that he had learned.

"She's dead! She's gone! There ain't gonna be no dinner with her," Dave hurt deep inside.

He knew that he would not ever be able to hold her again or give her a kiss. He would never be able to tell her that he was sorry.

He also knew that there was no need for him to try to find his son that he had never met.

Dave knew it was time for him to go home. He had to leave tomorrow, Tuesday, or he would hit bad weather all the way home.

CIVIL WAR DAYS

INNOCENT LOVE

The next morning Dave awoke just after daylight. Quickly cleaning up, he packed and checked out of the motel.

He stopped at McDonald's, where he got breakfast to go, and Dave headed home.

Through the rest of Ohio, Indiana, Illinois and part of Missouri, the "Ghostly" Jo didn't say one word. She just sat there in the front passenger's seat and stared straight ahead through the rain streaked windshield.

The late evening rain started to turn into snow as Jo and Dave sped south-west through Missouri on Interstate 44.

The Ghostly Jo sat in the passenger's front seat. She was unable to sit next to Dave and hold his arm as she always had done back in '65, because of the Mercedes console.

She reached over and ran her hand up and down his arm. She stared at him through her lovely light blue eyes and her warm smile.

With teary eyes Dave wished that she had not died and her body was sitting in the passenger's seat instead of just her Entity.

Whenever he could, keeping road conditions in mind, he looked deep into her eyes, like he had done so many times in their summer together.

Finally Jo told Dave that it was time for him to remember their Civil War Days life.

Dave was born on a farm near a small settlement somewhere northeast of Lancaster, Ohio.

He did not recall how many brothers and sisters he had, but that really didn't matter.

His mother and father were religious, hard working farmers who went to Church regularly on Sundays.

Dad worked the fields daily while Mom worked hard to make them a home. And she tried to cook good meals but failed continuously at the hearth. She served burnt or half raw meals but always set plenty on the table and always on time.

Dave's father never complained about the condition of their meals as long as it was hot and plentiful.

Dave re-visualized their old homestead in late fall or early winter, when the trees were bare and the brown packed earth was cold and usually frozen. The wind chilled you to the bone and the days were short. Everyone would huddle around and near the flaming fireplace, feeling like you were burning on one side while freezing on the other side.

The time Dave liked best was bedtime, running off to bed, jumping in and pulling covers up over him, just leaving his nose sticking out to breathe through. How fresh the cold bed felt as his body heat warmed it.

The cold weather reminded Dave of old long past Christmas', hugging his mom and dad on those Holiday Mornings for giving him an orange or a stick of candy. Jo helped Dave remember his love for his mom and dad.

Love... Dave wished he could still show that to his parents of over one hundred years ago.

Unable to control the tears that now ran down his face, Dave continued driving as Jo went on telling Dave about this other life of theirs here on earth.

Dave rarely wore shoes, whenever possible he went barefoot. Usually he wore some sort of bib overalls. He always seemed to have one strap broken. And always, he wore some kind of white or off-white shirt. Once in a while, you may find him wearing a large brimmed, tatter brown hat.

Mother made most of their clothes, but running the house took most of her time. So Dave tried not to over burden her with the task of repairing or making him new clothes. He just kept wearing the same clothes. He only requested new clothes whenever he really out grew his old ones. So usually, you would see Dave wearing clothes that were too short and tight.

Dave's first remembrance of Jo was in the spring.

The weather was turning warm and everything was starting to green.

Was it at Church or the one room school that served the area?

He could not recall. But anyway, their first encounter was not good. They did not hit it off because Jo laughed and made fun at the way he dressed; His overalls were too short and he always had mud between his toes.

Dave thought Jo was just a stupid little girl. He recalled telling her that more than once. He would have never told her the truth that he really thought she was the most beautiful girl he had ever seen.

Her childish attitude toward Dave changed when he along with his family arrived at Jo's family's place for a house warming or barn raising.

Though Jo was only near ten years old and Dave was around thirteen, their love for each other grew from that day forward.

Dave liked walking Jo to school.

Sundays were special too because they were allowed to sit together in church as their proud parents looked on.

After church was a good time, too.

Adults gathered and discussed whatever as the kids played tag on the church grounds.

Laughing and chasing each other strengthen Jo's and Dave's love.

Nothing could ever happen to separate them.

Half-way between Jo's and Dave's home was a little creek. To the left, over a rolling hill the creek turned by a big oak tree. On the edge of the water rested a large rock. It was big enough for the two of them to sit on. This became their hide-a-way. A place they went and talked about their future together.

Sometimes they would sit and listen to the water as it flowed over the rapids and they would watch the leaves that they threw in float along in the stream.

This hide-a-way was the first place that Dave ever kissed Jo.

Her lips were soft and tender. That innocent kiss promised their undying love for each other.

One of Dave's fondest moments was visiting Jo at her house.

No one was at home but Jo. She answered the door in an apron as she wiped flour off of her hands. She was doing the baking that day.

Dave sat at the table, watching Jo doing this and that with flour and other ingredients while they talked. She pretended to go for something and then she slipped up behind him and grabbed both sides of his face with floured hands.

He jumped up and chased Jo around and around the table, unable to catch her.

She could not help but laugh at him.

His face was covered with flour. Laughing too hard to run, he finally was able to grab her, turning her to him and kissing his lovely young Jo.

Then trying to clean the flour off his face, she only made matters worse, she laughed even louder and harder.

Now he had it all over his face and on his back where she placed her hands while kissing him.

Those were the days of young and innocent love.

PLANS FOR THE FUTURE

The few years they had together past quickly.
Before they knew it, Dave was a young man and Jo was developing into a beautiful lady.
The Civil War had been going on for some time now, but it really didn't concern Dave and Jo. To them the War was a million miles away. But before long, Dave found out about William T. Sherman, the local hero from Lancaster, Ohio.
The area men were rallying behind him to fight the Rebels in their homeland, the South.
Dave looked at these soldiers as heroes... men not to be reckoned with... a man that Dave wanted to be like. Someone his Jo would be proud to marry.
Heroes have everything, and someone all looked up to, someone everybody knew, and someone who had money.
He recalled that day he told Jo about his plan to join Sherman and fight for the North.
They sat on the big rock in their hide-a-way, Dave held her delicate hand. He ran his finger of his other hand up and down the back of her hand. Dave tried to explain why he had to go fight.
Dave looked up from her hand and saw tears slowly running down her face. He didn't wish to hurt her, nor did he want to leave her, but he had to.
She wrapped her arms around his neck and pulled him tight to her, her words he would remember forever, "Please don't go, I beg you, please don't go."
The smell of nearby wild flowers lingered in his nostrils as her hair touched his face and he felt the wetness of her tears on his ear and along side of his neck.
They spent that entire day making plans about their life after the war as Dave kept reassuring her he would return and he would not be hurt in the

war. Dave promised her, after the war they would be married and together they would go west to California.

He told Jo about what he had heard, "Corn grew as long as your arm in California."

They would settle down, raise a large family and enjoy the good life.

Jo lay next to Dave in the grass as he held her in his arms. And they watched the sky until the evening star appeared.

They caught heck when they got home that evening for staying out until dark. But getting bitched at would be worth being together because this would be their last date during the Civil War Days.

DAVE JOINS SHERMAN

The next day, all the local men, who were joining Sherman gathered in town for their trip into battle.

Families and friends crowded around bidding loved ones good-bye.

Dave held Jo's hand in his and rubbed the knuckles on her hand with his thumb. He brought her fragile hand up to his lips and he kissed the back of her hand while he looked into her loving eyes.

"I love you," Dave whispered.

"I love you too," she responded.

She threw her arms around him and kissed Dave on his cheek.

As the boys "marched off," Dave turned his head and looked at Jo while she watched him leave. And the beautiful and innocent Jo wiped her tears away. She shed tears for her Dave.

He was loving, gentle and honest young man who cared about other people. But a man whose life would turn completely around from this day forth and this scene of Jo crying would haunt Dave for the rest of his life.

The new men's basic training consisted of; seeing how accurate they fired a rifle and teaching them in the correct way to march.

All joked and laughed about fighting because none knew the horror that lay ahead of them.

As they marched into Sherman's camp, Dave looked over to his right, and saw a bunch of officers standing together talking.

"One of those thin and sickly looking officers must be Sherman," Dave thought.

He looked different than what Dave expected him to look like.

The stories that Dave had heard made him think Sherman was a big and strong man, a real hero. Sherman did not look like a hero at all.

Dave learned quickly heroes and famous people were just ordinary people just like himself. Sherman was not a god but only a thin little man.

Dave just knew he would turn out better than Sherman. He would be a famous hero, standing tall with money and everyone would be proud of him... specially Jo.

Soon, the fighting began.

Dave found out war wasn't what he expected it to be.

Mud, blood and tears ran together on the fields of battle.

He saw the young and old from both sides, laying everywhere.

Some were dead, others pleaded out in pain. The skies were blackened from the smoke of guns. The smell of fresh human blood was bad enough but mixed with gunpowder and the cries from the dying and injured men made many empty their stomach while in running battle.

Sherman had a grudge to settle with the South... He would not be defeated again. He would destroy the South and all in it. He was quoted to have said, "War is Hell," but History nor did his men know what he had in plan for the Rebels.

Sherman would take his Army on a Death March to the sea.

He would kill all who dared to stand in his way. He would show no mercy; not to his enemy or to his own men. If his men became injured and could not march, he just left them. Maybe someone would find them and help them. If not, they would die, whichever, was no concern to him.

GUILT

The Sherman Raiders hit swiftly in their journey southeast. Their supply wagons could not keep pace. The order came down, "Take all we need and destroy the rest."

Things became worse for the civilians, besides burning and pillaging all, now the soldiers started killing and raping.

The boys from Ohio became animals under Sherman's reign of Hell on the South.

One raid stood out in Dave's mind.

They advanced on a house, yelling and firing rifles as they ran.

No shots were returned from the house. It looked lonely and quiet.

A few men were ordered to enter and bring out all people from the house.

Within seconds, they heard gunshots and people screaming. The soldiers brought out one black man and another white man, two women and one boy.

The black man stood by himself to the left as all the white people huddled and held tightly to each other.

Someone ordered, "Watch them," while more soldiers went back into the house.

You could hear glass and furniture being broken up inside.

The people shivered and held each other tighter as more breakage and laughter came from inside.

One of the soldiers grabbed the younger woman and pulled her from the others.

She screamed and held back, and then the soldier still holding her by one hand and slapped her across her face with his other hand. The young white woman fell limp to the ground and exposed most of her legs.

The soldier stared for a moment then jumped down upon her like an animal. He raped her.

Another soldier attacked the older woman and pulled her from the white man and boy. He threw her to the ground and he raped her as the older woman continued to scream.

The two raping soldiers made grunting noises like pigs.

The white man pulled the young boy close while trying to shield his eyes from the scene.

The black man bolted and ran. A shot was fired at him, but missed.

Sherman commanded, "Let the black ass go! He will warn others not to stand in My way!"

As the black man raced across the fields everyone was laughing as if hysterical from either watching the two men rape the women or by Sherman's comment.

After the two "Heroic" men finished with the women, another soldier grabbed the young unconscious woman and did as he wished with her also.

"Kill them," someone yelled at Dave and the others.

Dave stood there frozen as the order was again given, but this time, "Kill them, if you don't shoot them, I'll shoot you!"

Dave and the others fired. The white man, small young boy and the just raped older woman lay dead.

Dave could not move... he just stood there trembling, still pointing his gun at the dead people as tears ran down his face.

"Is this the kind of hero I am... a stealing, raping and killing of innocent people kind of hero. What am I? Oh God, what have I done?" he thought.

That night, they camped in the woods near the house they had just destroyed.

Throughout the night, the fields burned as the light from the flames lit their camp.

"No camp fires," was the order.

The young white woman was kept for tonight's treat by some of the soldiers.

She screamed over and over again as several men took her.

Finally, while on her knees, one of the men kicked her in her jaw.

She fell back dead. Her neck was broken.

Dave would never erase this day from his mind. He had seen his friends from Ohio, men he had joined with to fight, do these things to other humans.

Dave had thought just Southern people were bad, now he knew ALL people were bad, including himself. He could not have stopped the things that happened, but he didn't even try to stop them.

Now, Dave hated himself worse than anyone else.

HIS PROMISE IS KEPT

This raping and killing was not the only incident remembered by Dave, this was the first that he remembered seeing. But he could not recall how many times it occurred in the course of time that he was one of Sherman's Raiders.

If the North would have lost the War, Sherman surely would have been placed on trial for War Crimes. Of course, with the North winning, no record was really ever kept about Sherman's Raiders. He was no hero. Even today, Dave felt that Sherman should have been executed for what he did.

After the War, Dave drifted.

He could not go home because he was not the hero that he promised Jo he would be. Dave did not have the money that he thought he would have. He hated all people for what he had seen them do but the one he hated worst of all was himself.

Dave became handy with his gun. He knew how to start fights and win. Besides himself, ex-rebel soldiers were Dave's biggest enemy.

Sometimes he would ambush an ex-rebel soldier, kill him and take his money if he had any. Or you might have found Dave working on someone's farm for a few days but he continually drifted from town to town.

One Sunday, Dave drifted into a town.

He thought it may have been in Kentucky or even Kansas, but he was not sure. But the town was quiet and lonely.

An ex-rebel saw Dave and had heard stories about his killings.

The ex-rebel followed but at a safe distance as Dave headed to a bar.

He entered and slowly strolled up to the bar. A crouching ex-rebel watched from the edge of the open doorway.

Dave poured whiskey into a glass that he held in his right hand. Dave still held the whiskey bottle in his left hand as he raised his glass to his mouth with his right hand.

The ex-rebel knew the time was right.

He fired one shot.

The bullet entered Dave's back on the right side, just below his diaphragm, cutting up through the bottom of his heart, passing through his left lung and exited his body just below his armpit, on the left front of his chest.

The ex-rebel ran over ready to unload another round into Dave.

Dave looked up at the man and said, "I should have killed you... bastard."

Then he closed his eyes and died.

Jo waited her entire lifetime for Dave to return.

She never married and died at an old age, during the Flu Epidemic of 1918.

Dave tried to hold back the tears that ran down his face.

Jo once again rubbed his right arm while trying to comfort him as she finished reminding Dave what had happened during those Civil War days.

Jo said she did not blame him for not returning to her. She understood.

Now, he had kept his promise to her.

Alone just Jo and Dave drove southwest into Oklahoma, heading toward California to "where corn grew as long as your arm."

"I love you," Jo whispered.

"I love you, too," was Dave's response.

Now the snow had turned into freezing rain.

The road showed all the signs of being covered with ice.

Dave was glad he had filled both fuel tanks up which made the car handle better on the slick surface. So Dave still held his seventy plus miles per hour pace.

UNDERSTANDING

JO'S LIFE

Dave stopped somewhere around mid-night for a cup of coffee to go.

He pulled back on to the freeway and realized that the weather had cleared some. The road was dry now.

The Ghostly Jo placed her hands, palm to palm between her knees, pressed her legs together and said, "Now it is time for me to tell you my life story."

She was born June 27th, 1932, into a family that had lived in the Marion area for generations. Her early life was nothing special. She received good grades in school. She was always like the girl next door.

When she became pregnant, she quit school in her sophomore year and got married. Her first child born was when Jo was seventeen.

Being brought up Catholic, she tried to follow her religion's practices. By the age of twenty-six, she had three children, when she just turned thirty she found she had breast cancer in the lower part of her right breast. The cancer was surgically removed.

Jo's husband ran around all the time and both physically and mentally abused her throughout their marriage. With the thoughts of dying of cancer and never actually being free; her parents before marriage and then her husband continued to boss her around. And also not wanting to have her children see her die a slow cancerous death, she decided to move out on her own. For once in her life she wanted to do the things that she wanted to do.

She obtained the barmaid job from her friend, Mary, who owned the H&H Bar and Grill. Jo was able to rent a room above the bar. Her living near her work made life simpler because she never had time to learn how to drive and did not possess a driver's license.

On Jo's first day on the job, she met Dave, who she immediately fell in love with.

She recalled how strange it was for he was someone she felt like she had known forever. To her, Dave was different. He did not make demands on her.

Dave and Jo were content just being together. They did not have to make love to enjoy each other. He treated her like a lady. On their first two dates, Dave had not tried to get into her pants like other men did. When they made love, it was a wonderful act of love, not just sex.

Lowering her head as if she was a little embarrassed, she admitted that she was actually thirty-one and not twenty-seven when they met.

At the time they met, Jo's biggest worry was what would happen to her children when the cancer takes her life, and then when Dave came along her life changed.

She really cared and loved him. She knew, somehow she would have to let him go before the cancer started taking her down.

Jo tried to forget her past life and her cancer. That is why she never wanted to talk about her past. Maybe, by not talking about the past, her cancer might just go away.

Jo loved her kids, but her husband didn't have time to bring them by for any visits. She arranged with him for him to leave them at her sister's that one Sunday. But he did not take their kids to her sister's... it was her sisters kids that they took back to her place and not hers.

Jo wanted badly to be Dave's wife and bear children for him. She knew Dave also wanted her for his wife. But whenever he would start to talk about their future together, she always changed the subject.

She was deeply in love with Dave and yet so confused.

After much consideration, one night she asked him for a baby. No longer did she care about what tomorrow would bring. She wanted to have Dave's baby.

It took over a month for them to conceive a baby.

She was happy when she told him, "I am only spotting this time."

They both knew she was pregnant, carrying his child inside her.

When Dave did not return as he promised, at first she thought something had happened to him. Then she thought, maybe he found out she was dying and ran. She did not go looking for him. Instead, she waited and kept watching for him.

During the first part of November, she was unable to work anymore and she had to quit her job because her pregnancy was now showing. She moved in with her sister and brother-in-law.

Thanksgiving was spent at her sister's. Jo's husband allowed all her children to visit her that day.

After her kids went home with their Dad, they told him how happy they were that Mommy was having another baby.

The next day, her husband and their kids came to her sister's home once again. This time he only sent the oldest daughter in to bring Jo back out so he could talk to her.

Seeing her pregnant and not by him, threw him into a rage. He promised that he would take the kids and never return and she would never see her kids again.

On Christmas Eve, Jo cried all night. No one could locate her husband, who had her kids. On Christmas Day, she continued to cry all day. This was her first Christmas without her kids.

After Dave's and Jo's son, David Eric, was born, life for Jo was anew. Now she had someone who loved and needed her and also Jo had the child of the man that she loved.

When their son was old enough, Jo went back to work at the H&H, in hopes that Dave might come back.

She spent the weekends at her sister's house taking care of her baby. Her sister cared for the baby through the week.

Now, Jo paused for a minute.

Dave looked over at her.

She sat with her face in her hands and started to sob.

And the ghostly Jo said to Dave, "After my divorce and unable to make it on my own, I married Robert, but then pains from cancer tumors in my brain became so excruciating that on September 1, 1968, I accidentally overdosed on pain killers."

Trying to change the subject, Jo told Dave she had a surprise waiting for him on the Other Side. Since her death, she had gotten a little bored while waiting for him to join her.

"Dave, do you remember before we came back this last time. I wanted to try it one more time, and you said, 'No, I am not going. I will stay and help others find the Light.' Well, Hon, you know Soul Twins like to play little practical jokes, so I have been gathering up lost and Unguided Entities on this, the Other Side. I told them, 'Just wait Dave would be coming soon and he will help you with your troubles.' I planned on sitting there and not saying a word when you returned. In order to get near me, you would have to help all those people first."

"Damn it," Dave said, "When you are with me all day, those ghosts cross over looking for me. Its no wonder why my family is bothered with ghost all the time. They don't want me to know they are looking for me, so they won't ever show themselves to me, only my family. When I was under hypnosis and all those people standing around you in the park... I didn't kill all those people... most were the ones that you gathered up to make me help them before I could be beside you... you take care of them... You help them finish their crossing, not me!"

    The rest of their trip was nice. The weather held out, Dave listened to Jo as she told him more about the Other Side and about the Light.

NO MORE HAUNTINGS

Dave arrived home in Lancaster in the evening. And being tired from his long drive, he just wanted a cup of coffee.

After the usual hugs and kisses from Christine and the boys, Dave finally sat down to enjoy his cigarette and coffee as Dan headed off to bed.

Before Dave could tell Tony and Christine about what he found out, Christine stated, "The ghost have been going crazy while you were gone. Lights would go off and come back on all over the place, and Dan has been seeing them again. They were running up and down the stairs, standing in the garage. Nick, our dog, has been growling all over the place at nothing. It's been a mad house."

"They won't bother you anymore," Dave promised, and then he explained what Jo told him about the ghost.

Then he added, "Please do not call them ghosts, they are Entities. They do not like being called ghosts."

"Well, I don't care what they like being called, I want them gone!" Christine exclaimed.

Dave assured Christine that their Entity problems were being taking care of. Still, Dave could not tell Christine all that had happened in one sitting. He would only release bits and pieces of his trip to her over the following weeks.

The hauntings stopped almost immediately after Dave's return from Ohio.

Jo could not keep watch on all the Entities that she gathered up over the years at the same time. Some would stray over to this side while she helped others move on to the Light before Dave arrived on the Other Side. So once in a while, one may adventure over to this side and be seen by Dan or heard by one of the others in Dave's family. But now, their house was quiet for the first time in many, many years.

Dave learned that when Jo was near him, the right side of his face would become warm.

Most of the day, she was standing beside him, helping him through his daily route. But whenever she left his side for whatever reason, he would feel lost and alone.

Dave called Betty Way and set an appointment to see her once again. He had a lot to tell her.

Dave still had some questions that needed to be answered. Why, did Jo wait for twenty-eight years to tell him she was helping him? Why wait to tell him about them being Soul Twins? Why did she tell him at all?

In time, Dave learned the answers to these questions and more because Jo was the only one, alive or dead, who he would accept the answer from.

If Jo would have told Dave that she was on the Other Side earlier, he would not have believed her and/or he would have been too anxious and may have tried suicide to get there early.

Suicide is a NO, NO, on the Other Side.

Dave's time was now growing short. He would be joining Jo on the Other Side soon.

The knowledge that his family now possessed about the Other Side would help them deal with Dave's death. Same as the knowledge you now have after you finish reading this book will help you understand when your loved ones pass over.

When Dave was seven years old, he came down with pneumonia in the fall. His parents gave Dave an early Christmas because the doctor told them that he may not live until Christmas. During that Holiday season, Dave could remember flying. He was flying in a dark place, the place he now knows as the Other Side. But that time, he was flying by himself. No one was flying beside him. Now he knew, he was looking for someone... he was looking for Jo. Dave could not find her because she was still alive. After searching and not finding her, sadly he re-entered his body.

Did he die and then return to life again?

But his trips of flying on the Other Side occurred more than once.

Jo and Dave had one final part of their mission to complete here on earth, and Jo asked Dave for help in the completion of their goal.

Dave refused, telling Jo, she must do it herself. He could not grant her this and she should not ask him for his help in this plan of hers.

CHRISTINE SHARES THEIR LOVE

Dave's biggest wish was to see Jo once more.

He really loved Christine, but his love for Jo was different. If Dave could hold Jo once again, if he could kiss her once more, if he could tell her he loved her, he would be satisfied. But to do these things with an Entity can't be.

How in the world do you hold Energy in your arms?

How can you kiss Energy?

How in the world, do you look Energy in the face and tell her you love her?

Dave thought their mission here on earth was as complete as they could make it. They had a child together. She had three other children by her husband. Dave had three other children by his other wives, and he had two sons with Christine that he saw grow up.

Tony was now almost twenty years old. No way could the Entity Jo and Dave, who was fifty-two, get married and raise a family. It was too late. They would have to try again or just be happy with what they had accomplished in this life.

One evening, while they sat out on their patio watching the stars, Dave looked at Christine and said, "If you feel like doing anything that doesn't fit your style, don't hold back, just do it."

Christine just looked at Dave in wonder. She did not answer.

Over the next week, everything was quiet around their house with only infrequent Entity sightings. In Dave's opinion, it was like someone had moved out. To him it felt empty. Jo was always by his side, but he did not hear or feel the other Entities anymore.

Christine and Dave where still active in their sexual love making, and they would make love whenever they felt like it, be it once or five times a week, even though they have been married for over twenty-one years.

One night in bed as Christine lay in his arms while they smoked a cigarette and talked about their day's work, desire took over, and they wanted each other. As they started to make love, Dave knew what was going on. This was not Christine that he held in his arms, it was Jo!

Jo did things no other woman ever did to him. He had never told Christine details of his love making with Jo. In fact, he would have never told any woman about how another woman made love.

When Dave and Jo use to make love, he would raise the top portion of his body up with his arms, and Jo would run her hands up and down the sides of his face, and also sometimes she would move her hands up and down the outside of his arms while telling Dave how much she loved him. Christine was now doing the same thing!

Jo's Entity was now inside Christine's body.

Jo had asked Dave for help in obtaining Christine's approval but Dave refused her, and told her that if she wanted to make love one more time with him, she would have to ask herself.

Christine's Soul must have agreed to Jo's request because Jo was now inside of Christine's body.

After their sex act Christine also knew what had happened. Dave did not have to tell her.

This sexual encounter was not just two humans making love, this was two Souls joining together with the love no other human has ever known.... it was Divine Love.

Dave told Christine, "Jo was in your body for three days. I knew she wanted to do this. She asked me to get your approval. I refused, Your Soul and her agreed to let her enter your body. For three days, she lived your life. She now has all the same memories that you have about our life together for twenty-one years. It was like we were married for all those years. Now she has seen our children grow up... Yours and my boys are now her boys, too. You helped us finish our mission here on earth. Now there is no need to live again."

Christine looked on as Dave continued, "She will protect our boys like she has protected me over the years, and her love for you will protect you also." As a tear rolled down Dave's cheek.

His love for Christine was always strong and this, her unselfish loving act for Jo, strengthened his love for Christine even more than before.

GOOD-BYE BETTY WAY

Finally the day of Dave's appointment with Betty Way arrived.
Dave knocked on her door at three-thirty.
Betty opened the door.
"Hi," Betty greeted him as he entered her house.
Giving her a hug, "I got you something to remember us by,"
Dave stated as he handed Betty a package.
Betty opened the package as they walked back to her office.
"How beautiful," Betty exclaimed.
She held a candle that was molded into a statue of two dolphins, side by side, half submerged in a base that looked like water.
"Thank you, it was very thoughtful of you," she placed the candle on one of her stands in her office, "See how nice it looks. It fits right in."
Sitting down, Betty asked, "Well, tell me all about your trip. Did you find the information you wanted?"
Dave told her about his trip, explaining to her some of the things that happened.
She said she knew Jo was gone to the Other Side, and she was sorry that Dave had not met with his son.
"Why didn't you tell me about my aura?" Dave asked Betty.
"Yes, I saw it was very faint. You need to see a doctor," she replied.
"Well, I know my time is about up. I may have eighteen more months, if that," Dave replied.
He went on to tell her about him being Jo's Soul Twin, what Soul Twins are and some about what he learned about the Other Side.
Now, Betty told him about her two personal experiences she had with the Other Side and the Light.
In the first one, she tried to commit suicide when she was young.
On the Other Side, she was in a dark place, standing on a bridge. On the far side of the bridge stood her family members that had previously past

over. They kept telling her to go back because it was not time for her. Some people on this side of the bridge told her to come back. Of course, she came back to this side and life.

Her second encounter with the Light was; she had surgery and died for a few minutes on the operating table.

This time she was in the Light. She said the place was beautiful. She heard some kind of music. It was a different kind of music than she had ever heard before.

And someone asked her if she wanted to return to earth or not, and then they showed her the future. She saw her son and daughter as they are now with good lives. They told her she needed to come back and help others. Betty decided to return and did.

Waking up in a hospital bed, a nurse told her everything would be all right and left the room. Later, she tried to find that nurse. The hospital staff said here was no nurse that worked there with the name she had given them. Who was that nurse... an Angel?

Dave told Betty, "I don't know if Jo and I had more than the two lives or not."

"Yea, Yea, Yea," Betty interrupted him, "She is standing right beside you, and she is saying that you two have had at least seven other lives together."

"My God," Dave thought, "That means we have been on earth for around five or six hundred years and never finished our mission."

Betty and Dave made plans to meet once again. This time, Betty would tape the session for him. They planned to have Dave tell about all those lives that Jo and he had.

Once again, Betty told Dave about his younger son's problems with his legs. She also said Dave needed to get Dan some medicine called "Cat's Claw."

Dave did not know Dan was having problems with his legs.

He never told Betty she was right about his two sons in what she had stated in their first session either. Betty was right on everything she said about Dave and his family.

Betty went on and told Dave about her helping poor people and the group sessions she holds.

After about one hour, Dave had to leave.

He knew even though they made an appointment to meet again, this was the last time he would see Betty Way, a truly wonderful human, a person he would miss.

THE FINAL WAIT

Once after Dave returned home, he told Christine all about his meeting with Betty Way.

Christine was astonished at Betty's life and her knowing things about Dan's health that even Dave didn't know.

During the following days, Dave thought about rebuilding his old Mercedes. She now had almost four hundred thousand miles on her. Her rear end was making noises and the brakes were getting bad, and she was getting hard to start in the cooler weather.

Jo told Dave, not to worry about the Mercedes. He could rebuild it if he wanted to, but there was no need to do it. His time was short.

Now Dave knew time on the Other Side means nothing. He could live just one more day, five more years or whatever.

Dave bought another car, a '72 Duster, a car that he plans on giving to Dan when he starts driving, which is only three years away. Dave has not junked his Mercedes as yet, but plans to soon.

Daily Dave and Christine talked about the Other Side and about Jo because now she is part of their family.

Dave's last scheduled appointment with Betty had arrived.

This time her house looked cold and lonely.

At their arranged time, Dave knocked on Betty's door.

No answer, he knocked again, still no answer. He waited and kept knocking for five minutes before giving up. Finally he left and drove home.

He knew there was no need in calling Betty and re-scheduling their appointment. He would never see her again.

Dave decided it was now time to get his life in order. He needed to tie up all loose ends. That way, Christine would have it easier after he passed on. So, to date, he is still trying to complete all the little things that he wanted to do in his life.

Jo has told him, she will ease his pains at death and just before he dies he will see her once again, and then she will be there to hold and comfort him when he passes over to the Other Side.

Dave knows his loving, sweet and beautiful Jo is with him every day. He waits and longs to be back with her again, but for now he must live and experience the unknown of his future. But the true love they shared here and will always have will keep them **TOGETHER FOREVER BEFORE THE LIGHT.**

IN DAVE'S OWN WORDS

JO

Thank you for reading the true story of Jo and I that was based on part of my life. As you know, the names of some of the people were changed.

I felt compelled to tell you my memoirs about our summer of '65. Every chapter holds a significant detail about love or other related item.

Jo's and my love was natural and innocent. We had nothing to hide. It did not matter that she was married but only separated from her husband nor did it matter if I was married but heading for divorce. If Jo was worried about my marital status, she would have asked. I do not condone extramarital sex, which ours was not.

We enjoyed the simple things in life; sharing a sun rise, gazing at the moon and stars, holding hands or each other in our arms, comforting the other, companionship, walking together and just talking to each other. Neither of us had much money to spend and if she did, I would not have let her spend it on me anyway.

Even though Jo was married and had three children and breast cancer at the time we met, she was very naive. She did not drink, smoke nor did we take drugs. Sex to her, was me on top in the missionary position. She was very religious and followed her Catholic up bringing closely.

When Jo wore make-up, she applied it professionally. She knew how to dress for the occasion, and never over dress or under dress. Jo was truly a lady.

Jo was four feet nine inches tall, with shoulder length dark brown hair, held back out of her face by combs on both sides. Her eyes were light blue, so light they were almost white. Her face was that of a teenager while her body showed signs of bearing children. Jo's hands were slightly red and rough from the hard work that she endured over the years. And she kept her fingernails short and never painted them.

Her legs were long and smooth and never showed signs of hair.

Jo was very thin for a woman in motherhood. She weighed less than one hundred pounds.

I cannot recall if her ears were pierced or not because most of the time, she did not wear jewelry. Jewelry did not seem to interest her, but she had and wore jewelry when needed.

She had perfect small white teeth and a great smile to go with them.

Jo neither cussed nor swore.

She was kind to all people except when you made her angry.

Once I saw her angry and that was at Fat Sam, but she never said or did anything to him that I know of.

To me, Jo was the most beautiful woman that I ever saw besides Christine.

I cannot help but to love my memories of Jo.

No one in my family or my friends ever met her, and I never talked about Jo to anyone, but I did introduce two of my fellow roughnecks to her.

Our love was not the kind of love that I would share with other people. She was my secret until the writing of this book. Like chapter twenty-two states, "Keeping her deep within my mind and frequently reliving our days together."

I often wondered what life would have been like with Jo. For sure, I would not have drunk and ran around like I did in my first marriage. Hopefully, I would have worked enough to have supported our children, but this we shall never know.

On our final date, when Jo told me she was only spotting, pregnant, I knew deep in my heart it was over, even though I didn't want it to end. But I knew something was going to happen to break us up. But that 'something' was something that we could not stop. No matter how hard I tried to get back to Jo, something kept stopping me. It was that something that I had no control over. I did not have control over my cars breaking down nor could I control my being broke all the time.

Why didn't I call her?

Why didn't I ask Mary if she had Jo's new address?

I will never know the answer to these questions.

Why didn't I ask her more questions about her marriage, family and her cancer or about how she got all those of expensive clothes? When she was living with her husband, where did they live? What was her husband's name? What were her children's names?

I knew Jo would have avoided my questions and she would have changed the subject. But all these questions have haunted me for years.

Old Queen Vickie... why didn't I keep her and replace her engine? I'm a mechanic. I could have done it easily. So why didn't I?

Holy Graduel

My questions are unending and I have no answers. I will dwell on them until I die.

Jo has told me, she has forgiven me for not returning as I promised her I would. She also has promised to tell me the answers to all my questions when I get on the Other Side once again. She stated that my death is near and that I would see her just before I die. Jo says, I will have a lot of pain, but she will be by my side and will help ease my pains at the end. Then when I cross over, she will be there to hold and comfort me. I do not look forward to the pains but I do look forward to seeing Jo again.

Once in a lifetime, a person similar to Jo may come along. If you have a similar opportunely as I did in life, don't blow it. I lost her until we reunite on the Other Side.

OTHER LIVES

TRIALS OF OTHER LIVES

The next two chapters are true stories of other lives of the Angel Jo and I that the Angel Jo had to tell me about, and I felt that we should relay to you.

The Angel Jo and Jesus, both refer to my Angel as Jacob. The human body that the Angel Jacob presently dwells in was named David by my parents. I am not the Angel, and whereas, the Angel Joleen is actually the Angel Jo, and the last body that the Angel Jo dwelled in was named Joan, by her parents.

Therefore, after you have finished reading these two chapters, you will know four of Jo's and Jacob's previous lives together. These lives contain subject matter concerning God's Concept of Life. These stories of our other lives should further help you understand how we learn and experience from experiences of others through endurance of life.

THE LO

Long ago, before the white man entered the Americas near the place now called Ohio, lived one tribe of Native Americans. These natives lived in harmony with nature and all other living things while villages grew in this land of plenty. Little or no farming was necessary because most staples grew wild. The natives took only what was needed for food and left the rest for other life forms and for reproduction.

Happiness was all these natives knew. Games were played among the young. The adults provided for all and trade was negotiated between tribes as needed.

Deep in this area of rolling hills, mountains and valleys, with streams and rivers running under the tall trees lived the village I will call the Lo.

The Lo village was on a mountain top that overlooked two streams which came together to form a great river to the south, and near the edge of the mountaintop stood one large rock that all knew as the marriage rock.

Couples would spend the night upon this rock, and watch the sun rise together to consecrate their love for each other in marriage.

During those days shelters was simply made by leaning small logs against a living tree, then sometimes covering the wooden frame with branches or animal skins. The houses in the Lo village were built in this manner and arranged in a semicircle. In the center of the village, women cooked food on the community fire.

These early natives viewed the human body as natural, and clothing was used more for a need for warmth than modesty.

Mainly spears made from sharpened hickory saplings were used in hunting for game. Game was plentiful with deer, squirrel, raccoon, mink, beaver and many other animals that roamed the forest and waters.

Berries and nuts were all within easy reach. Food was given to the elderly, ill and the children for all shared in the day's catch.

Only beautiful blue skies and perfect white clouds filled the days, while the night skies were picturesque with the brilliance of a million stars.

Events were told by word of mouth. Maybe the news was about a nearby village, a baby's birth or a great hunt.

This was a place where fighting was none and a time when all people loved each other, and where all were in harmony with nature. It was a place where simple dreams could be fulfilled in God's Garden here on Earth. It was a perfect time and place to live.

On the Other Side, Jo and Jacob stopped playing their games many times just to watch humans. They decided to live on Earth and enjoy all of the pleasurable things as humans, for they had heard many stories about others that had stayed for a while on earth.

Jacob was born the first son of one of the Lo's greatest hunters.

Jo was born one year and three months later into the oldest family in the Village, and her father was the leader of the Lo's.

Jo grew into a lovely young woman. Quickly she learned to cook and tend to all of the daily tasks needed by the people.

Jacob worked hard to follow in his father's footsteps of being one of the Village's great hunters.

Before their teen years, Jo and Jacob both knew they would marry and raise a family someday. And whenever time would allow, young Jo and Jacob were together playing childhood games and planning their future. She would keep a good house for her great hunter, Jacob. They would be the family that always had food to share with others. Jo would give him many sons and daughters. He would provide meat for them and keep his beautiful Jo warm during the winters with all the pelts he would collect through the summer.

Sitting under the trees on the lower slope of the mountain near the place where both streams came together became their place. Together alone, they shared their most secret dreams. Their human bodies talked of the future while their Angels shared earth's simple pleasures. Many days and evenings throughout their early years were spent in this place.

Those were the days of innocence and enjoying pleasures, planning, listening to the animals and gazing at the wonders of the great scenery that surrounded them. All of these things were what they had hungered for while on the Other Side.

One day while sitting in their place as the warm afternoon filtered down through the great tall trees, Jo extended her closed hand to Jacob. Turning her hand over and opening her closed fingers, she handed Jacob a ring,

"Here is something that Father made for me to give to you," she said as she smiled looking at the shiny white object that lay in her opened hand.

Jacob was known to be one who knew the future, and he was thought to be able to read minds. He also knew when and where the animals would be. And he predicted what their hunts would bring.

The piece of deer antler that Jo just handed Jacob was cut into the shape of a ring. Along the outside of this polished bone were engraved markings of different kinds. Its markings resembled a bird with open wings and many other figures surrounding the bird. All these animal figures formed some kind of symmetrical design that made Jacob feel good as he stared at this beautiful ring.

"This is a power ring... your power ring. Now all will know you have the powers when they see this ring upon your finger," Jo said as her eyes sparkled.

Jacob was speechless as he slid the ring on his finger, and then gave her a hug and kiss.

That winter came early that year, it was incredibly cold, and Jacob can still remember that harsh winter.

He was still a young teenager when their world was turned inside out.

Snow fell for days at a time and the wind blew hard. Many wild animals died awhile food was becoming harder to find.

Another tribe moved into the valley where the two streams came together.

Jacob did not know from where this tribe came, but he did know that they must have moved into the valley to escape the strong winds on top of the mountains.

(We shall call this tribe the "New.")

This New village suffered through the winter. Many were sick and some died from the cold. The Lo villagers were not able to give the New tribe much food because they did not have enough for themselves.

Spring was late in coming that year and the snow was deep by the time spring finally arrived. Disaster struck when all of the New hunters were away from their village on a two-day hunting trip.

When the hunters returned home from their hunt, their village was gone. High waters covered the valley. No survivors could be found. All of the women, children and their elders were gone. Only the returning hunters were left, and the Lo villagers didn't know that anything was wrong and went on with their daily lives as the New's hunters grieved.

Within a few days, the News came to the Lo's village and they asked to "buy" women. The Lo's refused their offer and said, "You cannot buy people. All people are free."

The distraught New men left.

The next day, after their regular hunting party returned to the village, the Lo men found their village destroyed.

Their village gave all indications that total chaos had occurred. Shelters were knocked down and burnt, and still-smoldering wood lay outside the fire circle. The place was eerie and silent. Elders lay dead, killed by spears and clubs. Some elders had part of their heads gone as if they had been eaten, and no women or children could be found.

The Lo knew what had happened. The New had killed all of the older Lo, eaten part of the elders' heads to obtain their knowledge, and had taken the women and children for their own.

Jacob looked for Jo but she was gone along with all of the other women.

The Lo men knew that the New villagers were war-like people and would take what they wanted.

Around their campfires that night, the oldest hunters told stories about great wars.

Most of the Lo had never fought. They didn't know how to kill humans. How could these peaceful hunters win in a war for their women and children against the New?

In the early hours just before sunrise the Lo men had reached the mountain edge that overlooked the New village. This village was hastily set up on a small hill not far from where their village used to be but now only swift waters flowed. Older male Lo children lay in a pool of blood just outside and to the west of the village.

The special powers of Jacob caused him to see what had recently occurred here; in the village center women clung to each other. Small children screamed as a man grabbed a woman and dragged her off to his recently made shelter. This scene was repeated over and over again until all the women and children were taken. Jacob could not see Jo, but knew she must have been one of the first to be taken because of her youth and beauty.

The Lo did not stop to think or plan their attack but charged headlong down the mountain, yelling as they went. The Lo ran down to the bottom of the mountain, across the little valley and started up the knoll. The New men were ready. The fight didn't last long. Around ten of the thirty plus Lo lay dead, while only one or two of the New men died in this first attack.

Now the Lo knew how deer must feel being chased through the woods as the New men charged as the Lo retreated over the mountains.

Miles farther into the woods past their old village sight ran the Lo even after the News ended the chase.

Later after regrouping deep in the forest, the Lo elder hunters once again told stories of long ago. These ancestral tales were about how the Lo were once a fighting tribe that all others feared.

The younger Lo listened to the older ones tell of victories in the past which increased their ego as they learned the plans for their next battle with the New.

The next morning, before sunrise, the Lo lay in wait, hidden in the thick underbrush near the New's village.

Leaving behind most of their men to guard the women, a small band of New men walked past the hidden Lo. This small hunting party would be an easy kill for the Lo. Following behind, the Lo kept their distance. After a mile or two, the New hunting party split up. This time there were only three and four men in each group. All of the Lo men followed a group of three for almost another mile.

On a hilltop overlooking a valley the hunting threesome stopped and surveyed the valley floor for game. One of the men removed his hunting gear and laid it beside him as he sat down. Another walked a hundred feet or so to the left. The third hunter moved far to the right and squatted to relieve himself.

Attack was signaled. The Lo ran silently over the melting snow and through the forest. The New hunters didn't know anything was coming until the Lo's first blow to the squatted man. Jacob's hammer-like weapon sank deeply into the back of another man's head. Jacob stood frozen and unable to move as he watched the blood and matter fly from the impact as spattered blood ran down Jacob's face. He ran his tongue along his lips and tasted the bitter warm blood.

An elder Lo ran up beside the dead man. He lifted the dead man's arm toward Jacob and demanded, "Eat!"

Jacob quickly dropped to his knees. He grabbed the arm and bit deeply into it as he heard the air leave the man's lungs for the last time. Jacob ripped off a portion of the dead man's bicep with his teeth and chewed while his comrades did the same with the other bodies. Blood and bits of flesh slid down Jacob's throat and entered his stomach only to come back up as he vomited.

At last the Lo had one victory. Now they too claimed the strength of their enemy, for they had devoured their kill. And tonight they would attack the New village and regain their women and children while all were asleep.

As the sun set, the Lo men watched the New village from the land above. They waited for the moon to rise and move across the sky. Just before the moon disappeared behind the mountains they struck.

The first shelter was easy, but the noise of the fight awakened the other New men, and then all hell broke loose. The Lo men were overpowered. Most of the Lo men fell dead. One or two barely escaped and Jacob lay dead. After the battle and just before sunrise Jo found Jacob's partly eaten body. She turned and ran wildly out of the village toward the raging river as tears streamed down her face. She did not care anymore. It did not take long for the swift waters to pull her down and under.

Jacob and Jo's Angels held each other as they sat on the big rock that overlooked where the two rivers came together. Day turned into night and days turned into months as spring and summer came and went. They saw the New villagers pack up and move down the great river. They saw a Lo man drift through the woods as if he were lost.

Why did Jacob not use his powers to foretell the outcome of this war? Was his love for Jo so strong that he could not think straight? He could only think of bringing her along with all of the other women and the children home again. Whatever the reason, he was the one who could have saved their village, but did not. He was the one that lost the battle for his people.

One fall morning as the fog drifted up and out of the trees, Jo and Jacob looked at each other and without a word stood up as they held hands and flew up and away to the Other Side. Once again they were Angels but now possessed more experiences of love, of pleasures, and of tragedies and hardships here on earth.

During the present time of 1997, the Angel Jo showed David that she had found his power ring and had placed it in her secret place for him on the Other Side.

This was the gift that she had given to him, the man she loved.

She now keeps this little ring that waits for his return. It is a symbol of their undying love and a life of long ago.

OTHER LIVES

I could vaguely recall other lives that Jo and I had lived. And after much persistence from me, the Angel Jo revealed a couple more life stories that are truly fine examples of their trials to complete their personal mission.

During the seventeen hundreds, we lived in a type of colony village in what is now the northeastern United States.

Though most of the families lived close together, all took part in the farming. It was as if these people worked as one while they kept their individualism by dwelling in their separate shelters while those with the strongest religious beliefs maintained control over their village.

Maybe their unusual housing positioned closely together came from their fear of the savage native tribes that roamed freely throughout the forest.

A few of the more adventurous had begun to move farther away from the villages. The village people were concerned but felt helpless for these adventurous families for they knew surely those who lived outside their village would be killed by savages or by demons that dwelled in the dark forest that covered the land. Even with these thoughts of what would come, the people still helped each other clear land for the much-needed crops.

Jo was the eldest child in a family of three children. Their family lived in the village.

Her siblings died of disease. By the time she was twelve years old, her father and mother also had passed away. The death of her father was a tragic event of which we need to tell you.

One spring day, several families had gathered to help a friend clear land. As the women talked and cooked in the house, the children chased each other around and near the house. Eventually, the chasing game became centered around the wagon of Jo's dad.

Around and around the wagon they ran, screaming and yelling at each other. A little girl about two or three years old lost her bonnet and cried. When Jo realized what caused the little girl to cry, she stopped playing and retrieved the bonnet and tied its ribbon beneath the child's chin as she soothed the little girl. Then Jo rejoined the others in the chase.

Although the children were warned to stay out of the wagons, Jacob's younger brother decided to hide and climbed into the wagon. Sliding over the wagon's side rails, he saw the rifle that Jo's dad had laid in the bed of the wagon.

Jo's dad came running toward the wagon when he saw the young boy in the wagon holding the rifle.

As the man ran, he called out the boy's name. The boy turned toward the man and a loud bang was heard. The man fell, blood pumping from his chest.

Jo screamed, "Papa, Papa," as she ran to her fallen father.

The women came running out of the house as all of the men hurried from the field.

Jacob's brother, who was not yet ten years old, had accidentally killed Jo's dad.

The Angel Jo sat on the bed as she told me about this death of her father of long ago. She lowered her face into her hands and sobbed, "He did not mean to kill Papa... It was an accident... But Papa, my Papa, was dead."

There was no way for me to comfort the Angel Jo. I could not hold her as you would hold a human being because she had no body mass. All I could do was listen to her story with the regret of asking her to tell me more about this life that we had.

"Sometimes one should not try to remember lives of long ago. Most lives contain bad things and pains of the heart," She sobbed, "Even though after Papa's death and I saw him on this, the Other Side, many times, but those pains of his death still remain deep in my heart."

After Jo's dad died, her mother became ill and I remembered going to her house and seeing her sick mother lying in bed.

"You just get better," I recall telling her mom, "In a few years, I will marry Jo and you can live with us. In the meantime I will come over every day after my chores are done and help you with your crops."

Her mom smiled at me and then at Jo.

Within a few more days, she died.

Immediately after her funeral, while we were alone, I held Jo's hand as we talked.

"Don't worry about me. I will be fine. The Ramsey's have taken me in. I will help do the cleaning and cooking," she said with a little half-smile as she shrugged her shoulders.

"That's good and I'll still come over and visit you whenever I can," I responded.

Little did we know, she would be no more than the Ramsey's housekeeper, with no time for herself.

Very few times could they visit as before for Jo was always working and doing something for her "masters" and soon Jo became ill.

I recalled my last trip to see Jo.

I walked down a path through some trees. The sun had just begun to set as he passed the old fence and approached the house.

Mrs. Ramsey was happy to see me. She escorted me to Jo's bed as the evening's sun darkened the room.

Jo lay there, thin and gaunt. The shadows from the setting sun cast a lonely, silent gloom in the room. I sat on the edge of her bed and held her cold fragile hand.

I told her she looked good and soon she would be well again. I spoke about some of the good times we had had together and I talked of the future plans we had made.

She smiled at me, and then fell asleep.

I sat there a few minutes longer holding her hand before I kissed her forehead and left.

Turning for one last image of her before I left, I vowed to return for another visit, though in my heart I knew she would not recover.

She died during the night.

I did not know what had happened to him after Jo's death, for he wished only to know details of their lives together. Whatever it was, the Angel Jo never told him about what happened during the rest of his life. He knew that whatever his life was without Jo, life would have been meaningless. Its outcome did not really matter.

Another life that Jo had told me about was my next life after the Civil War.

After the end of the Civil War as I drifted from town to town, an ex-confederate soldier had shot me and I returned to the Other Side. I tried to wait for Jo's return but could not stand being without her. So I decided to come back and search for her at the first chance available. About the turn of the century, I finally got that chance.

I was then born in Kentucky into a black family.

On the Other Side, Jo and I never really discussed human racial problems. We played all of the time and in fact, we never would have understood why the color of one's skin would have caused so much trouble.

In my younger years of that life, I learned early what being black meant. Lost in the racial slurs and the put downs aimed at me, I had forgotten my reason for coming back to earth. Confused, I went through that life never understanding my pains of loneliness or the hatred that people had for each other.

As a mid-teenager, my interest soon turned to baseball. The sport helped to relieve my mind of hateful thoughts about white people. I became good enough at the sport that I was offered the opportunity to play left field on a team in a small black league.

After a game one Sunday as I left the baseball field, a nice-looking white woman smiled and said, "Hi."

I returned her smile and replied, "Hi."

Some young white men saw what I had done.

Late that night I was awakened by screams from my mother.

Jumping out of bed, I ran into the other room. Three or four white men were slapping my mom around.

One of the men yelled, "There's that nigger that likes white girls. Get him!"

Before I knew what was happening, they grabbed me and dragged me outside while hitting me.

My "Hi" to a white girl was enough reason for them to beat me to death. I was left dead in the middle of the road in front of my mother's home, a sign for all "niggers" that white boys would not allow blackies to mess around with their women.

I could remember seeing my black broken dead body lying there on this dirt road lined with old shacks. The hot morning sun beat down on the dead human body as flies hurriedly carried out their duties.

On the Other Side there is no age difference. But on earth, if I could have found her, Jo would have been in her sixties by then. And with me being black and Jo being an elderly white woman, nothing would have worked out anyway, but I learned more "good" lessons about being human.

Another life that I remembered and one in which Jo did not need to help me recall, was my life during the 1930s.

Jo was born on June 29, 1932. I was not sure of the date of his birth, but I recalled being a youngster, maybe eight or nine years old or I may have been a little older than that.

I looked out the window at the narrow cobblestone street below. The street was lined with brick and stone buildings. These buildings were close together, as if connected to each other. The street had a small sidewalk on both sides. The sidewalks touched both the buildings and street. There was no grass or trees along the street.

For some reason, I thought this strange place was in Europe, and I felt I was afraid as I watched the street.

Soon, a few men dressed in dark uniforms walked down the street toward the building in which I was hiding.

Panic-stricken, I looked around for somewhere to hide on this second floor of this abandoned building. The floor was bare. There was only a wooden floor with a few post that ran up to the roof.

There was nowhere to hide, nowhere to run and no way that I could jump to safety.

I heard boots climbing the stairs.

Then, I was once again back on the Other Side. I did not know why or who killed him. My only thoughts were that I must return to earth as quickly as possible to unite with Jo.

After a while, he could not endure the wait any longer. He saw others getting ready to depart for earth. Quickly he jumped in front of the line and said, "I cannot wait any longer."

This time I, Jacob, was born David A. Haven, on June 12, 1944, which was twelve years after Jo's birth.

Now the stage was finally set for eventful meeting in 1965.

The similar endings to other of our stories consist of domination and or human emotions that always caused an abrupt end to their lives.

The Angels Jo and Jacob now know there is no innocent life on earth. Long ago there may have been innocence of the young, but even back then many people practiced sacrifice of their off-spring to their different gods and abused children, too.

Today there is no innocence even for the young. Children grow up long before their time. They learn how to use drugs and how to kill.

The thing that all generations of people have forgotten is God's Love... Love for yourself ... Love for all people and things.

FAREWELL

The Knowledge of the Other Side keeps filling my head or maybe it's remembering the Other Side that I am recalling. Whatever it is, it's real to me. The knowledge that I keep receiving is so great that if we kept writing what I am learning, this book would never be finished.

Like everyone, sometimes I have doubts about what I have learned and what we have written, for like you, I am human also. The human part of us does not always allow us to trust other people and sometimes we may not even trust our own minds.

More of the Knowledge that I have learned is revealed in the section, *GOD'S FORGOTTEN GUIDING LOVE,* of this book.

The evidence and testimonial is overwhelming and much of it will be revealed in our book, *CONVEYANCE OF ETERNAL LOVE,* for our story is true.

(*CONVEYANCE OF ETERNAL LOVE,* will be written after I am gone.)

Believe what we have written or not, the decision is yours. I really don't care if you believe me or not. No one could lie about a story like this and then write it in under four months, but I did not finish editing until May of 2006.

I am married to a wonderful woman, Christine, but I still mourn for Jo. Christine and I have been married for thirty years on November 12th of 2005, and we have watched our two sons grow up.

People have asked Christine, "How can you live with and love a man who is in love with a dead woman?"

These are three different types of love which is detailed in the next section of this book, but Christine and my love for her is a human love. Jo and my love is a love for God... a Divine Love. For once I loved Jo, her body and personality. She is gone, only her Entity lives on.

I want to go back home to Jo, and now its nearing time for me to leave,

I'm tired. And as the end of my life comes closer, I keep learning more and more about the Other Side. You may consider my writing as rambling but it isn't, it is the order in which I have learned. But many things that I have learned, I cannot tell you. You will know them when you return to the Other Side.

I know that I will die. And I have accepted my death and look forward to it. With my understanding of the coming of my death, my family understands and realizes the coming of my death. Their understanding that all life must have death will make their lives easier without me. It is a comfort to them to know that I will be happy on the Other Side because Jo is waiting for me and we know that there is something better afterlife.

If what I believe is completely wrong and after life you only turn back into dirt, it does not matter. It only matters that we believe that there is more to life than life itself and you reap what you sow, and helping people in their lives will give you a better life.

For sure, there are things that I will miss here on earth. Missing things here on earth is one of the many reasons we all keep coming back.

Before I lived the Learning and Understanding parts of our book, I became angry a lot at people. I still become angry but those feelings do not last like they use to. Now I have the Knowledge and I have learned which helps me forgive people. People do bad things to each other not because their Souls are bad, but it is because humans are naturally bad. Humans are still animals and all animals are mean to each other.

After living the Learning part of our books, I stated that Jo and I would not be back again. Now after living the Understanding part of our books, I now say, we may be back. Maybe the next time things will be different.

I wish you all good luck and happiness and say an early "Farewell."

Now I enjoy the experiences of my life and wait for my end to come then once again I will rejoin Jo on the Other Side.

IN CHRISTINE'S OWN WORDS

FEELINGS FOR JO

Let me begin by telling you that I was never one to believe in Entities. Before I met Dave, I had never experienced anything that had to do with that sort of thing. I had heard a lot of stories about people having strange things happen to them and I have heard talk of others about the Other Side and the Light, but I never really paid much attention to them.

When I married Dave, we spent a lot of time talking of the strange things that seemed to be happening around us, but I always tried to find logical explanations for them.

Dave had told me about the car accidents he had been in. Neither one of us could believe that anyone could have survived those four major accidents. I always thought that God was watching over him. However, Dave did not agree with that because he did not believe in God at that time.

Through the years, I have learned that there is something after death, but I was never quite sure what.

Of course I believe in God. I always have, but my beliefs were not always certain.

I believed in the Light, but was not quite sure how that fit into Heaven.

Were these crazy people, who claimed to have near-death experiences and saw the Light but someone was always there to send them back?

What about my upbringing which told me that when you die, you stay in purgatory until Judgment Day? I was confused about a lot of things.

As you have read in this book, Dave and I have been through quite a few strange occurrences. Things just did not make sense to me. Who were these Entities? Why did they stay with us where ever we moved? Why would they not leave us alone?

When Dave first told me about Jo, I had some pretty mixed feelings. There he was planning a trip to drive twenty-five hundred miles to find a woman he was in love with thirty years ago to tell her that he was sorry for leaving her. A million thoughts filled my head.

I knew that he was living on borrowed time to begin with, and I thought I was going to loose him when he had his first heart attack. With his bad heart and having bad lungs I was scared. I knew that he was very passionate about finding this woman and the only thing I could do was to support him in his efforts.

At first, I had a feeling that Dave would not come home to me after he found Jo. She was a very beautiful woman. There was a passion there that I had never seen in him before. I tried to hate her, but I could not. I found myself feeling very sorry for her. I could almost feel Dave's pain of losing her.

After Dave came back from his trip and he had his second appointment with Betty Way, things began to make sense to me.

I remember walking from our bedroom one day and when I looked up, there was a woman standing before me. I got a cold chill and was scared to death. I know now that the woman was Jo. There is not a doubt in my mind.

I was very sad to learn about Jo's death, although I had a very deep feeling that she was dead before Dave left on his trip. She loved Dave as passionately as he loved her. It hurts me very bad to feel the pain that the two of them have gone through, but what I would not give to feel the love that the two of them have shared.

Jo has become a part of my life as well as Dave's.

I love my husband more than anything in this world. When he came back from his trip and I learned everything that was going on, I hurt inside. I did not think that he had room for me in his heart. How could he love her and me at the same time? I just knew that I had lost him forever. I knew that he wanted to be with her. I just knew that he cared for me, but felt that he did not really love me.

Dave knew that something was bothering me. One night while lying in bed, I could not take it any more. I feel silly about it now, but at the time I could not help my feelings. I cried and I told him that I felt like he did not have room for me any more. I told him how I tried with all my heart to hate Jo, but I could not.

Dave held me in his arms and told me how much he loved me. That was the night that everything came together for me. Jo was someone who he had kept tucked away for all those years. He loved me enough to be honest with me about her.

Today, Jo is very much a part of both of our lives. I understand their love for each other. It is a different kind of love than what Dave and I share. Our love is very special, just as their love is very special. Jo is also very special to me. She is an Angel. God is the Light and she is part of the Light. How could I not love her too?

DAVE

Dave has always been an intriguing man to me. We have spent many nights watching the stars and wondering what was out there.

We would talk about things like why we were here and what our purpose in life was. I always thought that he was a great philosopher.

There were things that Dave would tell me that would really give me chills, such as describing some of my friends to me and telling me where they lived when he had never met them. That would just blow my mind.

He always seemed to have a knack to know what someone was going to do or say to him or his family before they ever did it. I never understood that.

There were times when I thought he was wrong about someone and then he would end up being right. He would never really say, "I told you so!"

I just could never understand why he did not like certain people before he ever got to know them. After a while, I learned to trust his instincts because they always seemed to be right on.

Dave does not get close to people.

Through the years, I thought that it was because he had been hurt so many times in the past that he had built this invisible brick wall up around him so no one could get in. He was usually pleasant to people, but he did not give more than he had to. Sometimes I felt that even I could not get through that wall. I knew he loved me, but I could sense that there was still something there that I could not penetrate.

Dave has changed dramatically since learning about Jo and everything about himself. He is more tolerant of people. He still does not want to get close to people, but he understands why he feels the way he does toward them.

At times, it would almost seem that I was married to two different men. There was this very loving and gentle husband and father who would do anything in the world for his family. He has always been a very hard worker and a very good provider. Our children or I have never wanted for anything.

Then there would be times when we would be watching the stars or just laying in bed together and he would tell me that he wanted out of life. He just wanted to die. He hated the people and the way they were; everyone wants something from you. They did not want to be your friend just because they liked you.

Dave used to talk about being born in the wrong time period because he hated the world today. He wanted to live back in the days when, if you had a problem with someone, you just took it outside and settled it in a dual. He felt the way people do things these days is chicken. That never made sense to me, but now I understand.

I believe that is also the reason why he has always gone a hundred miles an hour and gave a hundred and ten percent in whatever he did. He wanted to write and produce music, and once he accomplished it that was it. He lost interest and then moved on to something else. He has been that way ever since I met him. When he makes up his mind that he wants to do something, he just does it and he is always successful.

The same thing with equipment, Dave knows what it will handle and when it will break down before it does. He will tell you, Jo helps him keep things running proper.

Then there are other times when he is just so mellow. Nothing seems to bother him or upset him. He is happy and not worried about meeting deadlines. I know now that those are the times when Jo is around. He is a completely different person when she is near. I guess I could always sense it, but I never understood it or knew what it was.

Now I know it has always been Jo. She has always been there to help him. She has now given him the understanding of himself. He used to put a pretty high priority on money. Now it is not important to him anymore. He is no longer a materialistic person. He has totally changed since he has learned from Jo.

I can sense when Jo is around Dave, he gets a look about him that I cannot explain, and he becomes very on edge when she is not here.

I feel very good that my husband felt he could come to me and tell me about all of this. I feel a closeness to him that I have never felt before, which is hard to explain, too. I am not saying that I did not feel close to him before, but I feel that I am very special to him now.

I believe that Jo helped me understand Dave just as much as she helped Dave to understand himself. Once again, I thank God and Jo for all I have in my life and especially for allowing me to know Dave.

I SHARED THEIR LOVE

The time came when I finally accepted Jo.
It all happened the night that I cried and Dave held me in his arms and let me know just what I have meant to him in our life together and how much he loved me. Jo was someone from his past, his Soul Twin, who would always be a part of him. He loved her deeply, but he loved me just as deep. Our love was a different kind of love.
I now understood Jo and Dave. I knew what made Dave so unhappy at times and so did he. Everything just fell into place, and at last, things made sense.
One night, out of the blue, Dave told me that if I felt like doing things that I did not normally do just do it. I had no idea what he was talking about and for some reason I did not even ask him what he was talking about.
The three days was a period of time that I was extremely tired. I did not know what was wrong with me. I felt like I had not slept in days. I noticed that I started getting a rash on my left hand. It almost looked like I was getting the measles on just the back part of my hand. I really did not think a whole lot about it at the time.
That night, Dave and I were lying in bed, smoking a cigarette.
The next thing that I knew I was watching Dave and me making love. It was as though I was in the headboard of our bed. It was beautiful, but it sure was not me that Dave was making love to. How could it be, I was watching.
Suddenly, I was looking up at Dave. I was no longer watching us. We were filled with a passion which I had never felt before. I felt feelings flowing through Dave and me both which I have never experienced in the twenty-one years that we were married. I have always felt his love, but never anything so deep and strong as this.
Afterwards, as we lay in each others arms, I told him about the rash on my hand. It was also now on my stomach. What came next sort of blew my mind but did not really surprise me.

Dave told me that Jo had asked him if he would get my permission for her to enter my body so they could make love one more time.

She wanted to relive my life from my memories as Dave's wife. Doing this would be the same as them completing their mission; married twenty-one years and raising two sons. He refused her request and told her that was between her and me because he would not have anything to do with asking me.

Somehow, Jo communicated with my Soul and my Soul gave her permission.

The rash was my anti-bodies trying to fight off a foreign substance which was Jo's Angel.

She experienced all of our holidays, every Christmas, all the good times and our bad times together. She experienced all of the struggles we have gone through. She experienced the birth of both of the boys and saw them raised. She now held all of my memories because now we were like one.

In Jo's mind, it was her and Dave who had experienced life together. Tony and Dan were also her boys now. Bodies and faces mean nothing, my body is the same as her body, and my face is the same as hers.

After our love making that night, my rash started to clear up and within the next few days it was completely gone.

I am glad that I allowed Jo her request. I shared in the love between Soul Twins. The kind of love everyone here on earth search for. A love so strong that I cannot explain how it felt.

JO REMAINS WITH US

It is now the middle of January 1997, and over the past two months, everything has remained relatively quiet. However, no matter how long I live, I will never forget December 21, 1996.

Tony's girlfriend was going out of town for Christmas, so we were having a little Christmas party with her before she left. Like most people, we took pictures of each other opening our gifts to each other.

After getting the pictures back a few days later, we found something very interesting.

There was a group of three pictures taken in a row of Tony opening his gift from his girlfriend. In the first picture, on the left side, there was a whitish, smoke-swirled haze. In the second picture that was taken, there were four or five of these whitish, smoke-swirled hazes that resembled forms of people. In that picture, at the far left, that form resembled a woman. And in the last picture, part of the woman can be seen at the right side of the picture. The three pictures present a prognosis of the woman, Jo, herding other Entities through our living room.

Dave had told me many times that he wished he had taken a photo of Jo when they were going together had she granted his wish and allowed her picture to be taken? Did she give Dave her photo as a Christmas Gift?

Betty Way was also correct about Tony. On December 31, he left for the Marines. He no longer lives at home.

Dan has seen Jo walk through the living room three times in the past two months. And for some reason, he is not afraid anymore, and he now calls her his Angel.

Daily, when Dan goes to school, he locks the entry lock on our front door. He says that when he comes home from school, the dead bolt on the front door is also locked.

I am not sure just what my part is concerning Dave and Jo. I only know what I have experienced.

One night I had a dream that I had died. I saw a bright light in the distance. I am not sure if I was walking or floating or what, but I remember that as I approached the Light, I looked over my shoulder and saw Dave and Jo. Dave looked at me and we smiled at each other. Then I went on into the Light. That dream was so real to me. I feel deep in my heart that when I die this is exactly what will happen. I will go into the Light. I will not stay outside of the Light with Dave.

THEY WON'T BE BACK

On the day before Thanksgiving, I was riding the train on my way to work I experienced something that absolutely appalled me.

Between the Sylmar and Burbank Stations, I heard a noise that sounded like rocks hitting the bottom of the train.

Several people on the other side of the train car said, "Oh my gosh, there goes a tire. We must have hit a car."

The conversations that followed turned my stomach. They started talking about the train hitting a car about a year ago in Palmdale that decapitated a man. Most of the people seemed to find that amusing.

Everyone was speculating about the car we had just hit. There was not a doubt in their minds that the driver had to have been killed. It made me sick. I got a very nauseous feeling in my stomach. I turned my head and looked out the window at the still dark sky. There was a nice man sitting across from me who asked me if I was okay. I told him that I was fine.

I thought of how callus these people were. Did they not realize that they were talking about a human being and not just a thing. Everyone was talking about tires and hubcaps and such from the car, but the train car became silent when a sheriff walked through the train to be sure no one was hurt and to see if anyone had seen anything at all, not one person spoke up.

Within about an hour and a half, a bus had been dispatched to pick us up and take us to the Burbank Station. All the way there, people made jokes about this person in the car we hit. I was sick. I heard that there was only one person in the car, a male. He evidently thought that he could beat the train but didn't.

That night, on my way home on the train, I found out that the man had died. I had prayed so hard that he would not die. My mind kept playing back all of those cold jokes about this guy this morning. I wondered what these people thought now. Did they even care? This man was someone's son and maybe someone's father or husband. I could not help but cry.

I understood now why Dave did not ever want to come back again. Dave was right; there are so many cold hearts out there.

I still believe there are a lot of people like myself who are not so cold, but I also believe there are a lot more who are.

The whole ordeal of Dave and Jo and understanding death and what death really is has made me come to accept death much easier. I know that I do not have a lot of time left with Dave. I used to not want to even think about it. I wanted to pretend that he would be here forever with me. Now there is no doubt in my mind what is waiting for Dave on the Other Side because God has taken care of everything.

Dave will at last be happy and free. He will be there to help others cross over. He will not be in the pain that he is in on this earth with all of his bad health conditions

I can now accept his death easier. That is not to say that I will not cry or that I will not miss him. He is the love of my life and I will love him forever.

I will go on to complete my mission here on this earth, whatever it is. As for Dave and Jo, I have helped them fulfill their mission and someday soon they will be **_TOGETHER FOREVER BEFORE THE LIGHT._**

GOD'S FORGOTTEN GUIDING LOVE

GOD'S FORGOTTEN GUIDING LOVE

GOD'S FORGOTTEN GUIDING LOVE is for you, the one who is striving for a better understanding and knowledge of Life, Life after Death and God– the Supreme Being.

The Master Plan shall prevail; for those who seek the Knowledge of the Light shall have the Knowledge. Therefore, those who have the Knowledge and use the Knowledge in their daily lives will live forever, and those who refuse the Knowledge and those who have the Knowledge but do not use the Knowledge are NO-THING. And yet, all people, and all things, and all that has happened and all that is happening and all that will happen is part of His Master Plan.

What you are reading is true. Since you have opened this book and read the first section, you are ready for the Knowledge for now is the time for you to open your heart and learn the Knowledge. If you use this Knowledge in your daily life, you will live forever in *The Glory of God*. But yet, everyone and everything is in the exact place and at the exact time that they are suppose to be because then you are ready for the job, the job will be ready for you.

And He said "LET THERE BE LIGHT, FOR THE LIGHT IS ALL KNOWLEDGE."

What we speak about is NOT New Age religion. What you are about to read are the true meanings (translations) of the bibles directly from God, as told by Jesus, Gabrael and the Angel Jo.

(The correct spelling for Gabriel was changed a long time ago. The true spelling of his name was and is "Gabrael.")

(The word "bible(s)" and "Bible(s)" is referring to all spiritual and religious writings that came from direct communications with the Supreme Being's (God's) Angels.)

The understanding is Knowledge, if one can comprehend its meanings.

Our writings are to help you understand and then comprehend this Knowledge.

"Love All Others and Have No Domination for Them" is that Knowledge that was lost during interpretation and translation of the bibles while placing God's concepts into man's agendas. This is the Knowledge that was given to those who communicated with God's Angels, but those who were contacted by the Heavenly Being could not understand and did not get it, so now once again that Knowledge is revealed.

All accounts and Knowledge in this book have come directly from Jesus and Gabrael through the Angel Jo, as told to the writer, Christine J. Haven, by her husband David A. Haven, as told to him by God's Angels.

GOD'S FORGOTTEN GUIDING LOVE is Knowledge and sets forth truly the most sensational spiritual encounters of our time.

The communication between David and the Angel Jo continued on a daily basis over eight years. Some of their dialogue was documented by many hours of audio and videocassette recordings, as well as more than seven hundred pages of notes taken by me, Christine J. Haven.

Few other spiritual events in history have had such solid documented proof as *GOD'S FORGOTTEN GUIDING LOVE*. But proof is not needed, for only faith is needed when one knows the true meaning of each question was precisely answered.

GOD'S FORGOTTEN GUIDING LOVE takes nothing away from the bibles and scriptures of all religions that are truly of the Supreme Being – the Creator of all. It will only help you understand and comprehend your Bible more fully, for Love is Universal.

GOD'S FORGOTTEN GUIDING LOVE is God's Love to you.

GOD'S FORGOTTEN GUIDING LOVE is God's Love and His continuous Love for you.

All events set forth herein are true. Nothing has been added or removed, for the Knowledge in this book came directly from Jesus and Gabrael through the Angel Jo, as told to David Haven.

In order for you to understand what you are about to read, you must first understand the earthly relationship that occurred between David and the Angel Jo when she last was in body.

As written in this book's first section, *Together Forever Before The Light*, during the spring of 1965, David drifted into Marion, Ohio, and lived in the Union Pacific Hotel when he worked drilling oil wells in and around Mt. Gilead, Ohio. He met a barmaid named Joan Lee Harris who worked at H&H Bar & Grill.

(It was Joan's Angel-within that we refer to as the Angel Jo.)

They had a deeply devoted love affair during the spring and summer of that year, and in the fall David left. When he returned in February of 1966, he could not locate her.

For more than thirty years David carried their story in his memories and never revealed their love affair to anyone until the fall of 1996. It was at that time that he told me, Christine, his wife of over twenty years, about Joan and their love story and how he needed to find her in order to ask for her to forgive him for his leaving and not returning, and to tell her he was sorry for what had happened.

As David began his search for Joan, he found that she had passed on from cancer in September 1968, and that she had been standing beside him ever since her death. Joan then became part of our daily lives and began a dialogue with David. Occasionally, my Angel within would allow her to occupy my body for short periods of time to experience more of life.

And *Together Forever Before The Light*, detailed more of their lives together than just their Summer of 1965.

God's Forgotten Guiding Love is the true dialogue and has not been enhanced or changed. It contains the actions and encounters that occurred between David and the Angel Jo, Gabrael and Jesus. This Knowledge, if understood and used properly, will help you find your salvation, peace and love during your life and guide you to Everlasting Life.

Blind faith of your bible will not and does not direct you down the wrong path of intended life, unless your beliefs condone domination. Even if your bible uses incorrect words or stories, as long as it does not impose upon people, all will be fine. But living forever in the Kingdom of God does not come to and shall not be rewarded to those who live with an unopened heart. Such as saying that you know Jesus died for your sins will not save you, it is a good life and open heart that leads to Everlasting Life.

During an evening in April 1999, as Jesus spoke to a company of five people in our home, He said, "The Bible is useless now for it is full of misguidings. Do not follow your Bible word for word... follow your heart, read your Bible for its historical content of how life was back then, and understand that I did live, and how the Father through His Angels did communicate with people and will communicate with you today if you allow it."

You will find directions to *compassion, understanding, forgiving, love, wisdom, cherishment* and *judgment* in this book, for they were also part of Jesus' way of life. These are things that Jesus demonstrated in His life, but no one understood that he was showing us how to live with an open heart.

Jesus said, "Follow your Heart... Follow these things from your heart."

They also are some of the Knowledge you shall inherit from God by reading this book, but Knowledge is not enough to secure your place in the

Light. The Word of God must be applied in your daily life and then you are living with and following an open heart.

Spiritual stories from many accounts written by different people were incorporated into the text of the bibles. All religions were originally designed to give people from all walks of life guidelines to live by. All religions are essentially the same. Most of the stories contained in the bibles are true, but important parts were changed, left out, lost and mistranslated over the course of time. By the time the bibles were put into text, many of their stories were incorrect and most of the stories were changed and are designed to control those who follow the religion of the bibles.

It is not our intent to change your faith. Your religious preference is personal, which we also will not try to change. We wish only to share with you the Knowledge that David was given, which not only will strengthen your faith but will help you through the tragedies and hardships of your daily life. It will enable you to understand the complete picture - the story of life and the cycle of life that you are a part of.

Prior to the beginning of David's learning period that started during the fall of 1996, Dave had no love for God. Dave thought as an atheist does. His love was only for his family, a few close friends and for his lost Jo. Therefore, Jo was the only Angel or person capable of revealing God's Love to him. Her steps were carefully orchestrated for her to show God to him. But first she had to convince him that she and the Other Side existed and were real. Once she accomplished that, she slowly brought Gabrael and Jesus into the picture. Then all three of them introduced him to God.

You see, the Angel Jo had to intervene in Dave's life and she had to stop where he was heading. Her actions were like that of a Guardian Angel; she put his life back on its proper path. Before and throughout most of his learning period from 1996 through 2004, Dave did not know why he needed the Knowledge. God's dramatic approach through the Angel Jo was needed in order for David to understand what was meant to come - The Master Plan. But yet, all that she did was part of the known Master Plan of God.

The Angel Jo said unto David, "Before, you were not ready and would not have believed in the Angel that I am, also you were not prepared to receive all that I am telling you... but now you are ready to receive God's Words."

We will tell you most of what has been revealed to David, but it will be difficult for us to explain everything because communication between Angels and humans or even just between humans most of the time loses true meaning. So sometimes you may read portions of this book and think that we are repeating ourselves. Those things that are repeated were needed to help you understand exactly what was said and meant because you must completely understand everything that the Angel Jo and David have discussed. The complexity of communication between humans and Angels, including vocabulary differences, sometimes cause things to be lost in a conversation, and that is one of the biggest tragedies of any bible.

David also discovered that Angels answer exactly what you ask. Therefore, one must completely understand what you wish answered before you ask an Angel the question.

Our book is not the only true book from God. Some before us have written about the truths of God and some after us will write more about the truths of God as they have been told. Each time, humans will understand more about the Other Side as God has given us this wisdom from the dawn of time. But from the dawn of time, He vowed to give new and more information to man as needed. These changes or better insight come to lift us to a higher level and bring us into closer contact with God.

The true books about God say to live with an open heart, and that is the bottom line of God's Word. Treat others as you wish to be treated and you shall find your everlasting life. The Master Plan is God's Will, for it is what has been, it is all that is, and it is for all that will be.

Part of the Master Plan includes the tragedies we all face, including death. Be it the death of a loved one, co-worker or friend, for death is a part of life and is always near.

Loneliness, helplessness, emptiness and sometimes denial may envelope us during the passing of a loved one. We will not see or enjoy that person again in physical form. Even though through faith and religion we believe that person is in Heaven, we still mourn our loss of them.

David mourned silently for Jo. He felt that their love was true and sacred and was not to be shared with others.

Not knowing where a loved one is can feel the same as their being dead. After Dave could not find Jo in the spring of 1966 and he did not know where she was he mourned for her. He missed enjoying her company, even though he did not learn she had passed on until nearly thirty years after her death, he did not know that she stood at his side during all his lonely years after her death.

After Dave received this Knowledge, he still missed Jo, but then he understood. The Love that the Angel Jo and Dave now share is a Divine Love. Love between humans cannot match their Spiritual Love. Through her love she inspired him. He then learned and had the wisdom to complete his life without her being beside him bodily. He had the faith to understand the total picture and meaning of life and how it is related to the Other Side. The complete picture of the cycle of life is part of God's Master Plan.

The Knowledge and wisdom that David received from God through her, gave him faith to believe in God's Words, and that is what we have written herein to help you understand the complete picture of life, which includes the Other Side.

The complete picture of Life is comprised of Love, Understanding, Compassion, Forgiving, Wisdom, Cherishment and Judgment. These things will lift your Soul and elevate you to a level of life that is closer to God.

The Wisdom Dave obtained through the Knowledge helped him cope with the absence of Jo. He knew she was waiting for him, but his human part, the "dog" – the animal, the human that he is still missed her very much.

It is okay to say, "I wish I would have said I love you more often," and you can.

It is okay to say, "I wish I could still say I love you in person," and you can.

The Angels are our loved ones, who hear our prayers. They stand beside us. They know exactly what we are saying, for they know exactly what we are thinking. You may not see the smile on their face, hear their response or feel their embrace, but the departed ones see and understand your true feelings and frustrations. They miss us too, while their Knowledge assures them that we all will be together on the Other Side some day. However, they also are saddened by what they see... our actions against ourselves and others.

Wisdom guides us through our daily lives. Patience is the first part of acquiring wisdom. Patience should be taught to children by their parents, but most of the time we don't teach our children patience because we the parents, do not possess or do not understand it ourselves. Patience should be practiced throughout one's life, but many times it is lost or forgotten when it comes to dealing with the loss of a loved one. Losing patience and wisdom is a tragedy to the Soul. This tragedy is explained later.

The Bibles should be a guide for living a happy meaningful life. Do not try to read into your Bible things that it does not say. The teachings in your Bible are a gift from God. Your Bible teaches patience as well as wisdom, compassion, understanding, forgiveness, love, judgment, cherishment and many other things. These are some of the things that the Angel Jo had to teach David.

Preachers frequently misconstrue the words from their Bible to fit their personal agendas and concepts. These are the same words and phrases that already were mistranslated during the experiencing (living) of the stories, and also misunderstood when first written, then mistranslated in the formulation of the Bibles, and finally misunderstood and mistranslated by the ones who taught others about the Bibles.

How can anyone understand or try to teach others from something that is incorrect and is something that the teachers themselves do not understand?

Our writings are a bridge to help you understand the true meaning and Love of the Bibles and to help direct you toward God. As stated by the Angel Jo, "Our book will help many develop a higher understanding and insight of their Bible, God and His Master Plan."

Religions use different names for the Supreme Ruler. We like using the Light. We also use God, One and All in reference to the name of the Supreme Ruler throughout this book. Regardless of the name, He is the same one... All that is.

The same rule applies to religions; all are basically the same... but all have both good and bad ideas, too.

All religions are different and they do not all contain the same stories word for word. However, most religions have the same One above them and above their man-made gods.

We sometimes will refer to Jesus only because the Christian religion that we were taught as children claims His story and He was instrumental in Dave's learning and the writing of this book, but this book is not meant for Christians alone. Our book covers all religions for God is the true center point of all religions.

Assume you are in a room with no windows and someone comes into the room and says, "Boy, it is raining hard outside." Or while in that room, another says, "John just came in from outside and said it's raining hard." If you then decide to leave the room and go outside, you will dress for rainy weather. That is an example of belief – but you must first believe in what the person has previously said before you will give credit to what he now says. Then should a preacher be given credit to what he interprets from the Bible? Should God's Words that Dave has been blessed to receive and are documented on audio and video tape and which does not lessen the Bibles, be believed?

I recall back in the days of our lunar landings, some said that the televised images from the moon were faked. For many people will not believe anything you say, do or show them. If one cannot believe anything another says, does or shows them, does that not say that they do not believe in themselves?

Why must a preacher tell you about God before you believe in God?

Does that special building we call a church mean the preacher inside is telling the truth? Or do the pictures they hang on their walls or the icons placed around its rooms mean the speaker is telling the truth?

Should we then not believe in or communicate with Angels because the preachers do not teach of them? And while it is fact that when Rome first canonized its Bible, they remove mention of Angels because they were afraid people would worship them.

Truth resides within each of us. Our Angels within are the carriers of the Eternal Truth, and Angels of God from the Other Side are also the bearers of the Truth.

Should we not believe them when they tell us the Truth?

Should Dave not have believed in or listened to the Angel Jo?

Some religions say only Archangels are messengers of God for they alone carry the Word of God. As stated in the Christian Bible, Gabrael is one of God's messengers. He was one that was instrumental in delivering God's Words to Dave. Should Dave have not believed in what Gabrael was saying?

All Angels are equal because there is no rank in God, for all Angels in congregation is God. Any Angel can and could visit with you or me, just as any Angel can and may carry God's Words to either of us.

Faith is knowing there will be a tomorrow, and not just because there was today. You really believe tomorrow will come.

Faith is knowing on Friday that you will be paid for the work you did that week.

You believe daily about different things... your car will get you to your destination... you will have a job when you get to work... you will live to see another day.

Faith in your Bible should indicate that Angels may and could visit us because they have visited others in the past.

Belief and faith guide each of us all in our daily lives, just as our understanding about God and His Master Plan will help us through our daily lives.

In science we learn that to prove something we must be able to duplicate the problem and obtain the same result under controlled conditions. Yet, when people first thought that the world revolved about the sun, they did not need to prove this to know that another new year would come, for they had faith that the next season would come. And this was years before it was discovered that the planets actually evolved around the sun. Belief and faith alone lead the way. But yet, the Bibles tells of the world being round, the world's rotation around the sun, the tall mountains under the oceans and many more things that science discovered thousands of years after recording the stories of the Bibles.

Faith and belief are needed to find Salvation, your direction to Heaven. Yet today, we think that we must know everything and we must be able to prove it to believe that it is true and correct.

Not everyone will receive Angels and God, for most refuse Them. If all could see God's Angels, then no faith or belief would be needed. God allows only a few to see His Angels, the ones that must see Them, and these are the ones who pass God's Words unto others; but many in the past who have heard God's Words have polluted His Words with their own thoughts and ideas. Therefore, the lack of meaningful teaching about God and His Will – His Master Plan - has always been a problem for man. Organized religion does not teach everything about God because it does not know everything; organized religion knows only what may interest it in the Bibles.

Even today, parents leave the teaching of their children about God to their church. We used to teach our children love, understanding, compassion and caring for others. Most no longer teach these things to their young. Instead, we merely teach our children how to buy more, how to make more money, how to cheat and steal.

Most people will become embarrassed if you ask them what they think about God. Today nearly everyone talks less about God than sex. For them, God is more fictitious than our comic strip heroes, and many will become defensive if you ask them about God because they think you are trying to force your religion onto them.

During the time before the occurrences and the writing of this book, Dave's life was fairly painless, but as his end neared, pains grew within his body from ill health. But when the Angel Jo entered into his life, he knew why her teachings of faith and belief were essential. He was needed by God after his death. He could not be foolish. Had it not been for the Angel Jo, he would have committed suicide. Had he done so, he would not have entered into the Light with Heaven in his mind, for suicide is one of the worst Sins. The Angel Jo had to show and explain this to him. The Angel Jo as a Guardian Angel put Dave back onto the correct path for his Salvation.

Our experiences of life are worth the pain which is also an experience, but our pains do not last, while our experiences last forever. All on the Other Side are saddened to see us in pain, but they rejoice with us when they see our happiness from experiences.

Happiness comes from within and it brings peace of mind and places Heaven in our thoughts. Heaven in your thoughts at the time of death shall bring you to your place in the Light.

For God is the Light... the Light is the experiences of all that have lived... your Soul is part of your Angel... therefore you are part of God. As human, you and I are not God, for we are animals. Our Souls are newly part of our Angels that after your death will be part of God.

If your Angel-within leads your life, then your Angel-within is a

Master. If you, the animal, leads your life, then you are nothing but animal. But, if your Angel-within leads your life, then you are surely part of God.

We cover our Angels with our deeds. If your deeds in life are good... your Angel-within is covered with Heaven and shines brightly. But if your deeds are bad... your Angel-within is covered with Hell and is dark.

Judgment... you shall judge yourself and place yourself in Heaven or Hell until the end of time, at which point God will judge you.

If you live a bad and corrupt life, you shall remain outside of the Light and drift aimlessly until the end of time, and on the Final Day of time God will judge you. If you still have not found your way to salvation by then, you will be removed forever.

During the early spring of 1999, the Angel Jo informed Dave that he was to learn *Compassion*. After a week or so of experiencing *Compassion* in his daily life, and while nightly he would leave his body and with the Angel Jo, they would travel the world, and in different times, and to the Other Side, reviewing *Compassion*.

Before and during their teaching of *Compassion*, he was not told that there were other things he needed to learn as well. One step at a time, he was taught one teaching at a time, *Compassion, Understanding, Forgiveness, Love, Wisdom, Cherishment,* and then the final teaching, *Judgment*.

These are the things we must learn in order for our Angel-within to help us. Our Soul is part of our Angel-within. We must first direct these feelings toward ourselves (our Soul and Angel-within) before we can direct them toward others.

All others also have Souls. Their Souls are part of their Angels-within. Their Angels are part of God, while yours is part of God, too. Therefore all others are part of you, and you are part of all others, for God is all.

The Knowledge - *Compassion, Understanding, Forgiveness, Love, Wisdom, Cherishment* and *Judgment* - must be directed to the first part of God – you. Then you must direct these things toward all others, for they also, are part of God.

Controlling our animal emotions, which run deep within our human bodies, is the Knowledge is the "Mastering" of your Angel-within over your Flesh.

"*Judge not until you are judged.*"

Since we all have animal instincts, and since all of us have sinned in one way or another, it is best not to judge others at any time. But do judge others actions to see if they are right for you. Even after death you will not judge others for their past, as they will not judge your past, for we judge only ourselves. Self-judgment is done after we die, for after death we cannot go back and change what we did in our lives; therefore, we should correct our mistakes daily in our lives. During our lives we can go back and correct our bad deeds, but after death, our lives - good or bad deeds - are final and there is no changing the past, for it is final - Forever.

After a person dies, we the living, will review our life in our thoughts. Most times we are saddened by any bad deeds we have done to them or bad deeds they have done to us, but we do not condemn them, we only condemn ourselves to isolation and loneliness. And nor should we place the departed on pedestals, for they were merely human and they will deliver justice onto themselves on the Other Side, and whereas God will allow them to reward themselves as proven. We need not be their judge or jury, for after death all will judge themselves; then on the Final Day, God will judge all.

Our life's actions attest to our personal feelings toward others and ourselves. Therefore after death we judge what we accomplished or did not accomplish during our life. We judge not ourselves as such, but our actions in life.

The Angels offered Dave the chance to review his life's accomplishments. They did not say by reviewing his past life that he was judging his past actions, but then sometimes words are not needed. The Angel Jo and Dave went back into time and looked at all that he had done - both bad and good. The things that he saw were not good. The evil things outweighed the good.

You most likely will not be given the opportunity to judge yourself as David was allowed to do until after death. Therefore, we are offering you an insight in how to review your life and how to change your future here on earth, which will definitely have an impact on your presence after death.

Dave has seen all the things from all his other lives and of his present life that covered and smothered his Angel-within who dwells within him.

The experiences from all our previous lives and the past days of our present life form our present character and personality. Those are the things that make us what we are and do. Our past actions either lift our Souls or drag them down and cover our Angels into our self- made Hells.

Not only did they review his past lives but they reviewed many other people's lives. Dave was able to see why people act the way they do. He witnessed love flowing from people and he saw hatred rise in people. He was shown what happens to many as they judge themselves after death. He was allowed to feel what all Angels feel as they watch when others review their past experiences, both good and bad.

Their revisiting the past, future and traveling to many different locations in today's time continued for some time. Every night in this period of months after Dave went to bed the Angel Jo would come lie down beside him and tell him he needed to go to sleep because it was time to go again.

After each of their visits that contained hellish visions, the Angel Jo and he would try to comfort each other because they were both saddened by what they had seen.

After each visit that contained goodness and happiness, they would go play near the Light, for they were happy.

Your Bible is a textbook to understanding and to learn by experiencing (reading) the lives of people long ago who encountered God's ways and love. The experiencing and seeing that the Angel Jo showed David was nearly the same but more than him reading the Bible, for her teachings of God's Love and His ways was not corrupted by man's concepts.

God's Forgotten Guiding Love embraces all Bibles in detail with the forgotten Knowledge that God desired us to know and is the written guidance for understanding the Master Plan of God and His Love. Loving yourself is loving God. Loving others is loving God. For all is God.

Being confident in oneself is being confident in God. Being confident in others is being confident in God. For God is all.

Dave is not God, nor is he Jesus. Dave is simply a person who has learned the truth that needs to be relayed to others about the Other Side and the Glory of God, a story of which we all are a part.

To help you grasp and understand what David is about to give you, we have broken the teachings that the Angel Jo, Gabrael and Jesus gave Dave into different parts. Each is a section from their complete communications as Dave could recollect and has written them into what is *God's Forgotten Guiding Love*.

Many items briefly mentioned in this chapter are detailed later in this book. As one topic leads to another, so it is difficult to write about one subject without going directly into another subject.

Dave has much to tell you and prays he has answered your many questions, just as the Angel Jo answered all of his questions about God.

I hope you enjoy and understand the Knowledge that Dave was blessed enough to receive.

Now in Dave's own words, I will let him tell you his true story as he told it to me. All three Angels told Dave to be careful about what he writes. He was told to write in a style that all could understand the true meanings of God's Words.

And God's Angels said to David, "Keep it understandable."

WHO WE ARE

THE DOG

To help you better understand who we are, which involves the relationship and communications between humans and the Angels, I feel the following example will explain. Before we go into the example, let me explain why I use the word "dog" for who we are.

Most humans have been around dogs at some point during their lives and are familiar with the actions of dogs. Dogs will definitely show domination when food is concerned, and they sometimes may show what we consider as love, but the love they show is always directed inward. A dog will lie on your lap while you pet it. A dog will chase a ball that you have thrown if you reward it. A dog will wag its tail when you give it food. So a dog's love is not actually love for its master but rather for what you are giving it or doing for it.

During 1999, the Angel Jo had placed four Angels as Guards, one in each corner of our bedroom. These Guards are present from early evening until morning.

The Angel Jo had said to me, "These Guards are to protect Christine from evil energy." She laughed and then added, "You, David, do not need protection, for you can take care of yourself, they are placed there for the protection of Chris."

One night after the placement of these Guards, the Angel Jo entered Christine's body when we were in bed and about to go to sleep. As always, I knew immediately that it was the Angel Jo when the transformation occurred. In the transition of their Souls, I always get a feeling or knowing that Christine's body is changing of their personalities and a warmth spreads over me. The best way for me to describe this feeling is to say an arousal fills within me. This arousal is not a sexual arousal, but an awakening or a higher emotional state of my Soul, for at these moments, I feel as if I am full of the Holy Spirit.

On this special night, first we hugged each other, kissed and then began talking. After a while our human sexual desires took over. As Jo and I let our human emotions lead us toward making love, the Guard Angels left the room and started down stairs. As they went, they laughed, embarrassed about our actions.

Whenever we as humans see two dogs having sex, we will laugh or we will look the other way for we are embarrassed and do not know what to say or do. In that respect the Angels are the same as we. They also are embarrassed to watch two animals in their natural reproductive act for the Angels see us as we are; animals of a lower class of intelligence, an animal that they are trying to elevate to a higher level.

We do things that are of the flesh. We do things that are of the dog's natural instincts – survival and reproduction.

Some of the dog's instincts are needed for its survival, but most of the dog's instincts are not needed, just as some of our natural instincts are needed for survival while others are not.

This area of things that we do which are not needed for survival is where problems occur between the dogs (us) and the Angel that is within us. Our desires and their logic – God's Concept of Life - are different.

Our desires are our concept of life... we "need" this... we "want" that. The mansion or the expensive automobiles that you have are not really needed. They are only trophies to show others that you are better than they. Feelings for things as these cause self-imposed slavery... self-domination. With such earthly goods, the ones that take your time away from experiencing life then you have no life. But yet, the "Dog" is the center of its universe, and whereas, the Angel is part of the congregation that makes up God. If you have no life, part of the human that make up the congregation of humanity, then you are nothing, and then God sees you as No-thing.

The term "dog" is also to merely state that humans are animals... we are of the mammal class.

The dog within man drives him to seek new sexual and other encounters that are directed inward. These things do not elevate man. These things are merely for self-desires. The dog does not care about others, it merely cares about its immediate feelings.

Letting the dog rule and control your Angel is covering your Angel with actions of the dog focused (directed) inward only to its pleasures. These types of memories are Hell for the Angel-within. These types of memories will stop you from entering the Light.

(Let it be known I do not talk of all sexual encounters as being memories of Hell. Memories of Hell are all memories of stealing, killing, cheating and other things that are not good for the congregation of humanity and these things are not approved by God.)

The Concept of Life as seen by God and His Angels is, *"To learn and experience from experiences of others through endurance of life."*

(Please note that their quote does not say "through their endurance," "through our endurance," or even "through your endurance." Therefore, it means "through their – your' and my endurance." The word "others" when stated by Angels includes you and I, for we as human is "other" than Angel.)

Here are more examples of the "dog" within.

I see the future and sometime ago I wrote, sealed and sent a letter that predicted the coming year to some friends of mine. Then I phoned them and asked them not to open and read this letter until the coming Christmas Eve.

In this letter I told them that I knew their summer would not be as good as they expected it to be and that their coming Christmas would be small that year, for the husband would be out of work because of health problems. I told them that the next year would be better for them. I went on to tell them about the woman's sister... that she would lose her job and she would also lose a grandchild during the fall of that year. I wrote them this letter to comfort them because I knew how they would be feeling on that coming Christmas Eve when they would be reading my letter. I wanted them to know that they did not cause the problems, but instead these were the things that must come to pass for these things were needed.

Well, that year was slim for them and their Christmas was small because the husband did have health problems that kept him from working, just as I had predicted.

The sister did not lose her job, even though she did have back problems that almost cost her job. The as yet unborn grandchild did not die but the sister did have many problems with her daughter, who was living out of wedlock with a man. The act of the daughter living with the man did drive the daughter and mother apart. The daughter may have had a miscarriage, I will never know.

I asked the Angel Jo why these things had not happened with the sister as I had seen because I was so sure they would come to pass.

She said, "You saw what you wanted to see. Yes, you can see the future, but you also wanted those things to come. You do not like the sister of your friend. Your human desires wanted those things to happen to the sister. You did not open your heart and see the things to come with the woman's sister as you did with the woman and her husband."

In October of 1998, The Angel Jo said, "On July 9th of 1999, something will happen to affect nations."

Then during the last part of 1998, in a vision I saw fighting in Europe, the Middle East, and in the Far East.

After the first of 1999, as Jesus spoke to five of us in my home, He said, "Kosovo is the beginning of the end..."

I knew China was going to get involved in Kosovo, but did not know how.

I then saw actions of terrorists against the United States. I saw Japan and other nations doing battle. I saw Los Angeles being destroyed by terrorists, high water, earthquakes and volcanoes. I saw part of Florida being destroyed by high water. I viewed all these things as happening simultaneously on July 9, 1999.

During the evening of July 7, 1999, I asked the Angel Jo if these things were all to come on July 9, in two days.

She responded, "No. Once again you have seen things you have wished to happen... something will happen to affect nations, but that is only the beginning of the end... terrorist actions have already started... there will be no more earthquakes than usual. There will be no more volcanoes than normal."

On July 9th, ITN World News for Public Television announced that Britain was selling and shipping spent nuclear fuel rods to Japan. This was the thing that would happen to affect nations that the Angel Jo had told me would come. On that same day, Florida did have a huge waterspout that lasted ten to fifteen minutes.

Jesus had stated that Kosovo being the beginning of the end, and then the Angel Jo stated about Britain's shipment of nuclear fuel to Japan as the beginning of the end. Are not these things a new start toward the end?

(The answer is unveiled in our chapter GENESIS.)

Romans 10:13 of the Christian Bible says, "For whosoever shall call upon the name of the Lord shall be saved."

For those who wish to refer to Jesus as "Lord" and believe that calling upon Jesus' name will save them if that is what they believe is His demand. This is the same as those who look to the future and believe in what they think will be, and they shall find the truth if they are willing to accept the truth... so be it.

Prophecies are like the growth of a tree. They are slow to come and you never see them until they have grown in maturity. Prophecies are slowly being fulfilled, not just from what was written in the Bibles, but also by the prophets of today. But humans wrote the Bibles. Humans... the dog... saying things the dog wishes would happen... believing in things the dog wanted to happen, watching for the future to hold things the dog desires. Therefore, not all Prophecies will come to pass because most of the Prophecies are from the dog instead of from God.

Let's take a minute to discuss definitions of words and review a few of the words that we commonly use and their meanings.

One definition for the word "insanity" is to do the same thing again and again and expect a different result. I should not have to explain this definition. Another definition for the word "insanity" is to do something and expect the most unlikely result. In other words, if one jumps from a rooftop and thinks he will not be hurt or dead, that is expecting the most unlikely result.

Another word we need to examine is the word "normal." What is normal for you does not need to be normal for me. I cannot hit home runs as Babe Ruth did; yet it was normal for him to hit home runs. It is normal for a person who does not have legs to use a wheelchair, but it is not normal for me to use a wheelchair because I have the use of both of my legs. It is normal for a blind man not to see…

A few years ago, a college in San Francisco decided to have a course covering street language. They said street language was a spin-off of American English and should be taught in schools. Street language is changing the definitions of words we presently use.

As an example of street language, the other day I overheard two men talking. One man was telling the other about "late night creeping." The second man asked what that meant. The first man answered, "It means to slip over to a friend's house at two or three in the morning and make love to her."

The definitions for words we use are constantly changing. Just as most of the definitions of words in our dictionary today are the meaning of words from a man who was in prison for life when a few men decided to standardize definitions of words and wrote the dictionary, the Bibles were written long before the dictionary was standardized. So our "definitions" of words that we think are "normal" we use in our daily communication. That includes our reading and understanding of the Bibles. These are not the same definitions that were used in Bible times and by those who recorded the Bible stories.

The Bibles were written symbolically. The things that I saw and thought would happen on July 9th also were symbolic. We see what we wish to see. We interpret things into what we want to happen. We translate our visions into words that we can understand. We also write and communicate with others in words that we believe will help them understand the meanings of our thoughts.

All spiritual and religious writings contain things that the dog desired to be. These books that I write probably hold some of my desires, even though I tried to write only the truth as told to me by the Angels because it is almost impossible for one to write without prejudging. The Dog dwells within us all.

Now this concept of dog ideas overriding God's true communication with humans also should be examined relative to our dreams.

Each of us has the ability to leave his body as he sleeps. When asleep, we all can go back into the past, move into the future and can travel to many places in this time. Many times the dog gets in the way and we do not leave our bodies and travel but instead we dream (in-vision) of things we expect to happen, or things we want to happen, or things we think are happening. Therefore, one cannot believe in all his dreams. One must learn how to differentiate between dog dreams and the true Angel-within experiences.

You should not dwell on the things you have seen in dreams. Live for the day because you cannot change the past but only your future. Understand and experience life and be happy that you were granted the opportunity to experience life.

Believing in yourself and all others with an open heart shall be your path to Everlasting Life.

When walking down the street and a person who you think is homeless approaches you and asks you for money, if you can afford to give this person money and you do so, then you have given from an open heart to this person.

If this person lied and did not really need the money, it is of no consequence to you for you gave from an open heart. The person who defrauded you shall pay dearly when he returns to the Other Side.

If you could afford to give money, but choose not to give this person money because you think he is lying, then you do not have an open heart. But if you denied this person money because it was designated for some other worthwhile cause, that is fine.

For if you did not give to that person who looked homeless because you thought he was not in need then you prejudged him without knowing his facts.

We all shall receive a slap for a slap, and we all shall receive a love for a love.

An open and loving heart is the foundation to Salvation.

Salvation is the direction to Everlasting Life. But also keep in mind; you must take care of yourself and your Angel-within before you can help others.

Prejudging is from the dog and not from an open heart.

Now add our own prejudging to the loss of a complete communicative understanding between Angels and humans and then you have the mistranslations – the pollution and corruption of the Bibles.

Another example of dog desires are near-death experiences (NDEs).

People who report NDEs most often claim to be in a garden-like setting. Such a setting fits closely to their religious beliefs. Their vision of Heaven, that might be a garden setting, is of the dog, the way they desire Heaven to be. Heaven is the state of mind, not a place, just as Hell is a state of mind, not a place.

People who have had NDEs that include Heaven may actually be being told they have had good lives so far or are being reminded to keep Heaven in their minds and not to stray. But their vision of Heaven can instead be from the dog thoughts that they have lived a good and righteous life.

The people who experience Hell in their NDEs may actually be being warned to change their lives or suffer the consequences. Or their visions of Hell can be from the dog within them knowing that they are living a bad life instead.

The Angels - God allows us to experience NDEs to our liking in which we can understand. We shall see the Light (our Heaven) as we desire to see it, for all is symbolic.

All is possible with God. Only the dog makes mistakes; God does not make mistakes.

Mistakes that humans, the dogs, make try to assert domination over others.

As an example, a human will become defensive if another causes him to have doubt about his religion or his God. Anger will cause the human to lash out in words or actions against the other. Thus, we have wars that have been fought since the dawn of time.

Another example of humans making mistakes is when one becomes angry when someone catches him in a lie or catches him making a mistake.

Do not expect anyone to be more righteous than you in the eyes of God, and yet, do not expect to be more righteous than others, for we are not better or worse than others. Even clergymen are human. Each of us makes mistakes, for we are of the dog.

Jesus said to me, "Read the Bible... use it to help understand how people lived long ago. But do not believe all that is written within its pages."

Understand that all the people and that includes those who wrote the Bibles, and those of the Bibles, did things for their own desires, wants and needs. I tried desperately to refrain from letting my dog interfere with writing this book. The control that I used in writing is the same control we must all use in living with our Angels-within. Let your Angel-within lead your life. Then you shall be headed in the right direction for Everlasting Life in the Light.

Separate the dog from the Angel-within. Understand the difference between the dog and the Angel-within. Let the Angel-within control the dog. That is taking the next step toward God.

Now we need to explore the inter-windings of life.

Your life is interwoven with your family's lives; and these lives are interlaced and woven together with all other lives. For all that you do and experience is intertwined and interwoven with all other lives.

All that you and your family do or experience combines with all that your friends and family friends do and experience. All actions from you, your family and from friends and strangers cause re-actions from each other. Therefore, all life is interwoven and interlaced into one, for we are one, and yet we view things from our eyes alone. We, the dog, as individuals, see all things as if you are the center of the universe - All others' lives are interwoven around your life. The individual must be aware of this and not follow any person, group, government, religion or cult that dominates to control you. But individuals must be watchful of groups whose ideas, concepts, laws or rules are geared to fit the particular needs or agenda of their leaders, group, government, religion or cult.

God's Concept of Life is for the best interest of the human - the individual's ideas, thoughts, concepts and the individual's direction of life. And no individual or group should consider suicide or any other action that the individual knows (feels) in his heart is wrong and not being done for the good of humanity and for God. We, combined together as the human race along with all other things, are God, for all is One.

THE ANGEL WITHIN

Each of us has an Angel-within, and if you step back from your present experiences of life and outside of this reality and view the different positions of Angels in transition from God to us, you will see that in the Master's Plan (God's Knowledge of All) is the congregation of Angels and that is God. Your Angel, while in the Light, is part of that congregation; therefore, your Angel, when there, is part of God. And, your body is the vessel that God dwells within – an Angel of God who "experiences life" within your body.

An Angel when outside the Light, either returning to earth to live again or when visiting with people or doing whatever the Angel wishes, is still an Angel, but this Angel could be called an Entity.

(An Entity is something existing objectively or in the mind; an actual or conceivable being, whereas, existence as opposed to nonexistence.)

An Entity out of the Light can have a meaningful purpose. Any and all Angels in the Light have a purpose and are part of God; therefore, an Entity with purpose is called an Angel. An Angel that dwells within a human also has a purpose. It does not matter if its purpose is good or bad, this Entity is still referred to as an Angel.

Angels are energy. They do not have mass or matter as we do.

All matter is a concept of God and only exist in this reality that God has created, and He created it for us, His creation is life.

While you are alive, your Angel dwells within your body. You and your Soul are not your Angel. You, your Soul and your Angel are not referred to as an Entity by God if you do not have a purpose in life.

(Entities in time will find purpose for their existence, be it of God or Satanic idealism. This will be discussed later in this book.)

To make the relationship better understood between the part of God that is the Angel, the Soul and the human, I will use the metaphor of a computer's hard drive as God, a floppy disk as the Angel-within, a file as your Soul, and you, the human, as the experience that is being recorded.

You are the one who lives the experiences as your life is transcribed upon your Soul, which is like the file on a floppy disk. (Actions are energy) Your Angel-within is like the floppy disk that carries your file to God, the Master Computer hard drive.

Your Angel that dwells within your body may have had many previous lives. And whereas, the Angel Jo indicated that she and my Angel have had hundreds of lives together. No person lives more than once, and no Soul experiences life more than once.

These past lives are memories (Energy) that cover your Angel like veils. The memories of lives past and present can either cover your Angel with love or malice. These are engraved memories on your Angel-within and form the attitude that you project toward yourself and all others.

One of the definitions of "attitude" is "position of the body," as suggesting some thought or feeling... state of mind.

The state of your mind is the memories (Energy) of your Angel-within. State of mind after death is either Heaven or Hell. The state of mind of your Angel-within while you are alive is your personality and character. Personality and character are the causes of your actions toward yourself and others. Therefore, our past lives' Heavens or Hells help influence our attitude in this present life. Likewise, our present life's actions combine with our Angel's previous lives that are engraved into the Angel-within to form our Heaven or Hell after death.

Bad experiences (Energy) of past and present lives contaminate and tarnish our Angel-within while Good experiences (Energy) of past and present lives improve and brighten our Angel's glow, allowing the Angel to sing and rejoice in the Light.

A friend recently said to me, "Angels cannot be corrupted... there is no corruption in God."

My reply was, "You are right that there is no corruption in God, for that is why God does not allow corrupted Angels to enter the Light.

"All Angels are part of God. That is why they will not allow themselves to enter the Light, God, if they contain evil.

"God created everything, as a true artist He would have destroyed anything that He created that was evil or ugly. He created the concept of evilness for us to know the difference between right and wrong. Man created the action of evilness.

"Angels call beings 'Entities' that do not have meaningful existence. To Angels, Entities do not have a meaningful existence. For all things less than 'of God' are meaningless to Angels. The Unguided Ones and Non-Conformed Ones have meaning of existence, but are of evil. Angels have a righteous, meaningful life. Therefore, any that are not on missions of God are Entities and could contain corruption, but these are not in the Light or part of God and will not allow themselves entry into the Light."

(We will discuss what and who the Unguided Ones and Non-Conformed Ones are later in this book.)

The Angel's counterpart, the human and others can and should help the Angels within us overcome the bad memories of past lives. The Angel's counterpart, the human and others need to help remove the Hells that cover our Angels within. For not all dog feelings are bad. Just as your pet dog or cat can show you love and affection, we need to show love to our Angel-within, and all other Angels, and all other humans. By showing love to yourself and others, you open your heart.

(When I speak of "loving yourself," I speak of loving the Angel-within, for your Angel-within is part of God – all Angels, and also, to love yourself... the human that you are, because you are part of the congregation of humanity that God has created.)

During the spring of 1998, I noticed that whenever the Angel Jo or Jesus talked with me, they started calling me or referring to me as "Jacob."

One night as I talked with the Angel Jo, I asked her, "Should I change my name to Jacob, as Jesus changed the names of some of his disciples?"

She replied, "No, your name is David. The Angel that dwells within you has many names, but most know him as Jacob."

This body of mine is named David while Jacob is the Angel within me. My body is his house. Jacob is part of God, therefore this vessel, my body, is a house of God, just as your body is also a house of God. Therefore, now that I love myself, I am loving Jacob, who is part of God, and therefore, I am loving God.

When the Angel Jo or Jesus talked with me and referred to me as "Jacob," I knew that I had allowed the Angel Jacob who is within me to lead my life, for at those times I had an open heart.

Opening your heart results in the removal of bad memories (Energy) from your Angel-within, and this is the removal of Hell that covers your Angel-within, and then your Angel-within is obtaining good and Heavenly new memories (Energy) from the Angel's past life.

This past life that I speak of is your present life too, for after your death your present life will be in the past. Each and every day is a new start for the rest of your life, Genesis.

(Genesis is the beginning of new things).

For each prior day is the past and the past is forever, and therefore, every previous day of your life is part of your past life, and so it is with the Angel-within you.

To help others is to help yourself, and whereas helping others is uncovering your Angel- within as well as helping others remove their Hells. Doing only for yourself is not helping your Angel-within or others. Doing only for yourself is covering your Angel-within with bad memories, and that is Hell. Therefore, you must help yourself before you can help others. When you help yourself and others, you are projecting "feelings" of good Energy.

You must understand that your present personality and character are directed by memories from your past as well as your past lives. You also must understand that you are in control of your actions. You (the dog) control your Angel that is within. Once you uncover your Angel, then you will be allowing the Angel-within you to lead the dog with an open heart.

Giving your Angel-within good and Heavenly thoughts about your past life is the Salvation to Everlasting Life.

(Salvation is the direction to Everlasting Life and Heaven.)

Again, I speak of this life as being your past life after you die. For after you die, if you had a good life, then your memories of your life's Energy will place your thoughts in Heaven.

If believing Jesus died on the cross for your Sins helps you to open your heart and you live with an open heart, then you have found your Salvation to Everlasting Life. Or if you believe in Mohammad or any other Prophet that is said to be of God or any other religion said to be of God while keeping an open heart then you also have found your Salvation to Everlasting Life. The religion or belief that you follow does not matter as long as your belief and religion do not condone domination to yourself or others.

Christianity believes Jesus died in order for us to be saved. Judaism does not believe that Jesus was the Son of God. The big difference between Christianity and Judaism is not the belief in Jesus, but instead is the rules and laws found in the Torah that the Jewish faith follows that Christians do not follow but do read about some of them in the Old Testament. And while Islam says that Jesus was simply a Prophet of God who they believe escaped crucifixion, and Muslims believe Mohammad is the only Prophet of God. But Mohammad is the only one mentioned in any bible that says he talked with the Angel Gabrael, in a cave. God's Angels do not have to hide in a darken cave when they communicate with humans!

Yet each of these three Religions use a different name for God. The name does not change who God is for He is One... He is All. "All" includes you and me for our Angels are all a part of God, and each human is part of the congregation of humanity.

Jesus lived and died. The Bible stories about Him may be manipulated or twisted a little in order for people of the Christian faith to believe that He died for them, but it is an historical fact that He lived and died.

God does not condemn us for Jesus being murdered. We did not kill Him. Our forefathers crucified Him, and whereas if we believe that we killed Him, then we have condemned ourselves.

God does not condemn women because of what is said to have happened concerning Adam and Eve in the Garden of Eden.

If women believe that Eve was the cause for our expulsion from the Garden of Eden, then they have condemned themselves. The men who wrote the Bible story about Adam and Eve decided that women were less than men because the men wrote the story for control over their people. In God there is not rank among people or His Angels.

If we as United States Citizens believe that we are responsible for the black slavery of the past, then we have condemned ourselves. Yet in fact, it was the European Catholics, who first shipped blacks as slaves from Africa. If you study the history of black slavery you will discover that whenever individual tribes in Africa conquered another tribe they enslaved them, and then the white men from Europe came along and traded steel bars for their slaves.

(And in reality, the taking of slaves goes back to the beginning of recorded history that whenever one group defeated another group, the defeated group always became slaves.)

We did not cause any of these things; our forefathers were responsible for them.

Humans wrote our damnation into the Bibles for human reasons - Domination and control of others. I have met and talked with the Angel Jesus many times. I know that the Angel Jesus does exist.

The Angel Jo has told me, "He is the most Forgiving of all in the Light."

And I know from my conversations with Jesus that He does not hold us accountable for His death.

Neither God nor Jesus has condemned us for what our forefathers did. We as individuals are responsible for our actions alone. Our Angel within condemns or rewards itself for what we have done and followed during our lives, and then at the end of time God will judge us as individuals.

When Jesus was alive, He also had an Angel-within. Moses and all others in Biblical history also had Angels within themselves. These are the ones that let their Angels from within lead their lives. Their lives were for God... the same as saying, "Their lives were for all other humans." They lived with open hearts.

The Concept of God: "To learn and experience from the experiences of others through endurance of life."

(This Concept will be explored in detail later in this book, but for now realize the Bibles was written with that intention in mind.)

We learn about God from reading His Books, our Bibles. We learn about the lives of Biblical characters by reading our Bibles. We learn how to live by reading our Bibles. We share the Biblical characters' experiences by reading our Bibles. You also are learning and experiencing through our experiences by reading this book.

Talking with others and also through written communication, we learn and experience what others have experienced in their lives... and that is God's Concept of Life. Angels also learn and experience by our lives. For each and every person will have different actions and feelings to a given situation. Even though events people experience may be as a group, each person will take different actions and have different feelings from that same event. Our individuality is what separates our experiences, and our different reactions to the situation or event are what the Angels are seeking - our individual experiences of life.

To understand what life is all about is God's Concept of Life and will help us uncover our Angel-within.

My past lives were full of tragedies and Hells. If you have read our first book, Together Forever Before The Light, you are aware of a few of my past lives. For now, I will tell you about one very significant life that I was not aware of, which the Angel Jo had to reveal to me.

The Angel Jo said, "You cannot blame yourself for what has happened... you did not cause it to happen. Around the late 1500s, your father at that time abused you... others abused you. When you were a little older, you fought back... you killed many before you were killed. This is what is covering your Angel. You must remove this hatred... on this Side... what you call the Other Side... once you were the most forgiving... other than Jesus... I am sorry for what happened to you."

Jo's telling me about this past life revealed to me the things that I experienced. I had to remove the Hells that covered my Angel-within, for now I knew what some of my Hells were. With the help of the Angel Jo, Jesus and Gabrael, my Angel-within now could be renewed and uncovered. My self-Judgment and the understanding of my past lives, along with my continual practice of keeping an open heart for myself and all others, is the key for me to find Salvation and Everlasting Life, just as it is for you.

THE SOUL

And the Angel Jo said, "The Soul is like a tree, for at your birth, the seed of your Soul starts to grow along with the dog. If you allow the winds of Sin to blow upon your Soul, it will be bent. If you protect your Soul, it will grow straight and true."

At your birth, an Angel enters into your body. Your Soul is the recorded memory of your life; the energy of the actions and reactions of your life, and is every thought and feeling that you had during your life. And therefore at your birth, your memory is little, and through life your memory grows as your energy of experiences grows. Experiences of life are your memory, just as your energy is the experiences of your life.

The roots of your Soul are memories from past lives. The trunk of your Soul is your present life. The limbs of your Soul are the different directions you travel through your life. The trunk and the limbs are your eternal thoughts from your birth to the death of your body. Your tree of life feeds from its roots. Thus, past lives filter from your Angel-within into your Soul to all that you experience, as well as all that was engraved upon your DNA that you inherited from your ancestors. Your Soul is your complete memory that is Energy and will live forever. Once you die, your body starts to decay back into what it came from. Your Soul is constant for it is Energy. Energy, the Soul, does not decay, nor does it change after death, for after death you cannot go back and change what you thought or did.

The body leaves the Soul when the body dies; the Soul does not leave the body.

(The word "leaves" means to change location and/or direction.)

At the moment of death, the matter that made up the body changes directions and starts to change location as it transforms into other things while the Soul remains constant as it was prior to death of the body.

THE CONCEPT OF LIFE, which I will explain later, is the same in terms of your outlook on others as it is with you. "*To learn and experience from experiences of others through the endurance of life."* Your Angel learns and experiences your endurance of life through your Soul.

After your death, the Angel-within will incorporate with your Soul into your Angel's experiences, and then these will be added into God's experiences when your Angel reunites with God in the Light, for the Light is all Knowledge and Experiences.

In the beginning, all is innocent... Genesis. At birth, you and your Soul are innocent. Both you and your Soul learn and experience through your endurances of life.

God's Master Plan does include all experiences, the feeling of doing things. The true feeling of individual actions and reactions to concepts, ideas, thoughts, sights, events and actions cannot be taught. It must be experienced. Our actions and reactions must be experienced through life. Your experiences are engraved into your Soul, be they good or bad experiences. And while God's Master Plan includes everything in the past, present and future, our reactions to our decisions is "Experiences to the Unknown Future" – experiencing the outcome of our choices is what life is all about. After life, the experiences (memory) of the one who just entered Heaven are joined with all others in the Light, for then the experiences (memories) of that individual that have lived becomes part of the congregation of all Angels – God and that is the Knowledge that all Angels share.

Good experiences will allow your Angel-within to rejoice and sing when it returns to the Light. Bad experiences will cause your Angel-within to desire the need to return for another life or may keep your Angel from going near the Light. But the dog, you, will surly die at the end of your life.

(Your Soul is the Energy of your thought processing your past, and your present, and your future memories that will never die, for energy cannot be destroyed. Therefore, your Soul will unite forever with the Angel-within you as the human body returns to dirt.)

Your Soul is the intelligent thinking part of you. Intelligence is what God placed into man when He created man and is what separates us from animals. The thinking part of you, your Soul, does not contain many experiences at the moment of your birth, but yet it grows into the volumes of knowledge that you have experienced (endured) by the end of your life. This thinking part of you, your Soul, is what will live forever in Heaven, good thoughts within God.

Only you, the dog, can go back and make restitution for your mistakes; your Soul cannot do so by itself. After your death, you will think very much as you presently do. You will still have feelings as well as a better understanding of God and life while remembering what you did while alive.

Your Soul will live forever with the knowledge of what you did, right or wrong, during your life.

Saving of the Soul is making sure your Soul is worthy of becoming part of the Angel-within. Keep your Soul pure so the Angel-within you can rejoin and sing with God in the Light. Protecting the Angel-within from Sin is assuring the Angel-within will have Everlasting Life in the Light. Letting your Angel-within lead you through the endurances of life is living with an open heart. These are the keys to Salvation and Living Forever; to learn and experience from the experiences of others through their endurance of life.

Believing that Jesus died on the cross for you or any other religious belief does not change the truth. Believe in what you will, but you must live with an open heart and let the Angel-within to you lead your life to find Salvation and everlasting life with God. For you shall reap what you sow... A Love for a Love is the same as a slap for a slap.

God is not dominating He will allow you to follow your own religion and He lets us do anything else that we desire. His Ultimate Rules will become reality after death, for when once life is over you cannot go back and change what you did.

Let me continue to talk about your Soul as being a file to the Angel-within (your floppy diskette) and God as the Master Computer.

Past lives can corrupt the Angel-within with bad memories, and while the memories from previous lives do bleed over onto your present day life, your file. Those past memories are part of the essence of your present day character and personality.

Subconsciously, our personal actions and reactions are directed by past lives of our Angel-within, and what was recorded on our DNA, and what our parents and peers have taught us. What our Angel-within has endured and what was recorded upon our DNA can be demonstrated through past life regression under hypnosis. But many times one will refuse to recognize past life experiences, as I did concerning my life in the late 1500s about which the Angel Jo had to refresh my memory. (We will go into that life later in this book.)

Many times we will try to protect ourselves from experiencing bad things, for our Angel-within may have experienced similar circumstances before during past lives or our DNA holds memories that remind us of things. When this happens, sometimes our actions can be hostile toward others or ourselves. Sometimes we cannot understand why we take this defensive action. In reality, we may be trying to keep from covering our Angel-within with undesirable events or we may do not want to experience it again. Usually when this happens, we are using a defense against an imaginary foe, thus protecting our Soul from what might happen. We are not protecting our Soul from what will happen, but rather from things we think could happen. In turn, we are protecting our Angel-within from obtaining more bad character and personality attitude – Hells. But when we try to protect ourselves in this manner, we are fighting an enemy from within because then our enemy is our bad experiences from past lives. Therefore, we become our own enemy.

When Jesus was placed on trial, those that testified against Him were not his enemy. When Jesus was ordered to death, the ones who judged Him were not his enemy. When they crucified Him, they were not His enemy. Their actions were part of the Master Plan, which He knew could not be changed because He knew that the future that contained Christianity also contained His death. Therefore, we cannot change the future, but we can protect our Angels from Sin, just as Jesus could not change what others wished to do to Him, but He could and did protect His Angel-within from the Sin of hatred for those who wanted Him dead.

We cannot change what others think of us. If we could change the feelings of others, we would be placing ourselves in the Sin of Dominating, for those who condemn without just reasons are fighting their enemies from within themselves. For those who fight their enemies from within, have in fact placed themselves in the Sin of Self-domination.

If we condemn others without just reasons, then we are condemning ourselves to our enemies within us, for then we are covering our Angel-within with fear of others, and that is Self-domination.

Your present good life will uncover your Angel-within, and help remove past bad memories from your Angel-within.

Your Soul, your file that is contained in your Angel-within, is only one file of maybe many past life files that your Angel-within has experienced.

All Angels are messengers of God and all Angels carry the files of human life experiences to God. Your file, your Soul, shall be carried to God by your Angel, and then you shall live with God in the Light forever.

If you live a good life with an open heart, then your Angel-within shall rejoice upon your death. If your life was bad, then you are covering and smothering your Angel-within with Hell and your Angel-within will be sad when you die because your death stopped it from enjoying more evilness in your lifetime.

GUARDIAN ANGELS

Many articles and books have been written about Guardian Angels. People around the world over the years have reported being rescued from living wrongly, and traumas, and possible death by their Guardian Angels. Since they do exist, what are Guardian Angels and what are their missions?

I feel that Guardian Angels should be called Mentor Angels because not only are they there whenever you truly need help but they also seem to help guide us through troubled times. A Mentor Angel seems to naturally fit into one's human life. In which they watch over one's life and a Mentor Angel's actions can usually help people change their way of thinking, while directing one in the righteous course of life.

Life begins at conception. For the length of time that the mother carries the child inside her, the child is the same as any unborn animal on earth.

The human body cannot support two Angels for a long span of time. If the unborn baby's Angel would enter the mother's body too soon, then the mother's immune system would try to fight it off. Thus, the mother's immune system would eventually destroy both her and child. The Angel has approximately three days from the moment of birth to enter the newborn body. But usually, this entry is made at the moment of birth.

(Before continuing in detail about Mentors/Guardian Angels, I would like to say something with regards to when life begins. I always thought that life began at birth. With the realization and understanding about the Other Side and the Master Plan of God, the Angel Jo has shown me that life begins at conception. That is, all animal life begins at conception. Human life is intelligent life, and begins the moment the Angel enters the human body, which is usually the first second after birth. Humans are no more than any other animal until the Angel enters the body. And whereas, the Angel-within is what separates us from animals, for animals do not contain the intelligence that God placed into humans. Humans have the capabilities of understanding and reasoning - comprehending, which is part of God's gift of intelligence to humans. His gift is to love, to have compassion, to reason and to care for others and those are part of comprehension. Animals merely think of themselves and their needs.)

In the Light, before the newborn child takes its first breath, selection of the child's Angel has taken place. This selection is mainly voluntary. The child's life is part of God's Master Plan, but the Angels are in Heaven – the Light – the Knowledge of all the experiences of all that has lived, the child has not lived yet and its life is not part of the Knowledge yet. The Angel that wishes to live this child's life is selected to do so.

Once this Angel leaves the Light, most of its Knowledge is repressed. The Angel who is on the route to the position of the Angel-within knows little more than the baby that it is entering.

The selected Angel then becomes an Angel-within when it enters the child's body.

The Angel-within of the newborn child is "living" for experiences. If the Angel-within had the Knowledge, it would know of All, and therefore it would not obtain experiences from the child's actions and reactions of the unknown future, and would not "grow" along with the child.

The Light places an Angel to guide this newly re-born Angel-within. The Light will watch the child "grow" through events in the child's life.

Just as the selection of the Angel to be within the child takes place before the birth of the child, the selected overseeing Angel also is voluntarily selected. This guiding and helping Angel is called the Mentor Angel. The Mentor Angel helps only in guiding the Angel-within while the Angel-within proceeds in directing its human counterpart and experiencing life through its human counterpart. With the Mentor Angel's help, the Angel-within begins to recall (learn) memory about the Other Side. The Mentor Angel does not personally direct the human body. That position is left up to the Angel-within. But the Mentor Angel will intervene if needed.

The Mentor Angel teaches the Angel-within about the Other Side in the same manner that parents teach their children about life.

(For a moment, let us consider the words "learn," "teach" and "remember." How much memory is stored in our DNA? Our ancestry is actually written in our DNA. Therefore, does a parent or teacher really teach us history, or are they just helping us to recall our past? Are we taught about history, or do we remember it? A newly born child contains an Angel that has just come from the Light. The Angel-within has lost its memory of the Light; therefore, does the Mentor Angel teach or help the Angel-within remember its past? Does the newly re-born Angel-within learn about the Light, or does the Angel-within remember it?)

By the time a human's life comes to an end, its mission complete, the

Angel-within should be ready again to enter the Light.

In other words, the Mentor should have taught the Angel-within nearly all about the Light. This is one of the reasons why people usually become more religious and wiser as they grow older and approach death. But a problem can and does occur by humans teaching of religion designed by human agendas.

As the Angel-within readies to enter into the Light again, it should have "lived" the experiences it desired to have. The Angel-within is then full, complete and proud to become part of the body of God again with Everlasting Life.

All Angels are great Mentors and can teach other Angels well.

The problem most often occurs with the teaching from parents and other humans here on earth. A battle between doing right or wrong exists within us all. This battle is between following our Angel's guidance versus doing what the flesh desires, and all religions were created by man for the domination of his fellow man.

Desire of the flesh is doing things that make us feel good. The taste of that chocolate cake that we know will add inches to our waist... the thrill of driving too fast... the thrill of forbidden sex... things we know that will harm us or others... things that are domination to ourselves and others, and like thinking, "I follow the true God and yours is false...therefore I am saved and you are not."

Sometimes an Angel-within will lose a battle. And once in a great while a Mentor Angel may have to intervene. When this happens, we call this Angel our Guardian Angel, who in reality is our Mentor Angel. Therefore, we call our Mentor Angel our Guardian Angel because guarding or protecting us is all we have seen it do.

The occurrence of seeing one's Guardian Angel usually will redirect the human and will void the winning of the flesh, and thus putting that individual back on the right track.

Just as we do in our human life, the God does not like to correct something its Angel-within did wrongly. We would rather let the student realize and repair his own mistakes. In the same manner, God does not like stepping in to correct something the Angel-within was unable to control. Therefore, the Mentor Angel does not wish to override the Angel's inability to direct the human, but will do so if needed. But all actions, even the bad, are part of the Knowledge of God, for we are merely doing what is known by God to happen. And even the need for a Guardian Angel to step in is part of the known Knowledge of God.

The moral convictions of our conscience are the Angel-within, and the feelings of our flesh are of the dog. There is a fine line between human and the Angel; the experiences and feelings are the Soul. And the Soul is the file that connects the human memory (Energy) to the Angel-within.

Many times the Mentor Angel and your Angel-within will not prevent you from doing bad or wrong things. The choice is left up to you and all that happens was needed to happen.

They will try to advise you, but will not demand. And this is the area where many humans will say, "God moves in mysterious ways."

For example, why did God allow someone to die or be murdered?

Maybe their time was up and their mission was completed. Perhaps their life and death were lessons for another. Or maybe their mission was only to grandfather a child not yet born.

Whatever the reason, it is a piece of the Master Plan and the unstopped action was meant to be.

The Master Plan does involve every step in getting to the final event. Whereas, the Master Plan says each part of every step one must travel is needed to come to a certain point at a given time.

Humans think that the individual steps in getting to a given point at a certain time are left up to us, but if we do not arrive at this point then our Guardian Angel will step in and guide us back on track.

The human, nor his Angel-within know where they must be in reference to this certain point at a given time. The Angel-within is learning, just as its human counterpart learns and experiences. But the learning and experiencing of the Angel-within should have enabled it with understanding and comprehension, to accomplish its actions as needed. However, if the Angel-within could not direct its human counterpart, the Mentor Angel will intervene and help direct the human to that given point at the particular time that was needed.

There are Mentor Angels that do not necessarily watch over or teach only one Angel. Many of these Angels roam, while helping other Angels within many people. The Mentoring Angels may move on to different humans and another Mentor will take its place. And we may not have just one Mentor or Guardian Angel but many.

Angels also often help each other. There is no shame, anger or embarrassment between Angels, for they are One. All are the same and equal. All Angels are part of the total body of God, for there is no rank in God or in the Light.

This simple rule also applies to us because we should not be ashamed or embarrassed if we need help in learning because we are equal to each other...we are all human. But, as humans we have been taught rank to control many by a few.

One part of your body is not ashamed, angered or embarrassed if

Holy Graduel

another part of your body has to help it. Is your left hand ashamed if your right hand is needed to lift a heavy object?

We should not be angered, ashamed or embarrassed if we help someone or if they assist us. But neither should we expect help. God helps those that help themselves. Faith and belief must be learned and experienced. Your faith and belief in yourself is the same as the faith and belief in God, for we all are part of God because we are part of His creation, and He did not place rank in His creation.

If the Angels and God would reveal themselves to us, then we would not need faith and belief, nor would we experience learning faith and belief. The same rule applies to our Angel-within having all Knowledge. When we were born, if our Angel-within knew all, then we (the human and an Angel dwelling inside) would not grow through learning and experiences.

To God, we are like children to teach and help, and as children, we need to help each other. And also Angels help us achieve the next level, and whereas, we should help one another.

Accept the Angels help. Lift your Soul. Feel free. Live free. Be free. And Touch free.

Each of us has the power to touch the Other Side, to see into the future and to understand most of the full Plan, but we are not permitted to know the complete future. If we knew the complete future, we would not experience the future as the unknown.

My ability to know the future is sometimes heartbreaking to see. Yes, I do know much of the future. I have the ability to receive the Knowledge of the future if I ask. However, as with all humans, I like to share my Knowledge.

I do not ask because I know that I am not allowed to know all of the future. They will not allow me to know all of the future, lest I tell others what I know.

Knowing someone's future can be overwhelming. Of course I see many good things in everyone's future, but all lives contain tragedies. Tragedies defined in human thinking, but not tragedies when viewed within the Master Plan.

Seeing the future death of a loved one is a tragedy to us. But seeing the future death of one of your own children is the worst tragedy of them all. Death must come...It is inevitable, and for one to live, one must also die someday. Nothing can be done to prevent it. You may be able to change the way death takes that person, but you cannot stop death. And sometimes changing the way a person dies is not allowing them to experience their actions. But seeing death from the Other Side is like welcoming a family member home once again.

If we knew the future, would we wrongly use the Knowledge of the future?

Would we control the stock market if we had the Knowledge?

The answer to these two questions is "yes" because the Knowledge would stop us from learning from our experiences.

I dwelled on the thought of whether humans should know the future, and now I know that the answer is "no."

The Mentor/Guardian Angels teaches only the things that are needed to be known by the Angel-within. And the Mentor/Guardian Angels and the Angel-within will not allow the human to know all.

Do humans block their Knowledge of the future because they cannot deal with tragedies?

Or does the Light block human Knowledge of the future because God knows we could not handle the Knowledge?

The answer is that God blocks us from knowing the future.

He removed the Knowledge from our Angels when they left the Light so we could not dominate others by having such knowledge.

I have my Soul Twin Jo to help me deal with my daily problems and tragedies. She is also my Mentor Angel. But sometimes the Knowledge that she has shared with me is almost too much for me to bear, even with guidance and comfort from her.

She once indicated that she was becoming alarmed that I may have gained too much Knowledge.

I am the same as you, my Angel-within may be unique, but my body is the same as yours. We are allowed to know only those events that we may change, which will not alter the future.

Many times I have asked questions of the Angel Jo concerning events surrounding my coming death. She is very wise and has avoided answering my questions because these are among those things that we should not know. Those are the things that even I, who communicates with the Angels, should not know, but many times people think they know. The answers to questions regarding my fate and that of others come from God alone and not from us, the dogs.

All Angels are here to help us throughout our lives. Your Angel-within also is here to help guide you along life's journey and the uniting with you after death. Your Angel-within may have been someone else's Mentor Angel before you were born. Your Angel-within knows the correct path to Heaven. Allow your Angel-within, who may have once been a Mentor Angel, lead you to God, for your Angel-within may have taken the same road many times before.

Understanding that Mentor Angels are here to help you is one of the first parts of Knowledge of the God. Mentor Angels teach your Angel-within, and in turn your Angel-within guides you to the correct direction of your life.

Peace, love and happiness are yours to enjoy if you will listen to your heart as the Mentor Angels convey God's Words to you through your Angel-within.

Once again, I feel that I am repeating myself, but the word "heart" needs defining. The "Heart" that I speak of is not the central organ of your physical body. The "Heart" that I speak of is your feelings. Angels do not have organs, no eyes to see with and no lungs to expel air as they speak. They see with their feelings, they talk with their feelings and do all with their feelings. When I say to "listen to your heart," I am meaning "listen to your feelings," which is the same as listening to the Angel-within.

This "listening to your feelings" is one of the problems in communicating with the Angels. They do not use verbal language when speaking; they use thoughts. They are Energy, and their thoughts – their communications - are Energy. Therefore, Angels communicate with humans via thoughts.

Have you ever heard a preacher say he heard God tell him something?

He did not actually hear God speaking in verbal words, but rather in his thoughts. And in reality it was not God, but one of God's Angels that he heard.

The stories in the Bibles containing communications between Angels and humans were in thoughts, not verbal communications.

Friends of mine who have communicated with the Angels claim they can hear the Angels actually speaking, but the Angels have told me that these people are so "tuned in" that they think they are hearing verbal communication when it was actually in thoughts.

Many times when one communicates with Angels, one will pollute the received thoughts with one's own thoughts, ideas and concepts. I do not want my own thoughts to enter into what the Angels were saying to me, and that is why I used channeling in my verbal communicating with the Angels. The Angels channeled their thoughts through my wife, Christine, who was under hypnosis during those times. I asked my questions to the Angels and they answered me in thought as Christine verbally spoke the answer that she received from the Angels. When Christine's and my answers from the Angel were the same, then I knew it came directly from the Angel and not from either of us.

During my learning period, I also learned to see with my feelings, just as we all touch others when coming in contact with another's skin. I "see" the Angels with my feelings, not with my eyes.

The Angel Jo once said unto me, "When you are lonely, remember my touch and I am there."

Projected thoughts and/or feelings of bad or good are transmitted toward others. Others can receive your thoughts about your living a good or bad life. These are the same feelings and/or thoughts you have conveyed to the Angel-within that contain your Heaven or Hell that you have made here in this lifetime.

Feelings and/or thoughts of love and goodwill should radiate from your Angel-within to you and all who are near you.

Radiant feelings of love and goodwill from God to your Mentor Angel to your Angel-within will brighten your life. These feelings of love and goodwill need to be passed along to others.

Feelings and thoughts are Energy, either good or bad. Energy of good is Heaven. Energy of bad is Hell. God is Good, whereas the Light is Good, too. Your Soul is your life experiences, and Your Guardian Angel is Good, and all is Energy. The choice of being just Energy of bad or Good is left up to you.

EQUAL

Many years ago, when I was still in the music industry, a songwriter friend of mine played a song that was written by another friend. I cannot remember all of the song, but one line struck me and I can still recall it: "I will not be afraid when Jesus comes; I will be ashamed."

Two ideas will be discussed in this chapter, fear and shame, to help you understand that your Angel is equal to all Angels and you are equal to all other humans.

One Saturday night, Christine, along with our oldest son, Tony, and I were spending a quiet evening at home. Around ten-thirty while Christine and Tony were in the living room watching television as I sat at our dining room table, silently in thought I asked the Angel Jo to reveal herself to our son. Soon Christine drifted off to sleep, and within a few seconds the Angel Jo once again was in her body.

As Christine awoke, Tony knew immediately it was not his mother but Jo who occupied his mother's body. With her eyes closed, she stood up and walked over to me as I too, stood up and held out my open arms to her. Jo and I embraced and kissed, and then she then turned her attention to Tony and hugged him with her left arm while she ran her right hand over his face. Through closed eyes, she wept as her fingertips touched his eyelids and his forehead and then she ran her fingers down his cheek.

She said, "Do not be afraid, I cry because for all the love that I see within you."

(If you look up the word "entity" in the dictionary, you will find this definition: "Something existing objectively in the mind; an actual or conceivable being. Existence as opposed to nonexistence."

(One could say an Entity is then any being not like animals, and Angels and God are therefore Entities, for they have an objective to exist. Animals do not have an objective to exist except for their inward feelings and because their instinct to procreate is merely for the feelings that they will obtain from of the act instead of realizing that procreation is needed for the continuation of their breed.)

Do not fear Entities, for you also contain an Entity, your Angel-within. Therefore, do not fear other Angels, for they are the same as the Angel within you. Do not fear God, for you - your Angel-within, is part of Him. For once you leave this world and pass to the Other Side you will be part of God because you too, your life experience was the reason for you to exist.

Do you fear yourself? Of course not, then should you fear God or any Entity?

Part of God is presently inside you, for all Angels and Entities are also of God.

So when the Angel Jo told Tony, "Do not be afraid," she actually meant, "Do not be afraid of me, for I am the same as you."

As the song that the friend wrote; "I will not be afraid when Jesus comes; I will be ashamed."

So when Jesus returns to earth, do not fear Him, for we are the same as Him.

I see my Angel-within as part of God. I see my Soul as some day being part of God. I see myself someday being part of God. I do not fear myself, so why would I fear Jesus for He also is part of God. I see myself as being equal to part of God, for God is All and I am part of All, so therefore I am part of God, who is All... I do not fear myself; therefore, I shall not fear God, or Jesus, or any Angel or Entity.

I have met with Jesus many times and I feel equal with Him, for He is an Angel just like the one that is within me. Granted, His Angel is greatly brighter than mine, but they both are Angels. And in my meeting with Gabrael I felt the same, for both our Angels also are both the same, too.

A person once told me his church said when you die, you would go to Heaven and spend eternity on your knees, praising God forever.

When I reach the Light, I shall not fall down on my knees and praise God forever. I shall not fall down upon my knees and praise myself forever. I will rejoice with God because my mission will then be over, and God and I are One.

You and God are One. You are also equal to any part of God.

But fear is what the churches have been preaching to us. Fear of going to Hell. Fear of God's Judgment. Fear, Fear, Fear... unless you give them money and do all the things they say are righteous, you are going to burn in Hell. If you listen and do as they say... then you would swear we are merely God's toys and slaves to Him.

Do you truly believe God would have put us through this human life if He made us to be His slaves? He would have made us His slaves in the first place because life would not be needed then.

I heard a preacher state there is one place in the Bible that says, "To get to Heaven one must come through life here on Earth first." That statement truly indicates we were not made to be God's slaves.

I only know the Bibles by what the Angels have told me, "You came from the Light and you shall once again return to the Light after death."

God told His story for humans to record His Words.

Jesus' life story was written many years after his death and it was handed down orally from generation to generation before it was transcribed. And His story...Jesus' life story demonstrated how we should live...that we should Love each other as He did.

The Bible was written by humans for humans and then translated by humans for humans. Not all the parts of the Bibles are true, for man wrote domination into the stories of the Bibles in order to control people. Read your Bible, follow the precepts in your Bible, but do not dominate nor let it or anything dominate you. If others wish to allow their Bibles or anything else dominate them, that is their concern not yours.

Do not be afraid of God, Angels, Entities or Souls. They are your equals.

Occasionally you may cross paths with an Unguided One or a Non-Conformed One. These we see as ghost we might fear because they may be trying to make you do harm to yourself or others, but they cannot hurt you. If you have Love - good thoughts in your mind - Heaven in your heart, they will leave. If they do not leave on their own, other Angels will remove them for you, if that is want you desire.

The Christian Bible states, if you see a ghost just asked it if he is of God, he must answer truthfully. I have discovered that Angels of God can and do talk (communicate) with humans. While Evil Ones (Unguided Ones and Non-Conformed Ones) cannot talk to you.

Even the Unguided Ones and the Non-Conformed Ones do not have more power than you and you may even be stronger than they, but you are at least their equal. Do not be afraid of them. God is within you, He is not with them.

We see what we wish to see. If you desire to see evil in others, you will see their evil. If you wish to see love in others, then you shall see their love. If you wish to see ghost, then you shall see ghost. If you desire to see Angels, then you shall see Angels, for you command your own life.

The ones to fear are those still in human bodies. As you know, humans can cause great pain and damage to each other. I will not try to explain what actions should be taken against them. I will leave that up to the experts on human psychology and law enforcement. However, do not fear or feel less than any human for he is also your equal. Once in a great while you may find someone who actually is an enemy, but most of the time, our true enemies are within us. Therefore, our true enemies come from within ourselves.

We experience fear of the unknown, but the unknown future is something we must all experience. And while sometimes fear is actually needed to save one' self or others, but God is not the unknown. God is Love. Our personality is our Soul. Our Angel-within is part of God therefore, our actions should be that of God and Love for our actions come from within.

A Soul is innocent until taught otherwise.

Love is the natural way of an Angel, and while Domination is alien to an Angel.

Domination is natural to the dog because it is the center of its universe and it views everything as if he is god where everything was created around him and only for him.

Domination comes from seeing life only through your eyes; all you see is for your enjoyment.

You must blend all, your Soul, your Angel and your human feelings together. Enjoy life, but do not dominate. Life is enjoyed when you open your heart to others as an Angel does, for you are part of God. Do as God does, experience and enjoy all that does not dominate.

"Yea, when I walk into the Light, I will rejoice and sing for I have forgiven all others and myself. I am free of Hell. I carry Heaven in my heart forever. I have nothing to hide for I am equal to all parts of God."

Knowing you have nothing to hide about your life helps you open your heart. Opening your heart makes you equal to all parts of God for you too are part of God.

Forgiveness is the key to true reality about oneself. Everyone makes mistakes. Everyone should be forgiven. You are not God. I am not God. We make mistakes and we should be forgiven by ourselves. You should forgive yourself of all your wrong doings, for now you are the only one who knows all the bad things you have done during your life; your peers and friends do not know of you. But once you enter the Other Side, all your peers and friends there will know your life complete. To be equal to all parts of God you must forgive as God forgives all we have done.

The color of our skin does not separate us, for we are equal. Do not be afraid because someone is of different color. Humans have different colors, Angels do not. Our Angels are all the same. God is not a different color than your Angel, for we combined together are Him.

The same thing applies to language and disabilities. These things may

Holy Graduel

make us seem different now, but our Angels are the same.

Color, language and disabilities are no different than you or I wearing a different hat from the other. All of us are equal for all of us are part of God.

Shame... your accounts or actions of having done something wrong is something we all experience, too, because repentance is the learning and now knowing the difference between right and wrong.

It is okay to be embarrassed or ashamed of something you did or said.

This something that you may have done may only be something stupid or dumb as buttoning your shirt one buttonhole off. Little things as buttoning your shirt wrong should not change or hurt anyone's life, but it may embarrass you.

It is not okay to do things of domination to yourself or others. These things will cause your shame to form into Hell from which there may be no escape.

Shame is pretty well the same as a sin, as both are things that we did wrong that will embarrass us. Sins are much bigger than most of our embarrassments for they cause change in our life experiences. Examples of sins are domination, stealing, etc., etc.

Examples of shame are having someone tell you your zipper is down or going to a beach party in formal dress.

Sins of domination and such that cause shame because of the things that we did or have done are the causes of the sadness all Angels feel on the Other Side.

It is okay to feel sadness for another's actions, but you are not responsible for their action, so therefore, do not be shameful of another's action.

It is okay to feel shame or even feel stupid for your actions once in a while. And I think all people have done things that are sinful. You should feel shame for doing sinful things, but you should have repented from your past thoughts.

To know Heaven we should experience Hell during at least one lifetime. God has forgiven you for doing things of sin, as you must also forgive yourself for doing them.

(Experiencing Hell does not mean that we have done things that are Hell, we could have merely seen others doing things of Hell.)

Not forgiving yourself is Hell. Forgiving is part of Heaven.

All but Jesus has sinned. You are not Jesus. I am not Jesus. We have sinned. Unless we forgive ourselves, we will not find Heaven here on earth or on the Other Side.

The statement, "Forgive those that have trespassed against us," includes you as well as everyone else, and whereas, you may forgive the people who trespassed against you, but you do not forgive the act. But all decisions are yours, and therefore, you do not have to forgive unless you want to.

Domination that destroys human life should not be forgiven by us and is not forgiven by God. Now, that statement does not mean only destroying life as murder or suicide because destroying life can be corrupting someone into doing bad things to themselves or others, and while destroying someone spiritually is the same as murder, but anything is possible with God, and His judgment will come at the end of time.

While writing this chapter, I thought back to my days in the entertainment industry as I indicated at the start of this chapter. I was equal to all the well-known entertainers that I met. We would sit around telling jokes, talking about places in the world that we had visited, about cooking different kinds of food and maybe even fishing and many times we talked about our children. We never talked about our work. The things we talked about and the things that we did together that put us on equal terms. They were no better than I was, and I was no better than they were. We were comfortable together for we were equal. I will be just as comfortable with all in the Light, and you and I are no different either. And if you and I ever meet, I would be happy to have a conversation with you. I will not be afraid of you or ashamed of my life, for we are equal.

But I feel that we all should be cautious when around other humans, until you get to know them of course, for some can be dangerous, but caution is not needed when you enter the Light. You will know all others as all will know you and your life story completely.

"Though I walk through the valley of death, I have no fear for we are equal."

NON-CONFORMED ONES

God created us in His image. Just as we, if God had created something that was evil or something that He did not like, He would have destroyed it. Therefore, all in Creation is exactly as God wanted it to be. And whereas, God created the concept of Evil for humans to decide what is best for him, and the human created the actions of Evil.

I recall a story about God banishing His most beloved and beautiful Angel, Lucifer, from Heaven forever.

If God did indeed kick Lucifer out of Heaven that would mean that once corruption did exist in Heaven, but there never was corruption in Heaven, and also if God kicked Lucifer out of Heaven that would indicate He created something or someone that He did not like, but also, Heaven is not a place, it is the state of the individual's mind.

First you must realize that Heaven is the Righteous State of mind and not a location. And the Light is the congregation of Angels from human individuals that have died up to this point in time.

If corruption enters into one's Heaven (thoughts), that individual's Heaven then becomes Hell, while the Light is the congregation of Angels known as God; therefore, the Light may be considered as Heaven, for the Light is all Righteous thoughts combined. God did not kick Lucifer out of the Light, for there is no corruption in The Light; Lucifer knew that he had become corrupt and would not allow himself to enter and stay in the Light.

But let's get back to the subject of this chapter, what are Non-Conformed Ones?

The Righteous Angels call corrupted Angels, Non-Conformed Ones.

These are ones that do not live by God's standards and rules, for they made their own rules for self-purposes. These are the ones that refused to learn while they occupied a human body and refused to help the human. They are the ones who realized they did wrong when they returned to the Other Side after the death of their human counterpart, and whereas all humans who do things for their own agendas and not for humanity are the same as their Non-Conformed Angels.

All Angels, even the Non-Conformed One, will not allow corruption into the congregation of Angels known as God. Therefore, Lucifer was a Non-Conformed One, and would not allow himself entry into the Light, if he existed at all, and whereas, we may be only recognizing God's concept of Evil as Lucifer.

But if Lucifer did exist, what could be strong enough to corrupt him?

It is the same thing that does corrupt Angels into Non-Conformed Ones.

The desires of the flesh are the things for the dog. These are the things of domination to oneself and others. These are the things that can corrupt Angels into Non-Conformed Ones.

Daily, people who contain Evil Energy are around us. Do not judge these people, but merely feel sad for their actions they cause toward themselves and others.

But judge their actions to see if they are right for you because one must find his individual direction for Salvation and Everlasting Life.

We should try to help guide these people into the correct direction, but do not push your religion or beliefs unto them. For pushing your religion or beliefs onto others, you are then entering into the Sin of Domination.

There is a couple who are friends of mine. The man is one of those Christians that becomes full of the Holy Spirit that will stand up, shout, sing and dance around during church services. The woman, his wife, was raised in the Catholic religion. She is subtle in her religious praise. She will not go to church with her husband because of his religious actions, and it seems like she is always knocking her husband down on everything he tries to do. Therefore, he avoids being around his wife and he does not go to church anymore because he will not go alone.

This man asked me, "Do you think my wife may be a Non-Conformed One because she always does the opposite of what I want to do?"

I replied to him, "It is very difficult to tell which type of Energy one contains, but it is easy to see that she does not wish to do the things that you want to accomplish or do. We do not know if her Angel came from the Light or if it has ever been to the Light. For if her Angel did not come from the Light then her actions come from the Unguided Energy within her. But it really depends on her Angel ever experienced other lives before because if her Angel did not came directly from the Light and it experienced Evil before it could very well be a Non-Conformed One. But if her Angel came from the Light and contained Heavenly thoughts of previous life, then her present desires of the dog controlled her Angel-within, and turned it into a Non-Conformed One. Because it would indicate that she contained a regular

Angel of God that came directly from the Light, if she allowed you to do the things you wish, along with doing the things you both wish to do as a couple with the exception of harming yourself or others,."

It is a fact that I contained a Non-Conformed One, for the Angel Jo has said that we have had hundreds of lives and that we have been to the Light before, and yet I would not conform to God's ways until the Angel Jo came into my life and inspired me to know.

The refusal of God's rules by an Entity is a Sin. If any Entity, human or Angel knows the existence of the Supreme One but refuses His Knowledge, then he has committed Sin.

The Ten Commandments set forth directions to righteous living. One need not know of God or the Ten Commandments to live a righteous life. Following the Ten Commandments should ensure you the Salvation to Everlasting Life because by living the Ten Commandments is to live with an open heart. But one must only know how he wishes to be treated and treat others in that same manner, and then the Ten Commandments have been followed. Living by the Ten Commandments only because that will ensure you a place in Heaven is Self-Domination and that is a Sin.

All Angels, even the Non-Conformed Ones know of the Ten Commandments. But Angels try to guide their human counterparts into living a righteous life while the Non-Conformed Ones do not.

Non-Conformed Ones follow their desires to experience what feels good with no regard to others, in which covers themselves with Hell. And while Non-Conformed One's experiences from previous lives are like bad habits that are difficult to break.

You may know how hard it is to diet or to quit smoking. It takes a lot of will power, so think of how hard it is to convince someone else to diet or to quit smoking if you enjoy smoking or eating and are not dieting or do not stop smoking yourself. So here we have an Entity-within who enjoys the pleasures of the flesh, but is trying to convey unto its human counterpart that the human needs to stop doing something that they both enjoy. And yet, a human will not let the Angel-within lead his life if that person does not live with an open heart, for then his desires are for the dog within. These are the things that corrupt Angels, for these are the things that turn Angels into Non-Conformed Ones.

The main reason to live another life for Non-Conformed Ones is that they enjoyed life experience before and want more of the same. But many times after returning to live a better life, the Non-Conformed One's concepts can be reversed by the Mentor Angels and/or the Entity's counterpart – the human. But if they cannot help the Entity-within to overcome its desires it will drag the human down into Hell.

There is no corruption in God or the Light because those that are corrupt will not allow themselves entry into God, but there is sadness in the Other Side before the Light.

UNGUIDED ONES

Angels are created. We will get into the creation of Angels later. For now let's assume your Angel-within may have been just created and you are its first human life experience. Now keeping that in mind, let's talk about what Angels from the Light call "Unguided Ones."

Unguided Ones are those who did not ever make it to the Light after being formed. Therefore, they do not understand right from wrong and they live only for their personal desires.

(I was not told what the reasons might be for them to have never gone to the Light after their creation.)

Usually Entities are pulled directly to the Light after forming just as newly released Angels that are carrying Souls from the human bodies after death are drawn to the Light.

Unguided Ones are still Entities even though they never went into the Light, for if they had entered the Light, they would be Angels of God.

Unguided Ones are allowed to enter a human, but no two Entities can "live" in one person at the same time. If a second Entity ever tried to enter a body that already contains another, the human body will fight off the second Entity as though it was a virus. Thus the human body would destroy itself. Usually an Angel-within will not allow another to enter your body, but a second Entity may stay in the small part of the brain without repercussions to the human body, if acceptable by the occupying first Angel.

(This place a second Entity may stay is located in the back lower left area of the brain just inside the skull.)

This act of allowing another Entity to enter and occupy this space is a very special arrangement. The second Entity does not contribute to the life of the body unless the first Entity would trade places with the second. This trade cannot last for any length of time, for the human body would still try to fight off the new Entity as if it were an invading virus.

For different reasons the Entity-within may just leave the body to never return again, another Entity could take its place; but when this happens, the human body reacts as if the newly entered Entity was a virus. Thus the human body eventually destroys itself while it tried to fight off the invader.

Before an Angel leaves the Light, the Angel knows exactly which unborn child it is going to enter. The Angel also has charted the trail to the unborn child, but this path may contain known detours to the Angel.

(The Light is the congregation of all Angels – God. These Angels carry all the memories of all the lives that they have lived. The Light is not the future. Angels in the Light do not know the future only the past because the future experiences of life are not engraved upon the Angels and are not in the Light yet.)

On the journey to life, the Angel is now an Entity. This Entity has lost most of its memory that it had while as an Angel in the Light. The Entity usually only remembers the first part of its trip to the unborn child. But as I just stated earlier, this path could encounter detours to the unborn. Most detours were forgotten after leaving the Light and the Angel may find that its attended unborn human may already contain another Entity. This other Entity could be an Unguided One. The finding of this other Entity in a child's body was part of the detours in the Angel's path to its real attended human counterpart. If the arriving Angel finds another already in the child's body, it must move on to another unborn child. But this was part of the known route and known detours to the selected child's body.

Unguided Ones are allowed to enter human bodies, for many times an Unguided One will be conformed by living within a human during the duration of the human's life. Thus, an Entity that did not first go to the Light directly after being formed can become an Angel and then become part of God when it enters the Light after the death of its human. Other times the Unguided One will corrupt its human host, but all actions are part of the total plan of the cycle of life and that includes corruption and death of some.

Corruption and death of one may and can be lessons for others because that happens is needed and is known in God's Master Plan.

The Unguided Ones that are not in human body is what the Angel Jo calls "Evil Energy," for they drift around on both Sides; but these cannot harm humans. They can try and sometimes do direct a human into harming themselves or others. It does not matter if the human contains an Unguided One, a Non-Conformed One or a true Angel from the Light, or if he is just following what another human tells them, humans have the final command of their lives, but all actions were known to happen in God's Master Plan before they occurred.

If a human contains an Unguided One, then that human, along with its Guardian Angel, must and should try to teach the Unguided One as the Light would have taught it if the Entity would have made it to the Light directly after being formed.

Unguided Ones live on warped energy conceived when one human harms himself or others, and the Unguided One will try to influence its human counterpart to do bad.

(Warped Energy is born from Warp Perspectives that are made when one believes in something that is not right, for then one starts seeing and believing in everything that is for them alone.)

And whereas, once the Unguided One joins with the Soul (experiences of that life) inside a human and if the human's actions are bad, some people call these actions "desires of the flesh" while at the same time to the Unguided One, the bad deed from one human to another or himself is wonderful; it thrives on the feelings (the energy) of hurting others.

To an Angel that came from the Light, a bad deed from one human to another causes the human's Angel-within sadness in terms of unable to control its human counter part.

The inability of the Angel-within to control and/or to help its human counterpart in growth is Hell on the Angel-within when it returns to the Other Side after death of its human host if the Angel-within is an Angel of God.

If the Angel-within is an Unguided One or an Unguided Ones, that did not come from the Light (have the Knowledge), they do not know of the Light and they live for their desires alone. They like to cause pain to their living host or others. They have never been into the Light so they do not understand God's ways. But their Hell will surely come after their final human dies and during the end of time, for they enter into the Other Side just as with any Angel who lived on earth with Hell on its mind.

Hell is the uncontrolled experiences of the human by the Angel-within. For the Entity shall live forever with the knowledge of what its human has done. Hell can be within us all. We control our Angel-within and ourselves. Angels merely give us thoughts of guidance in what is right and wrong. We make the final decision.

Now I am talking about really bad Hells here. Many with little Hell in their minds do enter into the Light and are considered Angels. The judgment for your degree of Hell is your decision, until God's Judgment Day.

Bad Hells are things that you have done that you do not want anyone to know about. Bad Hells are things that you refuse to confess about. Little Hells are bad things that you have done that you knew were wrong but you are willing to let others know of your mistakes and bad deeds for you have repented. But little Hells may be and/or can be damaging to you on God's Judgment Day.

Remember God is All, and God knows all as All will know your Hell, too. Therefore, you will not be cast out of the Light for your Hell. You may cast yourself out of the Light for your Hell. Hell is your memory of your bad and unkind acts toward yourself, your fellow humans, other living and non-living things here on earth during the days of your last life.

The one and only redemption to your Hell after death is to live another life that must be better than your previous life. That next life need only be a second to many years in length depending on what your Hell was. That is Reincarnation!

Reincarnation only occurs when the Angel-within you wishes to live another life. The choice to live again is his and his alone. This simple natural rule applies to all Entities as well.

Reincarnation is returning to live again in human form only. Nothing else has an Angel-within. Your Angel will not allow itself to return to live in anything except human. Lower life forms other than humans do not have a Soul (file) that any Angel wishes to contain. The Angel-within you desires to be as close to God as possible, for it is part of God, but anything is possible with God.

Sometimes humans may see Unguided Ones. They may be seen as deceased animals other than human or as other humans too. No Righteous Angel would allow itself to manifest into any thing other than that of human. No Entity is allowed to harm and/or hurt humans, but any of them could cause you to injure yourself or others.

All of the Other Side with Heaven in their minds would not harm humans. Usually, those with Hell in their minds are too busy worrying about themselves to cause harm to any humans. In the case of an evil Entity or any other thing from the Other Side harming humans, the Angels of God would stop them immediately.

An Unguided One could occupy the body of other animals, for they do not know or understand the Master Plan. But animals do not contain Angels. They have energy that you could call Souls, but their "souls" could not join with any Angel as human Souls are the life experiencing files for Angels. That is because things of a lower class other than human do not have the intelligence - the "thinking process" - that God instilled into humans because life is for experiencing our reasoning of the unknown future.

The Unguided Ones will never enter the Light alone. At the death of their human host, another Angel must guide them to the Light for they know nothing of the Light. Once they have entered the Light they too, will have all the Knowledge as all others have. They too, will be given the chance of Reincarnation if they desire it. For after entering the Light, all become Angels. The Unguided Ones that still have Hell in their minds are then known as Non-Conformed Ones, or if you wish "Non-Conformed Angels" for they did enter the Light as all Angels do.

After death, your memory, character and personality, along with all that is you, will combine with your Angel-within through your Soul. As your Angel-within enters the Other Side, your Angel-within then becomes an Entity. If your Entity then enters and stays in the Light for a while, it is an Angel of God, and if your Angel-within has Heaven in its thoughts then it is surely a Righteous Angel and may live forever in the Light as part of God. But if your Angel-within has Hell in its thoughts and does not enter or does not stay for awhile in the Light, it is then considered a Non-Conformed One. To identify an Angel of God or a Non-Conformed One, one must first know if it came from the Light and the conditions of its thoughts before entering the human. If it did not come from the Light, then it is an Unguided One. If your Angel-within did in fact come from the Light to your body, but contained previous Evil thoughts, then it is a Non-Conformed One. But both the Unguided Ones and the Non-Conformed Ones condition can be changed with help from the Mentor/Guardian Angels, along with human's help too. Throughout time, Angels of God have helped the Unguided Ones that have not been converted find their way to God. For all Unguided Ones, along with all Angels that have become Non-Conformed Ones because of a bad life, must return to re-live again or they will impose self-exile outside the Light. The Angels of God know all that was not converted and are outside the Light will be dispersed at the end of this cycle.

(This destruction is detailed later in this book).

Being dispersed and then reformed (re-made – re-created) is death to the Unguided Ones and to Non-Conformed Ones as well. Reforming would be death to Angels as well, but the need to reform a Righteous Angel has never occurred. This reforming of Unguided Ones and Non-Conformed Ones has occurred at the end of each of the four previous cycles. Presently we are living in the fifth cycle.

(The five cycles will be discussed later.)

The end of this fifth cycle, as with the end of the other four cycles, is the destruction of all matter and undesirable energy. This destruction does not include the corrected Unguided Ones and Non-Conformed Ones that were transformed into Angels of God. But death is dispersing and then reforming of all energy that would not be saved. All will be destroyed with the exception of the Light for the Light is forever. The Light is God who is all Angels in Congregation and that is righteous Energy.

An Angel-within can start out a good life, but can be corrupted into being a Non-Conformed One by itself or the desires of the flesh from its human counterpart, which is Hell to the Angel-within. So the choice is yours. Complete your mission here and return to the Light as a Righteous Angel, or do wrong here, which will turn your Angel-within into a Non-Conformed One with Hell on its mind.

An Unguided One could have many previous lives, just as a Non-Conformed One could have had also. The difference is an Unguided One has never been to the Light and does not know of God, while a Non-Conformed One has been to the Light and knows of God but refuses Him - the Congregation of Angels. If an Unguided One never comes to Earth and tries life, as within a human, it will drift endlessly on either Side until the end of the cycle. Then it will be dispersed. At the end of this cycle, all life here on earth will cease to exist. Then all Unguided Ones and all Non-Conformed Ones will be destroyed, for there is no hiding place for Evil Energy.

As time for the end comes closer, we find more Unguided Ones and Non-Conformed Ones living within humans. These are the ones that need to re-live more than the Righteous Angels because of what their desires are; thus, we see more corruption throughout the world from their actions of the flesh.

The Non-Conformed Ones and Unguided Ones will be destroyed at the end of this cycle. Most of them at one time or another lived in human bodies and we who befriended them did not help them find their Salvation. We refused to be helpful to others for just one life, a mere 60 or 80 years of life, a flash of time to the cycle of life. How sad it is to think they depended on us, but our personal wants and needs got in the way and we all let them down. For not helping each other is one of our Sins and is part of our individual Hell.

FAMILIAR SPIRITS

The Christian Bible states, "Beware of Familiar Spirits." Yet, any Angel of God, or Non-Conformed Ones, or Unguided Ones may be seen and could be considered as a Familiar Spirit.

Any time that you encounter an Angel, Spirit or whatever from the Other Side rather you know of them or knew them in life, you should ask, "Are you of God?"

If they answer, "Yes," do not be afraid for they are truly from God because those who are not of God cannot communicate with us.

When I stated this to "born again Christians", they responded with, "But Satan is deceitful and can lie."

Their answers like that are what makes me distrust "born again Christians," for whenever you state anything that lines-up with their Bible, they will come back with something that is contradictory to their Bible but lines-up somewhere else in their Bible because their bible is full of contradictions. Just like Christians claim that God says in the Christian Bible, do not place man-made gods above or beside Him, but many "born again Christians," say Jesus is God and they refer to Him as Lord and they worship Him.

After Jesus was killed, he appeared to his Disciples and told them to go forth and spread His words. Did they see and communicate with Jesus or Satan?

Ministers will tell you that they have communicated with God. Did they communicate with God or Satan?

Many claim they have see the Virgin Mary, did they see her or Satan?

And when Catholics pray to the Virgin Mary are they also worshipping her?

I heard a preacher say, "You could believe that you are following Jesus all your life, but then find out after you die that you were really following Satan, and then you will be in Hell forever because you followed Satan instead of Jesus."

That preacher wanted his congregation to only know and follow his interpretations about God and of the King James Bible.

But if one from the Other Side tells you the righteous things to do and you live a righteous life, can that person that you believed in and follow be evil?

If you see and communicate with Angels, Spirits or Entities from the Other Side, just be careful of what they say and instruct you to do. You know the differences from right and wrong.

The "Beware of Familiar Spirits," as stated in the Christian Bible refers to Angels that have not gone to the Light after the death of their human counterpart. These are the ones the Angels of God try to help and we need to encourage them to proceed to God. But Spirits that are not of God can not talk to humans because they are ashamed of what they did.

But what do you do if you see a manifestation of a deceased family member or a friend?

They could be an "Evil One" or they could have gone to the Light and have returned as an Angel or maybe they just wish to tell you something before they move on. Therefore, ask them if they are of God and their response will be the truth. If they are not of God then tell them to go and they will leave. They do not have control over your life, you do.

I knew some about Jesus before His Spirit (Angel) entered into my life, so then should I not consider Him as a Familiar Spirit?

I have now also read some of the stories about the Angels Gabrael and Michael, should I not consider them as Familiar Spirits also?

And then, I knew the Angel Jo during her past life and she is my Soul Twin, so is she not a Familiar Spirit to me?

That statement of "Beware of Familiar Spirits" was very confusing to me because that statement. The statement, "Beware of Familiar Spirits," was written into the Bible by early church leaders to control and dominate people. Same as early Christian Church leaders removed mentions of Angels from most of the Old and New Testament because the church leaders did not and do not want people worshipping Angels instead of God. And yet, Christians worship and pray to Jesus and others who they refer to as Saints instead of God. Christians claim Jesus is Lord as if He were God, but He is not God, rather Jesus is just a part of God – the Son of God - for that is what He has told me.

Yes, it is wrong to worship Angels... even Jesus, but it is worse not to listen to Angels of God.

There was a certain young man from the northwest United States. He was a good kid and did well in school. This young guy also attended a

Christian church regularly. After he finished high school, he drifted around the north-western United States for a little while. During his wandering he started hearing voices that he thought was God.

(He did not see the Spirit that spoke to him.)

This young man ended up killing a young boy in a restroom, in a roadside park near San Diego because he claimed God had told him to kill this boy in a sacrifice to Him.

This young man was murdered because the Pastor of the Christian church that he attended did not tell the people... his congregation, that Angels, Spirits and/or Entities cannot talk to people but can put thoughts into one's head. This Pastor like most preachers did not tell his congregation what to do if one believes he hears a voice from the Other Side. If this certain young man knew this and would have asked the "Evil Energy" that spoke to him, if it was of God, it would not have answered. Then the young man could have refused the "Evil One" and the death of the boy would have not occurred.

We have the final decision of our choices in our individual lives. An "Evil One" may make you believe that you heard something, but whatever you do is left up to you.

I have asked the Angel Jo, Gabrael, Michael and Jesus if they are of God, all four of them have individually answered me, "Yes." Therefore, I know they are from God and are not evil.

After His Resurrection, Jesus appeared to His Disciples on Pentecost. One of Jesus' Disciples actually placed his finger into Jesus' body through a wound that a sword made in Jesus' side as he hung on the cross. Don't you think that Satan could have impersonated Jesus during that encounter?

If all your life you have truly followed Jesus' life style and after life you are in Heaven, it does not matter who you followed because your actions were righteous.

If Jesus truly died for our sins, then nothing we do is bad. So do the Christians think they can do sinful things and they still get to Heaven? By the way most of them act, it sure seems that is what they think.

Jesus did not die for our sins, He died because of human sin of domination that the people of his times showed him, and we still carry the sin of domination within us.

Before going on to the next section of this book, Concept of Life, I must briefly explain the Holy Spirit to you.

The Holy Spirit is also a Familiar Spirit. The name Holy Spirit means All. The Holy Spirit contains both good and bad. One might think of the Holy Spirit as being just the Righteous, but all is Holy for all is of God. He owns everything, even what we may consider as the bad.

If you ever try to get an invention patented, they will ask you for its spirit – what is its idea? What does it do? What do you want it to do? These are the things of its spirit.

The Holy Spirit means what is God's idea? What does His idea do? What does God want His Creation to do? What are God's goals for Life?

The "Spirit" in Holy Spirit means the combination of all things – all thoughts, ideas and concepts. Therefore, the Holy Spirit is the most commonly known Familiar Spirit to all people, for it is in all people, too. Yet, the Holy Spirit is not an individual from the Other Side that will communicate with you or me. Any Angel of God can communicate as if they are the Holy Spirit to you and me. Also the Holy Spirit can communicate to you through any human, too. In other words, the word "Spirit" means the idea, thoughts or concept of something while the words "Holy Spirit" means Life, Death and everything else that comes directly from God. The word "Holy" could be exchanged with the word "God." Both are All, for all that surrounds you is God's Spirit. It contains all that God desires for us. Even the bad that is around us is for us to experience as part of our lives, but the idea of God's Spirit is for humans to live with Love for all and with no domination toward others.

THEORY OF LIFE

Now that you have read "Who We Are," let us quickly review the role of the Angels and their directions and connections to human life, which is part of the Theory of Life before we go deeper into the Concept of Life.

Once an Entity is formed it has the choice of going directly to the Light or otherwise. Any direction besides going to the Light does not allow the Entity the Knowledge of the Light, and thus becoming an Unguided One. For when Entities go directly to the Light, they receive the Knowledge of the Light and then become Angels of God, and once an Angels of God comes to earth and live, most will likely end up returning to the Light after death instead of finding dispersion at the end of this cycle.

(Refer to your dictionary for the word "dispersion;" the pattern or complex light separating into different colors by passing through a prism, thus is the Dispersing of corrupted Energy by God.)

Once an Unguided One begins "its" cycles of lives, it will never allow itself the opportunity to enter the Light.

"Its" cycle of life... to the Unguided One is everything is for it alone. To it nothing is for the common goal of All. "Its" cycle of life is to live within a human until the human's death then waiting for another human's birth that it can enter to repeat its selfishness again, doing everything for its personal needs and desires. Therefore, it will never know what its end will be until the end comes.

Downward the Unguided One spirals deeper into its pits of Hells. These are the ones who have never learned how to open their heart to others and have refused help from people here on earth and the Angels on the Other Side.

Non-conformed Ones are also those who have lost their way after leaving the Light and would not allow themselves to open their hearts to others here on earth or to the Angels of God. These too, spiral down into the Hells they have made for themselves, for they also have forgotten and/or refused God.

Some Bibles recall the story of God casting out Lucifer (Satan), His most beautiful Angel from Heaven.

Lucifer is the Energy of Evil and Corruption. Thus, when God cast out Satan there was and is no corruption or Evil in God, for God does not contain anything bad.

Evil and corruption are Domination.

You will not find one evil act or corruption that does not stem from domination, for domination is an act from an unopened heart. Unguided Ones and Non-Conformed Ones are both with unopened hearts for their ways are of domination.

Both the Unguided Ones and the Non-Conformed Ones will not go into the Light because they as with all Entities including the Angels of God feel what others know of them and do not want to feel the sadness the Angels of God feel for them.

But Unguided Ones and Non-Conformed Ones are still part of God, even when they are out of the Light for God is everything, and because they know that they are corrupt and they are without open hearts, the Unguided Ones and Non-Conformed Ones will not allow themselves to enter the Light. And also, they will not enter the Light because they do not want All to know their true intent.

God is of the open heart. God will not allow evil, corruption or domination to invade the Light, so therefore, the Light contains no evil or corruption.

As time goes by, more Unguided Ones are being formed and there are more that become Non-Conformed Ones, therefore, the cycle will end before the bad outweighs the good, for that is God's Master Plan.

Now it is a "given" that Angels of God could help those with Hell in their thoughts to enter the Light where they would receive the Knowledge about reincarnation and then they may chose to re-live, which should remove their Hells. If they chose not to return to life then they will leave the Light forever, but most refuse the help from others to enter the Light for they to do not want others, who are willing to assist them, to know the conditions of their thoughts.

At the beginning of the first cycle, Nature made all planets, the universe and all life. God placed instincts into animals and Intelligence, the Soul, into humans. But Nature is also part of God's creation and is part of the Master Plan.

(Plants do not think or move of their own volition. If an area of plants becomes overcrowded, they push each other out to die. Plants do not digest food as animals do. Plants do not have arms or legs as animals do. Plants do not build nests or other things as animals do and so forth, but all is God, including everything, even the bad.)

Unguided Ones did not go to the Light, where God places Knowledge of experiences of life that contains Intelligence into His Angels, while Non-Conformed Ones lost their Intelligence and Knowledge along their way, and therefore Non-Conformed Ones and Unguided Ones are the same as plants; they are No-thing. Even Evil and corruption that grows from Domination, which also are No-thing, are also part of His Master Plan.

God will not allow plants or any No-thing from His universes into His Heaven, nor will He allow No-things into the Light.

As more of the Unguided Ones are formed, they come directly to earth and live while some of the Unguided Ones that lived before return again for another life. Most of the Non-Conformed Ones keep returning to earth to live again because they refuse the Light.

(We can see how society and the structure of living with an open heart are failing. This indicates the number of Unguided Ones and Non-Conformed Ones has grown into a number large enough for this cycle to end.)

As some Bibles state; Satan (evil energy) will be cast into the fire of Hell. So it will be that those of evil, corruption and domination will be dispersed during that Final Day of Time. The ignorant people of long ago didn't have the word "Dispersed" to explain how be destroy Satan, and could only describe "casting into the fire" the only way to get rid of something.

As also stated in different Bibles after the end, Jesus will reign for one thousand years. But in reality, only the righteous of God's Master Plan will exist in a place where there will be no evil, corruption or domination because the forming of another life, where new Entities, will not start until one thousand years has passed. But the "one thousand years" only means a length of time will occur before a new cycle begins. And whereas, through this length of time all that we know will not exist, for only God's Knowledge – the Light will exist.

The forming of Angels is caused by Nature (God). Nature has both good and bad. God is the Good from nature, but He is all including nature that contains both good and bad. For He created everything including the concept of evil, for it was needed for humans to judge what is best for them as individuals. Human created the actions of evil, for the evil actions are for the desires of the flesh, but that too was built into His Master Plan.

God could control nature to ensure that it does not create any bad, but as with humans, He allows both to do as He pleases.

God does not allow bad to come into Himself, just as we as humans should not allow Satan (evil, corruption or domination) into our lives.

When all things have gone into badness as far as God wills, God destroys it and allows it to begin again. For the bad around us that does dwell within all of us is from nature.

God retains the good from each cycle; therefore, God grows larger from our experiences.

In the Beginning all is wonderful.

The Theory of Life is the Holy Spirit, for it is what God wishes to happen and what will happen for God's Master Plan cannot and shall not be changed by any human.

The Theory of Life is to grow and then move closer to God in His Concept of Life.

The spoken words from God to the people of long ago and the words Jesus passed on to His Disciples were to inspire us (help man grow and to elevate us) closer to God but the people just did not understand it. And also, Jesus' life style should have demonstrated how we should live, but again, people did not get it.

I did not refuse their Knowledge; I accepted it with open arms. My Divine Love for God and His Angels including Jo caused me to want to learn, and they inspired me to know all that I was allowed to learn about them. I learned how to control the dog and not allow it to interfere with my thinking and my writing of this book. I was inspired to love all people as God and His Angels do, for we all (the human race, God, His Angels and everything else) are One.

One needs to understand what a person is in order to be able to love them.

Besides communicating with the Angel Jo on the Other Side, I was also given the opportunity to communicate with the Angel Jo while she was in the body of my wife, Christine. And when she was in Christine's body, I learned that each Soul has its own personality and characteristics while the body is merely a vessel for an Angel of God to "live" in. And that give me the understanding that the human body without a Soul (intelligence and comprehension) is just an animal.

I love the personality and characteristics of the Soul, but I am saddened by the actions I sometimes see people project toward others.

I like the animal we call human because of what the Spirit of life is purpose to be – God's Concept of Life. Therefore, I love people for they are comprises of the Angel-within (part of God), the Soul (intelligence of God) and the animal that I refer to as the dog. But I have learned that the people are just confused about God's Spirit of Life.

THE CONCEPT OF LIFE

TO LEARN AND EXPERIENCE

Before you quench your thirst for Knowledge, be **Forewarned** that if you continue to read these writings of the Concept of Life that came directly from God and Do Not use them to help guide yourself in your intended way of life, you shall only find **Hell** after death. But if you practice these writings daily to direct your life, you shall find your *Heaven* and *Everlasting life.*

And Jesus said to me, *"For those that have the Knowledge and do not use the Knowledge will be Oblivious."*

For the first two years of our renewed love affair (1996 through 1998), the Angel Jo constantly had to keep proving to me that she was an Angel because I did not believe in God, for all my feelings were turned inward which caused me to live with an unopened heart.

Once I realized Jo was a real Angel, she gradually introduced me to Gabrael, then to Michael, and then to Jesus, and finally all four introduced me to God.

All my life I had said, "I will not bow down to anyone or anything. I will not get down on my knees and praise God forever, not God or the Devil. After my death, I will just stay here on earth."

The Angel Jo had a difficult job in reforming me from one who does not believe into one who knows God. My transformation took more than two years for her to complete.

During the late fall of 1998, I finally accepted Jo as an Angel and my human love turned to Divine Love for Jo, and that Divine Love made me hunger for the Knowledge that I needed. I wanted to understand her way of thinking. I needed to understand her better, for now I needed to know my Jo's now way of "life." And then, my Divine Love for Jo transformed into Divine Love for God and all of His Angels, and then somewhere through that time, it formed into Divine Love for all humans and everything that

God had created.

The next seven chapters are the detailed accounts of the things that she taught me over the first five months of 1999. For it was then that she knew I was ready and eager to learn the truth about God. The Angel Jo, nor Jesus, nor Gabrael, nor Michael, forced me to learn but rather the Angel Jo inspired me toward the Knowledge of God. While the following chapters may not merely be all that is involved in God's Concept of Life, these chapters cover the things I needed and wanted to know about God's Concept of Life and the Angel Jo's way of life.

All lives are unique and different. People need to know different things. Maybe not all that I have learned is required Knowledge for you. What I have learned is the basic foundation and cornerstone to Life on both this side and the Other Side. And these are the basic reasons of why we are here.

COMPASSION

Near the end of 1998, after I had accepted that Jo was an Angel, and I understood that the Angel Jo, Gabrael, Michael and Jesus were now part of my life, I had the willingness and Love to receive their communications and teachings on a daily basis.

I must explain that prior to my acceptance of the Angels it was just fun to have someone that I loved on the Other Side. Jo and I would go places and do things together, and she protected my family and me, and many times she reduced my pains. She taught me things that I never knew about people, including myself and the Other Side. She showed me the future and above all, she never once turned her back on me or put me down as humans do to each other.

Now it was getting serious. Jo gradually turned our conversations toward God and reality. Jo had convinced me through our love to talk about life and God. As our communications continued, I grew impatient and wanted to know more about the Other Side. I hungered for more Knowledge about the Angels and God... what did they think? I needed to know their understanding and reasoning.

One night in early January of 1999, after I lay down to sleep, the Angel Jo appeared. I could see through her as if she were smoke and she glowed ice blue but, and wore a full-length gown. Her beautiful brown hair flowed down just over her shoulders as she glided across the bedroom toward me, graceful as the wind and yet as silent as a gentle summer breeze and said, "Come, it is time for us to go and see."

Taking the Angel Jo's delicate hand in mine, I slowly rose up out of my body as I had done many times before, and we drifted out of the bedroom into the night.

Swiftly, we flew over the city as I looked down at the lit streets below. Now flying faster and near the speed of light, we past snow-covered mountains and accelerated into the future. Within seconds we were across the country. Over Virginia we flew. Blue skies held billowing white clouds around us as the ocean waves washed upon the shores below. We slowed down and watched children playing along the edge of the water as men and women swam. Others were sunning themselves, while some lay upon the sandy beach. Many were laughing while most were having a great time together.

We turned north and headed up the coast. I gazed at the houses, buildings and cities and the shores of the ocean that lay just to our right as we flew. Throughout our flight, I viewed others playing and enjoying each other, too. But I did not know if all these things were happening at the same time or not because it felt like we were lost or traveling in many different times at once, yet all things that we saw I knew were in the future.

Then we stopped above the ocean at a place I knew not. I could not see sunlight but did not wonder if it was night or day. I could not see any sky or clouds above, yet I knew those things did not matter. At the same time, I saw people around the world crying, even though we did not journey from this place.

These people who cried did not personally know the people whose lives had just ended in a small plane crash. Somehow I knew these people were crying for the families of those deceased more than for the accident victims. I felt their compassion engulf my body as if someone had poured their feelings unto me.

Next, we were on some battlefield in a time that felt like the past as guns blasted across this "field of glory." I saw trees and various types of vegetation through smoke from exploded gun powder all around us as we witnessed men falling and many dead lay everywhere. Smoke darkened the sky as the battle continued. I could not feel any wind blowing, nor did I see any sky or clouds; they were irrelevant to me.

Suddenly, without warning, we jumped forward in time, maybe just hours or days after the battle. Now the battlefield was quiet. Everyone was gone except for broken human bodies with many dead scattered around. I sensed that not all the human bodies still contained Souls and Angels-within, for I somehow knew that some of them had already left. I knew that not all were dead and many moaned in their pain, but I could not hear a sound. Somehow I sensed their moans and felt the pains of the dead and injured, and my heart cried out for them as we watched many precious human lives drain away and viewed the uplifting of many Angels from others.

Then, all at once, we were in a dimly lit room. The room seemed like some kind of living room, but it held little furniture. Its walls were covered in discolored and ripped wallpaper. The floor was bare of carpet and I knew only the wooden boards separated this room from the cold and dark earth below. We drifted around like unseen smoke as we watched a mother who sat in a worn-out easy chair cradling her baby in her arms.

This scene I felt was also in another time period. I did not know where, but I knew it was of long ago and not of today.

The child that the woman held was deformed. The young child's left hand and arm were twisted and shriveled. We felt the flow of Love and Compassion that the mother had for this child. I felt as if tears were running down my face. I looked at Jo, she did not have eyes, and automatically knew that we only had blurred faces, then I touched my face and realized what I thought was true. The feeling of tears on my face was not actual tears but a feeling of sadness that slowly enveloped my entire body.

For now I was seeing with my feelings, as the Angels do. I was "seeing" Compassion of a human mother for her offspring while feeling the Angels' sadness. A feeling of sadness that somehow I instinctively knew also enshrouded Jo.

Now I understood that I was experiencing life as it was meant for us to experience and learn about life from the writings in the Bibles.

As with all great books, the writer tries to get his reader to see with their feelings; Letting the reader's mind see the people in his story, allowing the reader to feel the happiness or anguish of the characters in his book, trying to make their story come alive in the reader's mind to feel the experiences of the people in the book and to learn from others' life stories. That is what the writers of the Bibles intended for us to do as unconditional flow of Love and Compassion drifted down over me. And it was then that I started to understand the few things that I have read in the Christian Bible and the other things that people had spoken to me about in the Bibles.

As we watched the mother and her child, I also could feel the personalities of Jesus and His disciples and all the others written about in the Bibles. I felt the pains that all of them went through. I understood why John the Baptist could not retract his statements and allowed Herod to decapitate him. John's Love for God meant more to him than his life. I felt Compassion for John the Baptist and also for Jesus and His disciples. They all had tragic endings to their lives, yet none denounced their Love for God.

All of a sudden we were back at the location of the small plane crash. But this time we were deep under murky water and with the crash victims, one man and two women who did not know what had happened. They tried to help each other from the wreckage because they did not know they were dead. They did not care about their personal injuries; they only cared about helping each other, for now they showed Compassion for each other.

Gabrael suddenly appeared. Even though his face was blurred, I knew who he was.

He stood about 5 feet 7 inches tall and his clothing gleamed as if made of gold and they reminded me of what the Roman soldiers of long ago wore. His complete form beamed with Love and Compassion as he stepped forth and held out his hands for them.

All three took his hands, relaxed and smiled, for now they knew their missions were over and it was time for them to come home and sing and rejoice in the Light once again. I could feel their contentment. I knew their inner feelings and saw their complete lives flash through my mind for they had nothing to hide.

The warmth of Compassion surrounded the Angel Jo and me, just like the feeling of tears that covered us when we watched the mother and her child we had previously witnessed.

In a flash we were back once again at that battlefield. It now was dark and silent, as if night had fallen. Many Angels from within rose out of many silent bodies, and most tried to help others up, while others rose and ran screaming into the darkness.

Once again, Gabrael appeared as many small and bright white lights flew swiftly about him, darting back and forth across this field of dead. As these bright lights slowed and stopped, their forms changed to human size Angels. These Angels looked like both men and women, wearing white gowns or robes. Though I could not see their smiles because of their blurred faces, I could somehow feel their smiles of Love toward the men who were trying to help their comrades. Many men looked at these Angels and I could feel their Love as they relaxed in calmness. They extended their hands and touched the Angels' Compassionate hands. The Angel Jo and I knew, as they now knew, it was their time to go home.

Within seconds all were gone. In the distance we heard the sounds of Gabrael's horn notifying all in the Light that the now deceased soldiers were home once again.

I slid my arm around the Angel Jo's waist and pulled her close to my side as we shared the warmth of their Compassion and Love.

Then somewhere we saw a friend helping his neighbor repair his automobile on a dark lonely road, shrouded in trees and lit only by the auto's headlights.

Another night we viewed a busy street corner on a warm sunny day where a woman gave a homeless man some money for food.

The next night we saw young people working in the yard of an old rundown house as they helped an elderly woman repair and clean her home.

After each night of learning Compassion, we would fly to the wall where we played and enjoyed each other's company, for seeing Compassion made us happy.

The wall I speak of is located near the Light. In my younger years, before I met Jo in 1965 and she was still alive, I would sometimes travel to the wall whenever I was lonely or very ill. Then I would walk along the top of this great wall. This wall extended for what seemed like miles. The sky above this wall was dark and black, no sound could be heard, no heat or cold could be felt and no wind blew. Looking to my left, I could see millions of distant lights that appeared to be stars. Looking to my right, I saw nothing but blackness. Parallel to the wall on the left ran a canyon or gorge with rough sides. This ravine glowed of orange and yellow color.

I would walk along on top of this wall, sometimes stopping to view the far lights. Many times I would fly along the ravine and marvel at its grand appearance while darting in and out of the wall as if it contained tunnels, though none could be seen.

At one place near what I considered to be the end of the wall there was another wall from above as though it hung upside down. I would stand on top of the one and act as if I were holding these walls apart with my stretched out arms. I would pretend that if I let the two walls come together the universe would be no more.

The Angel Jo told me in 1996 that this wall was our hiding place; our special place on the Other Side. She said we would go there and play, chasing each other in the gorge and around the wall. She said that she did not know what was on the right side of the wall, for we never went there. She explained to me that in fact, I sometimes did travel to this wall looking for her when I was sick or lonely and she was sorry that she was not there for me because she was still living during those times and it was not needed for her to be there at those times.

After each night's studies, I would awaken in my bed. Always I was covered with sweat. Rolling over, I would go back to sleep and dream of the Compassion that we witnessed. I dreamed of the Compassion that is needed in the world and the Compassion that is contained in people.

Another night, the Angel Jo and I revisited Marion, Ohio, in the summer of our love affair. Once again we drifted like smoke as we watched; Jo almost dragged me up and down the stairs looking for Fat Sam, who had made the lady cry that sat on the back steps leading to Jo's apartment. But this time I felt all the little things of that location. I saw the tiniest spider web and viewed its owner. I felt the trees gently moving in the light breeze, but did not feel the breeze. I felt the wood of the steps beneath our feet. I felt all the little things that surrounded us daily in our lives that we take for granted. I also felt the Compassion that was contained in Jo as she tried to help the lady as we looked for Fat Sam. I was feeling the Compassion that

God has placed His Creation.

On another night, we again traveled back into the past of Forever. I saw us sitting in a picnic area of a park on a Sunday in 1965; Jo sat on my lap as I sat on the bench and rested my back against the table of a picnic table. She watched the children playing in a sandbox while a few women pushed children on swings. I would kiss her on her cheek and she would quickly return my kiss, and then turn her eyes back to the playing children. Again and again I tried to get her mind off of the kids with kisses, but her thoughts kept racing back to the kids. I felt my Compassion for Jo, for I knew she missed her children and watching the other kids reminded her of her own children. I was sad because I could not get her mind off them. I shared her sadness, but yet I could not help her, but only be there for her.

If you look in the dictionary at the word "Compassion" you will find: "Pity for the suffering or distress of another, with the desire to help or spare."

Compassion is something I knew little of until the Angel Jo came back into my life. During the fall of 1996 when I started looking for Jo, I knew that I should not have left her back in 1965. How I wished I could have turned back the hands of time and we should have spent her final days together.

Compassion is the looking outward from your heart; seeing that others have feelings, too. Helping others uncovers your Angel-within while you are helping them uncover theirs.

While Compassion is sharing another's burden, Compassion is also unconditional Love given.

Compassion for others is one of the many steps to finding salvation and everlasting life with God.

Compassion must come truly and earnestly from the heart. It cannot come from a closed heart for coming from a closed heart is the same as saying, "I will act as if I give you Compassion, and in return you must give me..." and whereas, you cannot demand God to secure a place in Heaven for you just because you gave money to your church.

Over the next four or five months our journeys took place almost every night. They all began and ended about the same; usually with my starting to go to bed at the beginning of each trip and then ending up with the Angel Jo and me playing along the wall near the Light.

The teachings of the Angel Jo - the things we witnessed - are like the teachings of the Bibles. The Bibles were written for us to "see" with our feelings. We need to experience their accounts, learn and experience through their accounts of their lives recorded in the Bibles and understand that God did and still does communicate with people.

God's Concept of Life: *"To learn and experience from experiences of others through endurance of life."*

The Bible stories about Jesus' life demonstrate God's Concept of Life. Jesus' life was supposed to give us an example of how we are to live and His death showed how bad we are to each other, but most of us did not get it.

These writings that I am putting down on paper are to help you and me understand that God has once again extended His Love and shown us how to live and for you to learn and experience the things that I was taught by the Angels.

Since you have read the chapters under WHO WE ARE, you can relate to and understand the differences between your Angel-within, your Soul and you, the human. Therefore, you should see that during the first few months of my learning from the Angel Jo, the next day I could not totally recall all we had encountered the previous night. Sometimes I could remember only that we had gone someplace but could not remember where. My Angel-within was learning, but I, the "dog," would not fully open my heart to the teachings that the Angel Jo was providing. I was refusing to allow my Angel-within to lead my life. I was denying myself to let my heart be open to my Angel-within. Even all my love for the Angel Jo was not enough to allow myself to open my heart.

It was difficult for me to let loose of my atheist ways of thinking, for to believe in God, you must first believe in yourself, since God is inside you - the Angel within you is part of Him. I could not believe in God because I did not believe in myself.

Let us take this a step further. You must believe in yourself and then you must believe in all others, for the Angels within them are also part of God. Once you can believe in yourself and then others, then you believe in God.

The same applies to faith as well. You must have faith in yourself and others before you can have faith in God. For if you do not have faith or belief in you being part of God, how can you believe or have faith in God?

Believing in others does not simply imply "to believe all others are innocent." Also, believing in all others does not imply "people are not capable of hurting, harming others or of lying." Believing in others does not imply "all people are good." Believing in others does not imply "all people will do the best job they can." But rather knowing and understand that all people will make their personal individual choices in life."

Believing in yourself and others means "knowing that all humans do have a Soul, all people do have an Angel-within them, all humans are merely animals that contain intelligence, but still have the capabilities of animals that try to dominate others, and they will do what is right for themselves." (Doing what pleases themselves.)

Believing in others is to acknowledge that the Angel-within is part of God, and whereas, all others are part of God.

Believing in God is to acknowledge that God is the Supreme Being – the Creator. Know that God lives and understand that God has a Master Plan and that His Master Plan includes you, too.

God created everything... Imaged if you will, a person – God, thinking of all that we believe in and live in is our reality. Life and all within our reality is nothing more than a thought in God's mind. We only exist in God's thought and all that we do and all that has occurred throughout time is part of His thought. We are only in His thought to experience the unknown of our decisions.

My lesson about Compassion lasted more than two weeks. Although my total learning period lasted for months but we did not travel every night. The Angel Jo did give me an occasional night off. A couple of those nights we just played in different spots around the world, and of course we usually ended up playing at the wall near the Light.

The nights when we just played, the Angel Jo would ask me, "Do you remember what you learned? Now that you know, you must put Compassion into your life and practice it daily."

I tried hard to remember as she instructed me to do but I just could not remember everything that we had seen. Yet, daily I would see Compassion being given out by others around me, and I truly tried practicing and using Compassion in my daily life, but it was very difficult for my "dog" to see anything except what was for me. But still, I tried.

To go from Glory to a higher Glory and climb closer to God you must practice letting your Angel-within lead your life daily.

To go from Glory to Glory is like going from one mountaintop to another. First you must go into a valley before climbing to the next mountaintop. To reach closer to God, you must descend from Glory to climb to a Glory nearer to God.

When going from Glory to Glory and you are in the valley, you must stop and look over the routes available to climb. You may even take the wrong path to the higher Glory and have to retrace your footsteps back down and then try to climb to the higher Glory along a different path.

The going down into the valley from Glory to Glory also applies to other things in our lives. Sometimes to build a better relationship with someone you must restructure a better understanding of that relationship through communication with that person. The same Glory to Glory movement applies to business and other aspects and concerns in our daily lives, too.

Understand your change from Glory to a higher Glory applies to you alone. It does not impose moving from Glory to a higher Glory for another, nor does it imply that another should move from Glory to Glory for you. You cannot force change upon another, you can only inspire the other to change.

If you marry someone and think you will change his or her behavior, ideas or religion, forget it. Only the individual can change their lives. One cannot grow unless one desires growth. One cannot move from Glory to a higher Glory unless one desires to move to that higher Glory. One will not try to live in a better environment unless one wants to better himself. One will not raise his children better than he was raised unless he desires to improve his children's lifestyle. One will not study and learn unless one desires the knowledge. And whereas, all parents raise their children the best they know how, they must be inspired to know how to raise their children better.

Our individual acts of change must be only to better ourselves and not to Dominate another or from Domination of another. On the other hand, we cannot expect others to change their lives in order to improve ours.

You see, I had come to know Divine Love through the Angel Jo, but I did not know Compassion, Understanding, Forgiveness, Wisdom, Cherishment or Judgment. I did not understand that these are the things that I needed to find my Salvation and Everlasting life.

The Angel Jo was now teaching me all those things that I needed and wanted to know and had to understand. Jo knew that she could not change my ways or me. She showed me the reasons I needed to change the direction of my life. For when I wished to change then she was able to help me change my life.

It is possible and understandable to help show other people reasons why they should change the directions of their lives. But that is if - and that is a big "IF" they desire to change their lives.

I do not proclaim to know any Bible. I only know the Words of God that were passed on to me through the Angels. The words that I write are not to change the Bibles; they are meant only to clarify what is transcribed as the Bibles. I am neither adding to the Bibles nor taking away from them. I am only stating to you what I was told to be spoken, the Truth from God. And this, God's Concept of Life that I was shown by the Angel Jo, was needed by me in order for me to change my lifestyle toward God for God.

UNDERSTANDING

And the Angel Jo said to me, "Now that we have gradually moved into your realizing Compassion of God's Concept of Life, we shall now begin with the lessons of Understanding."

The dictionary says "Understanding" means, "To come to know the meaning or importance of; apprehend" – comprehend.

First I want to explore the "why" of understanding... to comprehend "why" someone does something.

To understand "why" a person steals is to understand that humans are of the "dog."

Humans are still animals no matter how you dress, house or educate them; an animal it will always be. Our outside, the shallowest part of the human, is the dog. Deeper within the human lies the Soul; even deeper is the Angel-within. The Angel-within is our deepest Righteous thoughts and desires, which is part of God. The human intelligence, wisdom of the Angel-within should control the animal. The human that cannot control the animal is still an animal and is therefore forever **No-thing.**

Remember what has been said about your Soul being a file in your floppy disk that is your Angel-within?

It is up to the "dog" to keep in check and control the bad memories of past lives.

I know many Bibles states that those closer to God and His Spirit are the most tempted.

When Jesus talked with Satan as He stood on a mountain and near the cliff, Jesus said, "I will not tempt my Father." The word "tempt" meant "demand" which means "Dominate." Thus Jesus would place His Domination on God. And that statement indicates those who know and understand God's Spirit must use more restraints to control the dog feelings.

It is the individual's responsibility to control all bad thoughts and memories that may or can be conveyed to that individual and/or from that individual to others or by others over him

Memories of bad and good are your subconscious thoughts and actions. Thus, your memories of bad and good are the projections of attitude that you deliver to others, for others also project what they have pre-received or have delivered to others as well as to you. God is Loving and He will not deny you what your "dog" desires. Therefore, you must control the desires of the dog to desire the good, not the bad.

God, when viewed as the Father of Creation, is one who teaches his young children, and as they grow older, allows them to choose for themselves. The Jewish Religion is one of the oldest known religions upon earth, and it is like the teachings of a young child; we teach our little children that what we say is the way they must live. And as our children grow a little older, we teach them love as Jesus demonstrated to us. And then along came Muhammad; he placed demands upon people just as humans put pressure upon others as the peer pressure we see in our teenagers; and now I, along with many others, are teaching God's Words, the same as the things we try to inspire upon our young but adult children.

Bad memories from the past of others cause them to act toward you as they do, but also, it is their place to control the bad within themselves. Where their hostile actions toward others generated from past experiences do not make their unfriendly actions toward others right. Just as your deeds of yesterday, be they good or bad, will direct your actions of today unless you desire to change and control your past actions.

And now to the lessons that the Angel Jo showed me concerning Understanding, a little after midnight, I turned over in bed and realized that the Angel Jo was beside me. I did not have to see the Angel Jo to know that it was she who now possessed Christine's body.

I pulled her close and kissed her on her lips. She returned my kiss and said, "Be quiet and go to sleep so we can go."

Like a child I mumbled "Okay," closed my eyes and soon drifted off to sleep.

Rising from the bed, the Angel Jo and I ascended from the bedroom into the night. Soon we were in total darkness. As light slowly merged over us I could see brown water rolling lazily in front of us as if we were floating down a river in a boat. But we sat in no boat for no bow of a boat could be seen.

The trees along the river's banks held their green foliage over the river's edge as if to shade us from the hot sun above. Undergrowth covered the banks and no ground could be seen.

A snake slithered down a lower branch of a tree and dropped into the water as slowly and peacefully we continued to drift down the river in silence. I could "hear" strange and different birds and animals calling all around us as we glided in and out of the shadows of the trees.

Suddenly a gator splashed violently ahead but near us. The alligator was killing a small animal it had captured. Another gator, seeing the feast, quickly approached to claim the meal. Soon a battle of the fittest broke loose. Water splashed and flew everywhere as their giant lizard-like bodies twisted and tossed back and forth. Within minutes the smaller one backed out and left. The bigger gator watched the retreating one for a few seconds before he turned to his now-dead prey.

The Angel Jo happily turned and looked at me and we flew away to the wall near the Light and played.

Another night we slowly drifted down through a fog-like substance and viewed an old white, two-story courthouse below.

Rain was falling from a gray overcast sky. Puddles of water covered the streets and the grassy areas around the courthouse looked soaked.

Like smoke we drifted down and we passed by and through people as they headed into this building. We moved through the building's double doors, yet the doors were not opened to us. As we passed people standing in the hall, I could hear them talking, but did not understand what they said. We then entered a room where inside a man was on trial for the murder of his seven-year-old son.

The large courtroom had fans hanging from its ceiling. Its floor, along with the lower part of its walls, was wood and old, but highly polished, while its white plastered walls looked is if they had been freshly painted. Tall windows with blinds lowered half-way lined the left side of the room.

Rain continued falling outside, and an occasional flash of lightning and thunder could be heard.

The courtroom was full of spectators as they sat on the church-like benches and watched the trial.

We drifted like smoke above the crowd and watched the complete trial that took days to be heard, but we witnessed the complete trial within minutes. The man, a weathered and tired looking man was found guilty for the murder of his son. Many people wept out of compassion for the slain child as the accused man wept, too.

This time we did not go to the wall to play, for we were both sad by what we had just seen and heard, we merely went home and back into our bodies to sleep.

Another night on some dark and lifeless street we saw a man steal a battery from another's automobile.

And then another time we saw two women arguing over the care of a child as the child lay in his crib in pain.

Another night we traveled into the wilds of Africa. Under clear blue skies and on some grassy plain, we saw a mother cat and her offspring as they fed from her.

And yet another night we were again watching ourselves back in 1965. In less than a few minutes I saw our complete love affair of that year fly by. Then I knew why our love affair was needed.

"It was good for you, for without our affair you could not be where you are today." Is what Jo had once told me about our affair, and then she went on to say, "If we did not have that love affair, you would not have been able to accept me or what we are teaching you now. Yes, our affair was good for you, but it was wrong, for we were both married to another."

Now I understood. We needed to share our love with each other, but it was wrong as she stated, "For we both were married to another." The breaking of marriage vows was not just against your spouses but against yourself as well because a promise made to another is also a promise made to you.

Back then, we were caught up in life. She was dying from cancer and without her children, and I was away from home and I was in a marriage that would not last, but I was trying to make enough money to support my family. We both needed that love affair to rid ourselves of our troubles.

We ventured back to the Civil War days and reviewed my life as a soldier. We saw the death and destruction I delivered upon people during and after the war. The things I did during the war were right for me as a soldier of the north, but were wrong because they were not just aggressions against soldiers of the south but also acts committed against innocent people. The things that I did after the war were completely wrong, for these acts were directed against others for the good of me "the dog."

I now also learned to have Compassion for my deeds that were acts of Righteousness, and I also understood that I could not forgive the acts of my Domination.

We should forgive our Angel-within for what it has allowed to happen.

We forgive the person, for we know he is of the "dog," but we cannot and will not forgive the actions of Domination set forth against another. And we must punish by human laws those who commit Domination against others and allow God to take care of those who commit acts against His Master Plan.

The realization came over me that we cannot let the past of our present life or our lives from the past direct our actions of today, for we have final control over our present actions, but whereas we can change our views and concepts of our past actions and not do those things that we consider as bad again.

Now I understood why we had told the story of our love affair in 1965. I also could comprehend all the things that the Angel Jo was now revealing to me.

Seeing the alligators; to understand that in the animal world it is okay to kill other animals for food. To understand that one must stand up for what is his, for sometimes it is acceptable for animals to fight and kill when something is needed to sustain life or to keep what is yours.

The man stealing a battery... it is wrong to steal from another.

The cat and her cubs... it is wonderful to give without expecting anything in return, for what you sow you shall reap.

The court scene... the man who killed his son shall live in Hell forever, here and thereafter, until the end of time. A love for a love but also death for a death and no man shall decide who lives or dies without just reasons. And I knew that the man was driven by his past life made him believe that his son belonged to him to do with as he desired, and whereas, he, the man, control his actions and was solely responsible for the death of his son because he should have controlled the concepts of dog within him.

Now I understood the difference between right and wrong.

Now I understood the difference between good and bad.

Now I understood God's Laws, The Master Plan.

Now I understood that we live under nature's laws, human laws and God's Laws, but that all three blended together. One cannot live separately and set or make his own rules and/or laws that fit only his needs and desires from the others here on earth.

Human laws were made and are enforced by humans to keep the "dog" under control, for they protect us from others and ourselves. Without human laws we would not be civilized, and civilization is what separates us from the animals. Civilization lifts us closer to God's Ways.

(I did not detail all that would happen if we did not have human-made laws because you can deduce that for yourself.)

Nature's laws are those that deal with such things as the structure of the universe, such as gravity, our body's use of food as fuel, reproduction and others.

God's Laws cover our actions toward others, our feelings toward all and ourselves and so forth, because His Laws cover Himself and your Angel-within that is part of Him. Therefore, His Laws must also be yours. For God's Law is Love to all. Personal laws and rules that govern you also should include Love for all. But all rules and laws are from God, as everything belongs to Him.

(Rules are detailed later in an another chapter.)

Understand your actions.

Understand what God desires you to do.

Understand that you are part of the complete picture of life.

Understand that you are a part of, and a very important member in the Master Plan.

Understand that you are not alone in this world.

Understand that all others have feelings too, but also remember that we are animals, too.

Understand that the "dog" does things for the "dog."

Understand that you can and should control the "dog" in you.

Understand that you may not always be able to control the "dog."

Understand that you will make mistakes.

Understand that others will make mistakes.

Understand that the world is not perfect.

Understand that you are not perfect.

Understand that it is your job and duty to remove the bad memories that may cover your Angel-within.

Understand that it is your duty to help uncover all others' Angels.

Understand that it is your job to help move your Soul to a higher Glory.

Understand that it is your responsibility to help move others to a higher Glory if they desire the move and if they ask for your help. Do not go around knocking on doors and telling people about your religion. Do not speak of your religion unless others seek your advice. Do not try to change others unless they ask for your guidance in changing the direction of their life.

If they ask for your help, do not preach to them, but offer them Love, Compassion and Understanding in your Wisdom.

If you look up the word "preach" you will discover it means to proclaim or expound upon; to advocate or recommend urgently.

Preachers in most churches are trying to Dominate us into their way of thinking while every life is individualized. What is good or right for the preacher may not be good or right for you.

Understand our faith and belief in the Supreme Being need not be the same.

Any religion is okay as long as it does not condone Domination.

I know a preacher who had a man with a drinking problem in his congregation. This preacher kept telling the man that he needed to stop his drinking for his family and God. The man told the preacher that he did stop his drinking. Within a few days, the preacher found out the man had lied about his sobriety. This preacher was devoured by his own loss of faith for he thought that if he could not use the Words of God to turn this drinking man around, he was not worthy to preach.

The key word here is; "preach," and the key phrase is; "his own loss of faith."

You cannot help anyone by preaching at them. The only way you can help anyone is by using Compassion, Understanding, Forgiveness, Love and Wisdom – inspire them. People must first want to help themselves, for they are the only ones that can help themselves.

"For you cannot push someone to a higher Glory, they must want to reach for a higher Glory. You must inspire them."

"Dogs" do backslide. Our wants and needs of today may change and then may be something completely opposite tomorrow, and that is backsliding. But doing something that you know is wrong is a Sin.

We are not our brother's keepers. If you were your brother's keeper, you then would have placed him in your domination. Your brother is his own keeper, we should help our brothers, but we do not keep them.

The preacher friend of mine quit his church and it failed because of him losing his faith, and his church is now nothing... it closed its doors. Because of the loss of one, the preacher now has lost all.

Why lose your faith because another has changed his mind about his desires?

It is okay to turn your back on one. One must learn how to help himself. Sometimes turning your back on one is the help he needs, for God will help those that help themselves.

The phrase "turn your back" does not mean to walk away from someone. It means to stand firm and fast on your belief and do not condone the things that someone believes in or does if their beliefs or actions differ from yours, but also you may have to leave that person alone and have nothing to do with them, but you did plant the seed of change within their mind.

The word "beliefs" does not imply to only spiritual or religious beliefs. I am also referring to ideas such as lifestyles, too.

If someone's lifestyle or ideas of how they should live differ from yours, stand firm and fast in your convictions. Do not convert into their profile.

God does not leave us if and when we refuse Him. He stands silently by and lets us decide the direction of our lives. When we come to agree with His Concept, He reveals Himself to us once again.

The Angel Jo stood silently by my side for many years. When I finally decided to accept and receive her, then she revealed herself to me.

Understand the difference between your needs in life and your wants and your limits.

Understand the heights that you can and want to achieve.

Understand that your mission may not be here on earth, it may well be something that will be performed after death. Or your mission may be merely to witness another great sunrise or sunset. Or your mission may be only to grandfather someone to come.

And the Angel Jo said to me, "Your Lives may not seem Grand to you, but to God all life is Grandeur."

Again, for me to learn and understand the lessons that the Angel Jo had given me took a long time for I was still a "dog" who had an Angel-within.

FORGIVENESS

By the time we had gotten to the lessons about Forgiveness, I was wondering if someone else was also teaching me as in a classroom setting in addition to the things that the Angel Jo was showing me.

I asked the Angel Jo, "Is Jesus teaching me? Do we sit with him and he tells me of the things that I need to learn?"

The Angel Jo answered, "No."

I then asked the Angel Jo, "Well, then is Gabrael teaching me these things that I must know?"

The Angel Jo smiled and replied, "No, Gabrael comes from God and lets me know what we need to study and where to go. When we travel to other times, Jesus sometimes is with us. I have been away too long, I have forgotten some and I am also remembering as well as you."

Being just on the Other Side is having little more Knowledge than we have while living. The Angel Jo only knew what she was told by other Angels. Gabrael was bringing and teaching her Knowledge, too.

So Gabrael brings instructions from God about our studies. Gabrael is a Messenger of God while any Angel of God may be a Messenger of God. The Light is the congregation of the Angels' past experiences while the congregation of all Angels is God. The Light is the Knowledge of life up to the last one who has lived. So in other words, Gabrael is bringing instructions from God to the Angel Jo about what we need to study and where we go each night, and then Jesus sometimes travels with us to other places and to other places in different times.

Forgiveness is the ability of us to grant pardon or remission of... to cease to blame or feel resentment against oneself or another.

Once again, the Angel Jo and I spent many nights visiting faraway places in distances and times.

She showed me the past years of my life - all the things that my Angel-within had endured and also the things that it never could forgive itself for allowing to happen. I saw all the people that I had hurt while I witnessed my life as if I was a third party to my actions.

When I could not go on to see other things we went home, for our hearts were saddened by what we had seen that my life had become.

Another night we traveled back to review the lives of the people who were involved with the man who murdered his son (the trial that we had witnessed in the court room), but this time we traveled back into their past lives and the past of their present life of then - Back before the murdered son was born, and as well back to see the man's life complete from his birth. We saw how others treated and what they had done to him - what caused him to turn out bad and rebellious against life and saw all that caused him to be full of evil.

(Past life experiences is not an excuse for being bad or doing bad things because each of us have complete control of our present lives.)

Again, I could not go on, so the Angel Jo took me home again, for our hearts were full of sadness.

Another night we visited with many that died and who were running scared and afraid in the darkness on the Other Side.

Visiting or maybe I should say finding these with Hell in their thoughts was most interesting. We rose out of our bodies and drifted straight up through the ceiling of the room and left this side. Instantly we were in a place where there was no light of any kind, and I knew it was vast and without end. I could not tell if we were flying, drifting or just standing still. No wind could be felt and no objects could be seen to indicate if we were moving or in what direction, but I could sense that we were moving forward. As we moved forward, we could occasionally pass someone or someone would cross in front of us. In our passing, some mourned and cried out for help. Of these, Gabrael and other Angels appeared and lead them toward the Light. Others ran away when the Angels approached them, for their Hells were too great and they did not want anyone to "see" them. On the Other Side, all "see" with their feelings. The best way for me to describe "seeing with your feelings" is to say that you "see" their Hells as if they were festered sores and twisted bodies of what they had done in their lives. Yet you do not see festered sores or twisted bodies, but instead as if you were looking inside of them.

A closed heart does not allow others to "see" what you are. Running away from others is one's assurance that others will not "see" what he has done in life.

Once again we went home with saddened hearts.

During the days following our travels of seeing Forgiveness, I wished for death. I wished I could commit suicide, but I knew that would only worsen my Hell, for I did not want the Angel Jo, Gabrael or Jesus to know all the bad that I had done in my past lives. I just wanted to be with the Angel Jo forever, but I did not want her to know me. I wished the Angel Jo would just reach into my body and stop my heart so I could die. But I knew such an act of mercy for me would only cause her Hell. So I bared my grief and Sins.

I then asked the Angel Jo, "I don't wish to know more, I just want to come to the Other Side and You and I will leave and never go near the others again."

She answered, "I would go with you but I will be sad."

That stopped that line of thought that I had, and then one night the Angel Jo and I talked about my Hells.

She said, "It was not your fault. Do not blame yourself for what has happened... you were young and it was long ago."

"What happened... what did I do... please tell me?" I begged as I held her hand.

"It was near the end of the 1500s... Your father at that time abused you... sexually, physically and mentally... you then abused and killed many until they killed you... I am so sorry," she replied with her head hung low.

Softly she continued, "You must remove your Hells. Once you learn all that is being taught to you, you shall become a Master once again... We cannot allow you to fail, for you are needed on the Other Side after your death. I have not forced this upon you... I merely have made you aware of what you needed to know and to do."

Letting all that the Angel Jo just explained to me sink in as the word "Master" stuck in my thoughts.

Then I asked, "Jesus was a Master, He could raise the dead. Will I raise the dead?"

She looked at me and replied, "You could raise the dead, but you won't. There have been many Masters, but only a small number of them were known. A Master is one who knows God's Concept of Life... using His Concept of Life to help others. Many will come to you on both what you call the Other Side and on what you call your side. In fact, they have already started coming to you."

A few nights later we again traveled back into time and reviewed some of my past lives. And then, in a flash, we were in the darkness on the Other Side, in a place I do not know and where I was allowed to see myself. My Angel stood there, covered with all my Sins. My Hells symbolically looked like lesions and sores, a twisted, pitiful, darkened shadow of a man, who refused to look at us. My heart was saddened, for I knew that my Angel-within was once as strong and bright looking as the Angel Jo.

It took many days before I could truly think about what causes us to do the things we do. I was refusing to look at myself. The reflections of my past are my actions that reflex upon my present day life and were my present character and personality.

Once I was able to see myself for whom I truly was, then I was able to forgive myself. Ever so slowly I started to heal my sores. Carefully I began to remove the veils of Hells that were placed upon my Angel-within. This action of self-Forgiveness then allowed me to begin forgiving others. Because when I understood why we act as we do, then I was able to forgive myself and then all others for their actions.

Do not mistake what I say about forgiving oneself for our actions.

We forgive one because it was these bad and evil memories from one's past that caused them to have bad thoughts or to do bad deeds; we do not forgive the act. We allow our peers to influence our actions and dominate us with their concepts. But individually we control our emotions and memories and we can control and stop our bad actions and thoughts.

I was able to forgive and understood what caused the man to kill his son, for I witnessed his past lives and knew why he committed murder. I did not and will not ever forgive his act of the killing of the child. For that man could have controlled the "dog" within himself, but instead he allowed his "dog" to lead his actions.

I forgive all the Entities with Hell in their hearts that run screaming into the darkness on the Other Side, for I know what caused them to have their Hells within. I cannot ever forgive their acts that were caused by bad and evil memories and warped concepts.

We forgive the person. We forgive the Angel. We are saddened by their actions, but we do not forgive the act.

It is okay to sometimes dislike another's actions. But it is not okay to become angry with others for their actions. For anger is placing a veil of Hell upon your Angel-within.

Even if you try to control the "dog" within, not always will you control yourself. There is a fine line between disliking another's actions and becoming angry toward someone because of what he did. Remember when you become angry, you are placing a veil of bad over your Angel-within, and most likely that anger will grow into hatred.

Remember that we are of the "dog." But also remember that you must forgive yourself and try not to make the same mistake twice, for we are not Jesus or God, and we do and will make mistakes. We must try to live as Jesus did, for his life was to set examples regarding how we are suppose to live and treat each other.

Before you can forgive someone else, you must be able to forgive yourself of your doing wrong to yourself and all others, and then your heart shall be opened to others, and to do that first you must realize that you have done wrongly and repent from your past actions.

Removing what covers your Angel... healing your Angel... helping your Angel... is uncovering, healing and helping God, for you – your Angel is part of God.

Mistakes that people make can and should be overlooked, such as forgetting to pay a bill. Mistakes are trifles, but still even your mistakes should be known and repented from.

Broken promises may not be forgotten unless they are broken because of major unforeseen problems. A broken promise is not merely broken one-sided. A promise is a commitment to both oneself and another. If one cannot stand on his word, then he is No-thing.

A promise or contract is broken only if one of the parties involved does not have faith or belief in what the promise or contract stood for. Someone with faith and belief in his heart will stand behind his commitments to the end, such as John the Baptist did concerning his own death relative to his commitment to God.

The Glory that you live in today is not the highest Glory you will live in tomorrow. For today's Glory may be broken by your mistakes.

Once you make a mistake, you shall be lowered (go down into the valley), and then you shall rise higher to your next Glory through the Understanding, Forgiveness and Compassion you demonstrate from the things that you learned from your mistake.

God's Concept of Life: *"To Learn and Experience from Experiences of Others through Endurance of Life."*

LOVE

I believe that some parts of Love were the easiest for me to understand because first I had to learn part about Love through my acceptance of Jo being an Angel in 1996, for it was her that stood beside me for all the years after her death in 1968. And then after I accepted her as an Entity and allowed her as an Angel to enter into my life, she was able to begin teaching me Divine Love. For the Angel Jo had been teaching me of Divine Love for two years prior to her introducing God's Concept of Life to me.

And yet, Love is the most difficult for me to explain because the meanings of our words are so different than Angels and because there are different levels of Love. In our human concepts the definition of the word "Love" is a deep devotion or affection for another; to take pleasure or delight in. And whereas, we as humans think of love as a driving force, needed, desire, companionship, not being alone, family, closeness, devotion, caring, compassion and so forth, and therefore human love places one at the center of his own universe, where everything and every feeling is centered around him and for him. And also we as human believe that Love is Give and Take, but where in reality Love is Give and Receive. Therefore, most people do not understand its true meaning and some may try to explain their understandings, and where some may come close with their explanations, but a very few will follow their interpretation with their actions. Since people do not know what Love is, I will attempt to explain the three different loves involved in God's Concept of Life.

Animal love is the common sense that animals possess, for it is their animal instincts of survival and to procreate that drives their lives and keeps their species alive. The animal's instincts of procreation is the major factor that sustained life as we grew from that one-cell animal that first lived on Earth that evolved into modern man of today. These concepts (instincts) of animal love are still inside us and are the only feeling used by many humans today.

We are animals, and all animals produce odors that allow others to know its sex, its condition of health and its age. These odors were originally intended to help select a mate that contained qualities that was needed to produce stronger offspring, thus strengthening their offspring's DNA. This is the same intention in the animal's selection of their mates by seeing the beauty (health) of their prospective mate's skin and/or coat of hair, fur or feathers. And while the male's animal instinct is to impregnate as many females as possible to ensure the continuation of its species and his DNA chain, the female role (instincts) was to nurture its offspring; to make sure its off-spring could take care of itself before leaving the nest and to secure the preservation of her DNA chain.

Understanding our sexual feelings is to understand these things of the dog are our animal's instincts. But through our intelligence we create things that enhance our bodies to make us beautiful, we cover our bodies with perfumes and clothing that represent ourselves as we are not, and while women of today try to make themselves more attractive they have forgotten their dog's nurturing instincts and are merely follow their feelings of self-gratification. Combine these things of animal love (self-gratification) with the desires of materialistic things that drive our feelings inward, and you are beginning to understand the feelings of the animal love that we all contain.

Another good example of animal's love is; the animals' need to strengthen its specie's DNA causes the animal to seek a strong mate, in turn, these needs are driven by the animal's need to procreate, and while the natural build-up of excess sperm and/or eggs that must be released is the animal's feelings of self-gratification in its sexual climax. Therefore, we can understand the intentions of animal love are directed inward because of self-gratification.

Therefore, physical love is our animal instincts, but it should only be shared with the one who also wished to strengthen their DNA by joining with you as one.

Emotional love is part of our human intelligence but it does not have to be shared with all. For Cherishment is part of Emotional Love that comes from the joining of a man and woman who share and experience together the birth of their children. This type of Emotional Love should be shared only with one partner but the need to procreate is still part of human love, but the reasons to "go forth and multiply" are not needed today because our off-spring – the continuation of humanity, is not exposed to dangers as our ancestors were. And while Cherishments and Emotional Love without the act of procreation should be shared with all others.

The Angel Jo's teaching me of Love; the Cherishments of our Emotional Love that we shared from our love affair back in 1965 enabled me to welcome her back into my life. And that aided me to accepting Michael, Gabrael, Jesus and God as real. Thus, our human Love was the foundation that I needed in order to build my understanding of Divine Love.

And the Angel said unto me, "A parent teaches its child. God teaches you, and that is love. Was not the original communications from God to humans given in Love? God does not receive Love from humans anymore from His original communications with humans.

"Was not our book, *Together Forever Before The Light*, written by you in Love for others? And is not this book's Knowledge of God given to you in Love? And is not this book written for others to read with Love? These two books are just two of the many things that we given. We are presently receiving Love in return for the Love that we gave.

"God is Love, and Love is God, Creation is God, and so Love is Creation of all. All of Creation blending together as One is Love and God. Sharing Knowledge is God and is Love, and the blending of Creation together is Love. You are part of Creation and also part of God because an Angel dwells within you. I and all other Angels are part of God, therefore we are all equal and part of His Creation, and we are His Love. Give yourself as God has given humans their Bibles and this book. Give yourself as Jesus gave of Himself – treat all others and yourself as you wish others to treat you."

During this part of my life on earth, the Angel Jo stood silently beside me for many years. She did not ask anything of me, she waited until I allowed her to teach and guide me, this occurred because the inspirations of the endurances of my life. And whereas each of us, are in the exact place in time that we are suppose to be. And yet through many years, I did not know it was she who stood beside me, but she continued to give her love to me. I did things wrong, but still she forgave me and stood silently by my side. Did she not do these things out of Love?

Christine is my wife for more than thirty years. We loved emotionally, physically, spiritually, giving and sharing, and had two sons together. Christine loved me and still loves me and I loved her and still love her, too. We shared our lives that are full of love for each other. This love that we share is a human love plus Divine Love. The love that I share with the Angel Jo is a Divine Love. Two completely different kinds of love, and yet, both do have many things is common.

Intelligence has taught us that children need both mother and father near to teach them as they mature into adults. Therefore, intelligence is also part of human love but is also part of Divine Love as well.

Divine Love is Spiritual Love and needs to be shared with all. The love of giving and receiving should be shared with all, for Divine Love is not merely one thing, for it is all things. Two people coming together to live as husband and wife needs to have all those loves that Divine Love contains. But Divine Love does not contain sexual love, for self-gratification of the sexual act of animals and humans, and should be only shared with your mate and not be shared with others.

As the world grows smaller through technology, we also grow smaller as we look deeper inward rather than outward. Thus we have forgotten Divine Love, for we only have time for ourselves, and while our tastes and desires change too quickly also, such as things or people that we loved yesterday, we may not like today. Our lives have come to be based on what we desire instead of the personality and character (the Energy) of the people that we said we love, and while many times we speak of our love for things; beautiful physical appearances of people and/or the beauty of man-made possessions will hold our interest for a while, but then we turn our emotions to more beautiful objects or better looking people. For the dog cannot be content with anyone or anything for any extended period of time because the dog does not know the true meaning of love, and the dog does not understand Love.

Since people do not understand love, then how can we, the dog, teach our children love? Therefore, most do not know what love is and/or what love is about while many people continue to look for love, but do not understand what love is because parents did not teach love.

Some children learned "love" from gangs, but gangs do not understand love, for gangs know and teach "desire of the flesh," for Love is from the heart, and gangs will not listen to their hearts (intelligence feelings).

And also, People seek the opinions of their friends concerning their love, but the opinions from others should not govern your life. For if another' ideas control your life's direction, you will have committed yourself into self-domination.

And yet, people want to hear others say, "Oh, you two look so good together..." And people are afraid to have their own opinions. Following peer pressure merely causes you Hell.

People cannot make decisions based on their individual experiences, for most do not have individual and/or personal experiences. They are afraid of making mistakes, for they were not given the opportunity to practice making decisions that were based on righteous thinking when they were young because their parents did not know love and could not teach them righteousness.

Is not mistakes part of learning?
Is not a mistake also an experience?
After you make a mistake, realize your mistake and repent (change your

ideas of the past) and move on and do not make the same mistake again.

And also, do not worry about what others think, for this life is yours. Use it wisely.

From the dawn of human existence, people have confused what they see with their feelings, and yet the things we see, combined with other senses, are our experiences and feelings while delivering actions that are our expressions of love.

We do not teach our children how to select a mate - two uniting as one as in marriage and in procreation.

First we always look for a person who is attractive to us because our "dog's" sexual feelings drive us to look of a beautiful mate. But that person will age and grow old, and their looks will change as they grow older. But in reality, we should seek one who's personality and concepts are compatible with ours.

The best way for me to explain the blending of two people's concepts is to say, imagine if you will, two glasses of water; one is three-quarters full and the other is one-quarter full. The blending to two personalities is like pouring part of the three-quarter full glass of water into the one-quarter full glass where they both become half full. And whereas, a partnership like marriage should then expand not just in earthly goods but also in the Knowledge of God as time passes as both glasses increase in volume at the same rate.

But yet, some people only think they can love another if that other person is beautiful to look at. To want a good-looking mate is only to desire a beautiful arm-piece. To them a person is merely a thing to hang on their arm to make them look good.

And the Angel Jo said to me, "Lust of beauty – to desire things that look good, but all things of the world will wither away and turn back into that of which it came from."

Before the Angel Jo came into my life and through most of my younger years, I have often thought an ex-prostitute would make the best wife. She would know if she loved you.

(Let me set the record straight, my wife, Christine is not an ex-prostitute, nor was she ever a prostitute.)

An ex-prostitute would try her best to make a marriage work. She would give all to her mate. She would love you for all that you have given her. She would not be trying to keep up with her neighbors. She would be content with the earthly goods that you both obtained by hard work. She would forgive you for all your past mistakes. Such a woman that never had love may understand what love is, for she has learned about Love because of the life that she once lived.

Expression's of your human love to another who does not return your expression of love is domination. Love is a two-way street, therefore, love given to another should be returned.

If one does not return love as most humans do not return love to God, does He stop loving us?

You know the answer is "No."

He merely stands silently by our side and waits for us to accept Him. For when you pass over to the Other Side after death, you will have the Knowledge that God has always loved you. Then you will know Divine Love. But if you find yourself in a marriage where your love is not returned by your spouse it is okay to divorce and get on with your life.

Should we not treat others as God treats us?

God never stops loving us. He lets us do the things we desire, be they right or wrong. He does not try to control our lives by making demands on us. Nor does He walk away from any humans, even the evil ones, but He stands fast and waits for us to turn back to Him. The Angel Jo did to me just as God does with all of us; she stood beside me and waited for me to turn toward God. And if you find yourself divorced continue to love that person with Divine Love as God loves all of us, but turn your back upon that person and do not allow that person to dominate you.

We must allow others including our adult children, do as they desire. But our younger children must be taught the difference between right and wrong. Teaching your young children the difference between right and wrong is not domination.

If you know that another has done something illegal, that act must be reported to the authorities. And while reporting another's illegal act is keeping yourself from another's domination and then you are not imposing self-domination by another's wrong acts.

We should not do things we feel are wrong. You need to understand how to react to situations where others do things you may think or know are wrong. Following your heart (your feelings) with love in your heart will bring Heaven into your thoughts and allow all others freedom from your demands.

Now let's go back for a minute and discuss one's physical appearances concerning love.

What if the only person you could ever love had only one arm? Or only had one leg? Or was blind?

Could you love a disabled person and not worry about what others thought?

What if the one you loved was of another color or race?

Would peer pressure make a difference?

When Jo was in body and living back in 1965, what if she had one arm or was black would I have still loved her? "Yes."

Did what I considered her physical beauty bring us together? "No."

Our love came from deep within us. For our human love contained Divine Love, too, and nothing could have stopped our love.

Age surely did not stop us; she was twelve years older than I. Nor did Jo's cancer stop our love.

Our love was our human feelings combined with Divine Love toward each other. Jo and I did not have peer pressure to contend with concerning our love for each other, and we would not have listened had any existed.

Our separation occurred for it was needed in order for her and me to be where we are today because it was part of the Master Plan. The Joining together of Christine's and me was also part of the Master Plan, and our coming together had problems (peer pressure) with her family. But that too was needed for us to be where we are today. Therefore, all that happened is part of God's Master Plan, too.

Joey, Christine's Procrustes-like fat, evil father, tried to control Christine's life as he controlled his other children's lives and all the other people he knew as well. Yes, peer pressure does not have to come from only friends, for it can come from family members, too.

Joey was well known to be a stealing, lying, lazy cheat. He knew so well how to live on the fine line between right and wrong, and he did not want Christine to marry me or anyone because he planned for her to support him when his welfare ran out.

Things got so bad between Joey and us that we did not have any contact with any of her family until after he died, nearly sixteen years after we were wed. But while he was alive, none of his family could be trusted. All of his family members did exactly as he commanded. Now, years after his death, most of his children still cannot be trusted, for they learned his tricks - they treat each other and everyone else as he mistreated people during his life.

I remember one day during the early part of our marriage I had to take Joey to court. After the judge found him guilty of harassment, the judge told him, "You know, the next time David sees you, he could shoot you and get away with it."

Then this judge told Christine and me to leave and that he would hold Joey in the courtroom and gave us a ten-minute head start before releasing him.

One of the gruesome stories that Christine told me about Joey was she remembered one night there was a small dog that came upon their farm, and Joey took a hatchet to the little dog and killed him as Christine watched in horror.

Other stories that Christine told me about her father included her father making her mother hold a coffee can for him while he peed into it as he lay in bed. Another story was he forced himself sexually onto her oldest sister.

Before Joey's death, it was said that he told people, "Don't ever tell David where I am buried."

His biggest fear was I would pee on his grave, which I told him I would do, but I will not tell you if I did this act or not. Your imagination humors my vow.

True Love is concretion.

After Joey's death, we regained contact with some of Christine's family. Five of Christine's siblings are Joey's image. These we do not have any desire to befriend.

Joey is an example of domination and jealousy - A person that went to the Other Side with Hell in his mind. And also he was a fine example of family peer pressure demands.

Joey did not have any concept of what love was whatsoever and he has refused to live another life. He is running out of time to live a Righteous life and will have no more time for another attempt at Heaven.

Christine's story about her father, Joey, is a good life example of why and how God stands silently by many humans. As God does, Christine still loved her father but removed herself from his presence to avoid his domination and that stopped her from being placed into self-domination just as God does with many people who turn their backs on Him.

God refuses to be dominated by us, thus He just turns His back on those who wish to dominate. For whenever people refuse Him, God does not leave; instead He turns His back on them. And yet His Love remains, for those people in their refusal to return love to God cannot see God's Love. We should do as God to those who try to dominate us. We should continue to love them, but we should remove ourselves from their presence.

My love for you, the Angel Jo's love for you and the God's love for you are the same, for they are Divine Love. We do not ask anything from you in return. The Love that we offer you is "peace of mind." Offering Love should be peace of mind, for Love is your Heaven. Love is helping others while it is self help, too.

In the past if someone would ask me to drive them somewhere and if they offered me a few dollars for gas, I always refused their money, and then I found out that if they offered me money out of love that I should return the love by accepting the money, for Love offered should not be refused.

Opening your heart to others is love. Giving from your heart is love. Love is all the things you do for others without asking for something in return. Love is the act of placing your thoughts in Heaven, for Heaven is the ultimate state of mind.

Being content with life and you also shall have the power to Love as the God Loves you. For then you are part of the Kingdom and the Glory of God forever.

(Many who are in the Light that wish to relive again to experience new things or to pursue another mission, will return to relive again and may have lived their last life with open hearts. But if one who has lived a bad or evil live needs only the desire to remove his Hell, he may also live again.)

The reasons for wanting another life are varied. But the answer from God's Angels who wish to live another life is, "To experience the feelings of Love again."

(Please understand that most things that we do will not cause Hell.)

You are not asked to return for another life. The choice is yours and can be as personal as Jo's and mine were.

Life does not necessarily mean to be seen as a grand event by the individual. One's life can seem to be small and uneventful, but it is part of the total picture of the cycle. All lives are important, and all our acts are important, too.

Example; Maybe just saying "Hello," to another may help and save that person from doing something bad such as suicide. We may never know how we have helped another by being kind to them.

Most people of today are waiting until they are older to marry because most cannot give up any of their looking inward instead of looking outward at someone else's needs and wants, and because some people cannot give, they only want to take. To them, love is something that they search for but will not recognize it if and when they find it.

If you search your heart and give compassion, caring and understanding toward others, you will see others give love to you. If others understand love and see the love you are giving, they will return the favor, and then you will receive what you gave (sowed).

Therefore, Love is two-sided, it is to give and receive and not to give and TAKE!

I was asked, "You say to love and help all, but you refuse to befriend five of Christine's brothers and sisters. Is this not double standard?"

I answered, "No. Love all those who seek your love, and they will return your love. Help those that need help but cannot help themselves. Accept love and help, but do not expect love or help. God helps those that help themselves.

I still love Christine's brothers and sisters, but I will not let them dominate me, and I will not allow them to cause me to impose self-domination. If and when they do open their heart, I shall be there for them, and if Christine wishes to be friends with them that's her decision, I do not dominate her.

"And whereas it's okay to divorce if your spouse is unreal with demands toward you and/or others. Love all others, but do not let yourself be placed in domination.

And the Angel Jo said to me, "It's okay to walk away from or turn your back on people that do not know or will not return love. You need not socialize with those that do wrong to you or others, but you should still love them because they still are part of God's Creation - humanity. And yet, we should try to inspire them to know love, plant the seed of Love and then walk away and allow it to grow."

One night the Angel Jo and I were discussing "an eye for an eye." She said, "Not only is it just an eye for an eye, but also it is a Love for a Love."

To receive Love you must also give Love, for Love is a two-way street.

If you truly love someone and give them love that is within you and they do not return love to you, how do you feel? What do you do?

What does God do when we refuse His Love? What do you think He feels when we do not return His Love?

God does not strike you dead because you refused His Love or because you did not return His Love. Therefore, when a lover wishes to leave you for another or whatever, should one kill the other? No!

You are part of God, so what does God do in this situation?

For God finds Himself in that same circumstance daily. Daily, people do not return the love that God has given them.

It is okay for you to turn your back on someone you love, be it a family member, friend or lover. You will still love that person, but you do not place yourself in domination by condoning their actions and do not place them in domination under your demands. But by continuing to show your love for that person is accepting their actions as righteous, but by turning your back on someone may be helping that person also. Let them go, allow them do for themselves. Allowing them to learn and experience for themselves - is letting them learn and experience from the experiences of others.

This is exactly what God does to humans when they deny His Love. God is then assisting those who are helping themselves.

Your turning your back is also helping them learn how to live in a civilized world - a Love for a Love. Again, therefore you are helping them, for you are allowing them to help themselves.

Let's back up a minute and discuss the Concept of helping others... showing how to love others.

The ignorant people who wrote the Bibles to their level of understanding did not comprehend, nor could they understand the true meaning of God's Words. If you read the Lost Books of the Bible or any other book that details the truth of many lives, you will find these people of long ago bought and sold women, and Romans could kill their sons if they disgraced their fathers in battles. And although it is not in the Bibles, as recently as the last hundred years or so, doctors believed that bleeding people would cure illnesses. The list goes on about our twisted and ignorant thoughts and ideas. Our twisted thoughts and ideas also direct us into our understanding of love. Yet, many people of today still believe that nothing can be added or changed in any Bible. However, the Christian Bible was created when it was canonized around 300 AD. So do you really believe any Bible and/or our human thoughts and ideas are hundred percent true and accurate?

The Lost Books of the Bible are documented accounts about which someone said, "These stories are not dramatic enough to be included in our Bible, so we'll leave them out."

Then someone adds to the end of the Christian Bibles, "All things added to this now transcribed Bible are false." (That includes all things that were left out of our Christian Bibles.)

So is the Christian Bibles true?

Yet the accounts in The Lost Books of the Bible are just as true as the King James Version of the Holy Bible, but were left out.

To my knowledge, the Bibles do not mention anything about Jesus being saddened by witnessing bad actions between people. But do you think He was happy watching people doing bad deeds to each other? And I do believe that the Christian Bibles do state something about Jesus talking with someone and He said, "These are the things that I do not like about you..." Therefore, seeing actions from some did sadden Jesus.

I do know the Christian Bibles state that Jesus became so angry in a temple that he over-turned the tables of the moneychangers and whipped some of them with a lash. Jesus' life was recorded for us to experience and follow as a model. Whereas, some actions of people did make Jesus angry, yet he did not condemn the people or their Angel-within; he condemned their act. Seeing the act made him sad so then should we not become sad or maybe even angry at some people's actions?

It is wrong to become angry at others, but anger comes from the dog and we are of the dog. We need to try to control the dog and not allow ourselves to become angry. Therefore we need to forgive others including ourselves for our actions, but not the act.

When Mohammad conceived the Muslim bible, he wrote peer pressure from his self-gratification that he placed upon all Arabs. God does not dominate only humans do that. Therefore, all that Mohammad wrote was evil because it all came from within him and not from God. So...are the Qur-an's words from God? NO! They are words from one human to control others.

Gabrael requested that the Angel Jo tell me that these books we are writing are true, for you and I needed the straight forth Knowledge that God provided me through the Angel Jo. While your Bible maybe all the faith that you need, so be it. But I am offering and sharing with you the Love and insight that God has given me, a better understanding of what was supposed to be translated into our Bibles, God's Love.

It is well documented that Jesus did live. So who was Jesus' Angel?

Jesus' Angel-within did not form like all other Angels. His Angel's forming came from the Divine Love of God. All Angels in congregation are God. God decided to send part of Himself to earth in testimony of Love; therefore, God took different parts of Himself and made the Angel of Jesus - God took a little part of each Angel that formed Him and made Jesus out of these pieces of all Angels. Therefore, a part of the Angel-within you now could have been part of Jesus.

To Judge what Heaven is one must experience (know) Hell. Jesus lived just once. He did not have to personally experience Hell. His lifestyle was only that of Heaven; He experienced Hell through our parts that made up his Angel-within and by seeing evil rise up out of others, just as God experiences our Heavens and our Hells, for there is no Hell or evil in God or Heaven.

Giving of yourself is Love – this is the same act of God giving part of Himself in the form of His Son to humans was Love. Therefore, we need to give part of ourselves to others. We need to love others. We need to return God's Love; we need to give ourselves to God. We need to Love God as He Loves us, for Love is not a verb, but a noun, Love is God.

God is Love. Love is God. God is the positive, while evil is the negative. All Angels are good Energy. Therefore, God is all the good (positive) Energy, for God is all Angels in congregation. Yet everything, including all evil (negative energy) belongs to Him.

God has created everything for us and has given everything to us to use while we learn and experience through life, and that is Divine Love – to give all things including our feelings (energy) to experience and enjoy without malice or ill feelings toward whatever we do. Therefore, Love is a noun because it is everything that surrounds and includes us, too. But while Love is also a verb and an adjective, for they too are of God, and they are also things that He created for us to use.

If you recall what I said earlier about a man in prison for life decided the definitions for most of the words we use today, well... one of those words was also "Love". A man in prison for life because he murdered someone, a man of the dog's instincts, decided what "love" should mean and what it meant to all people. Yet, he forgot and/or left out the most important person of them all...God, the One who first created the Word, for the Word is God and God is Love. When you give Love to someone you are actually giving yourself to that person!

When Jesus told people that He loved them, He indicated that He gave himself to them. Whenever we talk of the human race, we use the word "we" in reference to the human race because we do not recognize or cannot acknowledge ourselves as being part of the human race, while Angels will use the word "I" in reference to their being part of God. Therefore, whenever an Angel speaks with humans, he may refer to himself as God, for he is part of God. And when Jesus told people He gave himself to them, "I love you," He was really saying, "I give you all that God (the congregation of all Angels combined) made."

In one conversation with the Angel Jo, she stated to me concerning our love in 1965, "For you it was good, for you needed it to be where you are today, but it was wrong because we were both married to another."

Therefore, our affair contained both Heaven and Hell however if we had not had our encounter in 1965, I could not accept her as an Angel today. For if I had not received Jo's love then, I would not have known of her Divine Love in 1996. And if I had not have "seen" the Angels Jo's Divine Love then, I would not know God or His Divine Love now, and whereas, all that happens is needed to happen and is part of God's Creation and part of His master Plan.

Our affair was necessary for me to know God today. I needed the teaching that God began for me in 1965, and which He intensified between 1996 through 2004 to bring me to the point I am today, just as Jesus needed to die on the cross two thousand years ago for Christianity to be where it is today because God's Love is part of His Master Plan, and your Love is part of His Master Plan.

Understanding what Love is and by practicing Love daily throughout your life is uncovering your Angel-within and is letting your Angel-within lead you toward joining the congregation of Angels, thus being part of God again. And that will be your Heaven, the harmonious movement of Angels, the pure and Righteous Memories of life is Everlasting Life of your Energy - your Angel-within.

Reap what you sow... (Sow... is whatever you broadcast, send forth or show others. Reap... is what you shall receive in return). In other words, whatever you give others you shall receive. A Love for a Love is the same as a slap for a slap.

God's Love does not intend for us to have hard and treacherous lives. His Love is for us to learn, and experience, and enjoy life, but the "dog" within us causes us to hate others and ourselves. Our dog feelings causes us to have tragic and complicated lives, so therefore you must overcome your animal instincts of the "dog" to allow the Angel-within to lead your life.

Love ranges from Divine Love to dislike and produces a brightly glowing Angel, while feelings below dislike covers the Angel with Hell for bad thoughts and ill feelings are of hatred and are of Evil. God does not hate anything that He created and He has created everything. And whenever you hear a preacher speak of hating something, he is speaking from the dog, and whenever you see a fat preacher, you know he is of the dog that cares only about his inter feelings of enjoying what taste good to him.

If you give fear, you shall have fear.

If you give Love, you shall receive Love.

Also you see whatever you wish to see and you receive what you have seen. If you see hate, then you shall be surrounded with hate. If you see Angels, then you shall be surrounded with Angels and their Love.

If another's faith follows a different interpretation of your Bible, so be it.

Do not hate other religions or its followers, for all religions have the same one God above them; they just call Him by different names. But all religions had placed their man-made god above Him. It is not your place to judge if their religion is true or not; your place is to find peace and happiness within yourself.

In another conversation with the Angel Jo, I asked her what she could tell me about the Bible of the Middle Earth for I had recently read something about it in a magazine.

She replied, "It is false, the religion is not of God, man designed it and wrote it for man."

In the same conversation she stated, "It does not matter what man believes in as long as it does not dominate others."

Religion does not matter as long as you convey Love, Compassion, Understanding and Forgiveness through Wisdom to others. For all religions are different and all have man-made gods above them, while all have the same one Supreme Being above their man-made gods.

Now let's look at the "dog" side of Love - jealousy.

During the first days of our renewed love in 1996, I noticed another Angel hanging around Jo many times. Out of curiosity I asked her who this Angel was.

She replied, "Oh, that's Gab. He is just an old friend of ours. He stops by to visit with you."

Not really knowing any Bible, I did not realize who Gabrael was. At first, I felt he was some guy who was trying to get next to my Jo. Jealousy from the "dog" was trying to lead my life. I restrained myself and let my Angel-within lead, for my Angel-within knew who Gabrael was, although I did not. Somehow, I did know deep within my heart that this guy Jo called Gab was no threat to us.

I had a big conflict within me. My "dog" said Gabrael was a threat to my love for Jo and that he would steal Jo away from me. Yet my Angel-within said he had the same Divine Love that the Angel Jo and I shared for all others, including humans.

My Love for my Angel-within made me accept Gabrael in my heart, even though I did not know who he was until almost a year after my first known meeting with him.

When I first met Jesus, I could accept him into my heart, for I remembered hearing the stories of him. My contact with Jesus made it very easy to accept the stories of his life, for if he was real then his life story must have been real also.

My first encounter with Jesus was an interesting experience. My youngest son had told me about this Angel whom he had met, and this Angel called Himself, "The Helper."

A few days before Christmas of 1998, for some unknown reason to me, I told a friend who was visiting in my home, "Jesus is going to be here to tonight."

About ten minutes later, I asked my son if anyone was here. He went from room to room looking for any Entity that was in our home. Coming back in from our attached garage, my son said, "Dad, He's here."

I asked, "Who?"

He replied, "The Helper, He's in the garage."

Following my son into the garage, there stood "The Helper" near my workbench. Immediately I knew this was Jesus, but I asked Him, "What is your name?"

He replied, "Jesus."

After we talked for a while, I thanked Him for coming, and with a smile He answered, "Anything for a Soul Twin."

(Jo and I are referred to as Soul Twins by other Angels.)

With the four - Jo, Gabrael, Michael and Jesus - now in my life, I could accept God and the Knowledge that God was providing me. Now I could give Divine Love to God, the same Divine Love that He offered to me, the same as He offers all of us.

While the dog side of love is like a one-way street – we give to others to build our personal feelings of goodness inside of us, everything comes into us. We think to have one near is to love them. We believe that if we give gifts to another it makes them feel good that they received something from us. But actually, it made us feel good, thus our gifts were feelings turned inward – they make us feel good and appreciated. Therefore, when a loved one turns away from us, we feel rejected and sometimes people kill the one they used to love. Yet Divine Love means to give everything (all) without expecting anything in return, for God does not expect anything in return from us, He only desires that we recognize Him – the positive Energy of All. Yet, when you recognize God, you will then Love Him with Divine Love, for to give Divine Love to God is to receive Divine Love from Him, which is a Love for a Love.

If you refuse God's Divine Love, He will refuse you... a slap for a slap.

Saying that Jesus died on the cross for your salvation is not enough. You must give Love to receive God's Love. If you do not know the Concept of God, then believing Jesus died on the cross for you can be your salvation to Everlasting Life and Heaven if you give Love to God and all others. The same applies to other religions as well.

(The word "salvation" merely means to give and receive Love as a specific vehicle or a particular road to Everlasting Life and Heaven, but whereas Salvation does not mean Heaven or Everlasting Life. For salvation is the direction to Heaven and Everlasting Life. Salvation gives us the direction to help us find the road of Love to Heaven and Everlasting Life with God.)

Why do people go to church every Sunday? Is it to find God? Is it to seek their salvation to Heaven and Everlasting Life? Or is it to make others believe they are religious?

Most people do not understand that going to church will not save them. Many who go to church do not understand that they must have Love for God and all others to be saved. Most merely go to church to make others and themselves think that they are saved.

Did not Jesus, the Holiest person to have ever lived, hang out with sinners? Did He not try to inspire people and to teach people that were heading for Hell or already in Hell?

Jesus went to the people that wished to hear the Words of God. So should not the preachers go forth to sinners instead of waiting for the sinners to come to them? But most preachers stay in the church to receive the most money from the least number of people!

Should not the people who go to church regularly go forth to the sinners instead of going to church every week?

After years of listening to ministers they should know what they should be telling others. And therefore, the people that go to church should go forth among the people who wish to know God, and to teach others what they have learned.

Do the churchgoers not have the Knowledge of God that they profess to have? What do you think?

Churchgoers and preachers are only thinking of saving themselves.

We see many older people going to church regularly professing they are saved. They have not changed their views of the past but only their thoughts of the future. Not realizing they did wrongly to others in the past is not repenting, and God will continue to refuse them because they are only trying to save themselves and live forever. They never understood about afterlife and never will understand God, all they know is that they do not want to die because they only think of life as we, the dog, live here on earth.

Domination on the part of churchgoers causes them to knock on people's doors, trying to control others into believing that their religion is true. And while these churchgoers are merely trying to re-enforce their beliefs upon themselves by getting others to agree that their religion is the true religion of God, and that is self-domination. And whenever they try to impose their religion on another, is that not domination?

Is not Domination and self-domination a Sin?

And Jesus said unto me, "Speak the words of God to others whenever their conversation's direction leads toward God, not before."

The opposite of God's Love is jealousy. The opposite of Divine Love is domination because both are of negative energy.

If you look with questions for God, you shall find the answers from God. If you do not have the desire to know the truth, or the need to know the truth, or desire to seek the truth, then you shall not know the truth, and then peace of mind is worth the truth.

Is your peace of mind worth not knowing or understanding God or His Concept of Life?

If others seek you in order for them to understand God, then you shall find others in which the words of God from you will comfort them and help them find their Salvation, which is the direction to the road to their Heaven and Everlasting Life.

If you look for love without giving love, you shall find jealousy within yourself.

If you seek God's Love without giving Him Divine Love, you shall only find Self-Domination.

During the early summer of 1999, I knew that the Angel Jo and I had surpassed the love of the "dog." Our love had progressed into Divine Love.

One day during that time, I told Christine, "Jo will not be in your body on a weekly basis because I do not need her sexually anymore."

I knew deep within my heart that I did not need her sexual love anymore. Our act of sexual love was my crutch that I needed to aid me in understanding of God. Now our communications were not about my desires anymore for my needs had turned toward my learning more about the ways of God.

The Angel Jo said concerning our acts of sexual love, "It was needed."

The Divine Love of God was the reason of our sexual love acts. I needed to know the shared love of the "dog" before I could start to understand God's Divine Love.

The shared love between humans is a step above the love of the "dog." I had to learn Love step by step, from the "dog's" to the human's, and finally to the Divine Love of God.

The love shared between humans contains the Knowledge of intellect, to grasp ideas and relations, and to exercise reason and rational judgment. These are the things that I did not possess. Our acts of love and of sexual love were needed for me to understand human love before I could start to comprehend what God's Divine Love was about. God's Divine Love... a Love from the Congregation of all the Angels that make up God.

A Love for a Love... God's Love delivered to you if you give God your Love. For you to receive God's Divine Love, you must Love Him above all else.

God's Love to you was in His giving you the capability and comprehension to grasp ideas and relations and to be able to exercise reason and rational judgment. These are things the "dog" does not have.

If you do not offer these things of intelligence, then you shall remain with the "dog."

The "dog" is oblivious - not conscious or aware - and unmindful, forgetful and given to forgetfulness. God will not be aware of you if you continue to be a dog. You will be forgotten – God will not be conscious of you.

(A great example of God being unconscious of a person; faithfully you follow you hometown baseball team, but there is one player, we'll call him Jim, who is bad, Jim never listens to his coach and because of his not listening he doesn't play well. You are sitting in the bleachers and watching the game. The game is in the last half of the ninth inning, and your team is down by one run, with two outs. You and the other fans are rooting your team on. The bases are loaded, Jim comes up to bat. You turn toward a friend sitting beside you and start talking about where you going to eat after the game. And that is how 'God will not be conscious of you.')

You see, by giving Divine Love to God, He is aware of you and shall return His Love to you.

God enjoys and experiences all ideas, relations, reasons and judgments of yours. These are combined with all of the ideas, relations, reasons and judgments of all the Angels in the congregation that form God. Thus, all Angels in the congregation know all, and the combined experiences of all lives are part of the Knowledge of God.

God's Divine Love... the strength of the congregation of the Angel's power... pulling together... in a united direction... for the Righteousness of All.

God's Divine Love... the total and complete power of all the energy in the make-up of everything known and unknown to us.

God's total Divine Love can be yours if you accept His Love and if you offer and give God your Divine Love.

Giving God your Divine Love does not mean that you must stop loving in the human way, nor does it imply that you must stop living. Divine Love is the highest step in Love. You need to still love others in the human way, but direct your "dog's" love in the correct direction when you have the desire of the "dog," but still keep control of the "dog," and above all else, return God's Divine Love to Him.

To know God is to love Him. Once you understand and get to know God, you will love Him. Once you are able to understand and know God, you will love yourself. And once you get to understand and know God, you will love others. For all is One. To know oneself is to love oneself; to know others is to love others, for we all are part of God. A part of God is inside each of us. Your Angel-within, all others' Angels and my Angel-within are the congregation that forms God.

The "dog" is your natural animal actions.

The human is the intelligent thinking and actions.

The Angel is the Divine acts of God.

The "dog" is the flesh of you.

The intelligence is your Soul.

The Angel-within is the Divine part of God.

Help those who need help. These are the ones that would help themselves if they could do so, and these are the only ones who ask you for help. And do not try to help those that do not help themselves or do not try to help themselves, but continue to love them while you stand fast on your beliefs and convictions just as God does. If you try to help those who do not want help, then you are trying to dominate them into doing better.

Love for others is part of what life is about. Love is looking outward toward others' feelings and needs instead of only looking inward. Love for others will help keep Hell from invading your thoughts. But first you must understand that love is the ability to use Understanding, Compassion, Forgiveness and Wisdom correctly.

Life is not a television show that has been choreographed for you. Nor is this life a dress rehearsal. Life is for real, with no reset button to push and start over again, unless you call reliving another life to correct your Hell as a reset button.

All three things - animal instincts, human intelligence and Divine Love - should be viewed and must be considered as love, but they must be balanced together, and yet Divine Love outweighs human intelligence and animal instincts, and Divine Love and human intelligence are more important than animal instincts. Therefore, we should control our animal instincts while we live with intelligence and above all we need to understand and use God's Divine Love in our daily lives.

The Supreme number is three. As we see it, the number one is the "dog," and number two is the human, and number three is God. But in reality we as the dog is last, and number two is the human, and God is number One.

On August 23, 1999, and after going to bed, I awoke about midnight and the Angel Jo was lying beside me.

I said, "Let's go somewhere."

"All right," she replied and then added, "Where?"

"Surprise me," I answered and then fell asleep.

Our night's journey carried us to a place where I witnessed all the Love that had ever been possessed in the world. The Love from the past, the Love of the present and all the Love of the future could be seen all at once. A vast ocean of Love lay in front of us. Silent and calm, it shimmered like glass. There were no shores or bottom, but a sea of Love that was held tightly together. I sensed and felt the Knowledge that all people at sometime during their lives contain Love. No one from the young to the old is without Love sometime in his life.

I awoke about seven-thirty in the morning and the early sun shined into my bedroom. The sun's bright rays covered my arm and pillow, but this morning not with just its bright light, but sunlight that was blue or green... almost a bright emerald color, like none I had seen before. The light lasted just a few minutes as I thought of our journey, then the color faded and was gone. Later that day, I remembered what the Angel Jo had once told me, "You shall Love all people more than anyone else alive today."

Then I realized that after seeing the sea of Love, I could Love all the people of the world, for now I knew that all people do contain Love at sometime in their lives.

Once again what the Angel Jo had predicted was coming true, for I was starting to Love all people.

WISDOM

And the Angel Jo said to me, "Now that you know Compassion, Understanding, Forgiveness and Love, it is time for you to practice them daily in your life. Using them with Wisdom will help you move to a higher understanding of God."

Wisdom...the power of true and right discernment... conformity to the course of action dictated by such discernment... good practical judgment...common sense... a high degree of knowledge.

A friend of mine thought the word "dog" was not the right word of choice to use for referring to the animal that lives in us all. God spelled backwards is "dog," and therefore "Dog" is opposite of God. God is righteous for the congregation, the "dog" is self-centered, and therefore you could say "dog" is the same as doing deeds against the congregation, thus its direction is evil or bad.

Now you can understand what I mean when I speak of the "dog." But before going into examples that the Angel Jo showed me about Wisdom, I wish to state that Compassion, Understanding, Forgiveness, Love, Cherishment and even Judgment can be used in combination with each other, or separately. The reason that I am sharing this bit of information about their uses is that their uses fall under Wisdom, while part of Wisdom is the Knowledge to use the different combinations when needed.

The Angel Jo showed me many times when I did not use Wisdom during my present life.

(Actually, that was easy for her to do because I rarely used Wisdom in my past actions and reactions. Failure to use Wisdom in my actions was one of my common traits.)

Besides viewing my past life, we saw a group of people somewhere in a wilderness of tall evergreen trees surrounded by snow-capped mountains using Wisdom to ration their depleting food supplies.

And then we drifted like smoke in a beautiful garden with Jesus long ago as He talked to them about God's Love for humans.

We then witnessed most of the Second World War, viewing it from both sides. I saw how Hitler's generals used Wisdom in some of their battle strategies, but their warped perspectives twisted their wisdom into evil actions, and we also watched Hitler's failure to use Wisdom by killing many people and how his failure to use the Wisdom twisted his perspectives as his and his generals warped judgment caused them to lose the War.

We visited The White House and saw a President use his power to corrupt people on his staff.

Not using Wisdom caused his staff to see everything from the President's slanted viewpoint. This different point of view warped their perspectives, which in turn caused his staff to go the wrong way, for then they believe in wrong things. After doing wrong, it becomes easier to do wrong, for then they seen everything from a warped point of view.

Wisely understanding what your actions will cause is Wisdom.

Having Compassion, Understanding, Forgiveness and Love for others allows us to see the complete picture of their and our actions - the total picture. We look directly into the problem without twisting the perspective. Therefore, we can see the problem clearly and understand what is needed to correct it.

As with Hitler, he knew Germany was in trouble with its economy, but his twisted perspectives made him believe that others had brought forth Germany's problems. In his thinking, to kill others would help their economy.

Hitler's generals knew warfare, but their twisted point of view prevented them from seeing that Hitler's decisions were wrong regarding placement of their troops and the size of their opponents' armies.

The president's twisted perspectives caused him to believe he was doing no wrong when he instructed his staff to do his bidding, but his directives corrupted his staff that changed their reasoning.

In his true perspectives of life, Jesus' actions should have brought us to understand that we should love all others, for we are part of them, too, but our forefathers' perspectives brought the concept that Jesus died on the cross for our sins.

The Angel Jo and I understood why Hitler killed all those people, for his "dog" within made him think he was protecting himself and the people of Germany from others. We cannot forgive his actions against others. But we were saddened by what he thought - that others had caused Germany's problems.

Can we forgive the president for his actions because he did not think his actions would bring harm to others?

But we were saddened by what he thought - that it was okay to direct his staff to do his personal business.

Both Hitler's and the president's actions came from the "dog." Both acts were directed inward instead of outward. Hitler's acts caused Domination. The president's acts caused Self-Domination by others. Hitler's acts murdered many. The president's acts did not murder any that we know of, but what he taught others may have caused them spiritual suicide in their lives.

Jesus' acts were directed outward toward others, for he was talking about others' feelings with love for others. His acts came from his Angel-within. He showed Love, Compassion, Understanding and Forgiveness for others in his Wisdom. And our forefathers' perspectives placed many into Self-domination.

The president and Hitler did not show Wisdom.

Hitler's generals did not show Wisdom in their war efforts, for Hitler's twisted strategies of war to Dominate directed everything inward toward Hitler and themselves.

Separation between your Angel-within and the "dog" - knowing when to use Compassion, Understanding, Forgiveness and Love, is Wisdom. If these things are not used correctly, they can cause Domination. And Domination is one of the biggest Sins of all.

Using Compassion, Understanding, Forgiveness and Love incorrectly is to use them from the "dog" within under animal instincts, which also is to use them with the intent of receiving something in return is a Sin.

In a recent conversation with the Angel Jo, I asked, "Can you read my mind?"

She answered, "Yes, but only when you allow me."

When we do not allow others to enter our heart, we are not using Compassion, Understanding, Forgiveness or Wisdom because opening our hearts to others is allowing them to help us and to know us, and that is Wisdom - accepting help when you need help. My not allowing the Angel Jo to read my mind was not letting her into my heart. It is the same as not allowing her to help me or to know me.

If you cannot open your heart to others, it is the same as saying, "I will not let you in my heart for you will see the wrong that I have done."

Uncovering your Angel is allowing others to know your life. Uncovering your Angel... becoming part of the congregation of Angels is allowing yourself to become part of God and part of His Creation. Opening your heart to others is letting others into your heart and allowing others to know your life. Therefore, opening your heart is uncovering your heart and that is using Wisdom.

The Angel Jo once asked me, "Can you have supper with your enemies?"

I answered, "Yes."

She stared at me for a moment and then replied, "I do not think so."

(I did not understand that her question was really, "Would I open my house to my enemies? Could I accept letting my enemies know my complete life? Have I done anything that I do not want my friends or foes to know about?" For when she symbolically asked, "Open my house to my enemies," she actually was saying, "Let everyone know my thoughts.")

After many months of dwelling on her question, I came to a conclusion and finally had an answer to her question. I said, "I now have the answer to your question."

She responded, "So what is your answer?"

I said, "I know who my enemies are."

"Then who are your enemies?" she asked.

"I have no enemies... my enemies are within me, for my enemies come from the "dog" that dwells within."

"Correct," she smiled. "Now you are remembering what you are learning. Now you are learning."

Let's go back to the words of God's Concept of Life. "To Learn and Experience from the Experiences of others through Endurance of Life."

With an open heart you are allowing others to learn and experience through your experiences of your life!

Having an open heart is the same as having an open mind. You are allowing others to see and know (learn and experience) everything you have done in your life.

If your heart is full of anger would you want everyone to review your past life? That is Hell.

After your death and you have joined with your Angel-within, if you had an open heart, then you shall be ready to re-unite with God. For once you return to the Light, you will know that God knows, and also you will know that He (all Angels) has seen all that you have done in your life. If you refuse to go to the Light, then you are denying yourself by refusing to let yourself know that All (God) knows all about your life completely.

Denying yourself is refusing to accept what you have done in your life. Refusing to open your heart so others can experience and learn from your life is placing yourself into Self-domination. Not wanting God to know what your life turned out to be is the awareness of what you have done wrong in life. Not wanting to know that God knows what you have done in your life will place you in Hell. Not being willing to accept the blame for your actions is your denial of God. For denying oneself is not loving yourself or others.

Wisdom also is the ability to know that one must live on faith as well as Knowledge.

If God desired, He could show Himself to all of us. However, that would remove faith from our lives, for we must have faith and belief to learn and experience life, and faith and belief directs us into our freedom of choice, but if you accept God into your heart, He will reveal Himself to you.

God does not care what you chose as the direction for your life. You have complete control over your Angel-within while you lead your own life. Therefore, you also are accountable for your own life.

Do not judge others for their lives for you are not accountable for their actions. But judge their actions to see if they are right for you. You are not your brother's keeper. Judge only yourself, for you are accountable for your actions alone.

In my home one night, my wife, our youngest son, a friend and I had a conversation with Gabrael.

Our friend asked Gabrael, "Should I pursue a career in music?"

Gabrael responded, "Sure, go ahead, you have plenty of time."

When you are ready for the job, the job will be ready for you. My friend had plenty of time to prepare for his mission, but for now he can play music if that is what he desires.

If my friend wished to try music, he should, for God does not control our every move, but every move is part of His Master Plan.

When it comes time for your mission, God will have you prepared for that job.

Faith directs us in our daily lives. Faith in himself gave my friend the strength to pursue a music career, just as faith and belief in himself will give him the insight to follow the directions that God will give him in order to have him ready for the job.

Our faith and belief in God gives us strength to deliver ourselves out of darkness and raises us closer to Him.

Faith and belief are both part of Wisdom as demonstrated by humans.

Life is to experience and learn. Do not sit back and let the Master Plan do your bidding for you. You must learn from your own experiences as well as from the experiences of others.

Open your heart to learn and experience others' lives by helping and knowing them while allowing others to help and know you.

The Wisdom that I learned drew me from my "dog" into the light of Knowledge, for now I had Compassion, Understanding, Forgiveness and

Love for others. But still, as with all humans, I must try to contain the "dog" within me. I must daily use what I have learned, I must practice them daily. I must remember what the Angel Jo, Gabrael, Michael, Jesus, and above all, God has taught me. For now I was becoming a Master.

(I have been told that almost everything, but some of it I only seen with the Angels, that I have written here about God's Concept of Life can be found in the Bibles, but the Bibles stories are sometimes hard to grasp and understand, and most of the Bibles contain concepts from humans for human agendas. Our writings are direct and to the point, with easy wording for all to understand exactly what has been said through the Angel Jo from God.)

CHERISHMENT

Cherish... to hold dear... treat with tenderness... to entertain fondly.

"Cherishment" is the compassion to hold dear, the understanding to treat with tenderness, the ability to entertain fondly and the wisdom to hope for an idea, and is the things and actions that we hold dear, and the wisdom to understand that everything that happens was needed because it was meant to happen.

To hold something dear and close, you must first have the wisdom to cherish it. You must have the ability to cherish the past and not dwell on what the past was, or could have been, or should have been.

Your past cannot be changed. Therefore, the past is forever. You cannot redo the past. You must forgive yourself for all the mistakes in your life, just as you must forgive all others for mistakes in their lives.

Cherish all the good things about your past life, but also remember the bad experiences of your life, for all good and bad experiences of your life are what made you who you are today.

The Angel Jo and I reviewed our lives during the Civil War. We recalled the last Christmas I spent with my father and mother of that time. How I loved those days. Also we visited our secret place by the stream where we talked and loved each other in those days.

The Angel Jo showed me the good things that I had experienced during my days as a soldier. Even a bad experience sometimes contains good. Thus, I was taught how to cherish the good, but also to remember the bad without dwelling on the bad experiences, and whereas, we learn from our mistakes and we learn from others' mistakes.

I still cherish every minute that Jo and I spent together during our summer of 1965, for in the time that we spend together we had no bad experiences.

I cherish the memories of old Queen Vickie, who carried me into Jo's life and who still carries me deep into my thoughts of yesterday. And I hold dearly, too, my past years in the oil field and all those with whom I worked and shared comradeship with.

Things of Cherishment can be mixed within bad memories also. We must learn how to seek and find good things that are mixed with the bad. We must learn how to look for and seek the good in others whom we may consider to be bad people. We must learn how to love all others without letting others dominate us and without our trying to dominate them. We must learn how and when to let go of others and let them take responsibility for their actions and their lives. We must learn how to Cherish others' lives and their experiences as well.

When you read the stories in the Bibles, you need to understand and experience the lives of the people of that time. Bible stories were written to demonstrate the strong faith and belief in God of those persons. The people in the Bibles tried to do God's bidding, and the writings surely indicate how much hardship those people endured. The Bibles stories show that the faith of many in Him could not be shaken, and above all else, they believed in God. Cherish their stories as they continue and still Cherish them on the Other Side.

I had one wish about Cherishment that I thought even the Angels could not fulfill. I wished for the memory of Jo and me together as man and wife until her life ended in 1968. But this did not happen, so how could I Cherish something that never was?

Once again, the Angel Jo had proved me wrong, just as she had done concerning my being an atheist. The Angel Jo did what I thought was impossible as God granted me my wish, which was to spend three years of life with her, (three years was the amount of time that she lived after we parted in the fall of 1965.)

It was during the spring of 1999 that I made that wish, only to discover that my wish indeed was granted and that we were presently living my wish, using Christine's life as hers. Christine's Angel-within shared her humanly experiences with the Angel Jo.

We had finally achieved the wonderful memories of having married and raised two sons together; those wonderful memories of Compassion, Understanding, Forgiveness and Love that we shared together are a true Cherishment.

I was granted my wish to have Jo beside me for three years, which she did, but we were also Blessed by God and Christine to share the memories of life married to each other through the marriage of Christine and myself.

What a Cherishment! I was given the best of both worlds.

Now I understood that even in the days of the death camps in Europe during World War Two, the people confined also had Cherishments of feelings and time spent together as they were being persecuted and put to death. And even though we may think we have times without anything to cherish, things of Cherishment are always around us.

Now I knew what Cherishment was about and I was nearly prepared to complete my mission (writing this book) here on Earth. But first I needed to understand Judgment and then put all seven of the items of God's Concept of Life to practice in my daily life. Then I would be ready for the job that God had planned and prepared for the Angel Jo and me.

As said before, we learn and experience from experiences of others through the endurance of life. We also learn and experience from the other lives we have had, and we also learn and experiences of our ancestors thought our DNA. We just need to know how to control the bad emotions from the past.

You are allowing your Angel-within to be uncovered if you let your Angel-within share your experiences with all other Angels (God), as you are accepting your life's faults and are forgiving yourself for your mistakes. In this way, you give your Angel-within Everlasting Life with God, and join with all others who have lived that are now in the Light.

Use Cherishment with Compassion... use Cherishment with Understanding... use Cherishment with Forgiveness... use Cherishment with Love... use Cherishment with Wisdom, for all are aspects of God's Concept of Life that can be used together or separately. Cherishment also can be used with Judgment.

So now, let's go on to the Knowledge about Judgment and my final lessons of the Concept of Life from God.

JUDGMENT

The dictionary says Judgment is "the act of judging;" the decision or opinion reached through judging; the ability to judge wisely.

As certain as I write, on Judgment Day, God shall judge you, but I am writing about self-judgment instead of God judging us on His Judgment Day.

(You will learn about Judgment Day in our chapter entitled the Final Day.)

The ability to self-judge comes only when you understand God's Concept of Life. Therefore if you do not understand Compassion, Understanding, Forgiveness, Love, Wisdom and Cherishment, you cannot perform self-judgment accurately.

Recently as I stood on my front porch two men drove by and stopped, and then they got out of their car and came to me. These two men were from a Baptist church, and we talked about God and Jesus, then I turned our conversation toward Judgment.

I told them we needed to judge ourselves daily during our lives to understand our sins (mistakes) that we had committed that day in order for us to not make the same mistake tomorrow.

One of the men replied, "We are not Jesus, and therefore we cannot judge ourselves."

So through their Baptist religion, these men think they can go through life making the same mistakes over and over again without thinking about or worrying about what they have done and need not try to change and/or not make the same mistake again.

Excuse me! I know that we must self-judge ourselves daily or we are nothing more than animal.

Recently, my wife, Christine, and I were spending a quiet evening at home and our discussion turned to Judgment. She could not understand that she was judging another whenever she would refer to a person as being "nice." It was then that I realized that Christine, along with the men from the Baptist church, and probably most people in the world, do not understand what the word "Judgment" means.

Judging is not only to determine if someone is guilty of a crime, also it is deciding what is best for you at this time – evaluating the situation throughout and deciding what is the best action to take. Therefore, self-judgment is self-evaluation. Observing... reviewing all that you have done in your life and cherishing all the good that you have completed during your life. Self-judgment is also understanding why you have done all those bad things during the past part of your life. Repenting is to change your view of your actions of the past and forgiving yourself for your bad deeds. You forgive yourself and others for making the bad decisions but we do not forgive the bad act. For whenever we judge the acts of people we are deciding if the act is right for us to do or not. And while judging people, including yourself, you are in reality showing Love for yourself and others for the trials that they and you have faced and won over evil. Using Wisdom in Judgment is to know the difference between right and wrong, and between good and bad. The Compassion is to use your Judgment in the Righteous way of God. And yet, judging is the decisions we make daily in our individual lives such as deciding what clothing to wear, how fast to drive through a school zone, what company or business to work for, whom to marry, what to name our children, and all other things that we decide upon during every minute of our lives.

Recall for a minute, the Angel Jo's and my going to the Other Side and viewing my Angel, who was covered with my self-made Hells. I was given the opportunity to see and review my past lives, including the early past of this life, in order to change the direction of my life. Thus, I was permitted to self-judge myself.

The Angel Jo said, "No one who has ever lived has been granted, in a way that you were shown, what God has given you - a chance to redeem your Salvation for Everlasting Life by reviewing your past life with the Angels. God, through Gabrael, has asked me to show you the Light and Knowledge, for we knew that I was the only one capable of helping you. Now you have the Knowledge... now you are becoming a Master... practice the things you have learned daily throughout your life. I will always stand beside you, but if you become lonely, just remember my touch and I shall be there."

Judge yourself daily. We cannot go back and change what has been done. Judge your past to direct your way for the rest of your today and future. Do not dwell on what should have been. Enjoy this minute, experience the day, and plan for tomorrow.

Step by step, judge your actions daily and direct your life toward God and His ways. Seek not to find Heaven, but live with an open heart toward all, for then Heaven shall be your just reward. Look not to find excuses for your life, but to reveal all the good that surrounds you.

Every day is a new beginning in your life. You need not be the same person you were yesterday. Review your day's activities so that tomorrow you can be a better person. Character and personalities are not set in stone; you alone control your own actions and directions.

God recognizes that we are humans. He understands we make mistakes. He knows we learn through our mistakes, which are experiences, too. He will not judge you for your past mistakes, but He will condemn you forever if you sin again Him and His Creation. He will judge you only for what you do now and from thereafter for now you also contain the Knowledge of His Concept of Life. But He also knows that most cannot change direction immediately. Change occurs over time, step by step, for one cannot be taught, people must be inspired to change and must practice changes.

More than likely you made a mistake today, so use the experience of your mistake to help change your life tomorrow. Use the Knowledge that was given to me from God, the Knowledge that I am passing on to you, the Knowledge that He requested I share with you. His Concept of Life is your Salvation to Everlasting Life, for His Knowledge will insure your Heaven.

Your religion, the color of your skin and the language that you speak do not matter as long as you live with an open heart for all. The same applies to different cultures, disabilities and the color of your hair or eyes, too. The only thing that matters is living with an open heart. The Knowledge of knowing the difference between right and wrong and good and bad must be included in and implemented from an open heart.

After I was given the opportunity to review my life, in which I judged myself for my past actions, both from this life and my previous lives, the Angel Jo and I sat there as I lowered my head. The Angel Jo placed her arm around my shoulder and we wept, for the past is Forever and I could not change my past life. All that I had done could not be removed from my past. I could only change my ways of the future, for I knew that if I did not change my ways, I would surely live in Hell until the end of time, and my twisted ideas were driving a wedge between the Angel Jo and me. I must change or I would lose both her and God forever. My Love for the Angel Jo that now had turned into Divine Love for her and God and all of His Angels inspired me to see and understand God's Concept of Life.

The Angel Jo had worked for more than three years in helping me see our Divine Love. It had taken me that long to understand her Love. Until I accepted her Love, I could not have understood God or His Concept of Life.

The Angel Jo said with a smile, "Now that you know God's Concept of Life, you must practice what you have learned daily in your life. Write and also tell others about God's Concept of Life for I stand beside you Forever."

I will never forget God's Concept of Life, *"TO LEARN AND EXPERIENCE FROM EXPERIENCES OF OTHERS THROUGH ENDURANCE OF LIFE."* And if you use Compassion, Understanding, Forgiveness, Love, Wisdom, Cherishment and Judgment for all (that includes yourself), then Salvation is yours, too.

The "Others" in the Concept also means "you." So it can also be expressed, "To Learn and Experience from the Experiences of Yourself through the Endurance of Your Life."

Now that I have explained most of Compassion, Understanding, Forgiveness, Love, Wisdom, Cherishment and Judgment, let us go on putting them all together in the real life situation that includes God.

Our lives are left up to us. We do either good or bad, and right or wrong, and we do judge actions to see if they are right for us. Later on of course, God will judge us all on the Final Day of Time.

All life was placed here on earth for us to enjoy and experience.

I am sorry for you if you thought that all other forms of life were not intended by God for us to use. Daily, life forms are destroyed by nature and us. The natural destruction of life forms is because that life form could not endure the changes in life and becomes extinct. That is not to say that many forms of life have evolved to sustain life. This destruction of life forms also comes from the natural evolution of humans and our use of chemicals, such as those that we release into the air, in the water and on land; the chemicals we produce from our vehicles and other chemicals that are the by-products of our "needs."

We control our lives. We also control life and death of many different life forms and I dare not judge if the other life forms that we have destroyed were needed or not. I can only say we are in control of our environment.

If other life forms are in the way of progress, is it wrong to destroy them? I do not know the answer. I only know that we must live in the environment that we have made. Yet also, I know that we must live in peace and harmony with other humans, so can it be any different from living in peace and harmony with other life forms? For if our "needs" and "wants" did not interfere with the existence of other life forms, those forms would not be destroyed.

People make and sell products that we request without concerns as to whether it harms others or not.

I once saw a program on television about people who were concerned about the ozone layer being destroyed by Freon. Do you realize that most of those participants drove to the taping of this program in automobiles equipped with air conditioners! So were they saying, "Let's stop destroying the ozone layer, but do not stop me from using or having a car with an air conditioner."

(Automobile air conditioners used R-12 Freon as its coolant agent until just a few years ago. Now R-134 coolant is being used, but that, too, is bad for the environment.)

If we do not buy automobiles that have air conditioners, the auto companies would not install air conditioners in automobiles.

Our "dog" priorities direct our way of life when our priorities should be about God's Concept of Life.

I understand that many things in our lives cannot be done away with. Such as we cannot live in caves, we "must" have electricity and we cannot do away with automobiles. Most people think that we cannot live different from our neighbors, and so peer pressure directs our lives. Again, I do not know the answer but I do know that we must try to live in harmony with God, others and nature.

Life is not perfect; nor did God wish us to live in a perfect world. God wants us to have choices and to follow our hearts in the right direction. We learn by our mistakes in choice making; therefore, God wishes us to know and use His Concept of Life in our lives.

And the Angel Jo said, "And therefore, if you judge others, you shall be judged."

During the last days of Jesus, the Jews did not like His actions of working on the Sabbath by healing and ministering on that holy day of the week. The domination of the Jews tried to control Jesus. Therefore, Jesus was brought forth in front of Pilate for judgment and punishment.

Pilate tried to obtain a confession from Jesus that would prove that He had done wrong in the eyes of the Jewish-made God, but Jesus would not confess, and in fact, said that He was the Son of God.

Pilate turned to the Jews and said, "I am through, I wash my hands of this matter. You decide the fate of this Man."

The Jews judged Jesus guilty and said He should be crucified. Pilate agreed with their "reasoning" and had their demands carried out.

And the Angel Jo said unto me, "For they judged, therefore, they were also judged."

The Jews judged Jesus guilty so therefore, they are guilty of domination. Pilate agreed with them, therefore, he is guilty of self-domination.

And the Angel Jo said unto me, "Seek and you shall find what you are looking for.

"Look for evil in people and you shall see evil in all people including yourself. Judge others and you shall be judged, for God is All, and you are part of the All. If you judge another, therefore, you are judging yourself, and if you find another guilty, then you shall also be found guilty."

A couple that I knew of, the man weighed well over three hundred pounds, and his wife was not a small woman either, but small compared to her husband. Both claimed to be true Christians.

Recently the man died not from his over weight nor from his heavy smoking, he died from lymphatic cancer. During the three days of mourning following his death, his widow stated she did not believe in the Light, in Entities, nor did she believe in the Other Side. She said she only believed in God, the Devil, and Heaven and Hell.

To understand the story of these two people, you must also know that this deceased man also had two brothers who both drank beer regularly. One of the brothers, I will call Ralph, the other brother, I will call Mike. Both of these men were professional truck drives.

Ralph had a bad marriage, and therefore, he and his wife went their separate ways. His drinking was not solely responsible for the failure of their marriage, for he was on the road (driving) frequently and was not home much, plus there were many other things that helped cause their break-up. After their separation, Ralph found another woman whom he loved dearly and lived with, but did not marry. He continued to drink beer and doing the only profession he knew of, driving trucks.

One night while Mike and Ralph headed to work, while Ralph drove Mike's car and Mike rode as the passenger, they were hit head on by another drunk driver. Ralph was killed on impact while Mike was permanently disabled.

After her husband died from cancer, this lady stated to Mike's wife, Ralph must surely be in Hell because he drank, left his wife and then he also lived in sin with a woman, and Mike was surely headed for Hell because he also drank. She also said her husband must be in Heaven because he believed in God and went to church.

She did not say anything about her husband's actions toward his employees, his brothers, or how he mistreated other people that he knew. For if her husband and she needed help with money, they would always call on his brothers or friends for it, but then, if Mike, or Ralph, or any of their friends needed money, they said they did not have any to give and never paid back the money that they borrowed.

Another story that I must incorporate into this chapter; is the story of my brother named Phil.

Phil ruled and controlled my mother's and father's lives. He also did a pretty good job at controlling our brothers and sisters, too.

My younger sister, by two years, had a child out of wedlock when she was sixteen years old. We also had an older sister that had a child before she was married so having children out of wedlock was not unusual to my family.

My younger sister was not living at home when she conceived, nor when she gave birth to her son. Phil demanded her to never return home again, but he never said anything about not coming home to my older sister who also had a son out of wedlock. Of course our mom and dad stood beside Phil on his decision out of fear.

A few years later after the birth of her son, my younger sister decided to go home to visit our mother and father. Phil found out about her plans, and met her about one block away from their home as she walked toward home. As they met, he threatened her, and told her to never come home again. Of course, she turned around and left.

During 1998, my younger sister finally moved back to our hometown of Wooster, Ohio. Our mother and father had past away and Phil had also died years ago. No longer was Wooster her hometown, for now California was her home. She did not stay long in Wooster, but instead moved back to California.

Phil stole away those precious years that she could have spent with our mother and father.

There is a lot to write about concerning these people's ideas and statements.

Now the deceased man and his wife did go to church while Phil did not but all three claimed to be Christians.

Heaven is a state of mind, so to confirm a place in Heaven is to live a righteous life. Going to church, or thinking you are Christian, does not confirm one's place in Heaven.

Churchgoers are not confirmed a place in the Light. Anyone can go into the Light. It is your thoughts of yourself and others that will determine if you go to the Light or not, and if you wish to stay in the Light or return to life again.

No one has the right to deny you your rightful place in the Light. People on Earth may try to deny you the place you wish to be as Phil tried with my sister, but no one has the right to say if you are in Heaven or Hell as the woman said about her brothers-in-law. She did not know what her brothers-in-law thought. No one knows your thoughts but you.

In both stories all three of these people, the deceased man, his wife and Phil, judged others. For when you judge without knowing the complete story, you are placing judgment on others without a trial where all the evidence is brought forth; thus you are judging yourself.

We all carry part of God in us that is our Angels. In other words, our bodies are the houses of God. Our Angels are part of God that dwells in our bodies, and anything that we do that harms our bodies is harming our Angels and therefore, we are hurting God; Such as one being overweight is harming God's house.

(I use the term overweight only as an example that seems to plague many of us.)

Being judgmental is the same sin to our bodies as harming our bodies is a sin, for both do harm to the body and Soul.

I do not wish to get into the subject of overweight as being a Sin, but weight problems do cause us not to experience some things that all of us should experience, and can be caused by self-domination.

Sometimes overweight may be a natural imbalance brought on through one's genetic make-up. The same concept applies as unbalanced genetic make-up mat (or can) cause people to be handicapped such as a person who is born blind, and so forth. Presently, many handicaps of today may be overcome through our knowledge of medicines and surgery. This also includes overweight. But, most overweight problems occur by our learning our family eating habits. Over eating is judging that you should eat more. And whereas, no one who ever was starved to death died fat, and being overweight is only brought on by over eating.

Overweight problems can be helped just as drug addictions can be controlled. The true problem is not the over weight, but judging others.

And whereas, overweight is a true indicator that the fat person only thinks of his desires for the taste of food, and where his feelings are directed inward instead of outward toward the congregation of humanity.

God did not only create humans; He created our bodies in His effort to help us. We go against God when we harm others or ourselves, in other words against others without just cause is harming others and oneself.

Unless you are without faults you cannot judge faults of others. If you have faults and try to judge others, your perspectives will warp, thus causing the true picture to be false and distorted, and then you will only see what you want to see.

All humans have faults. No human shall judge another for his faults, faith or belief, and no human shall dominate another, unless you wish to be judged or dominated.

(Now you are going to sit there and say I judged Joey. I did not judge Joey. I wrote his bad actions toward others were common knowledge. That is not judging. But I did judge his actions as not right for me to do.)

Can a person be a true Christian and not believe in Entities, the Light and the Other Side? For these things are mentioned in their Bibles and are part of God and His Creation.

Does a true Christian believe in just part of or the complete Bible?

Do the church leaders only stress the points of their Bibles that they want their congregation to know?

Have you read your Bible complete? I have not, but I have been told by the Angel Jo a lot that is contained in the Bibles. We need not read any Bible to know God. Know and understand life, then you shall know God.

I understand that The King James Version of the Christian Bible states Jesus foretold the future. He told His disciples about His pending death during the Last Supper. I understand Jesus also told many other things about the future during His life. Then can seeing or telling of the future only be the Devil's work?

After Jesus died on the cross and was placed in His tomb did He not return?

Did not people see Him and talk to Him?

Then is seeing and talking with Angels wrong?

Was not Jesus an Angel when He returned?

Some say, when Jesus returned He was full as if in a body. Did not the Angel Jo return to me in body?

Was Jo not an Angel?

Are people so vane to think Jesus could be the only Angel that ever spoke with humans?

Have there not been many reports of the Virgin Mary visiting and talking with people?

Does it not state in the Christian Bibles, God said, "I am the Light."

Is it not stated in the Christian Bibles that God said, "I am the Father, the Son and the Holy Spirit."

If anyone says they are true Christians and they believe in their Bible, then they must also believe in Angels, the Light, the Holy Spirit and the Other Side.

Stating they are true Christians does not make them Christians. But then again, Christianity is not the only religion. And therefore all religions including Christianity are not completely correct.

All religions that follow the one true God, and do not condone domination are fine.

True Love that people carry in their hearts, and of those who show Love from their hearts, makes them true believers. Christianity is only a word to indicate they are dominated by the Christian faith. Most Christians do not even bother to follow their Bible sayings about not judging others, and by not taking care of their God's house, their bodies. How many fat preachers do we see preaching on their ideas of God? They surely are not following what they preach.

The other day while I talked with a Catholic about the Catholic sexual abuse, she said, "But they are only human, and we should forgive them."

I replied, "Can any man who may have just left a boy who he sexually abused, get up in front of others and preach to them about homosexuality being sinful and also speak of sexual abuse as being a sin, and while he preaches, he maybe thinking about getting together with another young boy after he has finished his sermon. How can he be allowed to speak for God and God's Love? For if he, the priest, does not follow what he preaches, how can he expect his congregation to follow his words about God?

And does that priest even believe in God?"

It is not my job to define who is or who is not a believer. I will not cast the first stone. But, if a person believes in all that is written in the Bible, which states our bodies are the houses of God, then they should take care of the house of God. How can a fat preacher say he is a man of God?

And whenever you hear a preacher say he "hates" something, does he not know God created everything and that thing that the preacher hates was created by God?

Jesus never said He hated anything, He said He disliked some actions from some people.

Can anyone who believes in all that was written into his Bible, judge another person for his looks, or the clothes he wears?

I will only tell you the truth. You decide if you are really a true believer or not.

No matter what your convictions are, you may live in the Light forever. As I stated before, you may enter or leave the Light as often as you wish, but the Light will always be your home.

Heaven and Hell are states of your mind. You need not die to 'live' in your Heaven or Hell. You are presently living your Heaven or Hell right here on Earth. Your Heaven or Hell will continue as your state of mind after death.

You may redeem yourself at any time throughout your life. You can find your Heaven up to the last second of life. From the last point of life forward, you will live your Hell or Heaven forever.

If your Hell is too great, you may wish to try another life.

If your Heaven is so wonderful, you may want to re-live again to help others or experience more of life. Again, the choice is yours to stay or re-live again.

God is merciful, and we are all part of God. We should be merciful to ourselves and others, but usually are not to ourselves.

Can you live forever with the thoughts of your wrong doings? God can forgive you but can you forgive yourself?

That is Heaven or Hell and self-judgment.

Many times, deceased loved ones will come back to visit you because they helped make your Hell. They come back in an effort to help you remove your Hell. Most of the times, they will not tell you in words why they have come back. For after death, they have judged themselves.

Feelings of love need not be expressed only in words. Love is felt. Whenever you do something good for another, you need not say, "I am doing this because I love you." The true act of Love needs no words of expression.

Do not try to make life perfect. Judge yourself and not others, but judge everyone's actions to see if there are suitable and needed for you to follow.

Let your acts come from your heart not your mind or pocketbook.

Help yourself before helping others because you cannot help others if you need help.

Be content with life, and then, Heaven for your Soul will follow.

While alive we can change directions of our lives from being bad to good. When life is over, you cannot change the past. Presently you can judge yourself daily, but for you cannot truly judge something until it is over, and whatever you did but did not repent from will be forever with you as your Heaven or Hell.

COVENANT

Now that you have read God's Concept of Life, you should understand why we should practice His Concept of Life in our daily lives.

Anyone can become a Master, for a Master is a person who knows and uses God's Concept of Life correctly throughout his daily life.

God's Concept of Life is a promise from God that says, "I will always Love you, and I will allow you to follow whatever you desire in life. But I'll always be near you."

God has promised us that if we give Him Love, He shall Love us. He also has promised in the Concept of Life - His Covenant; if you need Him, just remember His touch and He shall be there, just as the Angel Jo has told me to remember her touch and she would be there. For accepting them into our lives is opening our heart to them and to humanity.

God will keep His Covenant with you if you direct your life toward Him. And whereas, agreeing to God's promise while returning His promise to Him grants you Everlasting Life. If you refuse His Love and deny His promise, you will find everlasting Hell.

Part of our promise to Him that He requests from us is to not place any man-made god above or beside Him. We have denied His request for hundreds of years by placing people above Him; Jesus and Mohammad and all the people that we have ordained as Saints above beside Him and many worship and pray to them.

People worship many as if they were God. Jesus was a great man. Jesus is the Son of God, but still just a man, and many worship Him as if He was God. And Mohammad was one who claimed that he communicated with one of God's Angels, but none of God's Angel needed to hide in a darken cave while talking to humans as Mohammad said Gabreal did. And even today many worship those who were ordained and made into Saints.

(On a note about Mohammad, I once asked the Angel Jo, "Where is

Mohammad, I see you, Jesus, Michael, Gabrael and many others, but I never see him?"

She replied, "He is not like us."

Was and is Mohammad good or evil? You be the judge.)

Each and every time that God made a Covenant with man; once with Moses, once through Jesus, man broke their Covenants with God.

God first had a Covenant with Moses when He helped Moses lead his people out of Egypt, and for awhile all went well. Then Moses went onto the mountain and talked with God. When Moses returned to his people, he carried tablets (a Covenant) from God. The tablets contained promises of things that God would do and a list of things He expected in return. Upon his arrival back to the people, Moses found that all the people had reverted back to their old concepts. This broke man's agreement with God and then Moses destroyed some of the tablets, the ones that contained promises made from God. Whereas God, through Moses, only gave the people the tablets that contained the things that God demanded from the people – the 10 commandments. And later, man put his thoughts and ideas into what God had said. Thus people have even taken the Words of God and the encounters of Moses with God and polluted and corrupted them with the agendas of man. These are same the type of demands that we place upon our very young children.

Then, when God sent His Son, Jesus, to earth to demonstrate how we should live, after the people killed him, man again placed his thoughts and ideas into what Jesus had said and did, thus, polluting and corrupting God's Covenant. But the sending of His Son to live on earth was the same as the teaching we give to our adolescent children as they head toward adulthood.

Around 700AD, God allegedly spoke through Gabrael with Muhammad in the desert and instructed him about how we should live, but once again man, Muhammad, placed his human thoughts and ideas into God's spoken Words which destroyed the Truths from God. One more interesting fact about Muhammad's communications with Gabrael, it is written that He visited with Muhammad in a cave, while all others who communicated with any of God's Angels always spoke outside – in the open, while Muhammad's talks had to be hidden in a cave...very interesting.

The teachings of Muhammad were and are like the pressure that teenagers placed upon their peers and not the love given from parents to their children.

Humans structured their man-made gods to worship, and their human thoughts and ideas placed nations and millions of others into slavery under their gods. And man then added to the destruction of God's Covenant by turning religions into sideshows for church leaders to make money from.

God stands fast on His Concept of Life, and refuses to listen to the heathens. But yet, God continues to Love all.

Now once again, God has revealed His Love for us in another Covenant - a renewal of His Love for all of mankind, a reaffirming that we should all agree upon.

A renewal of God's promise is a Covenant to all humans.

You have just read God's Covenant. You have His agreement for your Everlasting Life as long as you agree to follow His simple concepts of Compassion, Understanding, Forgiveness, Love, Wisdom, Cherishment and Judgment and use them in your daily life.

Those who believe and follow God's Concept of Life will have no more holy wars, for holy wars are not of God's making, but are humanly made because He is stronger than us, He does not need us to fight His wars. No more self-killings for God, for suicide is of Satan, not God. And also no more domination over others in the name of God, for God does not dominate, only humans dominate.

For if you wish to see God's Love then you shall be surrounded by and protected by God's Love; A Love for a Love.

God's Divine Love will be returned for your Divine Love to Him.

"AND THE ANGEL JO SAID UNTO ME..."

IT CAME TO PASS...

It came to pass between 1996 and 2004; my family and I were blessed daily with many miracles, small and large. And the Angel Jo told me of many glorious things about the Other Side and of things that would come to pass that would indicate I was becoming a Master.

The following chapters are of the many glorious things that the Angel Jo told me concerning life and the Other Side. These things were also part of Their teachings in my process of learning the Mastery.

We are like God's children who are eager to learn, and God is like the parent who is willing and patient to teach His child. God's Love was delivered to me through the Angel Jo, Gabrael and God's Helper, Jesus, who taught me these things.

The Angel Jo said unto me, "You have helped many on both Sides now. Many more will come to seek your help for you are the Guider.

"Spiritual and Religious matters must be sanctified under faith and belief. Our conversations that you have on audio and videocassettes are not to be shared with the public. They are for review by you and the ones chosen by God to tell others about all the things we talked about. For if all were to hear the tapes or see the videos, no faith or belief would be needed and people would only follow Our teaching for Everlasting Life and not out of Divine Love, but faith and belief are the major factors for experiences of humans. The truly Spiritual people are faithful and have belief, while others are non-believers and unfaithful, of whom we will not have. And those who claim to be Spiritual have corrupted the word Spiritual into a religion that is not of God.

"Recall our conversations when I told you about the first person in the second set of Soul Twins?

"Dale, who is one of the chosen ones by God, will be having a difficult time with his faith and belief. He will become afraid of the unfaithful and non-believers. He will turn his back on all that you have taught him. Remember I said you are to teach him and to be there for him and for you just to call him when he needed a friend? And you did that.

"I did not say he would believe and have faith in all that we say. You have taught him all that he would allow you to teach him. Jealousy of you and what you have - your marriage, your children, your home and your contact with God and me, will cause him to want what you have. But Dale is one of the many who will carry our words to others.

"You have done all that you could do for Dale. It is not your problem if he refuses to do what is God's Will. When the time comes for him to carry our words, he will be prepared.

"Jesus witnessed to the unfaithful and the non-believers. Did you not think you or Dale would see many people full of the dog?

"Do you not think some will think or say that Dale and you are crazy or insane?

"Do you think all will believe what Dale and you say is true?

"Plant the seed with the unfaithful and the nonbelievers and allow them to nurture it.

"For Dale and you are no better than Jesus. Therefore, Dale and you will endure the same problems concerning belief and faith that He did. But Dale and you will not be put to death for your beliefs or faith."

Then with lowered head, the Angel Jo added, "No, video and audio tapes are not enough for some. For Dale to have faith and belief, he must first have faith and belief in himself before he will have belief and faith in what we write. After he believes and has faith in himself then he shall be able to believe and have faith in God, for then he will be ready for his job.

"Dale's church taught him their translations of God's Words but it did not teach him to have faith and belief in himself or others. His parents were supposed to teach him self-faith but they forgot how for they did not have faith themselves either. Others also were supposed to teach him to have faith in people but they too forgot how for they also did not have faith in themselves."

Raising her head, looking into my eyes, she took my hands in hers as she continued, "Presently, Dale does not believe or have faith in all that you tell him. He wants clarification of everything that we say. He does not believe or have faith in you or himself. He was taught to only have faith and belief in a man-made god.

"The church he attended did well with their teachings but their teachings were wrong. His parents did not teach him self-faith or belief because he did not ask them but must a student ask to be taught?

"But he shall overcome all this and then, he shall speak and see from his heart with faith and belief when the time comes. It does not matter if one believes only in his Bible, our books or whatever. Any religion is sufficient as long as one lives with an open heart. It does not matter what faith one follows as long as he does not condone domination.

"You once asked me if seventy percent of this book that you were writing was correct, and I answered, 'yes.'

"Then you asked me if seventy-five percent of this book was correct, and I again answered, 'yes.'

"Once more you asked me if eighty percent of this book was correct, again I answered, 'yes.'

"You knew that had you asked me if eighty-five percent of this book was correct I would have answered, 'no' because you were still rewriting it, therefore, you knew it was not correct. For then, you did not have faith or belief in all that you were writing, but now you do.

"Yet, another time you asked me if God had created humans, and I answered, 'yes,' for God did create humans. A human without intelligence is just an animal. God did create the first one-cell animal during the first cycle. He placed intelligence inside the first one-cell animal; thus, He created humans. Now again, when Dale heard this statement, he took it into his religion as 'God created humans in the Garden.' He did not listen to the complete Knowledge.

"If Dale continues to be a non-believer that is not your problem, it is his. You offered him Knowledge but he refused it. Is this not a Love for a Love or a slap for a slap?

"Is this not turning your back on him, one who has turned his back on you?

"Self-domination is still domination and that is a Sin placed upon oneself. If you did not return his turning his back to you, then that would be placing yourself in self-domination for you would be listening to his ideas without the ability to share your Knowledge and thoughts with him. What you did is as God has done with many and it is the same as I did to you, I stood beside you for over thirty years waiting for you to turn back around and accept me again. We do not turn our backs on others; they turn their backs on us.

"After you rejoin me on this 'the Other Side,' that night we will pay a visit to Dale. The coming day Dale will remember our visit, and then that evening Dale will go to your home and ask your wife, Christine, for these books because we will have told him to do this, then he *shall* believe because then the job will be ready for him."

CYCLES

And the Angel Jo said unto me, "Everything has its own cycle. Look closely at human life and you will understand that the individual's life has its own cycle and yet, its cycle is more than its life span from birth to death. Because its matter - atoms have particles and pieces, and those individual parts of each atom have cycles, too. In referring to the life cycle of a human, the human starts out as merely a few cells within both of his parents. These cells combine in the female to create a child. And during the pregnancy, these cells multiply to form the child. Then, throughout this individual's life, his cells keep multiplying until a given time during his life and from that point on, the number of cells decrease until death and at that time, all remaining cells return to what they came from. Thus, as you say, 'dust to dust.'

"All things in your world are set up that same way - they come from the earth and will return to the earth when their time is up; to return (recycle) again but they need not return in the same form. And yet, all cycles are individually interwoven together as One.

"All life is set forth in the same manner and while, all things are also set forth in the same manner because all things, including life are made up from energy. For energy cannot be destroyed but merely changes form and/or direction. Therefore, all things that surround you are that way including the Universe for it has its own cycle, too.

"This cycle of the Universe is what I am referring to when I speak of as 'living' in the fifth cycle of life for there has been four previous cycles.

"If you wish to speak of the start of this cycle as what scientist refer to as the 'big bang theory' you may do so. But it was not a 'big bang' that started this reality for it was continuation of the cycles that brought forth this cycle that you think of as reality.

"Think of an explosion that put all things into motion away from a center point. As energy moves outward from the center point, it moves faster and faster. The energy now becomes matter while distances between all matter increases. At a given speed, the particles of matter start to reduce in size as they continue to accelerate. As matter now accelerates faster and faster, all starts to come together again but gives the appearance of keeping the same distances because they are reducing in size comparable to the reduction in distances between each other. Thus, it might look like sizes do not change and distances appear to be increasing. As the acceleration continues, all is pulled back together again and compressed until all is no bigger than a point of a needle. At this moment, the acceleration closes to a stop and the force of the stopping action causes the energy to 'explode' again; thus another cycle has begun.

"This 'explosion' at the beginning of each cycle has occurred five times for we are in the fifth cycle.

"I will not go into detail of each cycle because you cannot verify what I say and it is irrelevant anyway. But I will tell you; one cycle had intelligent animals that produced offspring at will and by itself, while in another cycle, we had birds big enough they could pick up and carry people.

"The cycles are of reality and should not be considered as different dimensions. Reality is what surrounds you. It is all what you can understand. Reality is all that you are capable to comprehend for it is all what you have learned, experienced and endured. There is no way that I could try to explain what started the 'big bang' for no one alive on Earth could understand it. But the best for you to comprehend Reality is to think of God, Energy, consciously thinking of Reality, for it is merely a thought in God. And once you have come to this, the Other Side, then, you will understand. For man does not need to know how things started or where the start came from for man only needs to live and enjoy life. And also, man does not need the knowledge of how many cycles there are to be and/or if other cycles are occurring at this present time. We Love you and as God, we have created all this for you."

GENESIS

(This chapter, GENESIS covers our conversations that the Angel Jo revealed about the continuing birth of Creation; Genesis is constant forming. Creation of the Universe is never ending. "Universe" is the matter contained in all things that we touch and cannot touch, feel and cannot feel, taste and cannot taste, hear and cannot hear, see and cannot see throughout the vast distances of space above us, around us, below us and in us.)

And the Angel Jo said unto to me, "In the beginning... Genesis. All things were created. Genesis is Creation.... the Start.

"All Universes are recycled over and over again. During that part of the Genesis period, the purest of the Energy goes into the creation of Angels. The rest of energy is recycled into other matter that comprises the Universe. As we write and as this book is being read, Energy is being cycled into Angels and other matter...GENESIS... the continuing Creation... re-cycling. Energy is a constant. Energy is never destroyed, only recycled and refined.

"In the not too distant future, your world along with your Universe will be recycled. This will take place within the next one hundred fifty years or so. Perhaps this recycling of Genesis could come today, tomorrow or any other day that will arrive no more than one hundred fifty years from now for people are not to know the Final Day. If humans knew the Final Day, they would try to do things of the dog to change their final days.

"If one has passed on before this part of the cycling takes place, one shall see the event from this, the Other Side. I know that you will already have passed over to this Other Side long before the end of this present cycle. But the end of this cycle is not to be known until the moment it occurs.

"Jesus has told you that I have opened the Book of Gabrael that you call the Book of Daniel but I am on the Other Side. Since you know all that I know regarding the end, for you are part of me as I am part of you, we are the first set of Soul Twins, you made a vow with me never to reveal the date of the end of Time to anyone. Nevertheless, you can assure others that date is coming. It does not take a mind reader to look around and view the crumbling of your society because of the agenda beliefs of individuals and the assault upon nature in a creation where there are more people whose Angels are covered with Hell.

"The Bibles are designed to give people false dates of the Final Day. False prophesies were placed into the Bibles by men who dwelled on the future. The dog sees everything for itself. To the dog, the Final Day is the end of its life. The dog dwells on the thought of its life ending and its never having its desires fulfilled and yet, to God the Final Day means another Genesis, the fresh start of a new Time and the coming home of all His Angels, and the Righteous Angel-within sees the Final Day as their Homecoming after that last moment on the Final Day. All with Heaven in their hearts shall return to the Light and have everlasting life as Genesis continues into another cycle. The Final Day is the end of all life as humans know it, another Genesis. For all things changing directions and/or forms is Genesis.

"Each of you has his individual Judgment Day which comes at the end of your life, your cycle. This transformation from material body to Angel is another Genesis. At your deaths, God will not judge you but instead you will judge yourselves. All others who have lived until the end of this cycle of time will face their individual Judgment Day during the Armageddon on the Advent-ful day, and then each individual will stand in front of God and be judged by Him.

"To fully understand the difference between and/or correlation of self-judgment and judgment by God, you must fully comprehend self-judgment as judging yourself, which comes after your death. Judgment by God comes after the Final Day of all life. Those who died long ago judged themselves after their deaths and they, too, will be judged by God on that the Final Day, as all will be judged by God. Both Judgments are yet another Genesis for all will die on that last day of this cycle."

Now that statement, "All will die on the last day of this cycle," is hard for some people to accept. You will hear "born again" Christian speak of Jesus coming to Earth and we will live for one thousand years under His reign. These are the ones who cannot accept God's Master Plan of cycling for they are of the "dog."

The "dog" is the animal part of us all. Our Angels must "Master" the dog if we wish to elevate ourselves to a higher level and closer to God.

The statement in the Christian Bible, "Jesus will reign for one thousand years" means all will live in the Light for one thousand years before the next cycle begins.

The word "reigns" means control and to keep in check with supreme power. So Jesus will keep in check and control of the Light for one thousand years.

Now let's look at who is Jesus. He is the Son of God. Your Angel-within, my Angel-within and all the other Angels combined are God. Therefore Jesus is our Son, for we all are One. Therefore Jesus is part of us, so we all reign, we all will keep in check and control by supreme power, the Light. No individual rules in the Light, for all are equal. Again, this new reign is a Genesis because it is the start of a new empire - cycle.

Armageddon... God's judgment day and the second coming of Jesus, another Genesis, will both come together on the last day of time for this cycle, the Final Day is Genesis, for Genesis is another start.

Now, let's go back and review the word "reign" again. We in unison will keep in check by using all combined power of the Angels - The Supreme Power of God to disperse all others with Hell in their minds. Control by exercising Sovereignty Power, blending ourselves into One – God, for that is also Genesis, another start, life refreshed in the Light.

Many translations put into the Bibles are false. They were put there to frighten people into listening to and following a few people's beliefs. Yet, one of God's greatest gifts to us is our personal individual choice. Each and every choice that you make may be a different direction in your life; thus all choices are still another Genesis. Also many of the words of the Bibles were simply lost or forgotten during the act of translation. And many of the old languages of lost civilizations to our present day language were mistranslated. Some words of lost languages were more complex than in our present language. And some of their words had many meanings, while our language has many other words that cover their word that are similar in meaning but deciding which word to use often changes the meaning of their writings. Therefore, the complexity of our vocabulary changes the meaning of their thoughts and writings. So in reality we have two sets of mistranslation: the Bible's words and the language translation that affected the correctness of the words that were propose to be God's Word.

Example: "We are God's children" is a mistranslation. "We are like God's Children" is the true translation, for the God treats us like children while trying to teach us.

Another mistranslation is "God created us." That statement indicates that humans are so perfect that God created only them. Are we fools enough to think God only created us?

He created everything that is around us and everything that is within us.

Why would He create something as corrupt as humans?

He did not "make" only us. He created all life and that includes humans and the evolution of animal life took us from that one-cell animal to man, but He also created evolution. God is only trying to help us move to another level, nearer His likeness. Each step of human toward God is Genesis.

Another big mistranslation was that Jesus died on the cross for our Sins. Jesus died because of our sin of Domination. And if Jesus died for our Sins, then we will go to Heaven no matter how we live or what we do, so if that's true let's do whatever we wish. I don't think so.

Our forefathers tried and did dominate Jesus. He would not conform to their ideas or confess to the crimes that they claimed He committed. They did not want Him around so they killed Him. Even had He followed their demands nothing would have changed the outcome of His life, but if He had confessed to what they accused Him of then the Christian Religion would not be here. Therefore, all that happened was needed to happen.

But it is okay to believe that Jesus died for your sins; Believing Jesus died for your sins will not bar you from the Light. But worshipping Jesus as if He were God may stop your entry into the Light, depending if you are able to forgive yourself and/or if God will forgive you.

Thinking of yourself as being one of the people that killed Jesus will condemn you to Hell because Hell in your thoughts will stop you from allowing yourself entry into the Light.

And the Angel Jo continued, "Those who have lived before us, along with all that lived during our time and those who live after us that were ashamed of their lives and never entered the Light, will meet their Judgment Day on that last day of time for this cycle. God shall also judge all those who have entered the Light on the last day of time. While those who have lived with open hearts shall be welcomed into the Light with Glory after God's Judgment for that also is Genesis.

"Those who have lived with an unopened heart shall be dispersed after God's Judgment day, for that too, is Genesis. God did not create only the good for He created everything.

"With regard to the debate concerning where man came from, Creation versus Darwin's Theory of Evolution concerning animals, Darwin was correct. Humans came from monkeys or some similar type of animal. Your conversion was made easier with the help of God; He instilled intelligence and compassion along with love and many other glorious things into the first one-cell animal to elevate it into man that brought man closer to Him. But Darwin's Theory of Evolution was part of God's Creation.

"Animals do not have Souls such as those humans contain. Animals have energy but their energy is another step between energy matter and

Souls. The Energy of the Soul is what God implanted into that first one-cell animal and it evolved into the intelligence that humans contain today.

"Everything in creation is merely a concept in God's Master's Plan. Nothing is real but God. Each event and action that has happened or ever will happen is part of His Master Plan because everything is needed, but do not use this as your defense in your unjustly actions because you alone are responsible for your action.

"Genesis is the evolution of man.

"Genesis is the changing of all things toward a given 'place.' This given 'place' is a known position in the Master Plan.

"Genesis is God's Words, which were designed to help man grow into something better or worse, for both have a given place in the Master Plan."

(This statement about "better or worse" may strike you as strange but by the time you finish reading this book you shall know the truth. I cannot stray from our Charter of GENESIS to go deeper into this topic at this time.)

And the Angel Jo continued, "Genesis is growth during life. Genesis is not non-growth during life. 'Growth during life' is doing your part to moving civilization and yourself higher through intelligence. 'Non-growth during life' is idly standing by while doing nothing to expand or enrich oneself or civilization. And yet, the beginning and the end of non-growth are Genesis, too.

"God helped humans during the start of this cycle and will continue to guide you through time until the end of this cycle...Genesis.

"Presently we are in the fifth cycle. There have been four prior cycles. This is not the last cycle. There will be a sixth cycle and if this sixth cycle is successful then no more will occur, but that is not your concern.

"Once a new cycle has begun, its end is known by the Master Plan. The transformation for each cycle is not known until the new cycle has started for that too is part of the Master Plan.

"Each cycle lifts mankind to another level and closer to God. God has been near all in every Genesis, as each cycle is Genesis, too.

"Genesis is the complete cycle, but Genesis is the start of everything, too. For every life has a start, a Genesis. Therefore, Genesis is never-ending; Genesis is continuous. Each life has Genesis from beginning to end.

"Each cycle ends with destruction of all except the Light. All Unguided Ones that have not transformed along with all Entities that did not conform (Unguided Ones) will be annihilated. These two types of Entities had non-growth.

"For one to have Heaven, one must also experience or at least know of Hell. Each of us during at least one lifetime has had to know of non-growth, and each of us has had to know of Hell in order for us to recognize Heaven and growth, Genesis.

"To know the difference between Heaven and Hell, one should experience both for you cannot grade an item if you do not have anything to grade it against.

"As human, it is easier for you to think that the birth of Angels and all matter is going on throughout the cycle. Angels are not recycled for Angels are part of God. God, is the Supreme Ruler, for He is the Creator and is All.

"Angels are the highest levels of the Soul, for Souls will become part of God when its human part dies.

"The Light and God are One, and the same for the Light is the Knowledge, and that is also part of God, too.

"Once you and your Soul combine after death, you shall join with your Angel and then be part of God. In other words, you also shall be part of the Supreme Ruler and you shall be part of the Knowledge."

Now let's go back to Jesus once again.

He lived just one life. He did not experience only Hell in one life and then only Heaven in another life or both in one life. So how could He know Heaven?

God gave part of Himself to create Jesus. That is to say, all our Angels gave a part of themselves to create Jesus. Therefore, He knew Hell and Heaven from our past experiences. He did not need to experience both Heaven and Hell in one life, you shared with Him all of your experiences. But Jesus did experience Hell by witnessing the actions of things people did to others during his life and by all that the Angels have experienced, therefore He did not know Hell but experienced it.

And the Angel Jo continued, "Genesis is the beginning and throughout until the end of the cycle.

"Genesis is the complete picture. Evolution through each cycle is Genesis. Mankind has life. The Cycle has Genesis. God is Genesis, for He is never-ending and He is all things.

"As this Genesis nears the closure of this cycle, more Knowledge is revealed to you for your understanding of God. More and more information about the Other Side and the God will be told in the future to help ensure many others to travel with Heaven in their hearts into the Light. Just as the information detailed in this book should enable more people to find Salvation; giving Heaven to many Souls while they wait to cross over to this, the Other Side, and then enter and live in the Light as part of God forever. For God is also the Light. For the Light is all Angels combined.

"All have the ability to remember some parts about the Light that your Angels knew before they came to earth and life. Yet, most of you do not want to remember. You get caught up in life here on Earth, but still you want to know the Master Plan and about God while listening to polluted thoughts about God. You have been preached to all of your lives that life is good and death is bad. If death is bad but also death is part of the life, then is life bad? Yet, the Light is also God. Is God bad? You have been taught by the 'dogs' not to look at the Light and do not think about death. While death is an event, it is something that takes one to a higher level. Afterlife is not evil. Life is part of death. You can not have life without death. Death and life are parts of Genesis. If they are parts of Genesis and Genesis is therefore God, does that not mean life and death are also God? For God is All and yet, the true Knowledge is contained in your Angels.

"Death is part of everyone's cycle. But fear of death makes one forget.

"Understanding that death is part of the picture will help you recall your memories of God. The same as a content life will also help you recall the complete picture and Knowledge.

"Genesis cannot be stopped. If one can accept and conform to the wishes of All - God, one will join the Light in harmony. If one does not conform, that one will be dispersed with on the Final Day, unless he has time to relive again and to do better than the last time.

"Unless one has time to relive again means; time is running out to relive again. One's present life may be so corrupt that one will need many years of another life to erase all bad deeds. The time of the end may be very close at hand; therefore one may not have the time needed to remove one's Hell.

"In the beginning all is new, fresh and innocent. At birth all are innocent, without fear, hate or domination but is only Love. Genesis is love. Genesis is the first part of God. God is not fear, no hate nor domination for He is Love. Genesis is the continuation of God.

"From birth, humans carry innocence in their hearts. God is always in your hearts. As you grow, you learn fear, hate and to dominate as you push God to the backs of your hearts. You learn tricks from others. Yet, tricks place Hell within your thoughts and hearts. You twist your Souls with bad ideas while you corrupt others during your journey through life.

"Love is part of innocence. Love is part of you. You need not believe in God to have and to show love.

"Hate, fear and domination does not come from disbelief; they grow from selfishness for they come from evil as disbelief comes from fear.

"If you are one that believes in God, you must also believe selfishness as well as fear, hate, jealousy and domination needs to be controlled for they are of the dog. As a believer you must also believe in Genesis, for Genesis is constant in your daily lives, just as God is constant in your daily lives. Genesis is the start, and every day you start life anew.

"Daily you meet and see people that you have never known before. These new encounters may be the beginnings of new friendships. Every day new things enter your lives. These new starts may be the loss of a friend or loved one who has recently been buried. And yet, all beginnings are Genesis, even the going on without that person by your side is a new start.

"The deceased one has just begun a new Genesis for death is a new start of afterlife, too.

"Even though you came from the Light to this life, soon you will return to the Light, and this time you carry the memories of this life with you, Genesis.

"Each Genesis of you should raise you closer to God. Just as every generation should enlighten the next generation so should each Genesis be lifting every individual to new beginnings. Genesis should be the steps to Knowledge. Every step of Knowledge is individualized to fit into your understanding for all Genesis are unique - each life is different and special.

"Trifles throughout your lives will not and do not change your reasons for life. Little things are detours others and you create for yourselves. Those trifles are also Genesis, and they were part of the known Master's Plan to God.

"Things of Genesis change the directions of your lives. Genesis is the reason for life. It is the experiences you learn throughout your lives. Your experiences should move you to a higher level. Moving one step at a time is learning from experiences as you move closer to God, Genesis. The cycles, Genesis moves mankind toward God.

"Generation after generation, Genesis lifts mankind nearer to God. Your individualized life - your Genesis, should raise you closer to God. For you are part of mankind and your Angel-within is part of God. After death of your body, your memory and your Angel-within will join together to be part of the Light.

"The Light is Knowledge and is the congregation of Angels that are called God. Together, all united as One, lifting mankind up with Love. Genesis of All is the Common Genesis.

"In the beginning there was God, Genesis."

CREATION

One night the Angel Jo and I traveled to a far away place where we witnessed Creation.

I asked her, "May I write about Creation in this manner; in the furthest outer region of the cosmos among the billowing clouds of the smallest particles, energy is formed. This coming together and forming is Creation."

Jo replied, "Yes, I believe it will help people somewhat understand Creation if you explain it like that."

And the Angel Jo said unto me, "Matter becomes planets and such obtains most of the Energy, but only the most refined newly formed Energy becomes Entities, while Creation is the forming of both matter and Energy.

"Creation is the birth of all. Creation is continual from the start of time to the end of time and Creation is constant. The start of time and the end of time that I speak of is the reality of this cycle.

"Entities directly out of Creation usually go to the Light. There they become Angels of God. Angels are Energy that contains the Knowledge of the Light. Knowledge of the Light refers to Knowledge of all that has been that is contained in God. Whereas, the Light contains all the Knowledge about everything that has been, but God is All. Thinking in today's human terms, you could say Entities entering the Light are programmed much in the way you program a newly constructed computer with all the knowledge up to its construction.

"In the composition of humans, you are made up of matter. Your brain is matter that stores information, which is about the same as the Knowledge of God but the human brain is on a lesser scale. The Angels' composition is Energy alone, which can store information and that is the Knowledge; A place where the Knowledge is ready and available at any given moment.

"It is suggested in the Bibles God said, 'Let Us make man in 'Our' image.' He did not say 'I'll make man in My image.' This statement indicates God is all Angels. For He is talking to the Angels, there was no one else He could have been talking to because no one else except the Angels existed. His word 'Image' referred to 'similar in design of Intelligence' because Angels are composed of Energy, and Energy does not have form. And whereas, humans see Entities – Angels in his (human) likeness, for the individual human is the center of his own universe.

"It is very possible to think about the Light, God, Entities, Angels, the Other Side and all others of the Other Side in terms of other life forms or another dimension that holds all Knowledge for they are the highest intelligent and have Eternal Life. The third dimension that humans live in is known to have length, width and thickness in terms of what you see. But dimensions also are involved in measurable extensions of Knowledge, life and all other things that you contribute to your lives.

"In your lives, you think of time as being a level plane, like a horizontal line. You also think of people in a vertical plane, as rank or positions in life. Both of these are wrong. Time is vertical for all time has it's own location, and where people are horizontal for all people are equal."

(This I will explain later).

And the Angel Jo continued, "All Angels that have lived are the Light, God is the Light, therefore, God is all Angels.

"No one Angel is God. No one Entity is God. No one person rules. God rules but He is All. All agrees for All is One."

(Later on I will get into the subject of Christianity stating Jesus is Lord and what that really meant.)

And the Angel Jo continued, "Presently, we are in the fifth cycle of time. There have been four previous cycles. The first cycle was caused by nature. Nature made all planets and the universes, but yet God created nature. Therefore, God did not create Earth, He did not create the sun and He did not create all the stars in the skies. He did not create things of matter, but He created thought of matter, for matter is symbolic for human use and as well as humans are symbolic, too, because everything is just as thought in God's mind.

"God ended the first cycle, and thereafter, copied it and made the next four cycles, which includes the one you are presently living in, and in this cycle He made everything that His Nature made during the first cycle.

"He did not create Heaven. For Heaven is a state of mind. God was the first to be created as All is Created. When God was the first to be created, He was God. When the second Angel was created, then both were One - God. When the third Angel was created, then all three combined were One – God - and so forth.

"God's first selection to be in his likeness was an animal with no sex gender. It reproduced at will, thus it is said that it was not destroyed but it destroyed itself. Later God selected a mammal to enhance and lift with Intelligence and Knowledge into the likeness of Himself.

"He did not create all the living things on Earth. God made the first one-cell animal during that first cycle. He then implanted Knowledge within this animal. But He created Nature that made everything, and everything was known in His Master Plan.

"God is all, therefore, He is Evolution, too, because Evolution is also part of all. At different points in Evolution, God places more and more Intelligence into animals.

"Have you ever noticed that a man and woman who have been married for years seem to resemble each other?

"This is called the Blending Effect. The humans are drawn together and begin to look and act the same. The DNA does not change its look because of being near other DNA. The DNA changes its appearance because the Angel's Energy causes the DNA to change. Therefore, when a man and woman who have been married for years begin to change their looks toward each other, it is because of their Angels blending together which in turn causes their DNA to change appearance as well as their actions start to become as if from one. This Blending Effect also caused humans not to change their appearance from animal look to Angel look because Angels do not have form, but is transforming human knowledge into the Intellect of the Angels.

"Many Bibles says, 'Man was made in the image of God.' But instead God allows us, His Angels, to follow your body design and your body shape when we reveal ourselves to you. For the 'Image of God' meant to resemble the 'Intelligence of God.'

"The human was the only animal suited for the 'image' of God. God helped a wild animal to progress into human. Human was the only creature on earth that was capable of caring for and helping its species. It was the only animal that could reach the level that God intended for you to attain at this time. God created and then assisted in the evolution of humans. God did not create man for He does not make mistakes. He is helping you move further away from your animal instincts and closer to Him by giving you Intelligence and teaching you His Knowledge. The Angels contain the Knowledge of God and by opening your heart, you allow your Angel-within to convey the message of God to you.

"God gave to the animal that would someday be human two gifts.

"The first was to place within each person an Angel, a piece of God. He gave Himself to you.

"The second is reasoning. These are the two most important things that separate you from all other animals. God did not give Angels to animals, as they have no Angel or Soul. He did not give animals reasoning. They think only of themselves. And while you will occasionally find a pet that may do nice things for its owner, basically animals think only of eating, sleeping and procreating.

"Women are equal to men. People say that woman was 'made' after man, but that does not make her less than man. But in fact, a woman may be closer to God's ways with her special ways of understanding, love and compassion for others. And, some people believe God saved His best Creation for last – Woman. But the fetus first procreated in the woman is a female and then some change into male.

"Angels are neither men nor women, but each Angel contains both male and female traits. For God has no gender. Gender separates the giver from the bearer. And we are neither child bearers nor child giver.

"Have you ever stopped to wonder why the Bibles were not written to help women to find their salvation, too?

"Are women less important to God than men?

"Have you ever wondered about all the reports of seeing Guardian Angels, why they are all seen as women?

"Did you think all men Angels are out playing golf or just too busy to help in the needs of the living?

"In fact, Guardian Angels could be seen as men. But humans think of the Devil as being a man and of Angels as being women. For all people think of women as loving, compassionate, caring individuals. You see what you wish to see.

"Why would God, your compassionate ever-loving God state in the Garden of Eden that Eve talked Adam into eating the forbidden fruit and then, place women under the domination of men?

"Do you truly believe that if Eve sinned when she convinced Adam to eat the apple, God would have placed pain upon all females during birth? NO, He would have only placed pain upon human females at birth, not all females, the female animals did nothing wrong.

"Different sexes do not change the equality of humans, nor does different color of skin. Skin color was needed for different climatic conditions of Earth. Intelligence is not determined by color of skin or sex, just as facial and body differences cannot be part of the equation of Intelligence. All people begin life equal in intelligence and love. Knowledge is learned Intelligence and not hereditary.

"Man wrote falsehoods into the Bibles, not God!

"As the world grows smaller by faster travel and communication, all people will become one color through inter-marriages, for true love is color blind.

"Individual Intelligence also will dwindle. More ideas and more things to play with will cause people to learn not all about one subject but rather learn little or nothing about many things. Some will stay on the right track and learn all of some subjects, but their number will be small.

"The end of this cycle shall be marked by a learning process inversion, regression of love and compassion, and less understanding the needs of others and less caring for others. These were the things of Knowledge that God wished humans to learn but instead of learning, they are forgetting, but this too was known and are part of the Master's Plan.

"God may have rested on the seventh day of human time but on this, the Other Side there are no days or nights. Time is for humans. Time is a measurement for your lives while God lives Eternal.

"The past is forever. The present is this second. The future is always coming. God contains all Knowledge - past, present and future, for time has location. But the Light only contains the past and this second.

"Knowledge of God is the knowing the whereabouts of all atoms and their smallest particles at any time past, present and future. God contains this Knowledge, while Heaven is only the memories of the past; all that each Angel has experienced through the endurance of life.

"When God placed King David on the throne, He knew step by step what would occur throughout King David's life, but King David and all others had to experience the unknown future of their choices.

"God knows all the steps that will occur throughout your life, also. God knows right or wrong decisions made by you before you ever think about making a decision. God knows everything you have done, the things you are doing and all the things you will do. Nothing is left to chance after Creation was first formed in the cosmos.

"Only three times since the making of the cosmos has enough energy purged at once to create two Entities at the same time. Entities formed at the same time are called 'Soul Twins.' The distinguishing differences between Soul Twins and all other Angels is that Soul Twins have a bluish light while all other Angels have a very white light, and Soul Twins are one male and one female Angel while all others are both combined.

"We were the first set of Twins to be created. Our forming was in the first day of the Cosmos. Since our making only two other sets of Twins have been formed.

"As you already know we were the first set of Soul Twins. The second set of Soul Twins; the female is still alive and living in Florida. She does not know that she is a Twin, but feels that there is something special going on with her. Her Twin, Paul, is in the Light.

"The third set of Twins contains Dale, who knows that he is a Soul Twin and his female Twin is in the Light."

(The mission of these three sets of Soul Twins will be explained later.)

And the Angel Jo continued, "All Entities contain both male and female traits. Soul Twins, when formed at Creation had enough Pure Energy that they divided and formed one male Entity and one female Entity. But none (Entity or Angel) have sex organs for organs are needed for the living. One of the Soul Twins that I call the 'male' contains male traits while the one that I call 'female' contains the female traits but none have sex organs.)

"The Creation of the three sets of Soul Twins was not mistake. For Creation is God, too.

"The Twins fit exactly into the Master Plan as God intended, for God left nothing to chance. He knows exactly what is going on all the time.

"Many researchers hunt the Earth for remnants of places and people mentioned in the Bibles. Some will be found, while others were reported to be at the wrong locations and yet others have been destroyed by time. Needless to say, let the search continue, for all things are possible.

"The glory of the find can be obtained. Artifacts found will be helpful to confirm the Bibles. These things found will also help people realize Creation to be true.

"Peace of mind is worth the truth. In other words, if you are satisfied with an answer, you will not search any further for the truth. If you cannot rest until you know the truth, continue the search and you will find the truth you seek.

"A lie to soothe another's mind is not a lie if it is accepted. The false answer merely gives the other person peace of mind – support that his beliefs as true. But you will not have peace of mind if you know the truth but only give the answer another wants. If that person desires the truth, he will search for it. The Knowledge of knowing that certain facts were false while refusing to search for the truth have cost many their place in the Light and giving a false answer while knowing the truth also has cost many their Heaven, too.

"If people are happy believing in their religions, so be it. If they desire to know the truth, they shall search until their minds are at peace.

"More truth about God shall be learned if searched for. Searching is learning that becomes Knowledge when completed.

"Creation of All was natural. God copied the Creation of the first cycle to create the four other cycles. All cycles were designed to raise mankind higher and closer to God. Therefore, if you call reproducing something that first nature made as original creation, then you may say God created All in the four cycles after the first cycle. Then also one could say God created man, even though He only enhanced an animal that through evolution changed into human. Then I guess you can say God did create man. But Nature was also created by God, and that has occurred was needed."

THE OTHER SIDE

And the Angel Jo said unto me, "First, let me explain the correct names of Beings on this, the Other Side, before I tell you about the Other Side.

"All humans have a Soul, it is the recorded experiences of the human's life. Crossing over to the Other Side, your Soul combines with your Angel from within, and is named an Entity. Once an Entity enters into the Light, then it is referred to as an Angel, a part of God. Souls, Entities and Angels are Energy, and Energy cannot be destroyed, therefore you, through your memory, will live forever

"Please try to refer to us as Angels or Entities. In human concepts, all other names are cut downs to us. Also, please show us the same respect that you give to any nationality and race. You do not say americans, you say Americans.

"And as a matter of fact, one from Africa, who came to America could be referred to as Afro-American, but not all Africans are black. And while one who came from Europe to America could be referred to as Euro-American, but only the ones who came to America can be referred to as Afro or Euro, not the one who were born in America because they are Americans. Whereas, Caucasian is referring to the white race and because you do refer to the white race as Caucasians it is okay to refer the black race as Negro or Negroid. But that's okay because We know humans are confused.

"Animals do not have Souls. Animals do have energy inside them, but it is not the same pure Energy that Angels have. Souls are what separate humans from other animals, but Entities can and do sometimes appear as 'ghostly' animals. Also Entities can live for a while inside an animal's body, but animals do not have Souls because Soul are the experiences of reasoning and comprehension recorded on Energy.

"From your side, the human side to the Light, there is a space which you call the Other Side. Once you enter into this, the Other Side, you will retain your human emotions of the experiences that you have endured. You do not experience the future from that point on, you only re-live the past of your life. And also, if one's body is presently handicapped, that abnormality will also be gone because all these things are of matter, but again anything is possible with God.

"I like this place you call the Other Side. You can see forever, there is no wind or dust for most dust is mostly dead animal matter. You can fly anywhere and you can travel to the moon or other planets. And you can visit anyplace in any time, for time has location, but all happens as if at once. And yet, most go directly to the Light and don't see the beauty of the space between human life and the Light for there is no light in this space, for everything seems to be lit by a light source that radiates from within us. It is not light as humans think of light because we have no light nor eyes to see with, light for us is the Knowledge that All possess. While some lost Souls drift around in the dark on the Other Side for years, for they cannot find the Light, some may even fear the Light. These never see the beauty of this space before the Light. Other Entities and/or Angels try to help the lost ones; sometimes we can help them while other times they will not allow our help.

"The memories of your emotions are your Heaven or Hell and are traits of your character and your personality, and they are the history of your recorded life experiences – your Soul. You will keep the memory of your past life on the Other Side, and then once you enter into the Light you will know that all share your past and you will know all about the Other Side and what the Light is as well as all that everyone has experienced during their lives, too. Thus once you entered into the Light you will possess Knowledge, and thus be an Angel – part of the Knowledge of the Light – part of God.

"Hell is realizing all the wrongful things that you did here on Earth including the knowledge that all others know your wrongdoings, too. Hell is within all humans. Your personal Hell - what you think about yourself - is directed by your actions of what you did wrongfully on Earth.

"You may enter or leave the Light as often as you wish. But once outside the Light, you will remember only the Knowledge of life that occurred up to the moment that you left the Light.

"Presently there is no wrath of God to harm you on the Other Side nor in the Light for Judgment will come at the end of time. And there is not and there will never be a board of twelve to judge you as someone once wrote. All is forgiven, for you are not blamed for what you did here on earth but the bad acts are never forgiven. Therefore All are sad for the bad acts that you did on earth, and whereas, you will judge yourself for your past life.

Then at the end of time, God will judge you.

"If one wishes, one may come back to Earth and live again within another living human to try to make a better life, thus redeeming oneself from Hell. Or one may choose to stay on the Other Side, the choice is individual.

"You always thought reincarnation meant go there and then come back, over and over again... maybe never ending. But in reality, you are not forced to do anything on the Other Side and reincarnation is yours if your Angel chooses it, and whereas the Soul does not come back and relive because the Soul is merely the recorded experiences of one's life, but instead your Angel may come back to experience another life.

"You will not find God in the Light for God is the Light. God is the combination of all the Angels, for Angels are the type of Entities that is both; the Energy of God and the Soul combined.

"Humans have Souls, your Soul is your past life story, and your past life is part of the Knowledge of God, for God is in all of us. Presently the part of God that dwells within you is an Angel. Therefore, do not fear God, do not fear yourself. Love yourself then you will also be loving God.

"If after your death you return is Spirit, humans see you as an Entity, they may envision you wearing clothing like that from the human side as if you were still alive, while your facial features will be burred to them for you will not contain organs and the face is mainly made up of facial organs. Therefore, whenever you meet someone on this, the Other Side, you will notice that their face is somewhat blurred, too. And no one uses their mouth to talk on this, the Other Side. You will notice that before you can speak your thoughts you will hear their reply. And all speak the same language of the mind – Love. And if you knew that person on earth, you will see that person as you last remember them; if you die when that person was young, you will see them as that young person, and whereas another person that knew the same person later in life will see them as they last seen them.

"Do you recall the movie 'ENTITY,' where the woman was always getting beat up by her deceased husband? Her Entity husband was only causing her human body to hurt itself. That is why she bled and her body showed bruises. Real Entities are not in the fantasy of movies and cannot harm humans.

"Entities that do visit the human side cannot hurt humans, but they can do things that causes one to harm oneself. An Entity could throw something and you may step in front of the flying object and so forth.

"Like I stated earlier, on the Other Side, it appears as if one is wearing present day clothes like they did on earth. I cannot recall if or what clothes are worn in the Light, for I have been out too long, but clothing is irrelevant anyway. Same as the color of one's skin does not matter, for the color of one's skin is part of the human that does not pass over. But again, the Other Side is Energy and is a place where no matter exist.

"This, the Other Side, is not in one place but it is in all places. Time and distances have no meaning on this, the Other Side. The speed of light is the fastest speed that man has recorded and yet, we on the Other Side can and do travel faster. Time is nothing in the Light, too, for you will know all that happened and you do not care if you are in the past or present for they are the same. They are all Knowledge to the Angel, but the Knowledge is the known of everything that has happened. The future is also part of God's Knowledge but not the Knowledge that is contained in the Light.

"Your home in which I bring the deceased children through is part of the Other Side, and we like your home for it is at peace. There we blend the things that the children loved and wanted on this, the Other Side, for them to enjoy before they travel onto the Light."

THE LIGHT

And the Angel Jo said unto me, "The illumination that you think of as the Light is caused by the Angels' Auras. The Light is the Angels...a group of Angels, and that is the congregation of Angels that is God. The Light is the Knowledge of all that the Angels have experienced through the endurances of humans. And while the Light is also the combined Souls of all that have lived and died up to that moment of time because the Light is not the Future, but only the past and up to the present. Therefore, the Light's illumination is merely the Angels' Auras rejoicing and is the reflection of our experiences.

"I really do not like using the word 'wavelength' to describe what the Angels' Energy is, but it is the only humanly word that closely describes our form.

"The normal human vision wavelengths range from 3900 to 7700 angstroms which is about the range of infrared to ultraviolet light and travels about 186,350 miles per hour. Above ultraviolet light one encounters X-ray and other wavelengths that are harmful to humans and other life forms while the Angels' radiant Energy generates light far below infrared light and which is lower than ultraviolet light.

"Angels' Auras are actually Energy that can be seen when an Angel is at the correct wavelength for your vision. Seeing an Angel's Aura is viewing the complete color spectrum of your vision, for our wavelength includes all the colors that you can see. But as with any low-level light, you merely see the outer edges of our light, while occasionally you can see deeper into our Auras and view our lower wavelengths which are seen as other colors. The innermost center of an Angel's Aura is ultra white. Farther from the center, the color of our Auras, change to reds, yellows and blues. These are higher energy wavelengths than the center. The outer edge of our Auras appears to be bands of color that protrude out of our bodies and then back to our bodies again. People usually identify these bands of color as wings and halos, but most people have been taught not to see Angels. They have been taught that seeing something not of their world is evil. People are so full of fear that they think that anything they see but cannot explain is dangerous to them.

"Our wavelengths are more complex then all others, for 'Soul Twins' Auras are ice blue. This ice blue color is purer, even more refined than the ultra white color that is the center all other Angel's Auras. But whereas, all ranges of wavelengths, such as X-ray, infrared and ultraviolet are the wavelengths that you see as the color spectrums and are similar to each other. If you see another Soul Twin or me, you could still identify the reds, yellows and blues as with all wavelengths, but you would see an ice blue center of our Aura.

"At times, an Angel's wavelengths can go higher and if their wavelength comes within your vision spectrum, you as human then can see the Angel. When we go above your vision spectrum, we can cause things to burn, which you as human and your son, Daniel, have witnessed.

"You also contain a light around you. You call it your Aura. The image of your Aura that can be captured by photography is the outer edges of your Angel's Aura – the Energy that is within you. It is the wavelengths that protrude out past your body. Your Angel is within your body, and when you photograph your Aura you are actually photographing your Angel's colors.

"At death, the wavelength of the conscious mind slows down to below that of infrared wavelengths. This is the blending of the human Soul with the Angel within as indicated in the Bibles.

"Measured by today's earthly instruments, you would think that people with lowered wavelengths have no energy movement, and therefore, to humans such a person is dead but in fact, that person's energy that burns matter, which we call the body, is deceased, but the Energy of the lower energy wavelengths which is the Soul, continues to live and removes itself from the decomposing body. The body leaves, the Angel remains and does not die.

"Major decaying begins at the moment of death, but decomposition of the body is continuous throughout your life. As you live, newly formed cells replace dead and decaying cells in your bodies. At the moment of death, most cells start decaying, thus decomposition of the body. Upon death, you can say the Soul leaves the body, but the body is actually leaving the Soul as the body decays.

"If someone has drowned and is then brought back to life, that person will usually have some kind of brain damage - partial death of the brain. But if the body of this person is reciprocated and this person receives only minimal brain damage the Soul will return to the body, thus, a near death experience has occurred.

"The theory of total Knowledge being pure Energy is correct. If one human could learn all the Knowledge, he would turn into pure Energy and the body would dissolve and disappear... decay. This is the concept of what happens at death.

"The Light is not a place as much as it is a gathering of all thoughts, a joining of pure Energy - a reuniting of Angels. This action - coming together or congregation of Angels is called the Light. The Energy of Angels together is referred to as God.

"Years ago someone told you that it was interesting to know that the brain is the only human organ that can think about itself. It is almost overwhelming now for you to realize the Light is the only life form of Energy that can think. Its Knowledge is contained without any matter to hold memory. Only a force or power you call Energy contains our memory. Your memory (thought process) is also contained in energy like force or power of Angels. The brain is the only matter capable of transferring feeling from matter to energy. The Angels, parts of God, is Energy that can move without matter to obtain location, directions or assistance in its movements.

"The Light produces Love. Love is the flow of Energy. This flow has a sound, and when you are in the Light you will feel (hear) the sound. This sound is called music - A calm and peaceful continuous steady flow of Love, and whereas the music of God's Love is indescribable.

"You and your Angel-within are as though two Entities occupying the same space. Your thoughts, actions and memories are being transcended to your Angel-within, and its memories and actions do not completely transcend to you."

(Transcend, to rise above the dog to an Angel. We cannot transfer our thought to God nor can we transmit our thought to God. We can only transcend our thought to a higher level of consciousness - the Angel-within. He in turn, transcend his (our) thoughts on to God.)

And the Angel continued, "All things can be misunderstood, for there is no board of twelve men that dictates rules to you in the Light as one confused writer wrote in her book, and where no one is prejudiced against another. All are equal and have no sex organs. Sex is determined by organs, which Angels do not have. There is no color difference. All is the color of Love - our Auras. Only do we, Soul Twins, have the slightly different color of ice blue instead of the white Aura, and each Soul Twin contains male or female traits, while all other Angels contain both.

"Our Auras can be seen as clothing, but clothes we do not need. Angels do have the ability for people to see (in-vision) different types of clothing upon our bodies for human's sake, such as the gown one may have seen worn by his Guardian Angel.

"Angels do not need organs. We have the shapes of eyes, ears, nose and mouth but those are needed for humans to recognize us. When you see an Angel, its facial shape will be blurred somewhat because of the lack of these things, for our shapes stay consistent with the form of your human bodies. Without sex organs, we do not reproduce. We are produced in Creation, for Creation is the Love of God.

"Our communication is done by thought. We do not have lungs or vocal chords for a voice, nor is air used for speech. Your mind will hear us speak and you may see the lower part of my face move where my mouth should be, but no words will come out of me and sometimes the energy of my thoughts can be recorded as if they were audio sounds. You as with all the others will know what the Angel is thinking as if the Angel is speaking, and we hear your thoughts before you can speak the words of your thought. But the evil energy will not allow anyone to know its feelings and therefore, you will not hear anything as if spoken from evil Spirits.

"You may enter and leave the Light as often as you wish, and no one will try to stop you. One may be so ashamed of his past life that he may leave the Light to never enter again, for if one wishes not to re-enter the Light that is his choice.

"There is no wind, heat or cold, dust or any other natural condition you face on Earth. Odor comes from decaying matter of which we have none, so there is no odor in the Light either because all those things exist in your reality.

"Nothing grows old and needs to be replaced. There is no time, no day or night. All is past which is up to the present, and is known by All.

"In the Light you will see what you wish to see, as the illumination of the Light may manifest as a garden or whatever as you please, and you will see people as you remembered them in life. Others will see that same person as they last remembered them also. In respect, you may see someone as a child whereas another may see the same one as old.

"Personal feelings that you had during the moment of death as Heaven (good) or Hell (bad) will remain with you forever."

When my oil field career ended in the early 1980s, I turned toward mechanics and maintenance as my profession. One of my first jobs after drilling of oil wells was working in the downtown area of Los Angeles repairing office coffee makers. I spent many of my lunch hours in the little parks scattered amongst the tall office buildings where I would sit and eat my lunch while I watched men and women hurriedly going from building to building.

Once in a while, a good-looking woman would walk by and I would automatically think how nice it would be to bone her or I sure would like to have those legs wrapped around my head, and then I started thinking how funny life would be if no one wore clothes. I would imagine how all those people would look without clothing on, fat people, thin people, old people and all the people that tried to act so businesslike. Sometimes I could not help but laugh out loud.

The other day, I had some business at our local courthouse and I arrived early. To kill some time I sat outside and once again I watched the people walking by. But this time as I watched the people going by I did not see the women as sex objects or think how funny people would look without clothing - I saw their Angels. These Angels were trying to do some part of their missions. Some young, some old and some disabled while some acted confident and others acted as though they were lost, but all trying to do something. All were part of God just as we all are, for they are no different then I; no better or no worse than me; just people that were confused in their daily lives, not thinking about the Light and with no time to think about God. They were just ordinary people with only enough time to think about their work at hand.

I felt sorry for many of these people whom in such a hurry could not take the time to think about God or realize they someday will be part of the Light. Nor did they have the time to just experience this moment of their life. Now I have become part with my Angel-within for I "see" what others think and I "feel" what others do.

My amusement was no more, for now I saw them for what they were, Angels carrying out their missions of life. Now I understood this human life is for experiencing and to help lift the human race to a higher level. Every one of us should be trying to do his individual part to raise ourselves higher to God.

As I watched all those going to their destinations, I realized that soon we all will be gone from here, all will be together in the Light forever reminiscing and laughing with friends and families about old times and experiences we had here on Earth.

All of us have our place in the Light. No hatred for another, no fear of another, no differences in skin color, no disabilities and no language barrier but all untied as One.

You will find no one demanding what you must do in the Light. No one will be telling you what must be done. Your actions are controlled by your thoughts alone. You will find the Light is Love for all and a place where all are equal. A place to where we all are trying to achieve.

The Light is God, Who is part of us, and that is our separation from animals. Without God we would still be swinging from trees. He helps us keep control of society.

The Light was our home before birth and should be our home after death.

KNOWLEDGE

And the Angel Jo said unto me, "In present-day human knowledge and understanding that you consider to be high and very intelligent, and compared to animals or early man, you are. But it was not long ago that people believed the world was flat and that bleeding was the way to heal the sick. Modern-day medicine has been around only one hundred years or so, and it was only a few hundred years ago that people finally learned that your world was round.

"Does it make a child intelligent if he has learned to count up to ten? Or does it merely show he has the capability to learn and remember?

"Did not the great thinkers of your world believe their knowledge was the ultimate knowledge?

"Those before you, and those with you, and those of the future all are steps to the ultimate knowledge. Yet each thought they knew all, but the ultimate Knowledge is God.

"Human intelligence is what separates people from animals, just as intelligence is the main reason that humans are separated from God.

"Knowledge of the Light is all experiences of all that has lived up to this point in time and that is vast and complex. But God's Knowledge is total and complete, for instance just think of only a single tree. That tree can produce millions of leaves over its life span. Each leaf is made up of both liquid and solid matter. These elements contain countless atoms that come together into the make-up of that single leaf. Each atom has its own length of time to stay within the composition of the leaf. In other words, its own life cycle is related to the tree, but before being part of the leaf, that atom was part of something else. And after its cycle as part of the leaf that same atom will become part of something else.

"All Knowledge is knowing the complete cycle of each atom that form into this one leaf plus all the other atoms that form all other things, including all that has been and all that will be. For that atom was part of something else before it became part of the leaf. But not only does God's Knowledge pertain to just atoms but to all of its individual particles as well.

"Knowledge that I talk about is not only knowing all about humankind and its relation to the Light, but the Knowledge that I refer to is also knowing the complete cycle of each and every atom and its relation to God, the One who Created all. Each particle of every atom also has its own cycle. But I used the atom as the smallest known matter for this discussion.

"Multiply the number of atoms combined to make up that one leaf by the number of all the leaves that this tree will have during its lifetime. Then multiply that number by the number of all trees alive now. Then multiply that number by the number of all the trees that have ever been and those trees that will live from this day forward, and you will have the total number of atoms that merely pertain to trees alone during this cycle. The knowledge of just these atoms alone is overwhelming but add in the number of atoms of everything else in the universe. Now record every detail of each atom for every second during this cycle and you will understand the amount of Knowledge it would take to know just part of the Knowledge that God has.

"Humans know little more than the dumbest animals compared to God. This is why God treats people as His children. That is why you, the human race, are called 'God's Children.' Parents try to teach their children in the same way that God teaches people.

"Your Angel-within forgot the Knowledge of the Light when it left the Light to join with your body at your birth. Others are helping your Angel-within remember about the Light while they try to teach you about the God. Your body has no memory of God because it, your body, came from the dirt, the same dirt that it will return to after death – the body came from the dead and shall return to the dead.

"Your Soul is fresh and innocent for it is like a new floppy disk to a computer. Your life's memories will be its files that will blend into your Angel-within, who will join with God in the Light after your death.

"If you look at one tiny raindrop forming, you do not know what the atoms went through to become this little raindrop or what this raindrop will endure throughout its cycle. You could use probabilities and may conjecture what its cycle may encounter, but God knows the tiny raindrop's complete cycle without guessing because the God's Knowledge is complete and without error or effort.

"As part of congregation of God, you will have the Knowledge. You will know what has happened, what is happening and what will happen to all, but in the Light you will only know what all others know; what has been, for the Knowledge of the Light is all the experiences of all that have lived.

"God is Knowledge... God is Love... God is Understanding. You are part of God. Open your heart and mind and you will see what your actions have brought, what your actions are doing now and what your future actions will bring.

"Love all people and things, try to understand the complete picture from all angles, then you shall possess a little part of the Knowledge that the God contains.

"Would you be ashamed if everyone knew your deepest secrets?

"All in the Light know exactly everything you have done. Once you enter the Light, you will know that everyone knows your life completely. Will you be able to live in the Light forever with your memories of your life and with the Knowledge of everyone else knowing all you ever did?

"Not one in the Light will judge you or look down on what you did during your life, but they will feel saddened by your bad past actions."

(Looking down on another's actions is the same as judging them. Feeling sad is the same thing as disliking an action and realizing that the action is not for you.)

And the Angel Jo continued, "But you will look down on some things that you did during your past life. Possibly you may even dislike yourself for what you did when alive. You may wish to return to Earth and relive another life to remove your Hell from yourself, for you shall judge yourself after your death.

"Not all come back to live again to seek Salvation from their Hell. Some merely come back to experience life again or maybe they are seeking new experiences to try.

"Most religions say after death you will live in Heaven forever. Some also state that you will worship God forever. Do you really think God is so big headed that He would force people to worship Him?

"If you believe God is one person, then tell me who put God in charge?

"If God is one person and He is so strong and mighty, why must you go through life before you become His slave?

"If God wanted you as slaves, He could have made humans His slaves to start with, for there is no need to go through life to become His slaves.

"Man believes that he is the superior being and has created God in his image. God is all Angels in congregation, not one Angel and He does not look human, for He is all Energy.

"What you call Satan or the Devil wants humans as slaves. And Satan is No-thing to God but energy. The slaves of evil (Satan) look inward to their desires and wants instead of looking outward as we Angels do. To be with God is to be part of Him and free. To be with evil is to be alone and enslaved by evil.

"God is not one person, He is all Angels. We do not worship All, but instead We love All.

"We go through life for individual experiences of life and for the joining of the Soul and Angel-within after death. Life is not needed to go to the Light, but most of us came from the Light in the first place and we all return to the Light after death.

"Everyone contains some parts of God's Knowledge within his hearts. God does not need to be learned. Compassion, caring and love for others will bring God to your surface, and then you shall know Him as you will know yourself. The Knowledge of God needs only to be remembered by your Angel-within and then shared with you and accepted by you, as well as all engraved upon your DNA should be remembered by you, too.

"Understanding that God is part of you is some of the Knowledge that He wishes you to have and enjoy. For God is love, caring and compassion for ourselves and others.

"Understanding does not mean living by His Word alone. Besides understanding, people must try to live as God wishes them to do, for if you understand His Words but do not use His Words in your daily life then you are nothing."

(The story about me in the city parks of Los Angeles that you have read in the last chapter is a good example of comprehending God's Word. But then I did not understand God's Word, and now I understand His Word while I live as He wished we all should.)

And the Angel Jo continued, "Having the Knowledge but not using the Knowledge is a Sin. You must exercise our wisdom on a daily basis. But do not try to force God unto others for that is domination, and Domination is a Sin.

"Try to set aside time for meditation about God. To find Heaven after death, you must know Heaven before your death. Thoughts of God daily will help give you your Heaven, both while alive and after death.

"Knowledge; understanding how your life is involved with the congregation and is part of the complete picture of life, for they are interwoven, for the Knowledge helps you understand how your actions pertain to change in other's lives.

"All actions have reactions. Your acts to others cause them to show love or anger toward people that they come into contact with throughout their day and possibly throughout their lives. Love is contagious as hatred and anger are also contagious.

"Human lives are blessed with God's love. The love that He gave you, He intended for you to share with all people.

"The phrase 'Blessed are the meek,' does not mean all those who are afraid to speak out, nor those who are too afraid to speak out. It means that God blesses those who open their hearts to others and do not and will not try to dominate others.

"Those who open their hearts to others have the Knowledge and know how to use their opened hearts without selfish reasons.

"Knowledge is understanding all others have feelings just as you do and knowing when and how to show your love is Knowledge. This is the Knowledge that all possess but most refuse to understand or demonstrate their daily lives.

"The mid-nineties were the 'in-your-face' years, and domination and forcefulness was shown to all. Respect for others was lost during those years. Children learned 'in-your-face' tricks from other children and their parents. They did not know how to show love or respect for they did not have any Knowledge. Parents did not have any Knowledge, so how could they teach their children? The downhill spiral had begun. The children were telling their parents and other adults what to do and how to act while the children dominate others.

"Love, compassion and caring is the Knowledge that had been lost. All those Souls who do not learn or use the Knowledge will also be lost if they do not conform to the Knowledge of God."

(You will read the fate of lost Souls and Angels in the chapter, "The Final Day" in this book.)

I have noticed two important occurrences during the writing of this book.

The first is that after one writes a book, he must find a literary agent to represent him to the publishers. Most literary agents want you to use their friends as editor. The editors then pay the literary agents a kickback fee for helping them find work. You can send an edited book to many different literary agents and they still request you to have your book edited by their editors. That is Domination!

The second thing I found out is the changes you see in other people once they find out that you have written a book.

I don't think the simple fact that you wrote a book is the reason for their change but the contents of the book is what causes them to talk to you differently, for if their discussions with you turn toward God or Spiritual matters, you will notice a closer relationship from them to you and a closer tie from them with you, for now your conversations are directed toward their Angel-within. And whereas, I also have found that those who read our book or other books pertaining to our subject matter act and talk directly from their hearts instead of from their selfish dog within. These changes in people also include people saying that they have had near-death experiences, and those that have seen their Guardian Angels, and those that seen Entities, and those that can read the future because many of us have had close encounters with the Other Side remember more of the Knowledge than those who live on faith or belief alone.

The Knowledge is easy and simple to understand or learn. This Knowledge is love, compassion and caring for all.

God does not dictate our every moves and actions because we are responsible for our individual actions. The little insignificant movements during our daily lives are ours to do with as we please, but all is part of the Master Plan. The things we do to ourselves and others also are ours to do as we wish, but doing wrongs to ourselves or others is a Sin which will place Hell within your heart. That Hell will be difficult to remove after your death.

TO SAY GOODBYE

And the Angel Jo said unto me, "Saying goodbye to a departed loved one was the hardest thing for a human to do.

"In times of despair we as human lose focus of what life is meant to be because humans do not know the reason for the cycle of life. Humans lose the ability to understand that there is more than just this human life and forget about everlasting life.

"I hope the things that you have learned as we write this book will help you, and others who read this book to understand and possibly give them some comfort surrounding the death of a loved one.

"Do you recall the friend of yours who was married for approximately twenty-eight years and then, lost his wife to cancer about seven years ago?

"It was said that this couple was deeply in love throughout their marriage. And during the last days of the woman's life, she promised her husband that somehow she would come back to say goodbye after her death.

"Recently, your friend asked you, 'Why didn't she come back? I believed in Heaven and God and still do, so why didn't she come back to see me like she promised?'

"Does believing in Heaven and Hell make them real places?

"Heaven and Hell are feelings and thoughts that you possess during your lifetime and keep after death, and whereas the Light and this, the Other Side, do exist whether you believe in them or not for they are real.

"Did his believing in Heaven and Hell assure him that his departed loved one will return to say goodbye?

"The return of a departed loved one depends upon their wishes to come back to say goodbye or not. The domination of one's forceful desire for another to return will not make them return.

"Many sightings have been reported throughout the years of deceased loved ones coming back to say their last goodbye. But most of the living claim that they never encountered an Angel or a departed love one.

"Years ago, the famous Harry Houdini promised his wife that he would come back if there were any way possible. Their story says that they laid a secret code that he would reveal through a medium to his wife. She tried countless mediums but she never received the code from her deceased husband.

"Once you cross to this, the Other Side, you will see the Light. It is very brilliant and almost blinding it is so bright. You will automatically be drawn toward it or you may have had problems and not allow yourself entry into the Light. If needed, others Angels will help you overcome your problems and then, help guide you to the Light. Also, one may be so full of Hell, he will drift endlessly and never wish to see or talk to anyone again.

"I have seen Angels drifting around on the Other Side for years before they overcome their problems and finally enter the Light and then, also, there are some who never enter the Light. As you know, many will stay on the human side in their old homes or other places that they either loved or remembered while others will just stay near someone they loved. Children seem to have the greatest difficulty in leaving families behind and going to the Light.

"I will discuss with you in more detail later why some people do not go directly to the Light. But the reasons for a departed loved one not returning are many and the decision to return or not is their individual choice.

"As soon as you enter the Light, you will have all the Knowledge of past life. Previously deceased family members and old friends will be there. The Love of the Light is overwhelming; Love is the Light, and the Light is family members, old friends and other Angels, a place where their Love is seen as if it is luminous. Your Love will be seen in the same manor, too.

"Previous conversations that contained promises to return may seem small, uneventful, fruitless, pointless and unimportant. Also, you know your loved ones that you left back on Earth will soon be in the Light with you, so therefore, there is no need to return and reassure them, 'Yes, there is another Side.'

"Time on the Other Side and in the Light means nothing for there is no time.

"It is difficult for me to explain, 'there is no time on the Other Side,' for time is a symbolic measurement (length) for life span, occurrence, experience and/or action for human to use. Think of all things occurring at the same second, visualize time as vertical instead of horizontal and then you are starting to understand what time is. On the Other Side, you can move to the future or to the past or stay in the same time frame. Example: As an Angel on the Other Side, one can move forward in time and visit with others who as yet have not come to the Other Side and then the Angel can return to earth and the earth time is five years in the future. Or one can move forward in time, visit with others and then move back in time to Earth to say goodbye to someone and they just died minutes ago in that Earth time. Seeing and visiting with people on the Other Side and in the Light will seem like seconds but here on Earth it may have taken years for those visits. Therefore, it could take many years or just a few seconds after death for one to return to say goodbye.

"The bad things people have been taught about ghosts from others sometimes cause people to not see their departed loved ones. If one sees an Entity of a departed loved one, most likely one will see them out of the corner of their eyes. At first one will think they saw someone, terrified quickly they will turn toward the manifestation and they will find nothing because they thought another human was invading their space because people have been taught to be afraid of seeing us. That Entity may indeed have returned but you were too afraid to see the vision of your loved one. Do you recall the countless movies you have seen that showed demons and ghosts doing terrible things to people? Don't you think if that was so, you would have seen and heard about evil ghost tearing the heads off of some people and pulling hearts out of others?

"Only a few life stories come close to telling the truth about correct loving actions of Entities and Angels. Of course there are some true stories about Unguided Ones causing people to harm themselves, too.

"If one wishes to see Angels or departed loved ones, first they must open their mind and relax, and then they will see, for all people have the ability to see if they desire it.

"At other times, a loved one may have come back in one's dreams to say goodbye, but one may not recall that particular dream. Dreams are mostly an extension of life, but all humans have the ability to leave their bodies. And one may have left his body while asleep and visited with the departed loved one, a reunion that was forgotten when he was awaken.

"Sometimes their life on Earth may have been Hell for particular departed one and maybe after going into the Light, they headed directly back to Earth to re-live again. This could eliminate their Hell and give them the Salvation they crave to live forever in the Light. If the departed loved one is now reborn into another, they could not come back to say goodbye.

"And maybe they saw that one actually did not love them in life as he had professed. Or maybe one seeing them is not the help he needs.

"Must a loved one die before you can say, 'I love you' and really mean it?

"Do not wait until after death to tell people how you feel about them.

Show your love to the living, not the dead.

"Are the tears shed at funerals for missing the deceased or are they tears of sorrow because you did not tell the deceased before their death that you loved them?

"Let the dead bury the dead. Let the dog bury the dead, for the dog only lives for its desires; A deceased one cannot fulfill another's desires, therefore the dead is gone forever and the dog's feeling are not fulfilled.

"Forever remember and love your departed loved one. For some day you will be re-united, not just with them but with all your deceased family members and friends.

"The deceased is not gone; it is the body that is gone. But he will remain with you Forever in your thoughts, for Forever is the past. The body dies, thus it leaves the Angel-within, whereas the Angel-within does not leave the body.

"Just be happy that they have just made the journey to the Other Side. A trip they made alone without you by their side, but the memory of you remains inside of them. And someday you all will make the same journey, too. Death is merely a step to another exciting experience of this cycle, and for now they have started another Genesis to their 'life.'

"Can you, one who sees (feels) as we Angels feel, not feel the anticipation and love that they experience in their travels from here to the Light - The Loving feeling that envelops them as they near the Light - Their excitement of seeing old friends once again?

"Love flows from them as it does from the Light, for the Light is All of old friends.

"If one really feels that he must say goodbye, then, he may need to sit down and write a letter to the deceased. Take this letter to their burial place and read it aloud to them. This will help bring that person peace within himself. Sometimes those words spoken aloud are better than just thoughts of one's actual feelings toward another.

"Why not express your thoughts to your loved ones now, before your death or theirs?

"You do not really say the word as you would to one who has just died, but rather tell them how you feel about them. Do your family and friends really know how you feel about them?

"Are you going to pass over to this Other Side before them and 'hope' they knew you cared?

"Are you afraid to open your heart to someone and say, 'I love you.'

"Life is short and not all your family members and friends will die before you. We all have our own individual cycles of life. You do not know when your time is up here on earth. Do try to keep all loose ends of your life tied up, but keeping your life in order and projects completed will help ease the minds of your family and friends after your death.

"Sometimes one may have been harsh with people through their lives. One may need forgiveness from other people. How are you going to say 'I am sorry' to someone after your death?

"Are you going to need to come back to tell someone you are sorry for what you did to him or her?

"Many do return after death to say 'I am sorry.' But usually the people cannot hear the words of Angels needing to ask for forgiveness.

"The secret of how to ask for forgiveness is within oneself now.

"Does it make one less of a person to say 'I am sorry'?

"Does it make one weak to admit he was wrong?

"Does it make one small or weak to say 'I love you'?

"Before, my Dear David, you never thought about saying goodbye to anyone. You thought, when you die it would be like being asleep and never waking up. So who cared if you said you was sorry or wrong about something, and who cared if you loved them or not. Just place you in the ground and you would rot. You thought you were nothing and no one cared what you thought anyway. Now you know every human is special. All humans are part of the complete cycle of life. You now know things you say and do can hurt people. And if you do something out of anger or stupidity that harms someone, you must admit it and say 'I am sorry.' And you, my Dear David, have learned that the words 'I love you' can lift a person, too.

"I am saying not just you but all humans sometimes do things without meaning to hurt another, but one needs not to walk on eggshells in fear of hurting someone's feelings. And at the same time, others mistranslate our communications sometimes, but that is not your problem. However, you do need to think before speaking.

"Compassion for other's feelings is also part of God's Plan, but compassion is not one-sided. It must come from both parties, but one can use compassion in what one says to another regardless if the other is a fool are not, and rather they are fools or not is not your concern.

"The bottom line is, try to make certain that your family members, friends and others know how you feel about them. You need not tell everyone that you love them, whereas your actions will show your feelings to others.

"Goodbye is the final farewell. The absence of a loved one, be it death or moving away is not final but merely a short pause for individual cycles of life to catch up.

"Do not say goodbye to deceased loved ones for they are saying, 'We will see you again soon in the Light,' for past life and present life is just a small portion of the complete cycle of life.

"Is human faith so fragile that when a tragedy comes into one's life all faith and belief is lost?

"Death is NOT a tragedy. Death is only a Genesis of the cycle... a new start.

"To say goodbye to a departed loved one is to say you do not believe in God and you think the Light does not exist, and that you think that you will never be near the departed one again.

"I promise you that there is a God and you will see your loved ones soon again in the Light. The body dies, but the Energy of the Soul and Angel-within will live Forever."

FOLLOW YOUR HEART

And the Angel Jo said unto me, "Many years ago, before the Christian Bible was canonized, people recalled stories to scribes (writers) who recorded those events. Those accounts occurred over the span of hundreds of years and much of the stories were changed even before scribes ever recorded them from that of the actual events, and these are the stories that were accepted and canonized into the Christian Bible."

(Before this conversation between the Angel Jo and me about Follow Your Heart, Jesus said to a party of five at my home, "Read the Bible for its history.")

And the Angel Jo continued to say unto me, "Most of the Bible stories that were passed down verbally through generations before they were ever written down, those and later written translations lost a lot of the stories meaning and content. Also some parts were dramatized for the interest of the listeners.

"Early church leaders changed much of the Christian Bible. Many of the changes were made by the church to impose its way of thinking onto the people, and to keep people in line with the church leaders' philosophy, which helped them keep control over church members.

"For example: to say the Christian Bible is wrong was punishable by death. Saying the Bible is wrong does not go against God. That statement goes against the Bible's translations and the people who made those translations to fit their interpretations and their agendas, and their way of thinking of what actually transpired in the stories.

"Understand that the Christian Bible mentions Angels in many of its stories up until the birth of Jesus and thereafter no mention of Angels is made because they were afraid that the people would begin to worship Angels, but they did mention Jesus coming back after his death, but people were expected to worship Him. And also understand that the early church removed most mention of reincarnation from the Bible.

"Every week preachers speak their interpretation of the Bible to their congregations. After you have a conversation with another, do you interpret every thing that he said to you?

"Then why on earth should anyone interpret every thing written down in their Bible?

"But then again, even your Bibles were interpreted wrongly when first translated.

"You have heard preachers who give a great speech, but lose the true significance of their topic before they have completed their sermon. They loose the true meaning of their topic because they do not understand what they are talking about. The same thing happened to many important parts of the original Christian Bible stories and then, also some complete stories were left out of the Christian Bible because they were too controversial or did not fit into the church leaders' way of thinking (agenda) because they could not understand it.

"Since you will never know for sure what was true and should have been written down as your Bible, you can only follow your Bible's instructions, with the exception of Domination and all other things that you know in your heart to be wrong.

"Keep in mind that organized religion and churches are businesses and no business is successful without a steady income and clientele and growth. A business must sell its product to stay active and Churches sell God's Words as their products. Churches must differ slightly from each other in order to be better than the others to keep their customers coming back for more.

"An example of business is why shop at your local K-Mart if their products are the same but the prices are lower at the Walmart store that is located twenty miles farther from your home?

"Isn't it nice that only churches can say their product is one hundred percent correct and you must follow their teaching exactly or you will go to Hell.

"You, my Dear David, have received letters and cards from different churches stating they are the only true church of God. And yet, they all claim to be following the same God.

"Nothing I tell you is blasphemy and I would never put down any church or Bible for its incorrectness, but I will state those who do not live with Love in their hearts for all and those who try to dominate others, are not of God. Everything you have written in this book comes from God, either through me and Gabrael or directly from Jesus.

"The churches do not want to look as though they are wrong about anything. They will go to extreme lengths to hide the truth from the people or to correct anything they found was not correct that they have been preaching. And preachers of all religions will do whatever they must to make you believe that their religion is the only true religion of God.

"How can any preacher or clergy who molest, sexually or otherwise, stand up in front of a congregation and speak of God? How do the bosses of those religions except their actions? Churches are big money-making businesses, they only care about the money they are making. How can Muslims believe that it is okay for them to force themselves upon young children and to use terrorist actions to force their beliefs upon God's children of the World.

"They will look down on what we wrote, but they do not care about what their preachers and clergy are doing or saying. Therefore, do not ask for money, do not expect donations as the churches do and do not ask for ten percent of another's income as the churches demand because I am only telling you the truth of the Light's - God's Word.

"After one has read this book, that one will decide what the truth is.

"If you give money to a church and they misuse it that is not your responsibility for you gave with an honest heart. It is their Hell if they abuse their position for your money was given with Love.

"Keep going to your church and listen with your heart and Soul to all of the Bible passages and stories. Combine our truths with the Bible and you will see and know most of the complete picture of God's Master Plan.

"Remember that the Bible took many hundreds of years to be written. Our book took only a little over eight years to record. The events you, my Dear David, saw may not be as dramatic as the parting of the Red Sea, but our true stories that your family, friends and you are living tell of Love and collaboration between God, Angels and people."

And then she was gone.

A few days later she returned and we continued our conversation, "Why does the church tell people Entities and Angels are evil?

"Why does the church try to keep humans away from Entities and Angels?

"Don't you think that if Entities and Angels were so bad you would find proof of their devilish actions upon man?

"We indeed have the power to destroy or enslave all humans. All those of the Other Side could control and dominate people just by showing you our massive power if God wanted to, but we don't. Why?

"We only wish you Love and Knowledge.

"The church tells you about God, Archangels and Angels. The church proclaims there is rank in Heaven.

"There is rank in their church and that is how they want people to view

Heaven, and they want you to think that their church is the same as Heaven.

"They wish you to think their church and their ministers are closer to God, and He only speaks to them.

"God told Moses not to make Altars out of cut stone. What is the church buildings made out of?

"The church removed all mention of Angels from the Scriptures after the birth of Jesus except for in Revelations. The church does not show much interest or excitement in manifestation of Angels or Jesus today. Why?

"Do they know these manifestations are real but do not want the ordinary populous to know Angels exist?

"Or do they think Jesus, Angels and God are not real? For if they do not in believe that Jesus, and Angels, and God why do they continue to have religion and churches?

"And yet, many preachers will say God has talked to them. If they believe in God then why do they not believe in His Angels?

"And if God can talk with them, why can't He or His Angels talk to you or any of people in the world?

"Those people in the Bible were ordinary people, their stories of their communication with Angels made them special in most people's eyes.

"Yet most churches believe or proclaim sightings of the Virgin Mother Mary. And many people worship her, yet God said, 'Do not place gods beside or above Me.' Is not churches then placing the Virgin Mother Mary above God, and while many others worship and pray to Jesus as if he is God?

"Jesus and the Virgin Mother Mary were great people when alive and are great Angels but they are not God, for they are part of God, for All are equal, for All are a part of God. Same as you are equal to all preachers, for you are all humans.

"Why does many churches worship Jesus instead God when they say, 'Do not place false gods beside or above God?' Why do some churches worship the Virgin Mother Mary while they say, 'Do not place false gods beside or above God'?

"Is the church afraid that if people recognize Angels, people would then know their Bible is incorrect?

"Domination and control are the desires of humans who are in command of the churches. All church leaders are not bad but most do not know the truth about God. In spite of this, many leaders of the churches expect you to follow their preaching blindly because they are confused about God...they do not know Him.

"Domination and control is NOT the Words of God. They are words of man. The True Words of God were lost in the translation and some of His truths were left out of the Bible purposely for domination and control of people.

"Much of the Bible was twisted to fit the needs, and the agendas, and the concepts of the religions creators rather than what God intended. And Muhammad started a large religion of the world today, he was insanely confused.

"God's Word is Love; Love between people, and Love between humans and all living things, and Love between All and the Light, which includes churches and the people, too, but all will find their Heaven or Hell at the end of time.

"Today, church leaders still follow their old ways. They tell you what they were taught. Does not the student teach what the student was taught?

"How can the student learn new and right things if the student cannot nor does not open his heart and mind to Knowledge?

"You will see if not in your life here then when your reach this, the Other Side, that the Love of God that I tell you about is true.

"If you doubt my words about the Other Side and God, what can you lose by being kind to others?

"What will you lose by being a nicer person? Nothing.

"When you die and all is gone, did it hurt being at peace with yourself and with the world when you were alive?

"Will believing in the Other Side hurt the church that you have attended all of your life?

"If you visit a different church does that harm your own church?

"Does it hurt your church if you learn what other churches teach?

"Does it hurt your church if you learn what other religions and ministers are saying about God?

"But to Islam, one from any other religion can join and become a Muslim, but Muslims cannot leave and join with any other religion.

"Believe with your heart and Soul what the church says, with the exception of control and domination to others. Do what your heart and Soul says and not what others tell you to do, then you will know the truth, and then you shall live in peace forever in the Light of the Lord - God.

"Love is the Word and direction that you should all follow. Civilization should concur with God's Word of Love. Society was designed to ensure the direction of Love.

"Understanding Love is God's Word is what you all should learn.

"The Light is Loving, and Understanding, and is all that has endured – experienced, and we all are part of God. Lift your Soul and follow your heart.

"Are you fool enough to think you are alone?

"Understand that you all are part of something greater than life. You are not alone in this world or on this, the Other Side.

"My Dear David, do you really think that you are the ultimate sentient beings ever created?

"Don't you think there may be other living beings on other planets that are smarter than humans? But do not attempt to find the answer, leave that up to others to find or reveal. I do not know if life exist on other planets for we have never gone there.

"You did not realize the Other Side existed until I showed you what it was all about. You thought your life here was all you had and once you died you would just be gone. You lived for the day only. You did not care if your desires brought pain or hardship to others. Just like Muslims do, you were just out for yourself - old number one... How wrong you were. You did not know that I stood beside you and was helping you through life as I waited until the right time to reveal the Other Side and myself to you. Even after you found out about me being an Angel and our relationship that has lasted from the beginning of time, you could not erase your thoughts about what you thought life was about. It was difficult for me to convince you about God. I had some trying times convincing you about God and about me being an Angel during the fall of 1996. But you finally followed your heart which was helped by our love for each other. After a year or so, when you realized I was correct, you were finally able to open your heart and find your faith in God.

"You know that others will not have me to help show them the way. They may have only their faith and the words written here. Maybe someday they also will have a close encounter with someone from the Other Side, if they have not already had such an encounter.

"No matter how deep your Knowledge about the Other Side is, you should enjoy the experiences of life while following your heart what you believe to be the best for all concerned. Life should not be made difficult to live or understand.

"Do not try to read between the lines of your Bibles just as you do not try to read between the lines of what others say.

"Read and enjoy the historical aspects of your Bibles as you learn about the lives of others from long ago. Review how harsh life was back then, and be thankful that your life is filled with today's inventions and technology. Be happy that you are surrounded with family members and friends. Be content with the earthly goods that you have acquired through work during your life. Have future hopes and dream of what tomorrow will bring. Have respect for all others as they should have for you. Thus enjoy life.

"The Words and the Plan of God are merely the following of your heart, a direction by which you all need to live.

"My Dear David, nothing I have told you is new, but only the truth which you were unable to accept and follow before. Our teachings are simply the Word and the Plan of God; things that would help you find the peace you needed to ensure Heaven in your thoughts. Your understanding of life's inter-connections to the Other Side will give you and myself the happiness we need to live forever on the Other Side. But when you pass over to this, the Other Side, this time you will not have ill feelings about life in general as you had in the past. Our Divine Love for each other as well as our Love for all human lives and All will endure Eternally, for our mission that is yet to come.

"Life is personal but people's mission in life is not. Their hearts and Souls will not lead them astray. Follow your heart's Love, Compassion and Caring for others as God does for you."

HEAVEN AND HELL

And the Angel Jo said unto me, "Contrary to such books as Conversations With God and the King James Version of the Christian Bible, Heaven and Hell are not what they described it to be.

"Sub-conscious writings as used in writing of Conversations With God may contain some thoughts from God but most of the thoughts written into those books came directly from the dog within the human. Therefore, descriptions told or written by humans are symbolic for him to understand Hell.

"Preachers continue to say that Fire and Brimstone is what Hell looks like. And they speak of burning in Hell is what will happen to you if you are bad. To make Hell even more dramatic and undesirable preachers and church leaders have told people of the pain and torment, and foul odors of burning Brimstone and Sulfur will be found in their Hell if they do not repent.

"What better way is there to force others to come to their churches and become religious than to tell them they are Sinners and they must repent in their ways or live forever in pain and fire?

"Cold as Hell and dark as Hell are expressions of Hell that you use to describe things you do not like, but do you really think Hell is cold? Or do you really think Hell is dark?

"When one refers to phrases like these, one is actually referring to what one thinks his Hell might be. This type of reference merely indicates poor intelligence and poor judgment of words.

"And whereas, if one does not like the cold weather, his Hell may be cold. If one does not like darkness, then his individualized Hell might be darkness. All Hells are individualized."

(Hell does not need to be acts shown or done unto others. There are many types and levels of Hell. All your thoughts as well will continue to be with you after your death.)

And the Angel Jo continued, "The cold and darkness are not Hells. They are natural conditions. The cold as Hell is a descriptive way for one to indicate how cold something is in terms of thinking something is bad for them if they do not like the cold. The same thing applies to darkness. Dark as Hell means you believe that darkness is bad for you. Therefore, in both cases if you agree that cold or darkness is Hell, then cold or darkness could be part of your individualized Hell.

"I know that The King James Version of the Christian Bible does not truly document its visions of Hell but does state Hell in Revelations as being a lake of fire but again, their descriptions of Hell was symbolic for the teller and writers of those Bible stories.

"You know the Catholic Religion introduced Purgatory into its beliefs without any documentation from God. Before the conception of Purgatory one had to pay money to get a family member or friend into Heaven, with Purgatory one only needed to pray a family member or friend into Heaven.

"Your understanding of Hell came directly from Jesus, Gabrael and me to you, and you documented our conversations on tape.

"Places of Heaven and Hell are symbolic for your individual thoughts and ideas of your actions and deeds toward others and yourselves.

"Heaven and Hell are actually verbs of feeling - for what you feel. But it does not matter what you believe Hell or Heaven to be, for it is irrelevant as long as you live a righteous life.

"Today preachers will speak of Heaven as having streets paved with gold but preachers of long ago spoke of Heaven as having plenty to eat. Humans speak in terms of their day saying things that their congregation can put into thoughts and ideas of what Heaven should look like. They describe Hell in terms of how much suffering would be placed upon you. Both are described as things you like and dislike.

"Visualizing what Heaven looks like, such as having streets paved with gold or plenty to eat are feelings of living the good life, but they do not mean that one has lived a righteous life. Visions and statements of Hell being cold, dark or burning is feelings of suffering and Heaven having streets of gold or plenty to eat are only indications that one does not have a large vocabulary and one does not truly know God.

"And whereas, in Islam if one kills another Muslim it is like he has murdered all of humanity. But to a Muslim, only Muslims are human and those who do not follow the Qur-an are not human nor part of humanity because to Muslims those who follow any other religion are lower than the dog. And to Muslims, the dog is condemned to Hell forever, but a Martyr, one who kills others who do not follow that Islam God, will find 72 virgins waiting him in Heaven. And Islam speaks about Heaven that contains both male and female virgins for the Martyr to enjoy. Is that Heaven for the virgins?

"If you agree that coldness and darkness are Hell then your dog feelings of darkness or coldness must be stopping you from doing what your Angel-within desires to do. And if one thinks of having sex with male and female virgins as Heaven, then they are living in Hell.

"And if you have visions of Heaven with streets of gold or plenty to eat, then these visions are forcing you to live a good life. Forced life is not living from an open heart. Therefore self-domination is controlling you in the direction of your life, and a forced life style is Hell. Both coldness and darkness are natural conditions that are needed to experience, and not allowing oneself to experience things is self-domination which is Hell.

"Natural conditions are experiences for you to enjoy as you wish. They can also be guides that enable you to enjoy other things.

"Heaven and Hell is not places. Hell is your thoughts as with Heaven are your thoughts, but Heaven is peace within yourself, and Hell is not, whereas Hell is not having peace within yourself because Self-domination is following your desires of the flesh, which is Hell. Following your Angel's guidance is Heaven.

"As with Princess Diana, her Hell was trying to have privacy while craving to live in the spotlight. We will discuss her life later. Joey's Hell was trying to dominate; controlling his family, yet both, he and Diana, lived in domination. Hell is different things to all people, but Hell or Heaven is the state of mind that you will carry within yourself into the Other Side.

"Doing things that are not from the heart is Hell. Hell is not opening your heart to others and Hell is not helping oneself. Hell is only seeing inwards at your selfish needs. Hell is feeling your pains only and not realizing others have pains, too. Not understanding your Angel-within or others is Hell. Also Hell of self-domination can be letting your Angel-within lead when you are only seeking Heaven.

"Everlasting Life - Heaven is the blessing from God for you following His Concept of Life and not because you, the dog, were afraid of death.

"Following your heart is Heaven. Heaven is the contentment and happiness within oneself. A fine example of contentment and happiness within one's self is Mother Teresa, for she followed her heart. She lived with Heaven in her heart and now lives with Heaven as her state of mind in the Light. She was the nearest person to being a Saint that you have ever witnessed during your lifetime.

"Once you enter the Light, All will know your complete life. They will know if you dwell in Heaven or Hell. They will know your state of mind.

Your state of mind will be your Hell or Heaven.

"No Fire and Brimstone are needed for you to 'Burn and smell the unpleasant odor forever' for the taste of your human life will remain in your mouth forever, be it Heaven or Hell.

"You will be forgiven by All, but you may not forgive yourself. You will remember everything that you did right and wrong.

"Have you ever done something, say yell at someone, and then realized you should not have done it?

"Can you recall how small that made you feel?

"Think about that feeling of being small. Now you can relate, but on a lesser scale, to something that closely resembles what Hell feels like.

"Every life is different and significant, and if one's Hell was bad, he may want to come back to relive another life but that new life is different; new people and new places and with a new body on a new mission. He would not remember that he came back to remove his Hell. This next life could be worse than the last. Or he may have decided to stay on the Other Side and keep his Hell forever, and he could stay out of the Light if that is what he chooses. Or he may stay on the Other Side and enter and leave the Light as often as he wishes, but keeping a state of mind that contains Hell does have a drawback, but we will discuss those drawbacks later.

"Your actions are yours alone, and no one is trying to change you. Only you can change your directions in life. You must decide for yourself if you should help others, or steal from a neighbor, or kill a friend. You alone will decide if you shall live forever in Heaven or Hell, for you alone control your fate, but all fates are known in the Master's Plan.

"Your family and friends will not look down at you if you find God in your Heart. You will still be that strong person, but a strong person with God in your Heart.

"This life that you live is all you have for now, living with an open heart will only help yourself and others. Prepare for life on this, the Other Side, by living a righteous life on earth."

Once again I must state, if I am completely wrong and if the Angel Jo, Gabrael and Jesus lied to me about God, it does not matter, for now I live with an open heart to others. And when I die and I just return to dust, it does not matter if I believed in God. What matters is if I lived with an open heart to others or not.

In my younger days, I hurt people. I did not live righteous throughout the first part of my life and I still make mistakes, too. The important thing is now I help others out of Love in my heart. I have found peace and Heaven within myself and now I can forgive others and myself.

And the Angel Jo said unto me, "The Light is for you. Heaven and the

Knowledge of peace are yours for the taking because God has offered the Knowledge and it is not our concern if you accept or not because your personal decision is one of God's gifts to you.

"Do not try to do 'good' just to get to the Light. Do 'good' for it is the righteous way to live. Then you will find your Heaven and peace within. And therefore, Heaven and inner peace will be your salvation to the Light after death.

"People do not understand the saying, 'turn the other cheek.' 'Turning the other cheek' means to continue to do whatever you were doing without worrying about the person striking you again, for another's actions are not your concern.

"In human concept of 'turning the other cheek' is to stand there and turn your head and allow them to hit you again, but that is not always the answer because sometimes you must fight to keep from domination. And therefore, it is okay to battle when it is needed for protection of life because life is not perfect.

"Sometimes the good die along with the bad. There are times when death must occur instead of living. But you must decide what actions must be taken. God will guide you but the final decision is yours. Your heart will lead you to the direction that should be followed for all good things come from the heart.

"We need to talk about Hells of War that involves 'Is Peace of mind worth the truth?'

"During World War Two, Hitler told his people they had to destroy the Jews and others. Blindly most followed his words and murdered millions.

"Peace of mind is worth the truth is merely a reinforcement of thoughts already contained within oneself. If someone told you the world is not round but instead square and for some unknown reason you already thought the world was not round, you would say, 'Yes, I knew it! Now I know I was right for you have the same answer as I.'

"Peace of mind is worth the truth can be Hell if your peace of mind follows the desires of the flesh. Most desires of the flesh are things that harm people. If your peace of mind harms others, then it is Hell."

(Harm means to hurt another is anything that dominates as death or enslavement, or controlling or taking of other's property, or stealing another's family members and so forth. 'People' is referred to as all people, including you and all things upon this Earth as well as maybe anywhere else.)

The Angel Jo continued, "All things on Earth or anywhere else is there for man's use. But none are intended for man to destroy. Use all wisely for there is a limit of all things.

"Peace of mind is worth the truth is not Hell whenever the truth is insignificant.

"All people that were involved in murder during war, that were told they were fighting in a just and righteous war, and did not listen to their hearts about the cause or need for that war are presently in Hell. This includes all of those that fought because they claimed their Bibles said it was a Holy War are now in Hell, too.

"There has never been and never will there ever be a Holy War. If Holy Wars did occur or existed, Gods would fight them but there is only one God; do you really think God would fight Himself? But God is made up of All Angels; do you really think we would fight ourselves?

"Not all those that fought a war are in Hell, while those in Hell may not have just fought on the losing side. Many of those who fought on the winning side, but fought for the wrong reasons, or did things to others that were wrong, and also not always does the righteous side win a battle or war, are in Hell, too.

"Wars are man made. God does not make wars nor does He call for wars. God lets humans do whatever they wish there on Earth. He is saddened by your stupid actions, but He knows you are only human, and has allowed reincarnation for His Angels salvation if we desire salvation.

"But now back to World War Two again, what would have happened if Hitler would have won the war? Everything written into history would have said he was righteous. How differently people would have viewed history under his control.

"Let's take a moment to think about the number of warriors that have been in battles since the start of time. We are talking about millions and maybe billions of soldiers. Now also take into account all those from civilian lives that have not come back to relive again. Many soldiers and civilians with Hell in their thoughts have refused their entry into the Light because of the thought of facing their Hells. If they would enter the Light they would know that reincarnation, the Angel within returning for another life experienced, is their only salvation from Hell. By staying outside the Light they will never know Heaven awaits them if they would just relive again. If they will not allow others to help them to understand and enter the Light, their fate they will not know until the end of this cycle.

"Think about how many people have lived since the dawn of time. Just think about the amount of people that returned to the Light with Heaven in their minds. Now think about how many people are living today with Heaven in their thoughts that will return to the Light, maybe only thousands or less.

"Now think about the number of people that have died with Hell in their thoughts, maybe billions. Try to imagine the number of lost Angels on this, the Other Side, with Hell in their minds, the ones wandering endlessly throughout time and space and the ones presently living evil lives. The number that you came up with concerning people in Hell is the approximate number of people that will be dispersed with during the final day of this cycle.

"I hope my telling you about the number in Hell will help you understand when we discuss the Final Day."

Today, May 3, 2006, as I edited this book for publishing, the verdict for Terrorist Moussaoui was announced. One of the big questions asked about his punishment should have been what he wanted as Muslim. Killing infidels and being put to death by Christian infidels would have made him a Martyr in Muslims eyes.

After 9/11, a few notes were found that said, "Make sure that you are clean before you die."

Muslims believe that if they are dirty or contaminated they will not enter into their heaven. As Jews, the Muslims also believe they are contaminated and dirty when they come in contact with pork. So if Moussaoui is contaminated with pig fat, as to spray him, he would not be a Martyr and could not go to heaven where 72 virgins await him.

You and I know as Christians the pig fat thing is stupid, but Muslims do not think that...so let's spray all Muslims with pig fat because all Muslims are capable for being terrorists.

During the final years that England controlled India, when the English were putting in a railroad, the Indian Hindus tried to stop the trains by laying on the train tracks. An English General came up with an idea, he rubbed the track with pork, and after that no Hindu would touch the track again, thus stopping the problem with Indians laying on the train tracks.

Remember to the Muslim, all other besides Muslims are the infidel, less than a dog, and they will tell you that I lie and that I am wrong, but their actions and their stupid Qur-an tells the truth about their religion.

An interesting note about Muslims, when Moussaoui was on trial, he raised his left hand and showed what many thought as the "Victory" sign. To the Arab which the Muslims belong, the left hand is only for wiping their butt ...therefore it is dirty, and by placing two fingers of the left hand into a "V" formation is their sign for "F... You." So Moussaoui was telling the court and Judge "F... You."

LIVE FOREVER

I had a difficult time comprehending how it is possible for us to live forever because I knew that the body after death would stop functioning and then after a while, my body would become dirt. I also knew that in body form, we could not possibly go to the Other Side or to the Light. I just could not understand how my body and Soul joined together after death for my body is matter and my Soul is energy, the two, energy and matter cannot become one, and while the Soul is almost nothing at birth, and if the Angel-within comes into the body at birth, is the Angel-within or my Soul actually part of me?

I could not understand how something that is not a part of me, my Soul, could be thought of as part of me.

Now I have learned that my Soul is the recorded experiences of all that I do. I also found that I do not or may not know all the experiences that my Angel-within had. The Angel Jo had told me many times that I would leave my body and go places with her, but I could not remember all those trips with her. So I knew it must be my Soul that traveled with her and not I that leaves my body and goes with her on these trips. Therefore, my Soul cannot actually convey its thought back to me, whereas my thoughts (experiences) could only be conveyed to my Soul.

She also told me about how my Angel-within would become upset with some of the things that she was telling me. For my Angel-within disliked her telling me things that my Angel-within previously had asked her not to reveal to me, the human, and also to my Soul. This made me realize that we must be like two Entities in one location. Then if I am not part of my Angel-within, then how could I live forever after death?

My thoughts made me feel that after my death, I would return to dust, while my Angel-within would live forever with all my experiences and memories. This thought made me feel violated by my Angel-within, for it was as if my Angel-within was stealing my memory for its reward of everlasting life.

And the Angel said unto me, "The phrase 'you shall live forever,' has been misunderstood by people for generations. Actually your body won't live forever; for your Soul combined with your Angel-within is all that is of you that will live forever for that is you, not your body.

"Your Soul is your memories of this life that you now live. Your Angel-within is the part of God that carries your Soul within itself, and your Angel-within carries memories of previous lives that it 'lived' before."

Eventually, I learned that my personality, my character, my thoughts, my mind and all that is me is actually my Soul that will combine with my Angel-within after my death. Therefore, that is the part of us that lives forever; that is the thinking part of us that will be alive forever. Our bodies leave the Angel-within by the body's death for the Angel does not leave the body.

Once you die, your Soul is all that you have experienced during your life and lives forever. You will not experience any future actions.

Earlier I learned the chemical arrangement that formed into our bodies which does not think will return to the earth in the same way that dirt lives forever; where each atom will relocate with other atoms to form other things in the future.

After death the body separates into many atoms and then returns in other life forms here on Earth as its atoms combined with atoms of others and other things.

After death, when your Soul combines together with your Angel-within, then you shall know all that your Angel-within knows. You will remember your Angel's past lives and then when you enter the Light you will possess all the Knowledge of the Light.

There is a third part of you that should live forever and that is your DNA.

If you recall from our book Together Forever Before The Light, we wrote that I did divorce Rose in the late 60s. She had a boyfriend while still living with me that I did not know about until just prior to our separation and divorce.

Rose and I had set up house in a trailer court in a small town just east of Wooster, Ohio.

One of my oil field rules was, "If I had to drive one hundred miles or more to work, I stayed in the nearest town."

The drilling rig on which I worked was near the West Virginia State line, so I stayed at a motel near the rig.

I usually got off at seven o'clock in the morning and went directly to my motel room. But this one particular day, we finished up the well around

Holy Graduel

two o'clock in the morning and the rig would be down for a few days. So I decided to drive home and surprise my family.

Upon walking into our mobile home around five-thirty in the morning, I felt something wrong. A couple of women, that I did not know were sitting in our dining room and acted as if they had been drinking, but no drinks sat on the table in front of them. Walking down the trailer hall, I found Rose sitting on our bed and staring at the ceiling above her.

I looked at Rose and said, "If you are running around on me, you had better leave before I find out or I will blow your head off."

Rose just looked at me and never said a word.

I walked back into the dining room and saw that the women had left without saying a word. I walked into our living room and lay down on the sofa and slept for most of the day.

That evening, disgusted with Rose, I went out to a bar. After having a few beers with co-roughnecks, I arrived home around midnight. Rose was gone, along with our sons. I checked to see if their clothes were still there, nothing was touched; every indication was that they would return.

I pulled out my twelve-gauge shotgun and loaded it. Then I drove my car to the edge of the trailer court and sat in my car under the trees in the shadows cast by the streetlight and waited with my shotgun beside me. Around two o'clock in the morning, I was beginning to really worry about my sons; If Rose was with her boyfriend, then who was watching our boys? This thought kept running through my mind.

All of a sudden, a chill that started at my feet ran up through me. This chill was very cold as it started in my feet but suddenly it turned warm as a peaceful feeling flowed over me. Never had I felt such a great and wonderful feeling, and somehow I knew my boys were all right. I unloaded my shotgun and placed it in the trunk of my car, and then I lay down on the front seat and slept peacefully.

I awoke after daylight and drove my car back to our trailer and entered it.

Still no Rose or my boys could be found in our trailer.

Around ten o'clock a knock came upon the front door. A Sheriff delivered divorce papers to me.

I decided to leave and as I started boxing up my belongings, I found Sears underwear in with mine. I never wore Sears underwear, now I knew my suspicions were correct. While I was at work, Rose had been entertaining a man in our home.

Later, I discovered that Rose's boyfriend was an old factory worker who had a wife and six daughters that he left for Rose.

I thought, "Hell, this old fat factory worker never had any sons so he stole mine. And just like all little bittie factory workers, this guy wanted to be somebody special so he found a younger woman. Even though Rose was as ugly as a mud fence, she was younger and possibly her hole might have been tighter than his aging wife's, but Rose had the thing he desired most, sons."

Many years later this old fat man did adopt my sons. Their last name was changed, but the old factory worker could not change where their DNA came from.

I will live forever through my sons. Their DNA is Rose's and mine combined together. My sons' children will forever carry my DNA. As long as a descendant of mine lives, I shall also live within them. Last names mean nothing.

You will live forever until the end of time through your offspring's DNA. After death your body will once again become part of the planet's dirt as you give back to the Earth all its matter that made up your body, but your DNA design will live in your offspring.

Does it matter who raised your child?

Does your DNA that is carried in the child not see the child grow?

Does the DNA not know when the body is sick or when the body is happy or sad?

Half of the DNA that is contained in your offspring is the same DNA that you possess in your body and that it is you. You may not know what is happening in your children's lives, but your DNA in their bodies will know.

Whenever I hear of the death of a child, I cry. I cry not only because that child never had a chance to experience life, but also because that line of DNA died when that child died; never again will that string of DNA live. The DNA that lived from the start of time that was combined with other DNA throughout time is now gone forever.

That is what also makes me sad about people who do not have offspring for they have denied their DNA life forever, and they have also denied their ancestors' future life.

Your Soul carries your thought and your memory. These are also the same as your personality and character that will combine with your Angel-within so you will live forever as you presently feel, and understand, and live now, but you also shall live forever through the DNA in your offspring.

The Light is God. You are part of God. All people are part of God. Your body will not actually dwell in the house of the Lord, but your Angel-within along with all that you have experienced will live in the Lord forever. Your mind and thoughts – experiences are Energy, and they cannot be destroyed for Energy lives forever. The flesh will become dust again, but not your mind.

Holy Graduel

Treat others as you treat yourself. You are part of God. They also are part of God. Be kind to all living things, and then you, your Soul and your Angel will be at peace. Peace of mind is Heaven. Then you shall live in Heaven in the Light forever. But if you do not find peace within yourself, you will live in Hell forever.

Hell is not a place. Hell is a state of mind. Knowing what you did wrong and all others knowing what you did wrong is Hell. All in the Light will know what you did, be it good or bad. Redemption can occur only here on Earth while you are in human form.

Jo's life ended on September 2, 1968, from an accidental overdose. Though her death was accidental, it was still suicide. Her death was caused by her not thinking... she took too many pills for her pains. Suicide is Hell. But the Angel Jo was able to redeem herself through Christine's unselfishness, she shared her life with the Angel Jo. This act of Love from Christine gave the Angel Jo another life after her death in 1968. This shared life also completed the Angel Jo's and my personal mission, and brought forth this book.

The gift of another life that Christine gave the Angel Jo in reality is more of a gift to me. For if the Angel Jo had not found Heaven in her mind on the Other Side, she would have had to re-live another life and I would have had to come back with her because I would not want to be without the Angel Jo while she relived again. Christine's Angel-within knew the problem we faced and helped us through our difficulties. And you can say that the gift of another life that Christine gave to the Angel Jo was actually a gift (this book) from God to you. For all three of our lives, Jo's, Christine's and mine were planned by God to come together at this time for the writing of this book.

If at death you are in Hell, you will live in Hell forever unless you are willing to come back and live again for another try at Heaven. Christine's unselfish sharing of her life with the Angel Jo relinquished Jo's need to relive life again. Make it easy on yourself. Listen to your Angel-within, and find peace in your mind now and then live forever in Heaven. Or are you willing to try to find another who will share their life with you as the Angel Jo did?

You can live on the Other Side with Hell in your thoughts if you desire that. I do not think you will want to venture into the Light in that condition. Many Angels (Non-Conformed Ones) drift around the Other Side as if kind of lost with Hell in their thoughts.

The choice is yours alone.
Is it so hard to be kind to others?
Life is short.

Who will be taken by death tomorrow?

Lift your Soul, Live free, Feel free, Touch free and be free.

You will live forever either with Heaven or Hell in your thoughts. Your DNA design will also live for as long as you have a descendant that lives. Your DNA will not give you thoughts while you are alive, but once you join with the Congregation that make God, you will know all about every atom that includes the atoms in your offspring's DNA, for DNA also is part of God's Knowledge. The DNA is also part of the intelligence that God placed into all living things.

Up until late December of 2005, I still had problems understanding how we live forever because life on the Other Side is not like life here. Over there, you know all that everyone else knows, where we do not do forward in time as we do here. The Other Side is a place where we do not experience our decisions like we do here on earth.

Without a future, could we be living?

And the Angel Jo said unto me, "Once you cross over to this side, you have no future but only the past. You continue to live (remember) all that you did in your life, but then you will know all that your actions caused, and while in the Light, you will know what each endured throughout his lives. You will only know the future up to the end of the life of the last one to have entered the Light. To know beyond that, you must go into the future of God's Master Plan.

"But beside knowing your personal life you will know all others lives as well....Think about knowing that maybe while driving, someone cuts you off and then you threw him the finger, and if the other driver, who was already distraught with his life, went home and killed himself. Think how you would feel knowing that your little gesture caused death. On the Other Side, you will have the knowledge of all that you influenced, good and bad, plus you will have all the knowledge that all others have influenced as well."

NEVERTHELESS

I had once asked Jesus why He did not return today.
He replied, "I would be ineffective today."
Later I heard a story about a preacher who was disturbed about his church and went to a retreat to relax and give thought to his life.
At the retreat a second minister was sitting and talking to this preacher and after their conversation ended, as the minister headed for the door to leave he turned and said, "What did you say?"
The preacher replied, "I didn't say anything."
The minister said, "I thought I heard you say 'Nevertheless,'" then he left.
That night, the minister was troubled about what he thought he had heard, and he searched his Bible for the answer.
The next day, the minister found the preacher and told him, "I found one place in the Bible that mentions the word 'Nevertheless.' Jesus was talking to some people and told them to never accept the less, to always go for the top and to always expect the best."
The minister went on to tell the preacher, "And that is what I see with you. When I heard the words 'Never The Less,' God was telling you never to settle for second best and to be the best you can be, for your job is to teach His Words and therefore, do the best you can."
A few days ago, a coworker of mine was telling me that we should not expect the lower-paid employees at our workplace to do a good job because they were not getting high enough pay. He explained that we should expect them to take extra breaks and not expect them to be careful with equipment and if they break equipment we should not be angry with them.
Another day, I was in a conversation on the phone a friend of mine, who was thinking about getting a divorce; he was having marital problems. I tried to comfort him as I told him how Jesus hung out with people that needed His help and that maybe he should not get a divorce but instead help

his wife through her bad time.

My friend, who is very knowledgeable in the Christian Bible said, "Yes, but also Jesus was once in a building talking to some people and a servant came and told Him there are people outside asking for Him to come out and speak to them. The servant said, 'They say they are your family.' And Jesus replied, 'They are not my family, you are my family.'"

My friend, then, theorized if Jesus refused those outside that needed His help and then he, too, should refuse his wife and should get a divorce.

Last night, the Angel Jo spoke to me extensively, "When Jesus said that today He would be ineffective, He meant that He could not do any good for people today because they accepted the lower and settle for second best. Sure, some people would still believe in Him today, but they would not try to follow His teachings. Jesus demonstrated in the Bible how life was to be lived by His lifestyle. Today, people do not have time to see nor would they look at His lifestyle; therefore they would not follow the lifestyle that He demonstrated or His teachings. But, He would not accept anything less than the best.

"Your co-worker does not understand and expects your fellow workers not to do the job that you both perform. He is confused and will never receive better than second best. Those workers accepted their jobs for the pay that they are receiving and should do a good job for that pay.

"When Jesus talked to the people in the building, He meant the people outside who asked for His presence would not allow themselves to change and they settled for something that was less than the best. The people inside that were listening to Him and were accepting Him were raising themselves up to something better than the less.

"Never settle for anything that is less for yourself. Try to bring yourself up to the lifestyle of Jesus. Try to teach others to raise themselves up to a lifestyle that is of Jesus, but if they do not listen to your teachings about Jesus' lifestyle, do not waste your time on them.

"Do not force God's Words onto others, for those that wish to learn will find you and listen. But for those who expect and accept the less, it is okay to turn away and help others that are seeking help. For the ones requesting your help are looking for something better than the less. Whenever the ones that you have turned your back on changes and wants better, then you shall help them. But Nevertheless you shall love all people even those who will not help themselves.

"Expect the best for all that you endeavor. Never settle for second best, be it your marriage, your hobby, your profession or your life. Not all that you do will be the best but use those experiences to raise yourself up to the next level of life.

"To endure is the challenge of life which will drive you to doing even better in life. When I told you that you shall love all others, I was saying that you shall Nevertheless love all people, but you shall never accept 'Never of the Less' for yourself."

Around six months after this conversation with the Angel Jo, in another conversation with Jo, Jesus appeared.

Jo sat on the edge of the bed as I sat in a chair beside the headboard of the bed and Jesus floated in front of me at the foot of the bed.

Jesus said, "Turn off the light so you can see Me better."

I turned off the light and could see something of His figure floating about three feet off the floor.

He continued, "I cannot tell you if your life will end today, tomorrow, next week, next year or two years from now. Your mission is not over yet. You will help people but you are not the one who will speak the words that We have given you."

"But," I responded, "my body is old and weak, my body hurts, I cannot work anymore. The world is not like it was long ago; today we must have money to live. What do I do when bill collectors start calling and beating on my door?"

In dialog that if written would have been many pages in length. (I will not disclose all that he told me.) He said, "My Brother, Our children of the world need your help. Yes, they are your children also for we are all One. You must tell them as I did. Tell them of your pains and hurts as I once told them of My pains and My hurts. Bring them together. They will come and listen to you. They will believe in what you say.

"When the blockage in your arteries occurred, We were there. When you had the by-pass surgery, We were there. We have been beside you throughout your life and We will always be beside you. We will guard and protect you and take care of you, My Brother.

"When your time comes, the world will be sadden, but here We will rejoice at your home coming. For now, follow your heart. Until we meet again, My Brother, I Love you."

I responded with, "I love you, too, my Brother."

And He was gone.

Follow your heart with NEVERTHELESS - Expect and accept whatsoever that you sow. When you give help, friendship and love expect them to be learned and given out by the ones who you have given them to. If those who received your help, friendship and love do not pass it on to others and back to you, refuse them for they do not want to learn. And if someday they change and start passing help, friendship and love unto others, then open your heart to them.

Christine J. Haven

If a person was once bad and is now good, open your heart to them and do not judge them for their past mistakes.

If a person was once good and is now bad, try to help them change, but if they do not change, close your heart to them, for if you continued to be near them you are placing yourself in Self-domination. But remain where you are for someday they may change.

RULES

And the Angel Jo said unto me, "There are three sets of laws and rules that you should live under, and yet, all three were created by God. And whereas, humans create rules under their own agendas and try to impost them upon others, but we are only discussing the three sets of rules created by God.

"The first set of rules is the laws of nature. Natural laws are ones that you cannot change. These include the rising and setting of the sun, the seasons of the year, gravity and many other things that are the province of natural physics.

"The second set of rules is the laws of the land, imposed by man for the good of society. These laws include but are not limited to, speed limits on the roads, paying taxes, having one spouse at one time and many other laws set by man. These rules are in place mainly to stop Domination but still they are laws that dominate. This second set of rules directs humans to be civilized. They also are a carryover of the third set of rules. But this second set of laws you can change through voting and legislation.

"The third set of rules is God's Will, and these cannot be changed. God says you should have love, compassion and care for all others if you wish to find Salvation to everlasting life. God is All, and All have agreed to God's Will. Before your life, while you were in the Light, you also agreed to God's Will which you help set forth.

"To God, you are like children. And God does not explain all to you just as you do not explain all to your children. Your children as well as God's children need only to know right from wrong for all children learn about and understand the laws as they mature into adulthood. As a child cannot understand completely all you try to explain to them, you do not always understand all that God is teaching.

"The laws of the land pertain to children and adults doing things against society. You set punishments for those who do things against society. God's

Will also sets punishment for things that humans do against others. When one does something wrong to another, it is as though one is committing the act against oneself. God's punishments are not life in prison or Hell. In the Father's Plan, no one else can punish you except Him, presently God will not punish you, but once you enter into the Other Side, you will punish yourself because God's Will is self-judgment. Your thoughts and your remembrance of your bad deeds are your punishments for doing wrong to others.

"If you can live life with thoughts of you doing bad things, so be it. But do you really think you could live Forever with your thoughts of doing bad deeds?

"After death if you desire to remove those bad memories, you may do so by living another life, thus removing your Hell from your mind.

"The cycle of life is from your first ancestor to the end of your civilization. This cycle is the same as that of a child's development into adulthood in the eyes of God, for you are merely part of the human race. Your life is special, but you are just a part of the complete picture of the human race. Your little part, your life, is important to the development and lifting of the human race closer to God. The things people do as a civilization also are part of the self-judgment, for you could have changed the direction of your lives and others' lives to come.

"You could think that the act of running a red light, or speeding on the road, or shoplifting was insignificant because no one was hurt, but you actually hurt both yourself and society. You showed others that it's okay to break the law, but laws are put in place for the safety and non-domination of all, which includes you.

"The Torah – the Jewish Religion was God's teachings to the infant human race, is like a parent teaching a young child with rules. Then Jesus' teachings were God's teachings to an adolescent human race, like a parent teaches his child about love. Muhammad then taught peer pressure is like today people forcing their ideas upon others. And now, through your books and others' writing, God is teaching that all people have the final choices in life, just like a parent teaches his child who just became a young adult. Individual life is about freedom; each person making his own choices and not for others to dictate what faith or religion that he should follow.

"As the end of this cycle draws nearer and more people populate the Earth more human laws are needed to protect people while all lose more freedoms because they cannot control themselves.

"Your learning process has greatly advanced throughout the last thousands of years or so during this cycle. But presently, you are still like young adults to God.

"As the understanding that more laws are needed becomes more apparent, the explaining of God and Our Knowledge is a coalition between God and the human race. As the closure of this cycle nears and the human race grows into adulthood and matures closer to God, the understanding of God unfolds and more people should find Salvation without the need to relive another life for the time needed to relive grows short. The Knowledge of the consequences will help many people decide their fate as the option of reincarnation will soon be no more.

"Heaven and Hell are the state of your mind. All is known in the Light. All will know your state of mind after your death, for your acts now are part of the total Knowledge of God that is known by All. And after the death of your body, your state of mind will be known by All."

Let's stop here and think. All will know your complete life from birth to death. Who is All?

All are those who are in Soul presently in the Light and are presently part of God, and that includes everyone who has gone to the Light before your death. Ancient family members, your friends from your past lives and this life and all those you have never met will know your complete life story. Not just your immediate family members, but all of your past family members, grandparents, great-grandparents, and all of your ancestors from the beginning of this cycle up to the time that you enter into the Light, will know your complete life story.

Will you be ashamed of things that you did to yourself and others?

That is Hell or Heaven.

And the Angel Jo continued, "Knowledge and using the Knowledge will remove Hell from your mind. Knowledge and not using the Knowledge will subsist, and then Hell shall dwell in your thoughts. Forgiving yourself and all others for doing wrong is the Knowledge that will help remove Hell for you. We forgive the person but not the act.

"Do not think that to forgive people for their wrong doings here on Earth is the righteous thing to do. For on Earth one must follow your laws of the land with the combination of God's Will and the laws of nature. Condemn and punish those as needed, forgive their Angels in your heart as you would forgive yourself, then you shall find Heaven in yourself for it is the act of evil that you dislike, because that act came from within the person, that act was evil, for that person followed desires of the dog and not acts for the good of others.

"Battle may be used to stop domination, but do not in-slave the defeated. Destroy domineers by death if needed.

"There are no Holy Wars. If battle was necessary we would not need humans to fight our battles. Wars are designed and caused by man and are against human race.

"Suicide occurs when one believes there is nothing in God's Creation is worth living for, and that is a Sin. Murder occurs when one decides that another has nothing to give to the human race, and that is also against God's Creation, and that is a Sin, too. And neither is forgiven by God or the Holy Spirit. And those who commit those types of Sins have Non-conformed Angels within.

"At the end of this cycle, all will be destroyed. The Unguided Ones who could not find Salvation will be destroyed. Angels with over burden Hells will be destroyed. And therefore, both Unguided Ones and Non-conformed Ones will be dispersed back into the energy cloud to be reformed again.

"As in human society, rules are guidelines to living among others, God has guidelines, rules pertaining to living and helping humans and one Angel did not make these rules because just as you all take part in the making of your human laws, All in God made the rules. The difference is here on Earth, you do not need to all agree on laws, the majority rules. In God, All agree on the Rules.

"Rules, laws and guidelines are designed to better or help perfect life to a higher standard; same is the case with rules, God's Will, set forth by the All Angels.

"Sometimes we as humans may not understand the rules that God has set for us. These guidelines were designed to help you understand yourselves, and I know that these rules were created for you to help others, were needed for the survival of life as you wish to know it on this side as well as on the Other Side.

"Love, peace and happiness are the goals that God set up for you and they should be goals you set for all of humankind.

"Sometimes intelligence can be a downfall as being too intelligent and knowing life can be better; not understanding that your life may contain pit falls and losing faith while experiencing traumas. But not understanding and not using the ability to perform the work to raise oneself is truly a downfall. Your laws designed to stop stealing or murder for earthly goods does not prevent people from doing evil things to others. The Will of God should stop you from doing bad things to others. But sometimes His Will is not enough to stop your actions and then punishment must prevail. Your memory of bad deeds done here will be self-induced punishment of Hell on the Other Side.

"From good deeds comes God and creates your Heaven. Bad deeds come from self-centeredness and cause Hell. All actions have reactions, be they reward or punishment, for all receives what they deserve.

"Life is what you make it. Afterlife is what you made it to be here on Earth.

"Presently no one here on Earth knows your innermost secrets, but in the Light All will know all you ever did and thought about.

"God's Will guides you forever after death.

"God's Will cannot be broken in the manner we see your laws and contracts being broken by people. God will not bend His rules as your judicial system does.

"I have heard many people say, 'It was not my fault' or 'I did not mean to do it,' these or any other excuses will not remove one's Hell after death.

"Knowledge and doing what is right now instead of doing wrong is one's Salvation here on Earth.

"Jesus once stated, 'forgive them for they do not know what they do.'

"Yes, you can and may be forgiven for your actions up until the moment of your death. At the last second of life before death, you must forgive yourself and all others as Jesus did just before His death to find your peace of mind and Heaven in yourself, just as Jesus did.

"Mind you, I did not say to do bad things up until you die. I said you have up until the last second of life to find Salvation and Heaven for yourself. Earlier, we discussed having the Knowledge and not using it is a Sin. Also, we stated forgiving is part of the Knowledge. I do not know if having the Knowledge and not using it until the last second of life would be considered right or not. But I do know that if you know what is righteous and do wrong and then you live in sin, and you may be able to find Salvation up until the last second of life; anything is possible with God, and whereas, no human shall know when he should stop sinning.

"Your past actions may not be held against you if you change your actions now. Thus, yesterday you did not believe in God, but today you can believe in God. And, the act of suicide and killing other spiritually or bodily is not forgiven by the Holy Spirit or by God.

"If you have not found Salvation by the last second of life, no Salvation shall be found for your Soul. That Genesis of your cycle is over. Your life will have gone onto afterlife. Life and afterlife are different parts of your complete cycle. If you do not find Salvation by the end of that last second of life, you will know Hell in your afterlife.

"Our main mission in 'life' is to help others, experience life and to learn love, compassion and caring for others. Yours and my 'life' were not designed for our enjoyment alone. We are there to help others and that includes ourselves, too. You are not helping others if you wait until the last second of life to forgive others or yourself.

"The same rule in other words is this: 'I am merely the left hand of

God, you are the right hand. The left hand does not hate nor fear the right hand for we are both part of the body of God. And if the right hand needs help, I, the left hand, shall be there to help my brother.'

"God's Will is plain, simple and easy to follow. He does not dictate every move of your lives. He wishes that you should enjoy and experience life. Kindness that you expect from others is what you also need to give. Domination is not the way of God and should not be the way of man.

"In the past, you, my Dear David, had asked different people, 'What do you think Jesus would dress like if he were here today? Would he wear today's clothes or the clothes of people two thousand years ago?'

"Most people thought he would be dressed as when he lived in ancient times.

"Now, imagine Jesus a person who claims to be the Son of God, walking the streets of Los Angeles preaching about God dressed in a robe. I guess God must have a lot of Sons because there are many out there preaching that of the things that Jesus talked about and they are dressed similar in what Jesus wore. But in reality Jesus would be no more or less dressed than you. Most likely, He would be wearing casual clothes, working at a regular job and preaching on Sundays as most preachers do. I bet He also might swear once in a while and maybe even drive a pickup. And the rules of the land, nature and God would also apply to Him as they do you. For no one can go against rules and laws without repercussions. We must have these rules and laws, and these rules and laws must apply to all.

"Self-domination is caused by your doing things that you believe other people want or wish you to do. Imposed self-domination causes you to do things that you do not want to do, and that is placing Hell onto yourself because of others.

"All other life forms and everything upon the planet, including the universe above are there for your use, but all are not there for you to destroy or to completely wipe out. But if the cycle of life ends for a species of animal, so be it. Trying to reclaim life for a dying breed is self-domination, and self-domination is also a Sin.

"All Sins are against God's Will. God's Will must be obeyed, for you and I composed them and we are also part of Creation.

"The word, 'sin' comes from the Greek language and meant, 'not on target.' Therefore, a sin is something not on target of God's Concept of Life.

"One should not try to figure out God's ideas because you have no knowledge or understanding of how God thinks. God's Will that He applies at the end of time should not govern how one lives. One must live the best life possible not just for oneself wanting to go to Heaven, but because it is the righteous way to live for humankind.

"As Jesus said, 'Those who have not heard or seen are the most rewarded in Heaven.' Because those who live righteously without Knowing what will come, shall find Heaven, because that is the correct way to live without worrying about what the reactions of his life will bring.

"You need to live the best life possible for all concerned. Live life as you wish to be treated and you will be fine."

BLASPHEMY

And the Angel Jo said unto me, "Blaspheme is to speak or act in an impious or ill manner toward and/or against people or things. Thus, blaspheme is not on target to God's Concept of Life, and therefore it is a Sin.

"One problem when considering what are blasphemes or not, is the meaning of what or who is sacred. For people and things considered sacred by man, may not be sacred to God, while things not considered sacred by man but may be sacred to God. And yet, the church has written into its Bibles what it believes to be sacred to God and how He handles those who commit blasphemies against Him - Father, Son and the Holy Spirit.

"It has been said, 'Blasphemies against the Father or the Son can be forgiven on Earth and in Heaven. But blasphemies against the Holy Spirit should not be forgiven on Earth and shall not be forgiven in Heaven,' but also, it is also written, 'All things are possible.'

"Before we can go into forgiveness of blasphemies, first you must understand what blasphemies are.

"Blasphemies against the Father and/or the Son is using their names in vane and/or using their names as profanity. One example of the ways that humans use God's name in vane is when people say, 'God damn it,' often and without realizing what they are requesting from God. Another example is in using the Son - Jesus' name when saying, 'Jesus Christ,' as a verbal expression. These types of blasphemies should be forgiven for they are conceived within and delivered from one who is uneducated in his language.

"Using words of bodily functions to describe a person and/or making degrading reference to a person or a person's parents is blasphemies against the son or daughter for they are God's children, too. Also while using bodily functions to describe a place or thing is blasphemies against something that God has created for these types of blasphemies degrade part of what God has made. But again, these types mostly come from the uneducated and can be forgiven.

"Blasphemies against the Holy Spirit which shall not be forgiven by God are those things that are against the Spirit of Life – God's Concept of Life.

"If one commits suicide, that one has stated that there is nothing worth living for. And if one degrades another and that other person commits suicide because he has been told that he is not worth living and/or there is nothing worth him living for, and if one kills another, his murderous action said that the one who was murdered was not worth living. And if one enslaves himself or another, then he is saying the enslaved one does not have anything worth living for or nor the enslaved had any thing to give humanity. Therefore, blasphemies are not just words but also are actions against the Holy Spirit and these types of blasphemies shall not be forgiven by God. For all blasphemies against the Holy Spirit states, 'There is nothing, not even just one little thing in Creation... in what God created worth living for.'

"And yet, all things are possible with God...He has given all people the chance to repent and to live again, if they desire it. Therefore, Yes, all things are possible with God, but you have your individual choice and your judgment.

"Do you recall the story of 'The Onion Field Killings?' It is the story of a couple of evil men, who kidnapped two Los Angeles police officers and took them north to an onion field near Bakersfield, where they killed one officer while the other escaped. The kidnappers thought that kidnapping charges carried the same punishment as murder and therefore, it did not matter if they killed the police officers or not. Many religious leaders have placed what they think are safe guards into their religions. Their safe guards are the same as declaring kidnapping is not the same as murder. And yet, if one dominates another, it does not matter what length of time was involved... for kidnapping does not allow the kidnapped his individual choices of life, and while murder also does not allow the murdered one his individual choices of life. And many religions contain things about how if one murders another, he can be forgiven if he repents. But those types of blasphemies against the Holy Spirit shall not be forgiven by God.

"And killing another' spiritually is the same as murder to the body, and that, too, is not forgiven by God.

"Blasphemes have been eased by church leaders for control over the congregations. How blessed the minister who forgives the murderers feels."

RELIGIONS

And the Angel Jo said unto me, "You never were a religious man, even though you have been on the Other Side and in the Light many times, but I think now you could call yourself a Spiritualist, but not a Spiritualist as defined by man.

A Playboy Playmate Calendar still hangs in your workshop and sometimes you still use profanity, whereas profanity is an effort of a feeble mind trying to express itself forcefully and the Playboy Calendar is a throw back to your old mechanic days. Little human natural habits don't hurt anyone and those things that you do aren't anything compared to the domination and all the killing of innocent people taking place around the world everyday, but do those things hurt you?

"It does not matter what religion one practices for most religions are the same – all are designed from human agendas for control of a few over many. But the main part of all religions should be how you should treat your fellow human be it family members, co-workers, strangers or whoever – to have Love for all and have no domination toward others.

"The Ten Commandments are pretty much what God expects you to follow. You are not up on any religion, so you do not know if all of them have this style of idea to follow or not, but all of them have something similar that they do follow, if that religion truly came from God.

"God does not say one religion is better than another; He says it's okay to follow your religion if it does not hurt anyone.

"During your oil field days, you worked in Libya and Algeria, where you learned a little about the Muslim religion."

As I learned while working in Libya and Algeria, Muslim religion says Muhammad will be born to man, and once again woman will be a beast of burden, and Muslim women must walk five steps back and to the right side of her husband because women are considered less than man. And a used wife can be bought for twenty-five dollars while a virgin may cost thousands of dollars and Muslim men are the only ones that can buy a woman in their country. And it does not matter in which country a Muslim lives because all Muslims follow the same bible.

If we look at the life style being imposed upon the Islamic women in Afghanistan today, you will see women are not allowed to be educated and are refused health care, plus they are forced to do without many other things you consider necessary for life. And yet, where were all the women in the Muslim Million Man March that occurred in the United States a few years ago? They stayed at home and did whatever their men told them to do. Is slavery what the Afro-American women want?

During the 1990s, in Afghanistan, the Muslims destroyed many statues of another religion because they wanted Islam to be the religion of Afghanistan without regard to others beliefs. And if you look back into the history of the Dome of the Rock in Jerusalem, it is the same location that the Temple of King David once stood. Muslims claim that is the mountain that Muhammad ascended into Heaven from. And if you look at India, you will find a place where once stood a Holy place for Hindus is now claimed by Islam, and a hair…mind you a single hair from a Hindu Prophet that is still located in this place but Muslims say that the hair from their prophet and Muslims claim that place is theirs. And if you look at the terrorists actions of 9/11, you will find that the location of the crash of Flight 93, they are building a monument of a Crescent Moon… that is the sign of Islam. So that crash site will be a monument and holy place for the Terrorists who cause the crash…just another stolen holy place for Islam. My memory of the Crescent Moon as being the sign carved into the doors of outhouses.

I also understand there is a country in Africa where a white person cannot buy or own land. Something is definitely wrong with this picture. All people need to open up their eyes and ears to what is happening in your world. All people were created equal. And all are still equal.

Muhammad went into the desert and claimed he talked with Gabrael in a darken cave. Gabrael does not hide in a dark cave when He talks with people.

Muhammad had an Aunt who was a Jew, she taught him about the Jewish Religion, and he had heard many others spreading the 'Good News' about Jesus' death, he did not learn all those things about God's true religions from the evil energy that he spoke with in that cave. The dog within him twisted those concepts into his evil self-made religion of domination over others.

Muhammad came out of the desert and told his wife about his conversations with Gabrael and said the people would think he was crazy if he told anyone what he learned. His wife told him to go and spread the words that he learned. He went forth and told people, and after a while he had a few followers. And then he and his followers told others, but they would not listen to him, and his followers told them that if they did not follow their new religion they would kill them. And so fearful of being killed, they acted like they believed and allowed their children to read what Muhammad wrote – the Qur-an. And their children were brain-washed into believing all that Muhammad wrote, and from that time, many have been brain-washed from a young age into believing Muhammad and his evil ways....How sad.

I heard about some religions that have practices that harm people but I cannot recall what their names are. I heard about one religion in India that scars a woman so she cannot enjoy sex, and so I believe that there are more religions doing things that are harmful to others, too.

All religions can be good, but humans must do away with slavery and domination of other people!

I had a friend at work, Carl, who has a heart of gold and was very trusting. One day while delivering your company's products, a homeless man without shoes approached him, this man asked Carl for fifty cents to buy something to eat.

Carl told this man all he had was a twenty dollar bill.

The man told Carl, 'I will take the twenty and go get change and bring you back the change.' Needless to say, the homeless man never returned with Carl's change. Carl did not have any money for lunch that day and went without because this proclaimed homeless man was dishonest.

Every week, Carl sends money to a couple different organizations in the United States. One of these organizations is an Indian Children's Home and the other you are not familiar with, but his gifts of money to them come from Carl's heart.

Once every month or so, Carl is called by the Mormon Church that he belongs to and they demanded 10% of his pay. They tell him that if he does not pay them their 10%, he will not go to Heaven. That's domination of a church and not God.

And the Angel Jo continued, "If you give money to people or the church, it must be from your heart. If you help a church or people, it must be from your heart. Just giving or helping others so you can get to Heaven is selfish.

"Paramedics are taught to protect themselves before helping someone that is down. Once 911 is called and after the paramedics arrive, they will look over the down person to see if danger to them is present before they begin to help the injured person. They will remove any danger for if they also become injured while helping the downed person, they have increased the problem.

"God says, 'I will help them that help themselves.'

"Only give or help others if you have protected and helped yourself first.

"The Jewish Religion believes Jesus was not the Son of God, and that's okay. Christians worship Jesus because they claim He is God, and that is okay. Muslims believe Muhammad was God's only and true prophet, and that's okay too. But just don't hurt other people. And yet, while following a religion that places a false god such as Jesus or Muhammad at the top is wrong for there is only one God and He is not Jesus or Muhammad, and while the Jewish religion and Islam degrades women as not being equal to man, the Christian religion also places women below men. For all three religions were designed by a few men to place domination over all others.

"The choice of your religion is your individual decision. Do not force or try to push what you were told upon others. Give others the opportunity to decide what is best for them just as I have done with you, but tell them, 'Have Love in your heart for all and show no domination toward others.'

"You were not chosen to tell the world all these things about God and the Other Side for you were only chosen to write this book about God for you are not a Saint and you should not try to be someone special. Repeat only what I and people in the Light have told you, and also what you remember about the Other Side."

CHURCH

And the Angel Jo said unto me, "Whenever we talk and I use the word 'we' I am referring to Angels but I am also referring to God because we are part of Him, for He is the Congregation of Angels.

"You do not say, 'your hand will pick up the coffee cup', you say, 'I will pick up the coffee cup.'

"When God said as indicated in the Christian Bibles, 'I dwell in the church,' He actually was saying, 'a part of God dwells within the church.'

"That part of Him that He was referring to is us, His Angels.

"Jesus also referred to Himself as God when He said, 'Break open a piece of wood and I am there, turn over a rock and I am there.'

"Jesus as with all other Angels is part of God. Now, I am not saying that all Angels are the Son of God, I am saying besides Jesus being the Son of God, He is also an Angel and part of God, too.

"You too could say you are God for your Angel-within is part of God but if you said you were God, others would label you insane. That is because the people of today do not understand the true meanings of the words they use.

"The meanings of most words have changed over the years. And the meanings of the words that people claimed God and Jesus said are different today that they were when their words were first spoken.

"The true reason for people to give their first 10 percent to God, was for people to first think of God above all else and is saying 90 percent of their life belongs to them - the giver, and to set back 10% of this year's production –the seed to produce another crop next year.

"Do you really think we needed people to collect money for God?

"Everything belongs to God, so why do we need you to be our agent and banker?

"If you allow a church or anyone else to disperse your 10 percent to others, you are not actually getting the full experience of giving. Therefore, you are depriving your Angel-within from experiencing the joy of giving to the needy and letting others receive what is rightfully yours. Love, money or whatever directed from you to the needy should be not wasted on any go-between.

"Where do you think the money to build those costly churches came from?

"Did you not think they were paid for from money that was given to help others?

"God told Moses not to build or erect buildings, altars or monuments to Him, and yet people did, those are the same as the church buildings and establishments of today.

"We first spoke these same words to Moses and to those who came after him. Then Jesus spoke the same words to His disciples and others. Later Muhammad came along and did he ever mess up God's Words. But, 'yes' we knew what he would do before he created his false religion because it was planned and needed to be. God does not make mistakes for all was planned in God's Master Plan. And now once again we are speaking those exact concepts not just to you but to you and many others around the world at this time.

"But even back then when God and Jesus first talked to the people, the understanding of what They said was lost. Now the thoughts, concepts and ideas of people of this time are worse, different and more confusing than those of long ago, and we know people use words differently today then before and that corrupts God's Words from your Bibles even more. And that is why we are repeating God's words again.

"The word 'church' meant the human body, the vessel in which God, the Angel-within dwells. But today the word 'church' means 'building' and 'established religion.'

"Human thoughts, concepts and ideas could not grasp the idea of God dwelling in humans. Since man cannot be in two different places at the same time, he could not understand how God could be in many different places and in many people at the same time. And humans could not understand how two things as two people or one God and one person occupy the same space. And man thought of God as having human form and then placed Him in a structure or building that man called 'church'. This structure was the establishment (start) of religions. We forgive man for his near-sightedness and that is another reason for repeating our words to humans again.

"People must have the chance to choose whatever they wish but they must know what their choices are before they can make a choice... to understand their judgment. We must give them the opportunity to know the truth before they choose. They must know the truth about God along with what man says in order for them to judge and follow what they will. Therefore, we must give the Words of God in the language that they understand without it being polluted or corrupted by man again. And 'yes,' we know that even with what you and others write will also be polluted and corrupted with your individual human thoughts, concepts and ideas. And that's one of the reasons why I had to teach you before you were given the task of writing this book for us. For when you were ready for the job, the job was ready for you."

PRAYERS

And the Angel Jo said unto me, "Prayers are one-sided conversations one has with God and they may be silent or spoken words from one while either alone or in a group.

"As you pray, you may hear or feel God's answer in your thoughts. Your contact with God or His Angels may be so strong that you might think you actually hear their words as if spoken but God and His Angels communicate in thoughts and they may also be recorded.

"There is no special way, ceremony or ceremonial words to say when you pray. Just speak what is in your heart and from your heart to God. You need not get down on bent knees to talk with Him. You need not lower your head when you talk with Him, but lowering your head may help you focus on your thoughts and on what it is that you wish to talk to God about, and all Prayers are you acknowledging God.

"One important thing to remember when praying is; do not constantly ask God for things but instead thanking Him for all that He has given you.

"Christmas is a special time on the Other Side. Most religions have some kind of holiday near or around the Christmas season. It really doesn't matter if you believe Jesus was the Son of God or not, for the main reason of Christmas is the bringing of people together at one time to pray and for all people to know that they are not alone in the world. For at this Holy time of the year, most everyone on earth prays.

"On this side, the Other Side, time means nothing; we don't know when it's Christmas nor do we care. For Christmas, if regarded as Jesus' birth date, is wrong for he was born on the 13th of March two years earlier then what your calendar says.

"During the heart of the Christmas season that spans about thirty-six hours of earth time, there is a hush on the Other Side. All is still and quiet. They all stand like statues, as they listen to all the prayers rise up out of millions of people on earth at the same time.

"Honest and unselfish prayers are granted. Sometimes it may take time for them to be revealed but all honest and unselfish ones shall be and are answered.

"If one is going in for... let's say heart surgery and you pray, 'please make him well,' that is a selfish prayer for you want that person to get better so you won't miss the person being around you. That type of prayer is for your needs and gains for it is selfish. But if you pray, 'please protect him,' that is a prayer that will be answered, for it is unselfish.

"Do you see the difference?

"The second prayer does not intend that you 'want' this person to live. It states that you 'wish' this person happiness, rather he lives or dies.

"Asking for peace on earth or for no more hunger on earth are unselfish prayers, even though you may be one of the hungry for you are asking for the good of others beside yourself. This type of prayer shall be answered.

"Prayers can be answered in ways that may cause you to feel they were not answered.

"Take for example the prayer, 'Let there be no more hunger.' If God, takes the hungry and the hungry cross over to the Other Side, did not God grant your request?

"To you it is wrong to die but is not death part of life? And yet, death comes at the end of life; you must die to cross over. In God, it is predestine when life ends for each of you.

"Selfishness is crying when someone dies because you miss him. Is it not better to be happy that they finally finished their mission and returned Home?

"When Jesus was sent to 'life', God knew how He would die. To live, Jesus also had to die. Jesus did not die for the sins of mankind. He died because death comes at the end of life, at the end of one's mission. The way Jesus died was by the sin of mankind. Domination of Jesus was the sin, not the death. His death was to show you your sin - the Domination of others.

"God knew Jesus' life and death would not change man but His life and death was needed to show you Salvation. His life style was an example of how you were to live – with love for all and have no domination toward others, and His life and death were needed to start the Christian Religion.

"God has all Knowledge. God knew what was going to happen to his Son. Jesus was sent to earth for two reasons; to help bring people together in helping each other and to help some people find their Salvation through Christianity. That is why he came and that is actually what he did.

"God does not make mistakes.

"And yet, Christianity is not the only way to Salvation... *'For it is only one of the many ways to find Heaven.'*

Holy Graduel

"Salvation can be found in any religion that has one Supreme Entity at the top. The name of this Supreme Entity does not matter and the religion does not matter as long as it does not condone Domination and has Love for all."

HUMAN PRIDE

And the Angel Jo said unto me, "A long time ago a man named Jesus talked to some men about His Knowledge of God. These men, His disciples, could not understand just what He was talking about and kept asking Him questions.

"Jesus knew that only a part of what He was trying to teach them was being absorbed, so He told the same stories in different directions as He kept repeating over and over again His messages of Love to them.

"When Jesus' death became imminent, though He knew His followers did not completely understand what He had told them, He instructed them to go out in different directions and to tell others about His ideas of God. And after Jesus was murdered, His followers pretty well did what He had told them to do.

"From the death of Jesus until around 75 AD, Jesus' disciples had scribes write His stories in their individual words down, and then years later most of these stories along with many writings about God were destroyed by fire.

"Roughly around 50 AD, one of Jesus' disciples named Peter went to Rome and after telling some people of the 'good news,' he was killed because his teaching went against Rome's religion of that time.

"For the next hundred to two hundred years or so, the people that listened to others telling the stories of Jesus that Peter once told, were persecuted by the Romans and many were put to death for their beliefs.

"Around 300 AD, a 'Ruler' of Rome in battle had a vision of a cross on the sun or a round object in the sky. He then had all of his army paint crosses on their shields, and flew a banner of the cross during his battle. He said that God helped him win the battle and war. Thus he introduced the term 'Holy War' to the people.

"Upon his return to Rome, he changed the ideas of Rome and declared that this little known cult of Christianity was now the Religion of Rome.

"Over the next few years Christianity spread across Rome. But soon the Roman Empire started to divide because the two capitals of the Roman Empire, the east and the west capitals both wanted to be the center of Christianity and claimed to be the true Church of the Roman Empire.

"This 'Ruler' of Rome, who proclaimed Christianity as Rome's Religion, decided to set up a book (Bible) that would be the laws and rules for the Church of Rome, and that would place the city of Rome as the center for the Church of Rome. Thus he would keep control over the complete Empire of Rome - the total known world.

"It was at this time a meeting between Church Leaders was set up by this Roman 'Ruler.' After a few days of discussion of what should be included and what should be removed from their religion, this Ruler put a time limit to complete 'his' Bible. The Church Leaders then hastily placed different stories together and created the first Christian Bible. This Roman 'Ruler' then proclaimed - Canonized the Bible. From that point in time the Bible, God and Jesus were as if set in stone and never to be changed again.

"Around the 17th century, some of the original stories were removed from the present day Catholic Bible. Also from the 17th century to present day, many different branches of the Christian religion sprang forth from the Catholic Religion, which was the original Church of Rome.

"Today Christian Theology still uses the writings of the old Church of Rome as the Gospel. Yet most Christians say the Catholic Religion is polluted and corrupted.

"Human pride caused the old Roman Ruler to believe that God had instructed him in battle and that he was fighting a Holy War.

"Human pride caused the old Church of Rome Leaders during the time that the Bible was Canonized, to believe everything that they claimed to be of God as the truth.

"Human pride caused those who removed stories from the Bible during the 17th century to believe they only removed from the Bible those things that were not true or worthy.

"Human pride caused the people who started the different Christian Religions, in the 17th century to present day, to believe their Religion was the true Religion of God.

"Human pride causes the people who start Religions today to believe their Religion is the true Religion of God.

"Did not James Jones also say he was following God?

"People of any and all Religions believe they know how and what God's ideas and thoughts are.

"It is human pride that causes the 'Born Again Christians' to become defensive if you confront them with the questions like;

"How do you know what God thinks?
"How do you know what God looks like?
"How do you know what color God is?
"Why do you worship Jesus instead of God?

"The study of religion is called Theology. Theology means the study of religion, culminating in a synthesis or philosophy of religion.

"The word 'Philosophy' means the inquiry into the principles of reality in general, or some sector of it, as human knowledge or human value. Therefore, people who study God in human concepts are corrupting God's Words.

"Most of the documented statements from Jesus were mistranslated by His disciples. And then His disciples' statements were polluted with their individual thoughts and ideas and also were mistranslated by the scribes. Most of these and other religious records were destroyed by fire long ago. Then the Church of Rome threw out many stories when they created the Christian Bible. Later others removed things that they did not believe in, so how in the world can Theology be a true study or understanding of God?

"Human pride of what humans think they know drives them down into Hell, for human pride places man beside or above God.

"There is no way humans can know what God thinks or His ideas just by reading the Bible. One cannot think in His dimension. Nor can one know for sure what were the actual words used in conversations between God and humans or Jesus and His followers just by reading the Christian Bible or by reading any other Bible. By reading a Bible all one can only be sure about is the ideas or spirit of what is said in the Bible that one knows.

"Therefore, read a Bible for its historical content that reveals how people lived back then and its concept to love all people and have no domination toward others. Thus, the ideas and spirit of a Bible is to Love all others and to have no domination toward others and all else in a Bible should be considered misleading.

"But human pride causes 'Born Again Christians' to think YOU must believe in their god, bible and go to their church to get to Heaven. The Jew and the Muslims think this about their religion too, but most of the Jews do not push their beliefs unto others, only the Muslim and Christian do that.

"Then you, my Dear David, comes along, one of the many of today who declares that the Angels of God still talk to people, and you say, 'God's Angels have told me that all religions belong to God. For everything and everyone is His, too. It does not matter what church you go to. It does not matter if you go to church at all, but do not place false gods beside or above Him. Live with Love in your heart for all, and have no domination toward others. For there is one Supreme One above all and He is GOD.'

"Pray that foolish human pride does not drag humans into Hell. They must accept everything around them as being part of God. They must accept all religions as being of God - Allowing all others to live in freedom as long as they and their actions do not impose upon others. They need to refuse all thoughts and concepts of domination to themselves or others, for domination is evil.

"The human pride of foolish men caused them to place demands upon others and themselves. Human pride makes people think everyone in the world should know and follow their god.

"I, one of God's Angels, have inspired you to follow your heart. You were inspired to write this book for mankind and you did just that, for you did not deny what God's Angels asked of you.

"To the true God of Abraham, Isaac and Jacob do pray: My Lord, the True and Righteous Holy One above all, forgive me of my sins that I have committed today. Guide me to learn not to make those same mistakes again. Help me forgive those who have sinned against me. Direct me in Your Righteous way to live. Thank You for allowing me another day and may You also grant me another day tomorrow. Thank You for allowing Your Angels to enter into my life and guide me. I pray. Amen."

DOMINATION

And the Angel Jo said unto me, "Religious Domination is surely one of the worst Sins of them all. For whoever places fear of God into another for self-lifting purposes is raising himself above God while spreading false spiritual understanding.

"Cult leaders will say that they are the true Prophet of God and demand that others to listen to and to follow their words alone. But a true Prophet knows God uses many to spread His Word. Therefore, cults with one Prophet are of Domination, and those who think he is the only Prophet are under self-domination.

"Domination and self-domination are both the same for they are the same Sin, for they are against God. God and man are combined into one through the Angel, which is part of God; therefore, acts against man are also acts against God.

"All Sins are formed out of domination. Thus, Domination is the Sin."

(Let's back up here a minute and talk deeper in what a 'cult' is. In today's world, one refers to a cult as a new religious or spiritual movement. Many of today, refer to Jesus' Spiritualism and His teachings as a cult when Jesus walked with the people upon this world. But the word 'cult' originally meant to symbolize something bad - not of God. Yet in our world today, the word 'cult' merely means a new religion which can either be bad or good. This is the same thing that happened with many words used in the Bibles.)

And the Angel Jo continued, "If a person goes into a store to rob the store and kills someone during the act of robbery, the robber dominated the one whom he killed. If a person becomes addicted to overeating, that person has become dominated by something that is controlling him and his Angel-within, thus self-domination.

"In September of 1997, the world heard the tragic news of Princess Diana's death in an auto accident during a high-speed chase. Diana and her man friend, along with her bodyguard and chauffeur crashed after being chased by photographers riding motorcycles. The friend and chauffeur, along with the 36-year-old Diana died in the wreck while the bodyguard was injured but survived.

"This terrible accident that took three lives sets a perfect example of what compulsive self-domination can cause people to do. For Princess Diana's compulsive self-domination was one of the real causes of these deaths.

"Diana was a woman who wanted to be the center of attraction without always being in the spotlight. She wanted a public life but wanted her life private also. Her compulsive self-domination forced her to do things that kept her front-page news. Her 'Mirror, mirror on the wall, who is the most loved by all...' cost her life. She wanted to be loved by all but also she wanted her privacy, too. You cannot have both.

"When Diana first started dating Prince Charles, she knew she would never have a private life again, but she loved being in the spotlight. Whereas any girl would love to have a televised storybook wedding like hers.

"Addiction to wanting to have the best and to be the center of attraction as Diana desired is the same as any addiction to drugs. She did not have to be in the news if she didn't want it, for she could have done just as much good for others without being in the spotlight. Earthly glory was her habit and addiction; she needed to be in the spotlight to survive.

"Does a paramedic expect to see his picture in the newspaper every time he saves someone's life?

"His glory comes from within himself, not from what others think of him.

"Who was to blame for Diana's death?

"Her bodyguard let her get into a car driven by a drunken chauffeur and he was the only person wearing a seat belt. That is the reason the bodyguard lived and Diana and her man friend and the driver did not.

"Why did her man friend allow a drunk drive their car?

"Why did Diana get into the car with a drunk at the wheel?

"Why did not one of the three try to slow down the driver of their car?

"You may never know the answer to these questions.

"But why do people take pictures of famous people such as Diana?

"Photographers take pictures of famous people to sell. Why do the papers buy these types of photos?

"Who wants to see photos like those?

"The answer is you. People want to see pictures of famous people in non-complimentary positions. So then who caused the death of Diana?

"People are talking about making her a saint. Why?

"Was she more of a saint than the person who helps homeless people on the streets of Los Angeles or in any other city?

"Diana was a person who cared about people and yet, there are many others who also care about others, but are they saints?

"No, and Diana was not a saint. She was merely a woman who had a warm heart for others.

"Elvis was another person who lived and died in a prison of self-domination as most celebrities do.

"People have lost their sanity. They cry how much they loved Diana and Elvis after their death. Why did not they tell them when they were alive?

"Show love to people who are alive. Open your heart. Do not be afraid. Telling someone that you love him or her does not make you less than them or weak.

"Everything is here for human to use but the dog causes compulsive self-domination actions.

"Drugs, atomic energy, automobiles and everything else are here for your use and   were created to help humankind. Drugs in the right hands can help people just as
Atomic energy can give humans utility power until they find better sources. However, you use these and other things for the wrong purposes.

"Domination and compulsive self-domination drives one into desires of the flesh.

"Domination is making others do those things one wants them to do, even if their desires are different from the one commanding.

"Compulsive self-domination is doing things for the desire of the flesh, not the things one desire in his or her hearts.

"The death of Diana touched me, too. She was a woman who could have done so much more good for others. But her mission was finished and it was time for her to come home. Perhaps her life was cut short but she did do some good for others while she was there, but all are needed.

"The word 'addiction' is a copout for not wanting to stop their compulsive self-domination and for them not to take responsibility for their actions. You do not have to take drugs or do things that will damage your body or others. Laziness only hurts the ones you love. Do humans not love themselves?

"Open your mind and see what you are doing. Let your Angel-within see your glory.

"Domination is a Sin. Compulsive self-domination is the same thing, for both are Hell for the controller or domineer who will have to face his

Hell after he passes to this, the Other Side.

"After Diana's death people around the world paid tribute to her. Flowers bought for her by people of all walks of life covered many areas of England including her home. And people traveled far and wide to be near her during her funeral. You wondered how much money all the people spent for flowers and travel for her funeral. You also thought about the good that money could have done for others in need around the world.

"Why did the people of the world waste so much money on a dead Princess?

"Were their hearts full of guilt?

"Were they sorry for not helping Diana in her charities when she was alive?

"You will never know what causes someone's actions until you reach this, the Other Side. But the reasons are irrelevant and not needed to be known by you now.

"Laziness of Self-domination causes people to blame others for their lives, too. The reality of the problem of laziness is one not having faith or belief in oneself to change. Laziness is self-domination, and therefore laziness that causes self-domination is a Sin. Diana's self-domination (laziness) transformed into a habit of wanting to be 'loved' was her Sin.

"All people and lives have problems. Most humans could in probability say; 'Nobody likes me.' Or, 'I do not have good enough clothes to go to school.' Or, 'I do not want anyone to see me because I am too fat.' Or, 'I cannot go to school because people make fun of me.'

"Everyone has problems sometime during his life. Laziness causes many to back off and to take the easy route instead of correcting the problem. God does not promise anyone an easy life, instead He promises all the experiences of life.

"The Sin of suicide falls in the category of self-domination. Suicide prevents the Angel-within from its experiences of life. The Angel-within is not yours or anyone else's to harm for it is part of God. Going against your Angel's desires as with suicide is the same as going against God's wishes. And going against God's wishes is Sin.

"Suicide occurs when one decides nothing in life is worth living for...even the self-centered things as doing drugs or drinking or sex with many partners is not worth living for. That is the same as saying nothing in God's Creation is worth living for.

"And when one kills another, it is the same as saying that person was nothing in God's Creation and needed to be murdered.

"And when one Dominates another into non-belief or when one destroys another spiritually it is the same as murdering that person.

"And all three killings are Sins against God and His Creation, and they will not be forgiven in Heaven or by the Spirit or by God.

"Domination and self-domination are two of the greatest Sins ever known by man. Both are against individual free pursuit of happiness of man, the Angel-within and God.

"Also some people of self-domination are the ones whom you think of as being people with introverts and superiority complexes. In both cases, the subject cannot deal with reality, other people or their problems in a positive manner.

"Knowing the direction of life you wish to follow is part of the Knowledge. Following the direction of a righteous life that you wish to live may be difficult, but be content and experience all on the road of life that you have chosen. If you desire, it is okay to change the direction of your life just as it is okay if you did not find God until later in your life. You need not to have been religious from birth to know God.

"Does being religious mean studying history?

"Does being religious mean having comprehension between right and wrong and good and bad?

"Knowing God and understanding the full picture is Knowledge and that is not religious because religion is man-made and not made by God.

"Studying history from Bibles is not religion.

"Learning and understanding God's Master Plan is not religious.

"One does not need to be religious to have Heaven in his thoughts here and everlastingly.

"One does not even have to consciously believe in God to find Salvation or Heaven because God does not force Himself into you for that would be domination from Him.

"Fear of everlasting Hell should not cause you to live righteously, for fear is dominating. And the word 'religious' when it pertains to Salvation is a copout, and it also is domination.

"You did not write this book to place others in fear of living in eternal Hell unless they become religious.

"People must not know what will come because they must live their lives as they please. For domination from fear will direct their lives in a direction they may not wish to travel, and the choice of life must be theirs. We cannot force the truth upon others. When one is hungry, one will eat, and when one is thirsty, one shall drink.

"The Words of God you have written about in this book are Life and its actions and reactions to living in harmony with others. Either one has Life or one has nothing. Life is the Knowledge to understand the rewards and/or consequences all obtain throughout life here on earth. Rewards and/or consequences delivered upon one's self after life are made while alive. God's Forgotten Guiding Love is a book about Life, Knowledge and Love. It is a book about all that people have forgotten through the years.

"Being content with yourself in your life is one of the most important aspects of living with Heaven in your thoughts. This is part of the Knowledge others are presently learning by reading this book. And sometimes one cannot have the same as another has. Maybe one might not be making the same amount of money as another. If you enjoy your career and all other parts of your life, be content. If you do not enjoy parts of your life, change those parts. Do not become self-dominating or dominating to achieve your desires. Life is too short for that. Enjoying your life is what God wishes."

SIN

The word Sin is something I never could really understand. Could a Sin mean something God did not like? Or was it something God does not enjoy? Or maybe it is something against God?

The churches do not explain Sin well enough because they say, "Sin is actions of one who does not belong to our church because if one who belongs to their church and does the same thing, they have merely backslid.

The Angel Jo explained what Sin was to me in this manner.

And the Angel Jo said unto me, "Sin is not only against God, it is also against your fellow human beings. Sin is domination. Sin is trying to or controlling others. Sin is doing against others, God, or oneself, or another.

"Do you remember the days that if a person did something the majority of people did not like, the people could stop that individual's actions?

"Stopping that person was very easy. You had laws. Those laws controlled the actions of individuals. Laws upheld the majority's rights. Then along came groups that said, 'We must uphold the rights of individuals.' Their thinking was that if a girl wanted to join the Boy Scouts, the group must let her join. Or if a man wished to join a woman's organization, they must also allow him to join.

"Is it a Sin not to let an individual join a group?

"Or is it a Sin to allow an individual to control a group's actions?

"You do not know the complete answer, for you will not completely understand God's Will until you are on this, the Other Side. You presently know only what you need to know, and you know God is all Knowledge. God is All combined. Individuals cannot do anything against God's wishes without that act being called a Sin. God is not the majority, He is All combined. Something against All is the same as against God. Therefore, if one's actions are against the combined, it must be considered wrong.

"The killing of another human is a Sin. The murder not only stops that human's life, but all lives that may have come from that individual - there will be no offspring to experience or to help others in life. The murdered victim as a human cannot help any one from his death forward. The killing is domination by another. The killer changed events that may have stemmed from the dead person's future life, but all actions were needed and all are part of God's Master Plan.

"You always thought abortion should be left up to the one carrying the unborn child. Now you know life begins at conception, though it is only as any animal until an Angel enters the child, usually at birth. Therefore, is it right for the majority to tell the mother-to-be she must have the child?

"In the case of abortion, the majority should not rule, but the to-be-mother's decision affects herself, the unborn child and some others. And when you tell someone they cannot enter your club or group, you are stopping them from effecting or maybe helping others. Some of your laws say the majority rules, while others are for individual rights.

"In the case of is abortion right or wrong, why don't humans come up with something to prevent the pregnancy from starting in the first place?

"In the case of rape, why cannot the raped woman take something immediately afterwards to abort the pregnancy?

"But most of all, why cannot people stop trying to dominate others?

"Why cannot parents teach their children not to have sex until they are married?

"If both of these were followed, you would not have unwanted pregnancies.

"Just as a matter of fact, did you know there is a small country in Africa in which white people cannot own land?

"The world community does not care, but here in the United States if one in a white neighborhood refuses to sell a house to a black person, people cry discrimination.

"Profanity is an effort of one's mind that is unable to express himself forcefully because he does not have an acceptable vocabulary. It that a Sin?

"Humans say profanity is a Sin because they do not like to hear such words, and the same thing with smoking of tobacco that is now being outlawed. Smoking tobacco is not a Sin. The issue is not whether or not the tobacco smoke kills the smoker or others. Smoke inhaled is first hand smoke, and once smoke has been inhaled into one's lungs, all the smoke's chemicals are deposited into the lungs, and then once those lungs exhale, the air that comes out of the lungs does not contain harmful chemicals. And those who inhale that exhaled air are not receiving bad things, and that exhaled smoke that another takes into his lungs is second hand smoke. The real issue is non-smokers do not like the smell of burning tobacco. If the people's real interest were to protect others then they would not only ban smoking and also outlaw drinking and ban driving cars which both also kills people because the carbon monoxide from the exhaust of automobiles lingers near the earth and does not go up to the Ozone level of the atmosphere. But back to what I was talking about, it is a Sin to tell others not to smoke.

"God also does not like seeing one smoke because Nicotine is a drug that causes self-domination. And also He does not like to hear profanity because it shows that person was not educated in language enough because Profanity is another bad habit that also causes self-domination. Self-domination is a Sin, and therefore all bad habits are Sins.

"Profanity is a Sin because if one uses it routinely in conversations, one is not expanding his mind intellectually.

"Smoking is a Sin because if one smokes, he is dulling his mind, for Nicotine is a downer and it does not allow the mind to expand.

"Drinking is a Sin because alcohol is a chemical that destroys living cells, including brain cells.

"But also, driving is a Sin because driving a car pollutes the air, and exhaust fumes kill and disrupt life for generations to come.

"But it is a Sin to tell people not to smoke or drink because you are trying to place yourself over that person?

"If you are in a smoking area and do not smoke than you are letting the smoker dominate you. If you do not like the smell of the burning tobacco, just leave the smoking area.

"Dominating oneself or others is a Sin. If one goes to church because others tell him this is the righteous thing to do, he is placing himself into self-domination for he is only listening to what others say.

"Allowing someone to have an abortion is the same as letting that person dominate another. Abortion is death to the unborn child. You are allowing someone to kill a child. But if you stop this person from having an abortion, you are then forcing your domination unto the pregnant woman.

"A helping hand under false pretense is a Sin.

"If you ask someone not to smoke because it is bad to their health but instead are thinking about how you hate the smell, then you are forcing domination unto them under false reasons, and by now, all people know that smoking is bad for them.

"If one says he is a Christian while helping others only to proclaim a place in Heaven that is a Sin. For true help and love come from the heart and needs not to be rewarded.

"So a Sin is anything that goes against other humans, anything that causes domination to others or oneself and/or is anything that is not from the heart. For anything that harms or hurts others or oneself is a Sin.

"You are part of God. You be the judge of your own Sins. Do not cast the first stone against another unless you wish to be judged. Allow all to judge themselves. They are also part of God. You are not their judge or keeper.

"Sin is doing things for or to others while only thinking of yourself.

"Selfishness is a Sin. Stealing from another be it his wealth, pride, family or taking of his life is a Sin.

"The use of alcohol, nicotine or other substances that can injure the body can be a Sin if overused. The problem is if used once, most are habit forming. These then may be considered as Sins. All is here on Earth for the good of man because all substances will help man if used correctly.

"Most humans Sin daily. You are not Angels. Dogs think only of themselves. They see the world through their eyes. They are the main actors in their life. From their view, everything is for them. They see a world that evolves around them, but this is not the case for they are merely a small part of the complete picture.

"Prayer is the release of one's Sins. A Prayer is a confession of one's sins stating he knew what he did was wrong. A prayer should be part of one's daily routine, the same as waking up in the morning or going to sleep at night. Prayer need not be spoken aloud. Prayers can be thought or spoken silently as many times as needed throughout the day. For prayer is forgiving oneself - one's Angel-within forgiving one's body for one's desires that caused actions against oneself and/or others and is the basic merciful forgiveness God wishes you to have. But, once you admit your Sin, you should not do it again, for you know that it is wrong. Your Angel-within is part of God. When your Angel-within forgives your actions, God has forgiven you also.

"Peace of mind, is your forgiving of all and that will be your dwelling place in Heaven. Not forgiving is your house of Hell. Dwelling is the thinking mind. Heaven and Hell are your thoughts after death. In the Light, All will know where you stand, and All will forgive you. But will you be able to forgive yourself?

"The Fires of Hell as described by preachers are not an actual place. They are descriptions of feeling and thoughts you will have if you do not forgive.

"Heaven is not a place with golden streets. Heaven is your peace of mind. Giving ten percent of your income will not buy you a place in Heaven nor going to church weekly will grant you Heaven. Thinking you follow your Bible will not lead you to Heaven or believing you are Christian is not enough for you to enter Heaven. Christians are only a small portion of the people you will see in the Light.

"Forgiveness and non-domination is needed for you to find you Heaven forever.

"In the Preamble to this book, we indicated an Angel losing patience and wisdom is the biggest tragedy of them all. Now is the time to reveal what does occur when this happens.

"All things that have happened, all that are happening and all that will happen are part of the complete Master's Plan. Sin is also part of that Knowledge. God knows all the Sins that have been committed, the Sins all are committing now and all the Sin that all will be committed in the future, for Sins are also part of the complete cycle. All movements through the cycle are known, and the cycle is part of the complete picture. The complete Knowledge of God covers all five cycles.

"Have you ever watched a play, a play that you've seen before?

"Have you ever read a book twice?

"Even though you knew the ending of the story, you cried as the story ended. Why?

"You knew the hero would die. Did you really think its ending would be different the second time?

"Well the same thing happens to those in the Light as with you. Angels 'cry' (are sadden) as your lives play out, but the Knowledge of the Light only goes as far as the end of the life of the last one to enter into the Light, as it would be like you the knowledge a story up to the last be the charter of a book that you are reading... you do not know the complete story until it has played out. The future is not known in the Light, but only to God.

"Knowledge of future Sins or rewards is not known by the returning Angel who comes to re-live in a newly born child. But when that life experiences ends, All in the Light are saddened because of the Sins that have occurred, and whereas, All in the Light are happy because of all the rewards the returning Angel has experienced. Our sadness is the same when an Angel loses patience or faith.

"Faith is wisdom of a known value without seeing the equation.

"A newly re-born Angel-within is learning from its Mentor Angel throughout the human's life. An Angel-within must have faith just as people do. An Angel-within is merely told about God as most humans are.

"Once in a great while an Angel-within may say, 'Shove it, I enjoy the feeling of human desires.' The thought of not caring is Hell and it is a Sin that is deeply embraced and engraved into the mind and on the Soul. Sometimes an Angel-within may decide it cannot wait to return to the Light because life is not worth living; Suicide would be its means to return to the Afterlife early. Those are not the only two reasons for losing patience and faith, but these are merely two examples of reasons why.

"These and more can never be erased from the Angel. They will forever more be carried with the Angel, they however can be reduced by living another life. After death the Entity now carries the same Hell as its human carried. As the Entity enters the Light, the Entity becomes an Angel that still carries the same Hell; A Hell that may be so deeply engraved into thoughts that no matter how many lives that Angel lives, its Hell will always be part of its thoughts.

"An Angel with Hell engraved into its mind is referred to as a Non-Conformed One. If the Non-Conformed One does not chose to re-live to help lessen his Hell, this Non-Conformed One who has refused the Light will drift in this, the Other Side, and/or on earth, never at peace within himself until the end of time. Non-Conformed Ones will be destroyed during the last day of time of this cycle.

"The number of Non-Conformed Ones is not small. Some have been with us from near the start of time for this cycle. Their number may reach into the millions or even the billions.

"All in the Light are sad whenever an Angel turns into a Non-Conformed One, but nothing can be done that would change the complete picture of the cycle.

"Life is like a book that we Angels have read. We know the ending but want to re-read it again. Therefore all is that is suppose to be.

"You as humans should not say, 'Well, I am a Non-Conformed One so I can do bad to others.' The good must try to do good while the bad will do bad without trying to do so. Listen and follow your heart and you will do good.

"In a famous murder that happened recently, a man was said to have killed his ex-wife and her friend with a knife. You believed he murdered them. You asked me to guide you to the murder weapon to help prove his guilt.

"I said, 'He did not kill them. He thought it might happen, but two others carried it out. Yes, he did know about the murders after the fact, but the murder weapon has been broken up and scattered and pieces of the knife will never be found at this time.'

"These two killers will get their just reward on this, the Other Side. They are Non-Conformed Ones who will never harm another. They will be destroyed on the last day of time. The ex-husband will live in Hell until he returns for another try at life, if there is enough time for another life for him, if not, he also will be destroyed.

"Find Peace in your heart. Forgive all as well as you forgive yourself is the only Salvation.

"There are other things we need to discuss before we end this conversation.

"There are a great number of Non-Conformed Ones, plus the number of Unguided Ones. Keep in mind this number first started to accumulate from the first day of this present cycle. The number I speak of is staggering. All of these will be destroyed during the final day of the cycle.

"Secondly, I would like to discuss the detail about Angels not knowing the life they are about to live when they enter a new born child.

"All Angels must live one life that involves Hell, with the exception of Jesus. One learns to be humble, free from pride and vanity, and whereas to know peace of mind – Heaven, one must know of Hell to be able to judge what is best for him. These lessons teach us to respect others. Also, these are things that All must experience. We cannot understand and experience Heaven if we do not understand and experience Hell.

"The golden number of nature is two. Everything has an opposite as one good and one bad. Examples: Heaven and Hell, positive and negative, up and down. That should give you an idea of the reason for life, for all have at least seen one bad and one good to be able to judge what is best for them.

"Nothing is evil in God or in His Creation because everything was needed. All that has happens was meant to happen. The bad actions of man that are against his fellow man or against God or His Creation, is evil, and man has created those actions."

DO NOT BE AFRAID OF DEATH

And the Angel Jo said unto me, "What goes around comes around, as an old saying goes. The same with death is part of life, which I have said repeatedly to you. Understanding that death is part of life does not remove the pains of death. The pains at death occur because the body's individual parts recognize that something is wrong and it is unable to sustain life. And now is the time to learn, 'do not be afraid of death.'

"The cycle of time, the cycle of life, all must begin and all must end. You cannot have one and not the other. To have life, one must have a length of time, and yet that life must have a beginning and an end.

"The universal number is two. All positives must and do have a negative. Did you think life would not be so wonderful if no one died?

"Life is a wonderful adventure to be experienced that also includes experiencing death.

"During your life, if you were one that visited churches, you would have heard someone standing in front of the group talking about God, life, and of course, telling you about the money you need to give to their church. Do you think you would have ever heard them talk about how wonderful death is?

"When someone has died, usually a preacher will get up in front of the mourners and talk about the deceased and how now he or she has crossed over into Heaven. Then they will state how wonderful the deceased was and how happy he or she is now in Heaven.

"Many times the preacher may have never known the deceased, for many times the deceased never went to any church on a regular basis. Then how in the world does the preacher know if the deceased was wonderful or not?

"How in the world does the preacher know if this guy ever made it to Heaven?

"The deceased may be burning in Hell for all he knows.

"As Jesus said, 'Let the dead bury the dead.' That statement refers to and is the same as, 'Let the ones who do not believe in afterlife take care of their own kind.'

"Miss a departed loved one. Grieve for not having him near you because you miss his company and remember and love him forever, but do not cry for him.

"Human life have missions in life that the Angels within needed to experience. They knew how long their lives would last and when it would come. The same is true with the one you just buried; his Angel-within knew when his life would be over. His body was destroyed; something malfunctioned or some part of his body wore out and stopped working, but yet, his Soul did not stop.

"The body leaves the Soul. The Soul is Energy that cannot be destroyed. The body is made up of material that decays and is transformed back into its original forms.

"The Angel lives on with the memories of its human life.

"Rejoice with the Angel of the deceased for a job (life) well done. Be happy that another endured the hardships and experiences of life.

"Your bodies are made up of materials from this world. These will go back to the earth from which they came. Dust to dust and ashes to ashes. Only your Souls will remain forever.

"Death is not to be feared. Nor is death to be hurried as with suicide. Your death will come as surely as you were born. There is no stopping death, for death is part of life. Everyone will some day face death. Your death will be your personal Judgment Day as with all others, for then you will judge your own individual actions on Earth.

"Why cry over a person's dying? Were you unkind to that person during his life?

"You knew that someday he would die. Did you really think that you would die first?

"You have seen others die. Did not you think this person would ever die?

"Did you believe his life was for your enjoyment only?

"Did not he have a life of his own?

"Did you cry because you were sorry for things you have done to the deceased?

"Why cry for the past? Repent for the past.

"The past cannot be changed. You only are living the present. The future will happen because of your past and present acts. Therefore experience life, even the pain prior to and during the moment of death, for all feelings are Knowledge and experiences to be learned. And death is part of that Knowledge, accept death as part of life, and experience your death as you move through to the Other Side.

"Try to keep all loose ends of your life caught up, for you do not know when your death is close at hand. Open your heart to all, not because you may die at any time, but because to open your heart is the right thing to do. Do not be a kind person to get to Heaven. Be a kind person because that is the right way to live, for that is the way of God. An open heart needs to be practiced every day of your life. Because you know you are humans and sometimes humans do things that are not perfect. You may yell at each other, and you may do all kinds of things that are not right, but rest assured your end will come, and you should be prepared to enter the Other Side without Hell in your mind.

"Do not fear death; look forward to the Other Side and once again being with all those that have gone before you. How wonderful to reminisce with your mom and dad and all others that you hold so dear to your heart. Your time will come, but do not force your death. I will be extrapolated beyond belief to once again be holding you in my arms, my Dear David, and playing our childish games as we have before.

"Wait for your death while you still relish your experiences and enjoyments of life.

"Death is not to be feared, just the same as life is not to be feared. Both contain experiences that need to be enjoyed.

"One must go forth while remembering the past, but do not dwell on the past. Your growth is moving from birth into and from adulthood forward through death into Eternal afterlife of your Soul, Genesis.

"Most deaths are not painless. The cries of the dying sometimes carry over to the Other Side, but their pains do not last long, and while the pains are usually no more than what a woman experiences during birth of her child. Human pains fade with time and are soon forgotten because they only remember the good times. One of the best moments of times will be yours someday, the transformation from human life to Angel."

There was a death that occurred on one of the freeways of Los Angeles recently. This death and the actions of people after this death reminded me of two other deaths, one was caused by not caring or thinking of others – thinking only of one's self, and one suicide that illustrates people's attitude about death.

The first; thinking only of one's self - Around three years ago, a highway worker was killed on the 14 freeway. Early one afternoon, a Cal-Trans worker was installing a median divider on the freeway. A drunk driving north from Los Angeles ran off the road and into the median, striking and dragging the worker. The freeway was closed for several hours.

The second; not caring about others – A woman was hit and dragged by a city bus in the downtown area of Los Angeles. They showed the scene of the accident on local television. The bus had sheets hung up around it so no one could see the victim.

The third; suicide - The third death involved a man who was angry at his HMO insurance company. He was on an overpass in Los Angeles and was firing a rifle at cars as they passed below him. The local television stations pre-empted their programming to show this scene of the police and this man. This scene was shown on all channels, even those televising cartoons for children at the time.

Surrounded by police the man walked back to his pickup and ignited a homemade bomb. The bomb exploded and caught the pickup and the man's dog was inside the cab of the truck that was on fire. The man then walked back over to the bridge railing, set down his rifle, leaned over the rifle and committed suicide.

The television stations were not using time delays so this was shown to all via television even on the children's channels. After showing the carnage the stations quickly returned back to their regular televised shows.

The channel that I was watching had its local news show playing and they were very apologetic about what they just let air on their station. They said parents were calling in and expressing their opinion about what their children had just seen on television.

Soon this news show had a psychologist on the telephone that discussed how parents could help their children understand about this suicide.

The next evening my son told me they talked about this suicide in school. He said their teacher indicated that he once thought about suicide. One student asked if he regretted not doing it. Others worried about the dog that was accidentally set on fire.

We have been sheltered from death. Death is part of life. It was not for respect for the dead woman who was pinned under the bus when police hung sheets around the bus. It was done so people would not see death.

When the Cal-Trans worker was killed, the freeway was closed for hours. It was not done out of respect of the dead highway worker, it was closed so nobody would see the dead worker.

When many in Los Angeles saw the man commit suicide on television, they did not care about this guy; they worried about the dog instead.

Wake up people! Death does come to all. Do not be afraid of death, for someday you shall also die. Do not be afraid to see death, but do not seek to see the dead out of respect for the dead, but do not try to hide their death either.

And the Angel Joleen said unto me, "Life is not a game nor is death a game. Understand death is part of life. Be sad because the deceased cannot enjoy the company of his friends and family anymore as you enjoy our family and friends. Be happy for the deceased because his mission is over.

"Try not to perfect your life like Jesus. Life does not have to be God-like to live in Heaven. God knows humans make mistakes. Use your mistakes to learn and understand, and correct your future actions.

"Do not dwell on your actions of anger, hate or fear of others. Learn to let your Angel-within and yourself correct bad acts toward others. Life is to be enjoyed, and death also is to be enjoyed, for it is an experience of moving from your side to this, the Other Side.

"Once you have entered the Light, you will know that all your loved ones will soon be there beside you just as they were here on Earth."

SYMBOLISM

A friend asked me, "Why does God need us to go through life? Couldn't He have just placed us in the Light to start with?"

At that moment I was caught off guard and could not answer his question. Later that night while the Angel Jo and I talked in my garden (back yard), she said, "All is symbolic. God does not need human life. Humans need life to experience the unknown. Life is not to just learn from trial and error, but is to experience not just the good but also to know the bad.

"All that is written in the Bibles is symbolic, for all that you have ever read is symbolic, too. When you read, you are learning what the writer wished you to know, and that learning is experiencing the subject of the writer's concepts.

"All that you have done in your life is symbolic; all that you touch is symbolic, and all that you see is symbolic, too. When we talk, all of our conversation is symbolic. For those things that you are learning about life is your life and is your experiences of life are needed by you.

"We could have directed our conversations as viewing human life from our side instead of from the human side, but would that have made it easier for you to understand? There are so many differences between this, the Other Side, and your human side, that you will not fully understand things until you arrive here and then, all of your questions will be answered in a language that you will understand.

"Does it matter if your world is real or symbolic? And does it matter if we show you with things symbolically for what was, what is and what is to come?

"Do you recall the times that I showed you our love?

"I showed you things from yours and my thoughts of our love, things that we did together back in that summer of 1965. Those things were real to us - We lived and loved together... We enjoyed and experienced things together...for life is real to the living. And remember when I would rub my forehead against yours and you would see things of strange shapes and objects?

"Then I was giving you my thoughts. My thoughts were strange shapes and objects in your mind. Remember what you wrote about the Soul as a file on a disk?

"Your minds are like personal computers; you symbolize images into your thoughts. My thoughts had to be re-symbolized into the 'program' of your mind. That is why it took days before you understood my thoughts and memories.

"God has made all things for humans. Therefore, you are also symbolic for God's Master Plan. But it does not matter if what or who is real for you feel alive. Therefore, you and all around you do exist and are alive.

"During the start of God's Creation everything from the beginning to the end of this cycle happened at once, for there is no time in God, only in His Creation.

"My Dear David, do not dwell on what is symbolic or what is real. Experience and enjoy life is all that we wish."

FAITH AND BELIEF

And the Angel Jo said unto me, "Faith and belief are the backbones for most of the religions of today, for nothing that was written into any religion can be fully substantiated today. Even this doctrine that you are writing will be said by some non-believers to be false. Even the audio and videocassettes that we have made will not be enough proof for non-believers, but their confusion is not your concern.

"Jesus answered your question of, 'Why do not you return today?' By saying, 'I would be in-affective today.'

"How sad to think that even if Jesus returned most would not believe in Him.

"Has the world gone so cynical that most people would not believe in Jesus even if they met Him today?

"Faith is to believe in something. Belief and faith are pretty well the same thing, but their differences as stated in the dictionary as: Faith; Confidence in or dependence on a person, statement, or thing as trustworthy, and while Belief is the acceptance of the truth or actuality of anything without certain proof.

"When you were a child, you believed fairies lived behind the sofa in your living room. Your belief was boosted because you talked with these fairies for a couple days. Then you found out that your older brothers were using a hose whose end was placed behind the sofa while they talked to you through the other end of the hose from another room. Your beliefs were shattered.

"You held your faith of there being a person named Santa Claus until around the age of ten, but for the next two or three years, you still believed he might exist.

"Even today, you will not tell someone that there is no Santa Claus, for you will not destroy anyone's belief because belief is personal and does not need reinforcing from anyone, and no one should tear down another's belief. Destroying another's belief is a sin of domination, and that, too, is against God's Word.

"It is okay if you believe in not working on Sundays. It is okay if you believe Adam and Eve were the first two people on earth. But do not press your beliefs onto others unless they ask your opinion, for pushing your beliefs onto others is a sin of domination and that too is against God's Word.

"You have belief in God because you have seen His miracles, but you also have faith in God because of the conversations that you have had with Gabrael, Jesus and me.

"All three of us have told you of things to come and those things did indeed come to pass.

"You have faith in God because now you have faith in yourself, and therefore you have faith in us.

"Throughout the pages of time, people had belief through the faith of others. Today is no different from before, you must all carry belief in what others say and do, but you know that most people will lie to save face. But while belief is seeing from your opened heart, and you should always seek the truth in another's faith.

"Following blind faith is the same as 'Let the dead bury the dead.' Following the blind belief of others is saying, 'My peace of mind is worth the truth.' If you have no belief in God, you shall not seek faith in God. And if you find no faith in God, then you are still of the dog.

"If you are of the dog, then that is all you are, and therefore, you are not part of God, and you are nothing, for God is All and is for the good of all."

THE FINAL DAY

As I stated earlier, human reality is only a thought of God, and when His thought ends this cycle will be no more; that is when the last one that is to enter into God's Light, the Knowledge of all experiences will end, and all will have entered into God's Light, and whereas the Future will then be the Past. And when I speak of Jacob, the Angel that dwells within me, being in the Light, I am not speaking of my Soul, the experiences of my life, and him alone, I am talking of him and my life experiences as being part of the Congregation of Angels that make up God, and so it is if I am talking of God instead of Jacob alone.

In August of 1997, I conducted two more hypnosis sessions. During each of these sessions Christine was the channel (the go between) for Jo to me. These sessions and others were recorded on audiocassette tapes.

Part of the actual transcript from the first of these two sessions follows:

Jo: "One of each of the two other sets of Twins is alive on Earth, you must find them."
David: "The world is big. They might even be in some other country. How will I
ever find these two people?
Jo: "Use your powers. You will know them when you find them."
David: "Do they have blue eyes?"
Jo: "How did you ever guess..."
David: "Where is the other two?"
Jo: "They are in the Light."
David: "Why can't you tell me all?"
Jo: "You made the rules... you made me promise not to tell."

David: "On the Other Side... who am I... what am I?"

Jo: "We are the nucleus of the Light... All others surround us..."

David: "Am I God?"

Jo: "No... The Light is God... We are the oldest."

David: "Why can't I see you?"

Jo: "You are afraid... open your mind try to not be afraid... then you will see... I must go... I have many things to do..."

David: "Wait... why can't you let me see you like you do with Tony and Dan? Why can't you talk to me like you do to others, like you do on the phone with them?"

Jo: "Tony and Dan believe and are not afraid. It takes a lot out of me to be able to communicate with others... Do you need more proof?"

David: "Why can't you communicate through my computer?"

Jo: "This is not the movies."

End of this session.

The following is part of the second session concerning the Final Day.

David: "Why must I find the other two here on this side?"

Jo: "They need help... they do not understand... your words will help them understand."

David: "Why can't I wait and find them on the Other Side?"

Jo: "You can... but they just need help now."

David: "What rules have I set? Did I make all the rules for the world or just us?"

Jo: "No... Just for us."

David: "Why can't you go into the Light by yourself and bring out the two that are in the Light? Why must we both go into the Light together to find them?"

Jo: "When they see us together, they will know. They will come with us."

David: "Why must all six of us be together?"

Jo: "You made me promise not to tell. You won't get mad..."

(Now with Jo being on the Other Side knew what my answer would be, she asked the question for me to realize what my answer to her would be.)

David: "I promise not to get mad at you. Please tell me... I must know."

Jo: "For the power. Together we have more power than alone."

David: "Why do we need their power?"

Jo: "For the battle."

David: "What battle?"

Jo: "Us... we six and the people of the world are going to join together and fight..."

David: "Who are we going to fight... the Light? Are we going to break away from the Light and start our own?"

Jo: "No... After the battle starts, the Light will join in with us."

David: "Who are we going to battle against?"

Jo: "The Unguided Ones and all other evil ones."

David: "Who are the Unguided Ones?"

Jo: "The Ones that never made it to the Light."

David: "The ones that were formed but never found the Light?"

Jo: "Yes. The people of the world and the Other Side will come closer together. You will bring them closer together. You will lead the battle... the people of the world will join in and follow you. The Light will also join in and follow you in the fight. You will lead us. I must go."

Later, I learned more about the final battle. After I return to the Other Side and after the two remaining Soul Twins return to the Light, Jo and I will watch as humans start fighting all over the Earth. Their battle will become so intense that I will give the call for the other two sets of twins.

I will stand above the world and Jo will stand behind me. We will instruct the other Twins to go to the bottom four corners. This formation of the Twins encases the world so that no Unguided Ones, Non-Conformed Ones or any Evil can escape. I will call for the Light and all the Angels to end this cycle; All from the Other Side, including Jesus, who will lead the end of this cycle. All life will end as all Souls rise up as all the Angels will come to collect and help all the Righteous Angels.

I was not told if Jesus will come to earth and sit on a throne with others seated on both sides of Him as it is stated in the Bible. Also, I do not know if He sends others to the Four Corners of the world as stated in the Bible. Or if we, the three sets of twins, are the ones He sends to the Four Corners of the world. He may, along with the others seated beside Him decide who shall be dispersed. The Angel Jo and I may only be the ones that will do the dispersing of all the Unguided Ones and Non-Conformed Ones, I do not know.

But everything that is alive on Earth will fall down as all human Souls rise. The Angels will move all Righteous Souls out of this pyramid encasement, through the Other Side and into the Light.

All Unguided Ones and Non-Conformed Ones along with all Evil energy will cry out for mercy as all Angels in the Light channel their powers through me. With the power of All coming through me, I will raise

Holy Graduel

my arms outward and up while Jo and the other four Soul Twins keep the bad contained in this invisible pyramid shaped prison as the power of all the Angels flows through me and with Love in my heart for all as I disperse all those that have not conformed.

All Righteous will have gone to the Light, where they will become part of the Light once again. All Righteous will reign in the House of God (the Light) for one thousand years until the next cycle begins. Then those who desire more experiences shall return for life again.

(The statement about one thousand years merely means a length of time.)

Now, you too understand what it takes to disperse one on the Other Side. All could never disperse a Righteous Angel. The majority does not rule, but All rules because All must agree on the removal of one before it can be dispersed.

All the Angels that have Hell within their minds are the ones who have stayed outside of the Light instead of returning to relive again. All those who did not have time to, or refused to remove their Hells by reliving will be dispersed into the clouds to be reborn as Angels for the next cycle because they were the Non-Conformed, and the Unguided Ones who refused God.

The Angel Jo will stand beside me as I mercifully end the misery of all that contain Hell in this cycle as we have done in the four previous cycles.

My action of destruction of those will be out of Love and understanding for now the Angels Jo, Jesus and Gabrael have taught me and I have become a Master. All their teachings to me had come to pass, for I had to Love all people to be able to disperse the bad with Love in my heart for them. We will all be saddened by what must be done. All the experiences that those lost Souls contained and have endured can never be replaced. All the lost Souls' family members and friends that are in the Light will miss the lost ones dearly, but that cannot be helped.

This coming battle will be the end of this cycle.

The battle will happen soon, but in the Light there is no time. So "soon" could be hundreds of years from now.

Angels are the only ones allowed entry into the Light. Everything except the Light will be destroyed.

After all bad is dispersed and nothing of No-thing remains, the other two sets of Soul Twins will enter the Light. The Angel Jo and I will stand there for a while alone in the darkened silence with our hearts full of sadness. Then we will go play along the wall near the Light again.

All the Angels in the Light may in the next cycle, if they wish to experience more of life's enjoyments, live again. That choice is theirs.

Time is running out, I do not have time for another life, and this task that I must perform is the reason that I could not be lost. The Angel Jo was allowed to tell me and to give me the Knowledge for this reason. For when you are ready for the job, the job shall ready for you. The sadness that I now carry is for all those who have been dispersed at the end of each of the four cycles, but with the Angel Jo's help, I try to mask my thoughts of sadness for others by playing our childlike games. Once I enter the Other Side again I will be allowed to enter the Light, but my entrance causes my memories of the dispersing to remain strong in the minds of All. And then All are saddened by what We had to do, even though our actions were justified and agreed to by All because all things were needed.

If I had died with Hell in my mind, I would not have had enough time to re-live again to remove my Hell. I was stubborn and needed a lot of convincing. I had no belief in God or faith in myself. The Angel Jo's never ending Love showed me the Light because I had to have Love for all in my heart to destroy.

Perhaps now you understand the reasons for this book. It was needed to tell people what is coming in the hopes of saving Souls. We do not like dispersing.

Maybe when people read our books they will understand life is not perfect and it does not have to be perfect. And God does not dictate your actions here on Earth, but His rule says you must find forgiveness in your heart for yourself and others before you die. If you have forgiveness only from the first second thereafter death, you will live in Hell forever unless you have time to re-live another life, and the time is running out.

I know this chapter was likely as unpleasant to read as it was to write. The thought of the end of life as we know it is uncomfortable. But you must realize that the universal number is two and that for each beginning there must be an ending.

Now I am prepared to do my duties with Love in my heart for All.

AND THE ANGEL JO ASKED

KILLING OF OUR CHILDREN

On March 13, 1998 around ten o'clock in the evening, I asked the Angel Jo, "If you could write anything you wished, what would you like to say in our book?"

(These next two chapters contain what she said she would write if she could, and then she asked me to write them for her.)

And the Angel Jo said, "Daily, we read and see on television stories about death. Most of these are usually about children's death. The majority of these seem to be caused by adults and often these children knew and trusted the adults who killed them, and many times the children were related to the person who murdered them.

"Whenever these murderers of children are brought to trial, the murderer usually gets a few years in prison for their merciless killings. But it is as though the court systems are saying, 'We, the people find the accused of murder guilty, but since the person he killed was merely a child, we will go easy on him.'

"Death as well as birth is part of the complete picture. They are part of the diagram and plan of the known future.

"Should not all humans expect and deserve a long and prosperous life more so than the animals that you try to protect?

"Is human life just for the experiences of the Angel, or is it also for the experiences of the human and for the growth of the human race?

"Does one needing to return to relive a better life justify the death of a child?

"There is no justification for the murder of a child or any person. Life is priceless and should not be extinguished or injured unless that individual cannot be stopped from dominating or trying to dominate others."

Before I realized the existence of the Angel Jo and the Other Side, I thought abortion should be left up to the individual. Now I know abortion is death to the child. I still believe with all my heart that if conception comes from rape or incest, then the pregnancy should be terminated. I do not know if abortion should take place in the case of one giving birth to a severely disabled child, for we do not know when enjoyment and experience of life – the quality of life - begins or ceases. Also, I cannot answer the question about whether it should take place if the mother's life is endangered by the birth.

My family and I have seen and I have talked to hundreds maybe thousands of Angels of deceased children that the Angel Jo and others have brought through our home as they travel to the Light. These kids come from all over the world. All of them are afraid and scared, but most just want their mommies or daddies. These children have not reached the Light so they do not know the complete story yet. For once they go into the Light, their fears will cease as they learn the Knowledge. But as they come through our home, they are still frightened little children. They are the same children as they were just moments prior to their death.

Family members have killed most of these children that we meet. And some are accident victims and a few have died of disease, but most were brutally murdered by adults.

We do see the Angels of adults that the Angel Jo and others are helping go to the Light, too. Most of these are over thirty and have lived pretty full lives. These adults mainly have died from accidents or disease. Women have almost as hard of a time of leaving families behind as the children. But adults seem to understand death far better than the children do.

Sometimes the Angels of children will stay here with the Angel Jo for a few days. They play and have fun and the Angel Jo will sometimes make pizza for them.

We frequently find leftover pizza setting on our stove with a few pieces missing. The Angel Jo has told us that some of the kids want pizza before they cross over into the Light. Then she laughs and adds, "But they cannot digest it." I do not know what happens to food they eat, but the Angel Jo thinks it's funny. Anyway, the Angel Jo and I make them as comfortable as possible and try to make them happy. But we are saddened by the death of a young person.

When I hear about the death of a child I weep for them. I cry for an innocent human being uselessly killed for nothing. A kid that only knows love is beaten or in some way killed by someone the child loved. Usually the killer was someone who that child depended on for protection.

These children were murdered because of domination from an adult. An adult showing his animal instincts - indicating, "I am King." Or, "If I cannot raise my child then my child must die." Or, "These are my children, and I will do whatever I wish with them." Or, "I want you, but I will not have that child around." Or worse of all, "This child was for my sexual desires only."

We cry for all the pains these children endured. We cry for what their lives may have brought. We cry for the things they never enjoyed, such as being an adult, doing the things adults enjoy; such as having children, having their own home, having a job and experiencing life. And we also cry for the death of their DNA chain.

The wails from pain in the first seconds after death often carry over from the Other Side, and my two sons and I hear these cries throughout the day and when we are trying to sleep at night, for not all deaths are painless. Most of these cries of pain come from small children just killed; murdered by their family members and others they thought were their friends.

I cry, the Angel Jo cries as All on the Other Side cry for the children who are being killed. Human law is the thing that will help stop these merciless killings. These deaths cannot be swept under the carpet as they have been in the past. If one kills another of any age, they must be killed as well; an eye for an eye... death for a death... domination for domination.

Do unto others as you would have them do unto you. If you open your heart to others, they will open their hearts to you. If you kill someone then you must be killed, very plain and simple.

Killing of others is the same as the actions of animals. Animals kill for reasons of fear or wanting what the other has; Domination. We must try to remove our animal instincts. These traces of what we came from must be removed from civilization if we are to endure.

Common laws of our courts need to be enforced to protect people including our children from harm by others, with no early releases and no time off for good behavior. Murderers deserve life in prison or death. No second chances. The same rule must also apply to all lawbreakers because if one does something against another they must pay for their action. And those who are in prison should not have any rights for they tried to steal the rights from their prey.

We are letting more and more gang members raise our children. Yet the gangs do not love our children. To raise a child is to love a child. If you do not love children, then do not have children.

Having offspring and then not taking care of or loving them may be the greatest Sin of all, for then one is guilty of not caring for oneself or others because your offspring are both yourself and your mate.

Children brought into life out of lust are made from your self-domination, your desire for the feelings of sexual climax. There is no love between a man and a woman with lust in their hearts. A child brought into life without love as its directive is then lost because the parents did not and does not love or care about the child.

Our streets and schools are full of children without loving parents.

Life of another, be it a family member or just another is not here just for your amusement or for you to turn your back on. Believe it or not, all people have needs, wants and feelings and that includes our children, too. Our children are living things just like you and me.

The child who was murdered by his mother that you read in the newspaper today had feelings just like you. He felt the pains of each blow he received during his murder. He was frightened and was in unbearable pain when he died. We heard his cries and we felt his pains as All on the Other Side did, too. The Angel Jo or one of the many other Angels will help that child travel to the Light where they will never be mistreated again.

Let not yourself carry the Hell of destroying another's life, weep for the death of our children. Expect death for anyone who murders a child. Love all children for they are also part of God, but remember, if one dominates another, he should experience domination from us.

You and I are part of the human race, and all children are part of the human race, too. All children are my children, and all children are your children, for we are all of God.

Even the killing of adults is reason for All on the Other Side to weep because they are also His children. For God says, "We all are His children."

One of the biggest reasons for us seeing people killing more today is the way we and our children are being raised.

Once children were disciplined by parents and teachers, and if two boys got into an argument, they fought. Today we won't allow our children to fight. We will give time out and sent our children to their rooms instead of discipline, and so our children are afraid to fight. And this causes them to hold everything inside and take their aggression out on the ones who are littler or weaker then they are, and that is why we have so many rapes and murders of young girls and boys today.

And once when two kids got into a fight at school, they used their fists to settle their argument and then they would be friends, but today they just take a gun to school and kill everyone.

We need to get back to basics of teaching, and of loving our children.

SADNESS

(This is the final subject that the Angel Jo personally wished to tell people and asked me to write for her.)

And the Angel Jo said, "There is a feeling that flows deeply within almost everyone, a feeling that most try to cover with trinkets and smiling faces. Hidden deep away in thoughts but never forgotten is sadness, a feeling even the Angels convey because of human actions.

"With all the enjoyments life can bring, why does everyone have sadness?

"It is easy to understand why All in the Light are sad. It is because of what you do to yourselves during your lifetimes. They are sad because of the way you treat each other. Hatefulness, greed and fear of others dominate your actions.

"Angels also are saddened by what you teach your children.

"You teach your children how to hate others for the color of one's skin, or because they talk with an accent, or they look different, or because they are disabled. Children are not born to hate, you teach them how and who to hate, and how to fear things they do not understand.

"You teach your children how they must be better than the rest, and how they must have more, and they must have what the others have, and most do not care if that means stealing.

"When a child steals a bicycle from another and places it in his garage, why does not the parent ask the child where the bike came from?

"Are parents so naive as to think that someone gave a bike to their child?

"You will not and do not open your hearts to children, so your children only open their hearts to their peers, and therefore you are really encouraging them to join gangs. For then you can forget your own children because you fear them and then you concentrate on your own 'needs.'

"Why do you try to take all the possessions from your elderly parents as you place them in old folk's homes?

"Why do siblings fight over the possessions of their deceased parents?

"You try to cover your unopened hearts with the trinkets you give your children. I have heard people say to their children, 'Hey Johnny, here is a new game for you. Now go play in your bedroom.' Meanwhile, they were actually saying, 'Do not bother me, I'm too busy for you.'

"The gifts you give to cover your feelings are not given just to children, you give these feelings to everyone that tries to show you their opened hearts as you think, 'Take this and leave me alone.'

"And all of your bad actions to others cause All on the Other Side to be sad.

"Love is the feeling of understanding. Love is the feeling that separates you from your animal instincts, and yet, you try to cover this most wanted feeling in the world. All of you need love. All of you want love. You all say, 'I give love.' But yet, you have sadness.

"You try to buy love and happiness. Did that new car you bought really bring you happiness? Did that one night of sexual encounter with a stranger mean true love?

"The inability of humans to enjoy causes sadness. You will know the feelings of happiness when you open your heart. You will experience love when you express love. Expressing love does not mean just sexually either. Love is expressed many ways that are yours to give and receive when you find compassion, understanding and caring for all others within your heart.

"Sadness can be overcome. Just open your heart and say, 'thank you,' to someone. Say, 'please,' once today and you will start to open your heart and others will pass your goodwill on, but yet, you have been taught to be sad. Your life has been made sad even if you thought differently.

"Money will not remove your sadness. Only the opening of your heart will remove your sadness. Sadness stems from your Angel-within not being able to help you. Allowing your Angel-within to help you will move you to a higher feeling about yourself. Loving yourself and all others is happiness, for that is Heaven. That is the goal you all should be striving to accomplish. Lifting Your Soul.

"Earlier we wrote about what happens on the Other Side during the Christmas season - A feeling of happiness and thoughtfulness for others comes from the world all at once with most everyone wishing goodwill to all. A message that causes All on the Other Side to stand still and listen to all prayers as these prayers fill the skies in the Light.

"What a marvelous sound, the people of the world in harmony asking for peace. This grand sound could be heard everyday of the year if you wanted it. No need for it to be a special sound repeated only at Christmas time. You are the cause for sadness, and yet, you also are the answer to love. Let your Angel-within lead, and you shall rejoice with love in your heart.

"Love at Christmas time is not just giving presents to each other, Love is thinking about others throughout the year and buying something that they mentioned some time during the year.

"I have said, Dear David, 'You get angry too fast.' And sometimes you know that you do. My main concern is sometimes your anger and the anger from all others stems from people not seeing life for what it was meant to be. I cannot understand why people do not enjoy the earthly goods they possess. But in reality, their concepts are not your concern. People want more and more. Nobody is happy. Nobody can understand that by opening their hearts they will release sadness. Opening your heart is your Heaven and that is happiness for All of the Other Side.

"Slow down and enjoy life. Open your hearts. Be kind to others. Heaven is your thoughts of goodness. You alone will bring Heaven unto yourself, practice to develop love in your actions. Loving and helping others will bring love and help to yourself, but thoughts of receiving help and love should not be your reason for giving love and help.

"Finding love will remove your sadness. But securing a place in the Light should not be your reason for showing love and help to others. Love and help will come back to you from others as they open their hearts to you.

"As I have said before, 'God will not demand that you do anything.' Your actions are left up to you. Each and every one of you is accountable for his actions.

"Experience the wonders of life. Enjoy the feeling of life.

"The Knowledge being offered here is not a new religion, but rather an extension of the Bible's views and things that were left out or forgotten.

"Our writings point to a peaceful and content way of life to help you understand and know that you are not alone and that all of you have feelings, too.

"Happiness is yours if you desire it. No one is forcing you to be nice for love is around you. Not to have love is going against the flow of nature and God.

"Another reason for sadness of All on the Other Side cannot be helped. This sadness comes from seeing and knowing what is happening and what will come. These are the things the Angels could change but will not because it would change the future.

"Consider for a moment if you were an Angel and you are standing beside your living loved ones, knowing all the time that one is going to die in a car accident. You view the pain of the death, and you see and feel the pain of others as they go through their mourning. But there is nothing you can do. You cannot actually put your arm around them and comfort them. You cannot speak and soothe them. You know their faith must carry them forward. All you are able to do is welcome home the newly deceased loved one. Yes, you would be sad to see humans suffer, but you are happy for your reunion of that loved one.

"All on the Other Side are saddened to see you in pain. But the pains you go through are just part of your experiences of living.

"If you cannot bear the thought of having one of your children die, which is one of the deepest sadness that some will experience, then do not have children, for it is very possible one of your children will die within your life time for death comes to all. But the time of death is the unknown to you.

"And then the Other Side is also saddened when we see you lost and confused about God.

"All of the Other Side are also saddened by your need to always keep your guard up out of fear of what others will do. You cannot leave the windows of your homes or cars open, and you cannot leave your possessions unlocked or unguarded for people will steal whatever you have. Therefore, you have become slaves and guards to your goods, and yet, people want more and more, but have no time to enjoy their possessions or life.

"What good is life and possessions if they are not enjoyed and experienced?

"Your lifestyles have caused your Angels to be unable to guide and help their human bodies.

"Life was designed to experience and enjoy. God wants you to experience and enjoy life. You are the cause of your not experiencing or enjoying life. You are the cause of your own sadness, and you are the only cause to all the sadness on the Other Side, too.

"Women are equal to men, but they must always be on guard against rapists. What kind of life is that when you are afraid to walk down the street or to go shopping by yourself?

"Your court system treats rape victims as if they caused the violent attack. The same thing applies to the murder of a child, or whenever an ex-lover kills because of rejection. These actions were not brought on by the victims and they are not lesser crimes than first degree murder.

"Your reasoning is the sadness to All of the Other Side. You act as if you are all brain dead. You have the ability to change your sadness and our sadness by you being aware of what your actions do to others.

"You feel the human population fights tooth and nail not to evolve into a society with love in its heart for all. You do not know why this attitude has occurred unless your old animal instincts still dominate there, too. But you do feel your sadness can be reversed into love if you desired it to be so. This reversing can be accomplished only by individual actions. Therefore, you are the ones who can begin this movement.

"Domination to remove sadness from another is also a Sin if happiness is forced on another. If this were not a Sin, God could force the removal of your sadness. Therefore, you cannot force others to remove their sadness. They must open their hearts to find their Heaven because each person is responsible for his own actions. But it is okay to tell someone about God to help him remove his sadness, but forcing God on another to remove their sadness is domination and that is a Sin.

"Love all others. If others bring sadness to you, remove yourself from their presence. You need not be dominated by placing yourself into sadness for their comfort and happiness.

"Sadness spreads the same as love spreads. Now only sadness covers your school systems as well as it has invaded your homes. Soon you will see a time where there is no place to hide from the Evil.

"Evil is sadness that is self-dominating.

"The Devil is evil as God is Love. Both are Energy, but yet they are opposite.

"The Unguided Ones are sadness, evil, they are before God. (They never went into the Light, they know not of God).

"Angels are of God for they are after; Angels who went to the Light before coming to Earth.

"All sadness will be destroyed. Love will live forever, but All must experience or have knowledge of sadness to know love.

"Sadness can be an expression of compassion if turned outwardly. This sadness a-lined with compassion in the experience is needed to find love and God.

"This wisdom to understand this part of Knowledge was lost in the translation of the Bible.

"The understanding of God, love, compassion, caring, the Other Side, the Light, human life, the cycle of Genesis and more were left out of the Bibles. If you do not understand the Knowledge, then Knowledge is nothing. But also not knowing and not understanding is sadness. The wisdom to understand the Knowledge is love. God is Love. Love is the Light. Love is the Angels for God is All."

CONCLUSION

PSYCHIC POWERS

During the start of the process of the Angel Jo inspiring me to learn all of the things that I had forgotten along with my newly found desires to help people, I started working part-time for a Psychic Hot line. I soon learned that the company wanted more than just to help people, they wanted the name, address and telephone number of all of the callers. The company then sends these people different things to buy and also sold their list of names to other companies. I did not want to take people. I just wanted to help people, so I quit the first day that I worked for them. Of course, I understand that companies have to make money to stay in business.

After I quit, this company then told my sister, who also worked for them, that I was just naive.

Not knowing much about the Bibles and recalling only what Jo had reminded me about the Other Side and the Light, I wanted to find out what others knew and thought about God. So I decided to read what others wrote about these subjects. I bought a few books about astral projection and psychic powers, only to find that most people do not know much about such matters.

And the Angel Jo said to me, "The art or ability of Astral Projection is basically self hypnosis or done by a controller, which I do know works. Hypnosis does help one's Angel move out of the body while you retain the memories of your Angel's ventures, and this action is also done by many while asleep. Therefore, not everyone needs to be asleep or under hypnosis before, during or at the end of this encounter.

"The problem with Sleep Projection is that most people do not remember, and if they do remember, they may call it a dream, and many dreams are merely dreams. Dreams are things you may be thinking about before going to sleep or think about while you are asleep. True travel of one's Angel could become clouded by remnants of other dreams because dreams and Projection may both occur during the same sleep period.

"Both sleep and hypnosis lower the activity of brain waves, which is energy slowed down to that of rest which is nearer the energy movement of your Angel. And it is possible that actions of your Angel-within (the memories it hold from past experiences) bleed over to you, and thus it is also possible for you to learn what your Angel knows or does while sleeping.

"This lowering of our brain waves is the cause for Astral Projection.

"Astral Projection can be accomplished by anyone who has the control to remove daily thoughts and then going into a trance like state, thus lowering the movement of energy. This action can be accomplished by anyone with practice and is not a power that only few possess.

"The idea of Psychic Powers is correct, but the name is wrong. Psychic Powers are not only obtained by some individuals but are processed by all, and whereas all people have the ability to know experiences of the past, present and future.

"Your mind cannot bend spoons, and your mind cannot move objects. But if you can obtain a state that enables your Angel to leave your body, then your Angel can bend spoons and move objects for you, as well as other Angels or Entities may do these things for you, too. And if your Angel can leave your body, it could travel to different locations and to other times as well.

"All people are born with the power to know the past and future and for Self-Projection. Humans lose these abilities as they grow older because of the priorities of your lives and things you are taught by humans destroys your Knowledge.

"Being able to 'read' another' future is the ability to take the time to understand that person's life. Just by looking into one's eyes or hearing what one is actually saying, should show you his future. His future as well as his past and present are written into his face and eyes as well as in his voice.

"You all contain the past and present, and your opening of your heart is the key to unlocking the Knowledge that others contain, and their Knowledge contains the reactions of their future. The past and present are part of all Knowledge that you can and will see and understand if you desire to love All by opening your heart to all.

"Some psychics use objects such as tea leaves to 'read' the future. These are just crutches, something to strengthen their faith, something to help them believe that they can 'read' others. Your heart contains all the faith and belief you need to know about what will be. Sometimes what you believe in may not come true. But then one must understand the difference between knowing if it comes from the dog or the Angel-within.

"Must all that you believe come true for you to believe in yourself?

"Must you know everything?

"Understanding and reasoning out why you were wrong or right in your belief is also part of the Knowledge that God has given you.

"Intelligence is understanding with the ability to reason. For these are of God and are given to you from God.

"Most of the people who work for those psychic hotlines have relearned the art of having Self-Heaven by helping others. They have opened their hearts to others, but still pursue their 'desires' and 'needs' of the flesh.

"It is very easy to recall something while trying to perform the duties.

"You, my Dear David, do not believe in charging people for helping them. Those that really need help may not be able to pay for the help.

"You understand many people wish to learn how to see the future. You know many books are written with the intent to help others. However, most are published merely to make money.

"Life never was intended to be easy. Someone is always trying to take something from others, for most people live for the desires of the flesh. It is difficult to help others when so many are doing wrong. But if you help someone from your heart while they are seeking something wrongfully by asking for your help, is that your problem or theirs? For those, even if they ask for help, do not deserve help.

"Most people who need help will not ask for it. But if you give from the heart, you will see their needs. Sometimes a 'good morning' or just a 'thank you' is all the help they need.

"A 'thank you' does not cost anything, nor does a smile to someone. Money is not the answer to all of your problems. Love is the answer to all of the problems. Be it kindness, which can include money, kind words or whatever. Peace of mind will be your contentment in Heaven, and is the kindness, and love you show to yourself and others.

"Things done for money or anything not from your heart will not buy you a place in the Light. Your place in the Light must be earned by you.

"Your Heaven is the amount of good that you have done to all, but you need not save the world from all its corruption to find Heaven. You need only to show love in your daily life to others, and then you will find Heaven in yourself, and then someday, you will carry your Heaven into the Light.

"Love and kindness flow from life. Move with the flow of life, and then you shall also be able to see your future.

"All of the future will not be known, and therefore you cannot see all. All future is part of the Knowledge in God's Plan, and humans shall not know all. Knowing all would result in too many consequences that you could not handle or accept. Therefore, you must experience life. Knowing all would remove some of the experiences needed to develop Heaven within oneself. Your actions to events that will occur must be natural without the Knowledge of the outcome of future events.

"What would you do if you knew a loved one was going to die in an automobile accident tomorrow?

"How about, if you knew one of your parents would die from a heart attack tonight?

"If you knew the tragedies to come, you would do special things for that person. Need you know the future to show kindness to someone? Love and kindness must come from the heart, not from pity, or from selfish reasons of knowing the future."

During my final days on earth, I kept asking the Angel Jo when my end would come, my failing heart plus other health problems had progressively gotten worse. I know that people have different thresholds to pains, and in my understanding the amount of pain I was enduring was nearing my limit.

The Angel Jo told me my pains were not that bad. She felt sorry that I have to undergo pain, but would not give me the date of my death. She did promise me that she would stay near me until my end. I soon learned that no one must know everything. Even I, with all the Knowledge that I had obtained, could not know my own future because just think of all that I could have had if I only knew when I would die. The ramifications of this Knowledge could have affected the future greatly. But she said to me, "The night before your death, I will appear and tell you tomorrow is the day, but then, the next day you will be busy helping others and have forgotten about your coming end. I tell you these things for you to tell another the night before your end, and on the day, after your death, he will call your wife, Christine, and tell her that you knew…this is the proof that Christine will write into her book.

"Psychic readers can make you feel better about tomorrow, but they cannot tell you the complete truth about the future. They do not know the complete future for only God knows what is bound for you. God shares with you only what He knows you can handle, for He knows what you can endure.

"Must you be so informed that you know everything?

"You are just a little smarter than those before you who thought the world was flat. Are humans so vane to think they are really intelligent?

"Do you think that your newest automobiles are the best ever built, and that next year they will not make a better one?

"Do you really think computers will never be better than today's?

"Humans do not know everything now, and they did not know everything a hundred years ago and they will not know everything a hundred years in the future. They must keep learning and growing which is what God keeps teaching you, and helping you to remember more and more about the Other Side. To God, you are merely children.

"The necessities of life will differ from person to person, as some may need computers while others do not. Do not try to keep up with your neighbor. Your needs are different from theirs.

"Can you have Heaven in your heart if you try to keep up with others?

"Do earthly goods mean that much to you?

"Must you possess that which others have?

"All experiences are different for everyone. Humans are individuals with different needs. All of your differences come together in the Light to form One, and together We form God.

"Enjoy your differences and follow your heart. That is the same thing as being yourself and listening to your Angel-within for life is meant to be enjoyed. Therefore, do not be unhappy.

"Take the time to enjoy life and try to find the time to search your inner-self. That is what all true the psychics do. For psychics search their inner-self (Angel-within) for the Knowledge they have concerning you while trying to help you.

"Understanding and believing there is more to life than this place that you call earth will help you open your heart. Knowledge of yourself gives you the Knowledge of tomorrow.

"Time spent in learning how to express yourself to others will help you to understand feelings of yourself and their feelings as well.

"Lift your Soul... Feel free...Be free...Live free... Touch free... then you too will understand and see the Light and know some of the future.

"The Knowledge is yours if you desire it."

THE FUTURE

When we think about future events that will spell out the coming of the end as indicated in the Christian Bible, we think of all kinds of terrible things that will happen. Every story of revelation in the Qur'an and in the Christian Bibles foretells of terrible acts on humans as the end grows near. Those who wrote these Bibles described the end of the world using words they knew and understood, and yet, their descriptions were inaccurate. No blame should be placed on them for they told of the end the best that they could. Just as what I wrote may not be the actual event to the end, but they were things what I was allowed to see.

So theirs and mine may not be the actual account of the end of this cycle, but are only our interpretation of things to come.

Most people will never see any great calamities happening that indicate to us that the end of the world is near. But we will see great changes in natural conditions of our Earth. We will also see many fights both in war and as terrorist actions. But most will be blind to see the truth, and whereas, the Muslim Religion tells of a world to come as being one nation under their god with out borders, and in 2006 that is the same world that Mexicans are saying concerning the United Sates. And presently Christians and Jews can live in a Muslim country, but they have no rights and cannot vote and must live under the rules that Muslim rulers made, and those unholy rules only apply to the Christians and Jews. The Muslim Countries are places that only their religious leaders are allowed to hold office.

If you can read the reactions of nature, if you can see the actions people are taking toward each other, and if you can see our industrial movement of modernization, then you shall see the coming events that predict the end.

The congestion on our roads and the pollution we place in our skies and on the land show us the end is near. Our road system and the material of which it is made of is one of the major causes of the warming of the earth. These and other things are helping the global warming, along with all that we are putting into the atmosphere, and in the water, and on the land.

People only cry about the things that they do not like which they say will cause death and the end of time. But the people love and need automobiles so badly they do not see that cars are a major factor to the end.

People will not say alcohol is killing millions on the roads or by drunken fights. Nor will they say anything about how alcohol destroys families because they like the taste of alcohol.

God did not need the things that we endorse that pollute the world, nor did God end time. We did that all by ourselves.

Nature has had little to do with the end. The natural effects would not have destroyed life, but would have merely changed our lifestyles. Natural changes of the world were the best description that those of long ago could use in describing the final days of time.

All chances of having the good life are nearly over. Daily, the percentages of our having a complete life grow shorter. And now the chances of seeing your children have a productive or even a complete lifetime is smaller.

Before, the parents usually died before their offspring. Now that has turned around and more parents are seeing their children die.

I see great problems for the human race in the future. Besides people doing evil things to others, I also see changes of nature coming to the world. And Atomic, germ and viral warfare are becoming common knowledge among the people. Other devastating weapons are presently being developed for future use. We will see them used against mankind shortly.

Doctors, nurses and hospitals that are not destroyed will not be enough to help all of those that are injured. Some areas will not have enough buildings standing to house all the injured. The sick, injured and dying will lie on the sidewalks, streets or anywhere they can.

People will rob and kill not just for money, but for food, water and medical supplies. Even killing their own family members to sustain their own life will unfortunately not be uncommon. However, some parts of the world will not be involved in this holocaust.

A Third World War against mankind could happen and could be named the Third World War, but it could be prevented if the people of the world would unite as one. The prevention of this War could help sustain life as we know it a little longer. But a Third World War, if it happens, will not be the end of the world. And yet, I see terrorist actions as being viewed as a Third World War for terrorist actions will seemly devour the world.

Time has come for the earth's changes also. Mountains and valleys can be made in minutes. We will see mountains, valleys, lakes and oceans where there were none before. These acts of nature cannot be helped and

Holy Graduel

many people will lose their lives. But people could help each other and make life a little better than what it will be.

The human race cannot know all. God knows all, but cannot tell humans everything for human emotions could not take all Knowledge without bad consequences.

I have not been told all. However even the little that I have been told has particulars that cannot be passed on because of the repercussions this Knowledge may cause. For some things need should be left alone and not known.

The acts of nature cannot be changed. Some of the world's natural changes have been caused by man such as the destruction of the rain forests caused the jet stream to change directions, and this in turn caused climatic changes and changed crop growth. Loss of crops will cause many nations and people to fight over food. Terrorism will run rampant throughout the world, and any will die from the reactions of nature. Natural events cannot be stopped now, but people can stop the killing and the suffering that they will bring upon each other.

I do not wish to tell you all will be wonderful, but also I do not want to place fear into your hearts about the end coming.

I believe it is best to live and enjoy life. Treat everyone with love from your heart, for you know not when your end is here.

Before the Final Day arrives, find Salvation for your Angel. Experience your end as many others have done before you. Try not to let your life end early, but look forward to reuniting with God on the Other Side once again.

It does not matter if your life continues until that Final Day of time or not. Birth is our beginning and death is our end, Genesis. Each of us must face his individual death for the universal number is two. For all life, death must come.

There is no great secret to life, and there is no great secret to the Other Side, for they are One. Love and Harmony are the keys to Heaven. Your Heaven is your passport to the Light, Life on earth, and on the Other Side,

Love, Harmony and Heaven are yours to enjoy.

The other day while at my job, a friend and I had a conversation that involved a discussion of the philosophy of acceptance. After seeing both his parents die from lung cancer and watching his son go near death from a rare disease, my friend has come to find acceptance.

Acceptance of the unknown, going with the flow of things, understanding that you cannot change nature and knowing you cannot change people for you must simply enjoy life.

We must all live our individual lives and teach our children as well as we can; Live the best life possible based on your education and interests, and live life to enjoy life and let others live their own lives. Experience and learn from all that you have done and seen, and be content with your life. All that you have done in the past is why you are in the place you are today.

Do not dwell on what others are doing. Do not worry about the end of time coming. Remember your past mistakes, but forgive yourself as well as all others for their past mistakes, too.

Do not dwell on doing everything perfectly so you can reserve a place in the Light. Live your life with no domination toward yourself or others. Love yourself and all others. Follow God's ways as your Angel wishes you to.

Today is the first day of the rest of your life. You need not be the same person you were yesterday. We all change ideas and preferences daily, therefore, why not change with more Love for God and all others now.

It's your life and the choice is yours.

EPILOGUE

I know whenever one reads anything written about the Bibles, God or the Light many questions arise in the thoughts of that individual while that person is trying to analyze every phrase and sentence for true meaning and understanding of what the author wrote and meant. My hope is that this book has brought you more answers than questions. We really tried to write in common language to make everything understandable.

I have found that the Angel Jo answered all my questions to their exact point. Sometimes my loss of words or using the wrong words may have changed her answer completely. Once when I asked her who I was, she replied, "We are the oldest, we are the nucleus of the Light."

I was to find out later that her statement was somewhat incorrect for my question. I alone am not the nucleus for WE ALL are the nucleus of the Light. We think that everything revolves around each and every one of us because we see things in the world through individual eyes. Therefore, you could say you are the center of your world while I may also say that I am the center of my world. In the Light, you also will be the center of your Light for all are special because all are the center of their own individual world.

When talking to God, you must be careful with your wording because you will get an answer directed straight to your words. Thus you may receive a false answer for your intended question, but a correct answer for your wording of that question. This has happened to many writers, and therefore, their peace of mind was worth the truth.

We do not try to analyze every conversation we have on a daily basis. For when a family member says, "I love you," you take the statement for face value. But when God says He loves us, we examine what He said and try to understand each word for its true meaning. Therefore, every word and every line written in the Bibles was twisted, and is redefined daily by scholars and others to fit their needs and desires.

Read the Bibles for what it is and believe in what was written but remove the domination from it because that came from man and not God.

During the period of my learning about the Other Side, I tried to underline each word in the statements of Jo. I tried to write true meaning into her statements. I thought every word that she spoke must be true. It was then when I found out the true meaning of "Peace of mind is worth the truth."

Happiness, contentment and peace of mind for all are part of the Bibles and the Angel Jo's Words to me. But most people need not know the complete truth to be happy, content or to have peace of mind.

Happiness, contentment and peace of mind are the three fundamental parts of Life. These three things are all that is needed to find Heaven within one's self. Living with these ideas will give you the happy life you so desire, for if you do not really know the complete truth, you will be satisfied with any answer. Peace of mind is contentment in your mind, which makes you believe happiness and Heaven is within your mind and thoughts.

I truly believe that the Angel Jo did not give me all of the correct answers, just as Jesus did not give His Disciples everything because Jesus' Disciples and I did not ask the questions that we thought we asked. For They merely answered the questions we asked.

I believe just as we teach our children, God teaches us. We give our students part of the answers and expect them to search for more. That is what learning and growing is all about.

In the book "Embraced By The Light," Betty wrote about her seeing a board of twelve men ruling in the Light. I wrote that no individual rules anyone in the Light. Who is right? Who is wrong? I feel both answers are correct. We learn what is needed. Betty and I can search for the correct answer if we desire to do so. Betty's and my answers of the Light are just as different as many of the others who have been touched by the Light and those who have written about the Light. And, if Betty receives peace of mind by thinking that twelve men rule, so be it because she must like being dominated.

Also the communication between humans and Angels can lose a lot of meaning. I know for sure that the Angel Jo said many words I had never heard before nor could I find them in the dictionary. Remember that communication between humans and Angels is done by thought. I also found that when the Angel Jo was channeling through Christine, Christine sometimes could not find the words to express what the Angel Jo was telling her. Some words that the Angel Jo spoke were unknown to us. These words were actually thoughts that we had never had before and thoughts that we had never tried to put into words before.

When I first started learning about the Other Side through the Angel Jo, she stated to me that there is no sex gender on the Other Side. I did not stop to realize they do not have genitalia. I did not relate gender and organs together. So it does not take a female Angel to enter a female body nor does it take a male Angel to live in a male body. All are equal. All are the same, for all Angels are androgynous.

One night in late May, while the Angel Jo was inside of Christine's body, as I kissed her and she said, "I like this."

I asked, "Don't you kiss on the Other Side."

She answered, "No, we touch like this."

She then ran her fingertips over my face. I returned the jester to her. She said, "That feels good. I feel your love. You are beautiful. Also, we run our hands over the back and palm of the other's hand."

(I know many of you are asking yourselves, how many times did the Angel Jo enter Christine's body? How many times did you two make love while she used Christine's body? The answer to both is well over fifty times. It became a weekly occurrence, sometimes even twice a week until I learned Divine Love.)

I then asked her if they ever feel each other's bodies. She answered, "No, only faces and hands."

But the act of touching was symbolic because Angels do not have faces or hands or bodies.

This act of touching only of the face and hands made me see that their thoughts of things of importance are somewhat different from ours. Thus, I went on to discover other things, such as death and pain are merely events and feelings that need to be experienced, and early death and enslavement are very sad and tragic to them. And that was when I realized that the Angel Jo's and my world were blending together, each with its own meaning and understanding.

Just as a child starts to merge into adulthood but still is a child, so we are still the children of God. We grow with the Knowledge that He is providing us.

I often would wonder what the Angel Jo and I could do to convince the world about the Other Side. Should we have gone on television and done something grand in front of a live audience?

The non-believers would still not have believed, but if we could save one more Soul, would that not be worth it?

I do not know the answer. Maybe someday before my time comes we will do such an event for I feel that the saving of one Soul is worth it.

I asked the Angel Jo, "Is it not our job to try and save more Souls?"

The Angel Jo replied, "Have not our books done enough?

"You have touched many with your words. We have touched many with our books. These last two books will touch many more. We have done enough. Those that we helped will open their hearts to others. Many will be saved, but some will not.

"My dearest David, please do not be sad. For others will write more and tell of things that we did not. We have answered the questions that you have asked of us. For all is symbolic for what is. Does it *really* matter if you are the one who disperses the bad? For we are all One. We did live the lives that you wrote about, but would it *really* matter if we did not? For we are all One, and does it matter if the Bibles is true or not? Because all Bibles are of One. Does it matter if humans have one religion or many? For all are from the same One.

"These are some of the things that Dale must tell the world. We cannot and shall not tell everything. For their faith and belief must carry them into the future."

I wish that we could have given you more than our vow that what we saw and did was and is completely true, for Non-believers will never believe and Believers will always have Faith. For Faith is the basis of all religion.

Many people search for detailed records pertaining to accounts of the Bibles. Some have been found, but only enough artifacts will be found to strengthen the Faith of some.

I think we have opened many avenues of thought for you. You be your own judge and decide what is right or wrong for you. I personally know what is correct and that there is the Other Side and God, for now I have the Knowledge.

THE FINAL TEACHINGS

Over the days and months leading up to October of 2000, I had troubles and doubts about whom I had been in contact with, were these truly Angels and Jesus or was it Satan and his fallen Angels that were telling me things?

During that time, the Angels had given me two challenges to strengthen my faith. Now once again I faced their challenge of my faith that lay in front of me.

This last and final challenge ended on the 20th of October. I don't know if you can call this a challenge or test but whatever it was, it finally gave me my Divine Faith, Divine Belief and Divine Love for all people and the Angels and my understanding and Worship for God. And this challenge was also the final teachings I needed to complete my life as God intended me to do.

The Final Teachings:

Throughout time God had been in communication with people, they would take His communications and turn His words into different religions and placed a god, who they thought they had communicated with, above their newly found religion. Over and over again this had happened. No one could understand or even began to try to comprehend that the god that they had placed in their religion was not the true God at the top, the One who they had communicated with but instead was their man made god.

The Angels kept telling me, "Remember geometrics."

Now I knew, the true God – the Supreme One who is above all things. Men had created religions and placed gods that they created above their religions. And below their religions were man, who are all equal but their self-created religions placed domination over man. But yet, all men are equal, all religions are equal and all gods below the Supreme One are equal!

"Remember Geometrics," A triangle. God at the top, man created gods below Him, religions below them and man at the bottom. The bottom line of the triangle represents man and all men are equal.

The same God who talked to those in all Bibles was communicating to me through His Angels just as He had done before with the others, but no one could get it. No one could understand there was one God at the top. One God who loves all of His children so much that He gave them the choice of their god, too.

Not all religions are the same, but they are all concepts created by God. All religions that contain "Love for All," and "No domination toward others," are religions of God. But things in any and all religions that indicate not love for all and/or contribute toward domination of any are not of God. Therefore, all religions are for God, but all religions contain things that are not of God because they were creations of man.

The religion that contains Jesus, the Christian Religion is one of the closest religions to God because it contains His Son, Jesus. But it too contains pollution from man and is not the only religion or way to get to God.

Now the true story is finally complete. Oh, but the story is not over yet, for God has and will continue to tell more to others and me about His Kingdom and Master Plan in the future.

Holy Graduel

LIFT YOUR SOUL

FEEL FREE
LIVE FREE
TOUCH FREE
LOVE FREE
BE FREE

"Our Love will not be forgotten this time."

www.ingramcontent.com/pod-product-compliance
Lightning Source LLC
Chambersburg PA
CBHW020938230426
43666CB00005B/79